THE UNEXAMINED ORWELL

LITERARY MODERNISM SERIES

Thomas F. Staley, Editor

JOHN
RODDEN

The Unexamined Orwell

University of Texas Press
AUSTIN

Requests for permission to reproduce material from this work should
be sent to:
    Permissions
    University of Texas Press
    P.O. Box 7819
    Austin, TX 78713-7819
    www.utexas.edu/utpress/about/bpermission.html

⊗ The paper used in this book meets the minimum requirements of
ANSI/NISO Z39.48-1992 (R1997) (Permanence of Paper).

Library of Congress Cataloging-in-Publication Data

Rodden, John.
The unexamined Orwell / John Rodden. — 1st ed.
p.   cm. — (Literary modernism series)
Includes bibliographical references and index.
ISBN 978-0-292-72558-4

1. Orwell, George, 1903–1950—Criticism and interpretation. I. Title.
PR6029.R8Z779 2011
828'.91209—dc22   2011001966

FOR

JOHN P. ROSSI

Friend, Teacher, Mentor

Contents

Acknowledgments

In the course of this book's composition, friends on both sides of the Atlantic gave me sage advice and trusting reassurance. In the United States, Thomas F. Staley, director of the renowned Harry Ransom Center at the University of Texas at Austin, showed early enthusiasm for this project and welcomed it into his book series on literary modernism. Jonathan Rose, a scholar of nineteenth- and twentieth-century British history, caught numerous small errors of fact and interpretation. William E. Cain, professor of English at Wellesley College, read the manuscript with meticulous care and offered me both intellectual and emotional support. When I was wrestling in the early stages of the project on how to approach one of the chapters, Ian Williams helped me understand the experience of British working-class men and the formative influence of summer school programs in Britain for leftists of the 1930s and 1940s. I am also grateful to Peter Stansky, Jeffrey Meyers, Vincent Kling, Ethan Goffman and Thomas Cushman for their conversation and discernment about Orwell over the years.

In Britain, Peter Davison, editor of the monumental twenty-two-volume *Complete Works of George Orwell,* has shared with me on numerous occasions his encyclopedic knowledge of Orwelliana. Loraine Saunders has become a wonderful new friend and has been a rich source of insight with the publication of her book on Orwell's fiction. Gordon Bowker discussed at length with me his challenges and struggles with Orwell biography. Ian Willison, a distinguished scholar guiding the book history program at the University of London, has corresponded with me and invited me to deliver lectures on various topics related to Orwell and British intellectual life. John Newsinger has written me several times with interesting observations about Orwell, many of them newly developed since his fine study, *Orwell's Politics* (1999). I am also grateful to Christopher Hitchens for his conversations with me about Orwell, and most especially for his willingness to subject himself to a lengthy interview that forms the heart of chapter 4 of the present study. Dione Venables, the charming and knowledgeable benefactress of the Orwell Forum website, has been a strong and steady voice of encouragement. Dione is the niece of Jacintha Buddicom, Orwell's first girlfriend, and has edited a second edition of *Eric & Us* (2006), the memoir that Jacintha published in the mid-1970s about her relationship with Eric Blair.

Four other friends have offered me wise counsel and assisted this book's growth to maturity. Ian Angus, the co-editor (with Sonia Orwell) of the *Collected Essays, Journalism, and Letters of George Orwell*, published in 1968, has not only spent numerous hours discussing Orwell's life and legacy with me, but also hosted me in his own home for several days. Now approaching ninety, Ian is a fountain of knowledge about Orwell and London intellectual life in the latter half of the twentieth century. He is a cheerful presence and an engaging conversation partner, as is his accomplished wife, Ann Stokes, who is a much-admired artist and sculptress. I also owe a debt of gratitude to Gorman Beauchamp, who read this manuscript attentively, improving it in innumerable ways thanks to his deep and comprehensive knowledge of Orwell's life and writings. Bill Heyck also combed through these pages, providing shrewd judgment and keen insight both about Orwell and modern British cultural history. Steve Longstaff, a sociologist and intellectual historian commanding a consummate grasp of the *Partisan Review* writers specifically and the American intelligentsia of the mid-twentieth century more generally, has been a valued friend for more than a quarter century. He and I first opened a dialogue on the topic of Orwell's "London Letter" to *Partisan Review*, and since then he has vouchsafed me the benefit of his nuanced understanding of Anglo-American intellectual life to enrich several of this book's chapters.

My last and deepest thanks go to John P. Rossi, professor of history at La Salle University in Philadelphia for more than forty years, my erstwhile teacher and ongoing friend and intellectual big brother. Although I was never formally his student—that is, I never officially enrolled in any of his courses at La Salle University during my student days in the 1970s—I learned an immense amount from him as an undergraduate and even more since then. We initially met after I had done work in Irish history, an area of special interest for him, and we soon found that we shared a passion for George Orwell and British history. During the last decade, it has been a joy and privilege to work closely with him on numerous articles devoted to topics ranging from Hemingway's relationship with Orwell to the legacy of Dwight Macdonald to the career of the eminent historian John Lukacs. The chapters in this book on those subjects emerged from our collaboration, and with characteristic graciousness and generosity of spirit, he read every line of the present study, told me what he liked and disliked, persuaded me to alter my prose (which I sometimes did grudgingly though I granted he was right), and emboldened me to reexamine my assumptions about Orwell and his times.

This book is for Jack.

The Unexamined Orwell

The Unexamined Orwell

Afterthoughts
on His Afterlives

A t the close of May 2003, just three weeks before the centennial anniversary of George Orwell's birth on June 25, the *Chronicle of Higher Education* interviewed several "experts" under the following headline: "Deconstruct This: George Orwell." I was phoned by a *Chronicle* staffer as the token "traditionalist," to use her word. The other two interviewees included a well-known Marxist critic of Orwell's work and a leading feminist scholar. Needless to say, I was alone in questioning the project of "deconstructing" Orwell as a way of commemorating him.

Of course, the rise of fashionable trends in literary theory, such as deconstruction, marks the sea change in literary studies and public culture itself since Orwell's day. To many literary academics and most of my students, Orwell and his work seem dated. After all, though he wrote extensively about class conflict and class issues, he never did so in explicitly Marxist terms, let alone with any sophisticated conceptual vocabulary.[1] More problematically, his oeuvre almost completely omits critical discussion of gender and addresses racial matters almost exclusively from the vantage point of Empire and the decline of British imperialism. So his work allegedly suffers from sustained, comprehensive inattention to the present-day mantra of "race, gender, and class." He did not live to see the rise of social and academic movements such as feminism, multiculturalism, poststructuralism, postmodernism, and other forms of literary radicalism that have come to dominate scholarly and intellectual life. As a result, he frequently seems to those in the academy—unfairly, I think—hopelessly irrelevant, even quaint.

That was certainly the conviction of my fellow respondents to the *Chronicle* (and by implication, the *Chronicle* staffer herself). Invited "to explain Orwell's enduring significance," the Marxist contributor essentially argued that Orwell possesses no significance today: "Orwell himself doesn't really have much of a developed economic or political thought," he said. "You can use the simple images of freedom and decency that he espoused, and it doesn't matter if you are on the Right, Center, or Left; you can invoke him. So Orwell is used more as a political weapon rather than someone we can critique and analyze." The feminist scholar agreed in the main. "Orwell has an enormous moral authority" that is largely unjustified, she said. "He was granted a kind of moral authority beyond anything he deserved."[2]

I

And yet, however much I might protest the misfortune, indeed the arguable absurdity, of commemorating a writer's legacy by "deconstructing" him—or even worse, the aim of "explaining his enduring significance" by dismissing him as intellectually simplistic and morally inconsequential—my colleagues' statements in the *Chronicle* prove nonetheless quite illuminating in a sociological sense. "George Orwell has been dead for more than 50 years," the *Chronicle* introduction began, "but his work and ideas continue to reverberate in political debates on both the Right and the Left." The subtitle of the article mused: "What Would George Say Now?" Such reveries constitute the abiding, apparently near-irresistible, preoccupation of participants in what I have elsewhere called the intellectual "game" of W.W.G.O.D.? (What Would George Orwell Do?).[3]

Without question, it is sociologically significant—if, admittedly, often intellectually embarrassing—that this game is still being played, even long after the Orwell centennial of 2003. For instance, the US presidential election campaign of 2008 witnessed Democratic objections to their opponents' "insidious Newspeak" and "doublespeak" (e.g., right-wing references to "Obama bin Laden") and Republican charges of their adversaries' "vacuous Orwellian rhetoric" (e.g., Obama's allegedly empty speechifying).[4]

Blared incessantly on the airwaves and mouthed repetitively by "duckspeaking" podcasters and talking heads, Orwell's coinages from *Nineteen Eighty-Four* are omnipresent. Battle-certified from the Cold War to today's culture wars, his neologisms are still bandied about freely because they are lodged securely in the cultural imagination. And that is partly why the question of "What would George say now?" remains so current.

II

Yet the status of the author of *Nineteen Eighty-Four* as a literary prophet does not alone account for the persistent longing and lament "If Orwell Were Alive Today . . ." It needs emphasis that it is the subject of Orwell himself and his would-be verdicts—and not only the historical accuracy of *Nineteen Eighty-Four* set against the much-publicized "countdown" to his "doomsdate"—that has occasioned widespread discussion. For until the 1980s, the speculations as to "where Orwell would have stood" were advanced chiefly by intellectuals engaged with "the man" and familiar with not just *Nineteen Eighty-Four* but with his entire life's work.[5] "What would Orwell have said about this crisis?" they asked. "What would his politics be today?" Numerous "old friends" implied that Orwell would have gone the way that they did. In Britain, within a few years of Orwell's death, as Raymond Williams once remarked, "Father knew George Orwell" had become a tired joke.[6]

But neither intellectuals nor journalists nor the reading public have tired of speculating about Orwell's posthumous politics—and the cultural significance of this compulsion is revealing. Scarcely a major Anglo-American issue has gone by since his death in January 1950 that has not moved someone to muse, "If Orwell Were Alive Today . . ." Orwell's enduring radiance as a literary figure is perhaps best exemplified by the insistent recurrence of this conditional headline, variously voiced as regret, wish, challenge, and tactic.

Of course, in at least one sense, questions about a man's posthumous politics are manifestly absurd. The fact is that Orwell has been dead for almost six decades, and it is impossible to extrapolate from an author's writings what he would say about events after his death.[7] But what is fu-

Afterthoughts on His Afterlives

tile can nevertheless sometimes be enlightening, at least for sociological purposes—and sometimes precisely because of its obvious futility. Many observers continue to pose questions about Orwell into the twenty-first century. That they do so—even while frequently admitting straight off that their conjectures are frivolous—testifies to the durable appeal of the Orwell persona and the ongoing relevance of Orwell's work. The recurrence of the question has helped keep Orwell's reputation "alive" and controversial—and illustrates, more generally, the rhetorical advantages of claiming a sizable figure's mantle and the crucial influence of news events on a reputation's shape and size. Both as an early postwar Cold Warrior and a present-day Culture Warrior, Orwell has proven to be, as he once remarked of Dickens, "a writer well worth stealing."[8]

Or rather, more accurately worded: "Orwell"—the amulet, not the author—has proven "a writer well worth stealing." Increasingly so in the decades since the man's death at midcentury, as the Marxist scholar interviewed by the *Chronicle* rightly observed, "What we have is not Orwell the person or the author, but Orwell in quotation marks, Orwell the image or myth."[9]

Indeed. That claim has been precisely my own contention for more than a quarter-century in my studies of Orwell's reputation.[10] I have been equally concerned with Orwell the man and writer and with "Orwell" the cultural icon and historical talisman.[11] And particularly with "Orwell" the "ideological superweapon"[12] in the pundits' wars—whether cold or cultural—of words. Moreover, I have also been concerned with literary matters intrinsic to Orwell's prose achievement, particularly his lucid style and distinctive, indeed pioneering, "plain man" persona.

That is to say, I have sought to maintain a careful balance between context and text. Throughout my work on Orwell and the rhetoric of reception, I have addressed the power-laden psychodynamics and contingent, conditional, social process from which literary works emerge. At the same time, I have emphasized the "objective" formal elements of the work itself, including those particular genres, styles, and properties of specific texts. Although biographers and scholars have chronicled, with near-definitive thoroughness, the life of Eric Blair a.k.a. George Orwell, the story of the unique afterlife of "Orwell"—not the man or writer or even the persona or literary personality, but the world-historical individual and universal metaphor for issues in the Zeitgeist ranging from language abuse to privacy invasion to totalitarian evil and far more—contains numerous intriguing chapters still untold. Chiefly devoted to "Orwell," this study presents a broad cross-selection of them.

III

A word or two about my title for the book is warranted here. First, I call it *The Unexamined Orwell*—but it might also be more precisely (if pedantically) rubricated: *The Unexamined "Orwell."* (Moreover, that frequently voiced yearning "If Orwell Were Alive Today" might instead be phrased "If 'Orwell' Were Alive Today.") For the fact is that "Orwell"—the myth, not the man or writer—is the object of readers' ceaseless fascination today. It is he whom newscasters exalt as a prophet, whom intellectuals invest with political (and moral) authority, and whom readers conscript in the blogosphere and in letters to the editor. It is the mantle of "Orwell" that polemically minded critics shamelessly snatch, his grave that they ruthlessly rob, his coffin that they surreptitiously shift to the Left or Right.[13]

And, lo and behold! this entity—"Orwell"—is indeed "alive today." In fact, he occupies a secure place in our culture that his intellectual contemporaries—and even noteworthy successors who have only recently passed away—no longer do (or never did). His significance is not just historical: both his life and his work still exert a shaping influence on contemporary culture. More than six decades after his death, his very name wields a rhetorical and political force still sufficient to stimulate public argument.

Secondly, this book devotes attention to "the *unexamined* Orwell." The choice of adjective is quite deliberate: I am not proposing to unveil an "unknown Orwell." That task has already been adroitly handled in a biography of that title by Peter Stansky and William Abrahams, a groundbreaking study that first disclosed the figure of Eric Blair behind the famous George Orwell.[14] Nor am I addressing a "neglected Orwell," for some of the themes and topics that I am raising here have already been touched on—and sometimes written about at length—by numerous scholars and intellectuals, including myself. Rather, this study attends to the "unobserved" Orwell/"Orwell," presenting scenes from both his "unexamined" (or perhaps "under-examined") life and posthumous reputation.

*Un*examined? I am well aware of the paradox here: in certain respects, both Orwell and "Orwell" have been *over*examined. As I have already suggested, critics as well as journalists have speculated endlessly about what Orwell might have said or done "if he had lived." They have played W.W.G.O.D., or what one PBS-TV commentator dubbed "that intriguing parlor game" of guessing where Orwell would have stood on issues ranging from McCarthyism and the Vietnam War to the 2003 invasion of Iraq.[15] Such speculation about his posthumous politics is only one example of the "over-examined" Orwell: both magazines and scholarly journals have been inundated—particularly during the two peaks of his reputation in recent decades, the mid-1980s and 2002–2003—with disputes about issues ranging from his (often scathing) criticism of fellow socialists to his literary intentions in *Nineteen Eighty-Four*.

And yet, all major writers receive selective, sometimes incongruous critical (and press) attention, with certain aspects of their lives and work scrutinized, and others little-studied. This book aspires to disclose an as-yet "unexamined" Orwell by furnishing fresh perspectives on him and his work, either by challenging broadly accepted appraisals of his achievement or pursuing new lines of inquiry about it. My concern is not to view Orwell within a single cohesive frame or to impose any monolithic, unified interpretation on his life and legacy, but rather to honor the diverse historical projects and critical idioms in which he and his work are discussed, many of which cut across several academic disciplines and intersect one another—often at strange angles. Some chapters explore biographical and literary sources of Orwell's work; others relocate him in the context of cultural history via comparisons with his intellectual coevals and successors; and still other chapters examine his reputation and impact beyond the boundaries of Ingsoc and Oceania (e.g., in "Orwell's Reich," a.k.a. the former East Germany). My hope is that these wide-ranging chapters will prompt other readers to reexamine Orwell and his legacy anew, thereby stimulating still further investigation of his rich corpus and ambiguous heritage.

Each chapter exhibits a distinctive "reception scene" of Orwell.[16] As in my previous studies of his reputation, I am concerned throughout to show how these diverse scenes represent case studies in literary and political reception as cultural history. Here again, my hope is that telling the story of a person's "afterlife" may be considered a modest contribution to the craft and criticism of biography, suggesting how we might profitably "extend" the traditional "Life and Times" biography in valuable new directions.[17] Each chapter of the book highlights a dimension of the "afterlife and times" of "Orwell," showing not just his virtuoso costume changes but also illustrating how the man and writer ballooned into a world-historical actor who has seemed to bestride every major post–World War II issue. It was this outsized figure who prompted PBS-TV in 2003 to title a centennial special *The Orwell Century*.

IV

So this book stages eighteen scenes starring "Orwell" as it considers the man, the writer, the literary personality, and the cultural icon. The spotlight in Part 1 dwells on the multifaceted afterlife of "Orwell" in scenes that convey the panorama of American intellectual history. I am especially concerned in this section with the obsession among intellectuals to propose candidates as "Orwell's successor." Titled "If the Mantle Fits . . . ," Part 1 addresses from different vantage points the conditions and contingencies that have given rise to Orwell's unique status among intellectuals. Each of the five chapters in Part 1 is devoted to a prominent postwar intellectual. The selection includes a trio of leading cultural critics associated with *Partisan Review*, a distinguished literary quarterly that became the house organ of a left-wing group of mainly Jewish writers and critics who became known as the New York Intellectuals, and two other naturalized Americans: the British expatriate Christopher Hitchens, who received American citizenship in 2007, and John Lukacs, the Hungarian-born historian. Each of these men—Lionel Trilling, Dwight Macdonald, Irving Howe, Hitchens, and Lukacs—has been nominated "The American Orwell." (Or better, in the latter two cases: "the 'Anglo-American' Orwell" and "the 'Hungarian-American' Orwell.") Each chapter addresses the similarities and differences between Orwell and his admirer as it pursues the disputes about Orwell's legacy and the biographical issues raised by the comparison.

Yet my task here is not to engage in an exhaustive comparative analysis, but rather to showcase this quite diverse quintet from an angle that mutually illuminates both their work and Orwell's legacy. All five of them are important intellectuals in their own right. Nonetheless, however original, productive, and influential their lives and works have been, none of them has achieved that consummation of stylistic brilliance, independence of mind, literary range, topical diversity, and moral authority that distinguishes Orwell's oeuvre.[18] As a result, they may occasionally seem to dwell in Orwell's long shadow. Still, I do not intend to reduce them to mere epigones, let alone disciples or acolytes of Orwell—even though it is also undeniable that these five critics occasionally cross the line from admiration to impassioned identification with, if not "claiming" of, Orwell.

In Part 2, titled "Politics and the German Language," we shift to "Orwell" in Germany—where he is an astoundingly pervasive presence, in English as well as in German.[19] Building on several scenes in a previous study devoted to this titanic, Teutonic, indeed sometimes Wagnerian fig-

Afterthoughts on His Afterlives

ure, Part 2 further examines his status in the former East Germany and post-reunification Germany in light of my personal experience there.[20] I concentrate on the role and relevance of *Nineteen Eighty-Four* in the now-defunct German Democratic Republic (GDR), the Communist-ruled state that proudly proclaimed itself *das bessere Deutschland* (the better Germany). The scenes range from the place of "Orwell" in the eastern German *mentalité* to the GDR regime's shocking abridgment of personal freedoms in the self-proclaimed "Land of Reading," a.k.a. the "Land of Little Brother." One chapter highlights the fate of several well-known GDR dissidents who were imprisoned because they had dared to read and circulate Orwell's work before the fall of the Berlin Wall in 1989—and even sponsored an Orwell centenary conference ("Books That Led to Jail") held in Berlin in 2003. Two other chapters deal with the ways in which official Party orthodoxies were communicated to school pupils through Ministry of Education textbooks in mathematics and geography, respectively. The closing chapter concerns the misfortune of a gifted female athlete who violated official GDR *goodthink* and paid a heavy price. Many of these and other stories emerged from my classroom visits to the region's schools, or from my conversations with graduates and erstwhile faculty in the GDR educational system.

Titled "The Un(der)examined Orwell," Part 3 addresses the myths about the man and writer, repeatedly traversing that fuzzy borderland that Erik Erikson famously characterized (in his distinguished study of Luther) "half-legend, half-history." The section opens with a pair of inquiries into the life and work of "the un(der)examined Orwell." Chapter 11 addresses Orwell biography, investigating what I conclude is the "more than half-legendary" encounter between Orwell and Ernest Hemingway in liberated Paris in March 1945. This storied "un-meeting" has been enshrined in both men's literary biographies and in numerous scholarly and journalistic articles. As we shall see, however, the details have been "rectified" to fit the literary imagination: the biographical facts have disappeared "down the memory hole."

By contrast, chapter 12 is a source study focusing on Orwell's work, primarily *Animal Farm*. It argues that a possible folkloric inspiration for two centerpieces of Orwell's allegorical fable whose historical referents have long fascinated readers—Sugarcandy Mountain and "Beasts of England"—can be confirmed via compelling circumstantial evidence. I suggest that Eric Blair was "Tramping toward *Animal Farm*" in his twenties, as it were, and that a famous American hobo ballad ("The Big Rock Candy Mountains") engendered aspects of both Old Major's beast hymn and Moses the raven's alpine apparition.

Orwell's widely taught essay, "Politics and the English Language" (1946), is the subject of chapter 13, where I argue that it is actually unsuitable for classroom composition courses—at least for beginning students. Despite the essay's firm place in American college composition classrooms as a revered prose model, my contention is that it is far too sophisticated to serve as an accessible guide for most young writers. Sadly, given the low levels of cultural literacy and verbal ability commanded by many college freshmen, and certainly the vast majority of high school pupils, Orwell's essay should be reserved for more advanced students—though it doubtless can be profitably read by the general reader who seeks to overcome poor composition habits and aspires to write "prose like a window pane."

Our attention in the next two chapters shifts to issues of genre and rhetoric in *Nineteen Eighty-Four*. Here we are concerned with exploring aspects of literary and rhetorical theory not commonly posed about Orwell's work, specifically as they pertain to "narratology" and to the genre of utopia, respectively. "George Orwell, Literary Theorist?" addresses the rhetoric of narrative, using selected extracts from *Nineteen Eighty-Four* to illustrate how narratives function as arguments—that is, to show "how stories convince us." The succeeding chapter, "The Architectonics of Room 101," looks at the narrative elements in the utopian genre, drawing from a wide range of literary works, including *Nineteen Eighty-Four*. Here my aim is to illustrate how the utopia and anti-utopia reposition the structural elements of prose fiction in a hierarchy of priority different from that prevailing in formalist fiction. If we can recognize how the utopia emphasizes theme and setting, and consequently traffics in familiar plot conventions and stock characters, we can better appreciate what it is attempting to do—and what Orwell did so magnificently in his "didactic fantasies," *Animal Farm* and *Nineteen Eighty-Four*—rather than devalue the genre *tout court* by applying criteria foreign to both its aesthetics and architectonics.

The next pair of chapters pursue a literary phantom, stepping beyond the unexamined Orwell into the Neverland of the "unimagined" Orwell. Titled "The Review Orwell Never Wrote?", chapter 14 witnesses the author of "Confessions of a Book Reviewer" taking on a challenging assignment: Orwell, who enjoyed book reviewing and had much to say about literary biography, reviews the biographies devoted to his own life and legacy. If we accept him at his word—that only he could write his own life and that he would never do so—what might he nonetheless have had to say about the biographies that *others* have written about him? Since Orwell's scattered reviews include some impressionistic criteria for how biographies should be written, I propose to conduct a thought experiment whereby we apply his criteria to the Orwell biographies themselves.

The penultimate chapter, "The Life Orwell Never Lived?" issues forth in another thought experiment, an exercise in what might be termed "virtual biography" prompted by the publication of Orwell's collected letters (*Orwell: A Life in Letters* [2010], edited by Peter Davison). The volume, which I call "the autobiography that Orwell vowed he would never write," includes a heretofore unpublished letter written to her cousin by Jacintha Buddicom, a teenage sweetheart of Eric Blair, which shows the relationship to have been far more serious than originally supposed. For instance, Blair apparently never applied for admission to Oxford and instead enlisted in the Indian Imperial Police because Jacintha rejected him, and on his 1927 return home, Eric proposed marriage to Jacintha, who demurred and thereafter suffered a "lifetime of regrets at turning [Eric] away." Such revelations provoke endless speculation. Indeed, we could reimagine Orwell's entire life and work on the basis of this (and other) new information about Jacintha's role in it. As I note at the close of chapter 17: "Her significance thus shifts from the minor status of forgotten, platonic friend to the role of leading lady—as potential wife and/or unrequited lover and soul mate."

Part 3 closes with a chapter devoted to "The Centenarian, Our Contemporary," presented in the form of an edited NPR radio interview that originally aired in May 2003 during the run-up to his June 25 centennial, just as the US-led invasion of Iraq entered its concluding days. The interview captures an important moment in Orwell's reception history—and in the historiography of the "If Orwell Were Alive Today" conjectures—and suggests how readers are responding to Orwell and "Orwell" in the twenty-first century. By and large, however, they—much like Orwell's intellectual "successors," who are profiled in Part 1—have resisted the urge to "convert" Orwell to their political positions, let alone participated in the "game" of "If Orwell Were Alive Today"—quite unlike the me-doth-protest-too-much author of the present study.

For in the conclusion, I return—and succumb—to that irresistible interrogative, doubtlessly proving the truth of Oscar Wilde's dictum that "one can resist anything except temptation." In a closing meditation on "Orwell," I indulge wantonly in speculation about his posthumous politics, imagining his "counterfactual afterlives" since 1950. In defiance of the plain fact that Eric Blair suffered poor health throughout his short life of forty-six years, I take the conjectures well past his biblical allotment of three score and ten, musing about the politics of the

"The Centenarian, Our Contemporary" even into his eleventh decade. In pursuing this ostensibly outlandish exercise, however, my sincere aim is to take up the so-called game of "If Orwell Were Alive Today" seriously and honestly. I do not simply toss off knee-jerk impressions about "where Orwell would have stood" on events since his death. Rather, I consider the governing themes and contexts of his work, and I assess the value and shortcomings of historians' common tools, such as counterfactuals and historical analogies. Approached with an insistence on concrete supporting evidence, my hope is that such an engagement in the "game" can yield both deeper insight into "Orwell" and serve as a case study in both intellectual history and the sociology of culture. For the fact is that the sociological phenomenon of "Orwell" holds the mirror up to us—indeed it represents "*Big Brother* Watching Us"—and thus discloses much about ourselves.[21]

Afterthoughts on His Afterlives

Part One

If the Mantle Fits . . .

Lionel Trilling, cigarette in hand as always, in his office at Columbia University, 1950s. With the publication of *The Liberal Imagination* (1950), Trilling soon became known as America's leading cultural critic.

CHAPTER I

Virtuous Men?
or "The American Orwell" (I)

n his 1952 introduction to the American edition of
Homage to Catalonia, Lionel Trilling characterized
George Orwell, in an oft-quoted passage, as "a virtuous
man," "a figure in our lives."[1] "We," Trilling said, "could be like him if
only...." And yet, despite his elastic use of the first-person plural, Trilling's charged prose, his choice of details about Orwell, and indeed the
very title of his essay—"The Politics of Truth: Portrait of the Intellectual
as a Man of Virtue"—make clear that he saw Orwell as an intellectual
ideal, the figure as intellectual hero.

For it was Trilling's imagination and spirit that Orwell's life and work
engaged. Orwell stood before Trilling as a man of "truth" and "simple
courage." By means of a remarkable "directness of relation to moral
fact," Orwell seemed to have resolved the problem of political commitment and intellectual integrity, the liberal intellectual's—and Trilling's—
agonized "politics of truth." First published in the March 1952 *Commentary*, edited by Trilling's friend and mentor Elliot Cohen, the essay
reads like a wishful portrait of the first-generation New York intellectual
as a "man of virtue," "liberated" from his "little group," his comforting

"cant," his "need for the inside dope," his intellectual "fashions"—indeed very much like a sketch of Trilling's ideal self.[2] To Trilling, Orwell was "the figure of not being a genius."[3]

A student's characterization of Orwell as "a virtuous man" seemed to Trilling an archaism especially appropriate for describing him.[4] "Somehow to say that a man 'is good,' or even to speak of a man who 'is virtuous,' is not the same thing as saying, 'He is a virtuous man.' That sentence's simple phrasing, by some quirk of the English language," thought Trilling, brought out "the private meaning of the word virtuous, which is not merely moral goodness but fortitude and strength." *Homage to Catalonia* was imbued with virtue in this most sturdy and old-fashioned sense, "a genuine moral triumph written in a tone uniquely simple and true." Orwell was not a genius, just a man who renewed in one "a respect for the powers that one does have, and the work one undertakes to do."

Trilling in fact found Orwell exceptional. "It is hard to find personalities in the contemporary world who are analogous to Orwell." In him "there was indeed a quality of an earlier day," Trilling lamented, for Orwell was "an unusual kind of man, with a temper of heart and mind which is now rare."

Orwell was "an intellectual to his fingertips," said Trilling. But Orwell was no self-important "thinker" trafficking in lofty abstractions and disdaining the daily, earthbound routines of "ordinary" people. He was "far removed from the Continental and American type of intellectual." For Orwell "implies that our job is not to be intellectual, at least not in this fashion or that, but as a man intelligent according to our lights." Trilling's Orwell, "the portrait of the intellectual as a man of virtue," was simply an honest, intelligent man.

It was precisely this sturdy, self-assured intellectual integrity that Trilling was still struggling to achieve in 1952. The "great word" during his student days at Columbia, Trilling later recalled in his memoir, "A Jew at Columbia," had been "intelligence," which "did not imply exceptional powers of abstract thought" but rather "a readiness to confront difficulty and complexity" and "an ability to bring thought cogently to bear upon all subjects to which thought might be appropriate." Trilling conceived "the intelligent man" as exemplified not by erudition and scholarship but by "an intelligence of the emotions and of task."[5] His teacher John Erskine's motto "The Moral Obligation to be Intelligent" became Trilling's too.[6]

Indeed Trilling's own reputation was not founded on brilliance. By the early '50s, the younger generation saw him as an example of humanist-critical intelligence and instinctive good judgment. Like Orwell, he was

If the Mantle Fits . . .

regarded as a "different" sort of intellectual. Philip Toynbee noticed a strong resemblance between Orwell and Trilling as "liberal-democratic critics." One senses that these similarities in position and temper did not pass Trilling's eye unnoticed. In his obituary of Trilling, Steven Marcus closed by naming five authors whom his onetime teacher "most admired." Orwell was the only twentieth-century writer on the list.

Of course, whatever his writings may suggest, Orwell was not so plain and simple, nor even so self-assured, let alone fully integrated into the "life of the family," as evidenced by both his marital infidelities and his strained relations with his family over his struggles to become a writer. Trilling was more accurate than he realized when he spoke of Orwell's "fronting the world" with his "simple, direct, undeceived intelligence." Orwell's literary persona was partly a front, but that is not to say it was deceptive. It was a carefully crafted projection of Orwell's literary ego ideal: the man of decency and simplicity. And the self-projection achieved its aim: Trilling, like others, perceived Orwell to be a "plain" man. In turn, Trilling's image of Orwell in his introduction to *Homage to Catalonia* was a moving, fully convincing portrait of an intelligent man of virtue. Much of what made this portrait so convincing was Trilling's own passionate homage to Orwell. At this moment in his life, Trilling identified wholeheartedly with Orwell, not only with his situation and status, but also with his character and destiny.

To some extent the two men did ultimately realize a common destiny: Trilling's image of the "virtuous" Orwell came to prefigure the *Partisan Review (PR)* writers' image of Trilling himself. "He was, to use the old-fashioned term, a virtuous man," William Barrett wrote of Trilling in his 1982 autobiography, *The Truants: Adventures Among the Intellectuals*, "and moreover, a virtuous man without any touch of the prig. And in the particular environment of New York in which we moved that was indeed an accomplishment."

That common destiny has continued to run on parallel tracks up to the very present. In fact, as we shall see, it has taken a surprising turn in recent years, with the posthumous Trilling "morphing" in the twenty-first century into "the American Orwell" in an ironic sense that his long-time admirers never imagined.

I

By the time of Trilling's death in November 1975 at the age of seventy, the judgment of Barrett and his *PR* colleagues had solidified into a common consensus within the Anglo-American intelligentsia. Even before his death, sentiments echoing those of Barrett were often heard. For instance, in September 1973, the British poet John Holloway wrote about Lionel Trilling: "In our literary-academic world, Trilling has to be called a heroic figure, almost the only one." The tributes to Trilling as a culture hero, at least among Anglo-American literary intellectuals, are widespread. Yet they occur within a narrower demographic than in the instance of Orwell—chiefly on the New York-London intellectual scene and among humanistic scholars in the American literary academy. Indeed Trilling occupies a place not unlike that of Orwell's within a broader cultural-political sphere. And it is also true that Trilling is the only American intellectual who commands respect across the ideological spectrum, from leading American neoconservative, liberal, and radical intellectuals.[7]

Perhaps unsurprisingly, that wide respect has resulted in Right-Left battles to claim Trilling's legacy that exhibit an extraordinary resemblance—in shape, if not in size and scope—to the skirmishes for Orwell's mantle. Neoconservatives such as Norman Podhoretz have memorialized Trilling as a foe of the New Left, an opponent of the counterculture, and a defender of humanist values and cultural literacy. The "godfather" of neoconservatism, Irving Kristol, has stated that Trilling is one of the "two thinkers who had the greatest subsequent impact on my thinking" in the early postwar era (along with Leo Strauss); later Kristol adds that Trilling was one of the "two intellectual godfathers of my neo-ism" (along with Reinhold Niebuhr).

Meanwhile, Left-liberals such as Morris Dickstein and Gerald Graff have emphasized Trilling's high critical standards and his Arnoldian aspiration to reinvigorate liberalism, not abandon it. Admittedly, a few academic radicals have scorned Trilling himself as the "godfather" of neoconservatism, whose work leads to "an intellectual dead end" (Cornel West). But other Left-leaning academics have honored Trilling with book-length studies devoted to his work and legacy, arguing that he was a conservator, though not a conservative: a "subversive patriarch" with conserving impulses (Dan O'Hara) and a liberal cultural critic whose compelling essays guided postwar intellectuals' rightward steps away from progressive politics (Mark Krupnick).

Like Orwell, Trilling left no explicit political "testament." Indeed, he died just before the culture wars between the neocons and liberal-Left began in the mid-1970s. And whatever his sentiments in his private conversations, he never publicly sided with emergent neocons such as Podhoretz. In an odd way—much like the inadvertent timing of Orwell's

If the Mantle Fits . . .

death in January 1950, just as the Cold War was heating up—Trilling died at precisely the "right moment" to become an object of contention for both American neoconservatives and left-liberals. For example, if Orwell had lived even until 1955, let alone into the 1960s, he would not have been spared the agony of taking sides on political controversies ranging from McCarthyism to the student movement. Inevitably, as happened with Bertrand Russell, Koestler, Sartre, Camus, Mailer, Paul Goodman, and numerous other socialist intellectual "heroes" in the 1950s and '60s, his positions would have compromised him in the eyes of several groups that today claim him as a forerunner. His patriotism, his democratic socialism, his anticommunism: these and other aspects of his work would have come under attack from different sides. Could he possibly have won or maintained his current stature on so many fronts? It is most doubtful.

Here again, Trilling's fate has been uncannily similar. If he had lived even until 1980, it probably would have been impossible for both liberals and neoconservatives to stake a claim to him. As an intellectual leader, he would have been forced to take public positions on a range of issues—feminism, gay rights, abortion, affirmative action, Reaganism, Nicaragua, the war on terrorism, and more—that inevitably would have compromised him in the eyes of some partisans who now claim his heritage.

II

Such are the accidents of history and the contingencies of reputation-building. Since 1999, however, Trilling's reputation has taken an unexpected turn—though its somersaulting trajectory ultimately, if bizarrely, intersects on another plane with Orwell's own. Let us step back from the comparisons between Trilling and Orwell as culture heroes to examine thoroughly the unforeseen—yet, given cultural trends, all-too-predictable—course of Trilling's reputation in the twenty-first century. We shall then return to compare the two men in light of this newest stage of his reception history—and glimpse how the mordant, iconoclastic zeitgeist has reduced him to a mock-heroic figure: a portrait of the intellectual as an "American Orwell" caricature. The development has witnessed the political controversy about Trilling's life and legacy transmogrify into the psychological "case" of Lionel Trilling. Or, rather, the historical case *about* Trilling has become the psychotherapeutic "case" *of* Trilling, at least in the eyes of some harsh critics.

Virtuous Men?

The turn—arguably, the downturn—in Trilling's reputation possesses for many observers an Oedipal cast. In a memoir in the spring 1999 issue of the *American Scholar*, Trilling's son, James, published an essay that proposed an understanding of his father's suffering that differs from Lionel's own self-understanding. "My father's worst problem was not neurosis, it was a neurological condition, attention deficit disorder," he writes. James Trilling is not a medically trained diagnostician; he is an independent scholar specializing in Byzantine art and the history of ornament. But he advances his argument by citing his own experience as someone who suffers from ADD, a cognitive disorder affecting the mind's ability to focus.

Some of the conduct that James mentions—most notably, Lionel's periodic rages against his wife, Diana—were described in her memoir, *The Beginning of the Journey: The Marriage of Diana and Lionel Trilling* (1993), her last substantial statement about her husband before she died in 1996. But Mrs. Trilling's four-hundred-page memoir simply mentions these outbursts as occasional incidents in a long marriage. James Trilling goes much further, not only adding much new information but also devoting exclusive attention and sustained analysis to his father's psychological condition—and diagnosing other family members (including himself) as well. James stresses Lionel's "near-total obliviousness to his surroundings," which James sees as the empty reality behind his father's social "mask." That word comes from a 1952 journal entry that Lionel wrote just weeks after publication of his Orwell essay in *Commentary*—in which he confessed that his own exalted status "really needs a mask."

And Trilling evidently accepted this fact—and donned it, at the price of masking himself even to himself. Lionel's self-alienation allegedly reflected fear of his own rage and "his struggle for self-control." James Trilling writes: "All my father's personality flaws, which continued to haunt my mother almost 20 years after his death, were symptoms of attention deficit disorder." He blames his father's absent-mindedness, secretiveness, anger, impatience, indecisiveness, bad driving, bad swimming, and bad tennis on the disorder. Then he lays out the diagnoses of the rest of his family. His mother's affliction was "panic disorder with agoraphobia, which made her an emotional cripple for many years." His aunt had Tourette's Syndrome. His grandfather suffered from attention deficit disorder. And so does he. ADD, he emphasizes, is "the most insidious culprit in my family." The son has few doubts about his diagnosis. "I have it, my father almost certainly had it, and in all likelihood his father had it too." Its main feature is "the inability to maintain a productive level of concentration ('focus') through the normal range of

If the Mantle Fits . . .

daily activities." (On hearing this, one Trilling admirer wrote jeeringly to the *New York Times*: "Gee, I wish I could have Lionel Trilling's disorder, the kind that is so crippling that you are forced to write important books, become a judicious critic, teach at a major university, and have a family too.")

Titled "My Father and the Weak-Eyed Devils" (the latter phrase alludes to Conrad's *Heart of Darkness*), James Trilling's essay concludes that Trilling Sr. was so blinded by his love of Freud and psychoanalysis that he missed his real disease and suffered unknowingly from attention deficit disorder. The most reductive charge that James levels against his father is the idea that Lionel Trilling's very thinking—not only his love of Freud, but his whole moral universe—was determined by ADD: "He saw the world as a practical and moral obstacle course, but it was the obstacles that fascinated him, not the ways around them. He loved to follow the path of most resistance, and where obstacles were lacking he turned all his ingenuity to inventing them."

James then challenges his father's literary judgment, particularly his attention to "complexity":

> During his entire career as an interpreter of literature, I doubt my father ever solved a problem, in the sense of marshaling evidence to prove or disprove a theory. On the contrary, he built his career on the mistrust of certainties and was rarely content with a simple answer when a complex one could be found. . . . Of all "simple" solutions he mistrusted happiness the most. The idea of living happily ever after must have seemed almost crass to him. Certainly it left him all dressed up with no place to go.

Even before its publication, James Trilling's essay triggered a firestorm of controversy in intellectual circles.[8] Paul R. McHugh, the director of psychiatry at the Johns Hopkins University Medical Center, resigned from the editorial board of the *American Scholar*, calling the essay "abominable" and "mean-spirited." "It is a clumsily written, meanly written article about a defenseless father," McHugh said in an interview in the *New York Times*, adding that James's diagnosis "is so palpably unwarranted that it hardly needs extensive criticism" and is indeed "not given anything [in James's essay] like the foundation a psychiatrist would give." (It should also be noted, as James Trilling does, that the symptoms attributed to ADD are manifold and sometimes contradictory, and that educators and psychologists still argue about its validity as a diagnostic category.)

21 *Virtuous Men?*

McHugh viewed James Trilling's essay as a case of psychiatric malpractice potentially damaging to the entire field. He warned that the essay takes the field back to a time when it was used "to get at people who were defenseless." "Here is a person who knows little or nothing about psychiatry using psychological terms and ideas to settle scores," he said. Furthermore, McHugh asserted, ADD is a childhood disorder that may reach into adulthood but that cannot be diagnosed without a childhood history.

While expressing regard for Anne Fadiman, the former editor of the *American Scholar*, McHugh added that she had treated him as mere "window-dressing" by publishing the article without consulting him, the only psychiatrist on the editorial board. "I didn't feel it was written in a spirit of vengeance," Fadiman replied in her defense. "I felt it was written in a tenacious desire to get at the truth. James Trilling has spent his life bending over backward to avoid trading on his parents' names."

Interestingly, Fadiman is the daughter of Lionel's friend and former Columbia classmate Clifton Fadiman, and she and James are personally acquainted. Moreover, James's piece appeared not long after he declined a request to contribute to my essay collection devoted to Trilling's intellectual heritage, *Lionel Trilling and the Critics* (1999). The accusations of exploitation, Oedipal revenge, and psycho-autopsy were not slow in coming. "A Son's Simple Diagnosis of His Father's Complexities: Critic on the Couch" headlined the *New York Times* in a prepublication advance report on James Trilling's article in April 1999. Days later, writing in the "Think Tank" column of the *New York Times* (April 24), Sarah Boxer accused the son of betraying his father's life and work by reducing them to symptoms of ADD. Since Lionel was an orthodox Freudian, and James had proposed another way of looking at Lionel's life, she argued, the son's aim must be to usurp the father's place. Boxer asked, rhetorically, "Why does an article about attention deficit disorder sound so Oedipal?"

Three weeks later, in the *New Republic* (May 17), Leon Wieseltier, the magazine's literary editor and a former Trilling student, took the attack a step further, charging that James was seeking to "relieve himself" of the pressure of a vocation demanding high aspirations. His memoir is "banal and low," an exercise in "filio-porn." Wieseltier emphasized the bigger "stakes in James Trilling's exhibitionism." As an intellectual son of Lionel Trilling, Wieseltier was challenging James Trilling's filial prerogative and asserting his own claim to the Trilling legacy. (Wieseltier and James Trilling are generational coevals, both in their mid-sixties.) By implication, Wieseltier was asking: What does it mean to be an intellectual today? Is it all just a "mask"? Here we return again to Trilling's "example" and his status as a culture hero.

For Wieseltier, James Trilling's essay was a social case of intellectual pseudo-toughness: a case of disillusion with the intellectual calling, given vindictive expression via a skewering of the major postwar American intellectual who had seemed to embody that calling. The "aim" of the son's essay "is to relieve himself, and us, of a certainly lofty notion of Lionel Trilling and thereby to relieve us of a certain lofty notion of the intellectual calling. . . . His diminishment of his father's view of life into a clinical condition is designed to bring us all the gift of relaxation." That intellectual slackness leads the son to "degrade precious things" by degrading nuance and promoting oversimplification. Wieseltier's indignation led him to a moving peroration in defense of Trilling's exalted conception of "Mind": "The idea of living happily ever after is crass, but still there is happiness. Complexity is the destiny of thoughtful individuals, from which they will never be rescued, but still there is love."

The intellectuals' outrage culminated in July 1999 with Gertrude Himmelfarb's *Commentary* essay, "A Man's Own Household His Enemies." Deriving her title from Rabbi Eliezer's prophecy in the Talmud (from Micah) on the coming of family betrayals and fraternal corruption, Himmelfarb interpreted James Trilling's analysis as a historical case of confessional literature, representing its newest stage, whereby the revelations bare not just one's own private life but that of helpless family members. (Himmelfarb included John Bayley's recent memoir of his wife, the philosopher Iris Murdoch, and Diana Trilling's *The Beginning of the Journey* in her indictment.)

Unlike other commentators on James Trilling's analysis, Himmelfarb (who was married to the late Irving Kristol) wrote with special authority. She is both a scholar-critic of Trilling's work and a longtime acquaintance of Lionel and Diana Trilling, who had much contact with the Kristols throughout the postwar era (until the couples fell out in the early 1970s over whether to support Richard Nixon's re-election bid for president). Much of Himmelfarb's scholarship has focused on the rise and fall of cultural fashions, especially the historical development of "the moral imagination" (a phrase of Trilling's, whom she keenly admires). A historian with a strong, conservatively toned revisionist sensibility, Himmelfarb is an outspoken defender of the leading values of Victorian morality. She is also opposed to the dominance within academic historiography of Left-oriented social history (which she criticizes as a form of covert radical propaganda), preferring instead traditional historical approaches that emphasize politics and "high" culture.

Virtuous Men?

Himmelfarb is usually identified as a prominent neoconservative, and she views Lionel Trilling as an intellectual model and neoconservative forebear. She dedicates *On Looking into the Abyss: Untimely Thoughts on Culture and Society* (1994) "to the memory of Lionel Trilling." Himmelfarb adds in the preface: "The spirit of Lionel Trilling hovers over the book as a whole." Titled "The Abyss Revisited," the opening chapter returns to Trilling's famous essay "On the Modern Element in Modern Literature" (1961), arguing its significance and relevance to Right-Left academic debates of the 1990s.

In her *Commentary* essay, Himmelfarb drew on her considerable authority as a scholar-intellectual and former friend of the Trillings. She was able to meet James Trilling on his own ground as someone who could draw on personal experience of Trilling the man. "To those who knew Lionel Trilling," she writes, "nothing could resemble the man less than this listing of his incapacities." She speculates that James waited so long to publish his essay because he "did not have the means at hand for the task" until gaining access to Diana's tapes about her marriage (after her 1996 death) and until ADD became a fashionable medical ("or pseudo-medical") diagnosis. Indeed, James admits that his father rarely had a personal conversation with him, and that most of his information was gleaned from his mother's tapes, which she made in preparation for writing *The Beginning of the Journey*.

Himmelfarb deplores what she sees as the indulgence and arrogance of the son's confessional mode of analysis. "What is striking about this memoir is the way its author implicitly places himself on a par with his subject, indeed puts himself at the center of the stage." To James's claim that he and his father were "in the same boat" as ADD sufferers, Himmelfarb retorts: "To the reader, it may seem more remarkable that at no point does the adult son acknowledge that, in terms of accomplishments, they are hardly 'in the same boat.'" In direct opposition to Anne Fadiman's view, Himmelfarb sees James as trading on his famous father's life in order to claim victim status and gain national attention.

Here it seems apposite to mention the response of another old friend of the Trillings', who informs me that Diana once said to him (about James) that "life is about accomplishment, not contentment"—and that James was failing in life "because he has accomplished relatively little." Diana did not hide her disappointment that her son had become a homemaker who reared the children and chose not to pursue his art history scholarship full time after being denied tenure at Brown University in the 1970s. (The language of "accomplishment" may mark a

If the Mantle Fits . . .

generational divide between the outlooks of James, born in 1946, and of both the Trillings and the Kristols.)

But Himmelfarb does not confine her critique to the son's essay. Indeed she contends that both James and Diana invaded Lionel's privacy posthumously. Writing about Diana's lengthy discussion in her memoir of Lionel's depression, Himmelfarb adds: "He was at pains not to disclose it even to his closest friends—whereupon she proceeds to disclose it to the world."

James Trilling's lone vocal defender was Mark Krupnick, a onetime sharp critic of Lionel who had become an ardent admirer by the 1980s. In "Diagnosing Trilling: Why the Critics Are Wrong," Krupnick adopted a sympathetic stance toward James's analysis and motives. Writing in the *Chronicle of Higher Education* (June 4, 1999), Krupnick valued "the sensitivity, generosity, and empathy that seem to me to inform [James Trilling's] understanding of his father"—qualities that Krupnick had not thought characteristic of Diana Trilling's memoir. Unlike readers who interpreted the son's essay as a form of Oedipal revenge, Krupnick judged it to be an act of compassion and reconciliation: "Despite Lionel Trilling's incapacity to see his own weaknesses in his son, the son shows himself able to forgive the father and wish that the father could have been helped to know and accept himself as the son has. James seems to be performing an act of reparation, not an act of parricide."

Did Lionel Trilling suffer from ADD? If so, did it limit his life and work? Krupnick argues, not implausibly, that Trilling's nuanced literary style and repeated appeal to the "complexity" and "variousness" of life represented a positive adjustment "to neurological problems involving attention and focus." Whatever critical consensus ultimately emerges, Krupnick's concluding statement about the newest turn in Trilling's reception is astute as a historical judgment about Trilling's "complex" reputation and heritage:

> His essays and lectures remain models for today's public intellectuals who aim, as Trilling did, to challenge the literary and cultural orthodoxies of our age. Now his son, James Trilling, an art historian, has dared to reinterpret his father's life, and critics have responded angrily to what they see as a challenge to the purity of his father's legacy.

Probably this inconclusive controversy about Trilling says much more about contemporary intellectual life than it does about Trilling himself: the hunger of secular intellectuals for "purity"—and for culture heroes.

Indeed I would go so far as to speculate that, quite ironically, it may well turn out that this odd debate ultimately elevates Trilling's standing even further—precisely by reinforcing the image that readers such as myself have long held of him: the writer engaged in the arduous struggle of shaping a self, the thinker who prized the life of the "Mind," the man who pursued a lofty vision of the intellectual vocation.

And those perceptions are, above all, why Lionel Trilling evokes—much like Orwell, though arguably in a more subdued, even more cultivated sense—such an intensely personal response in his readers. By both men's example, they implicitly challenge us to conceive our lives similarly—and thus heroically. They prod us to live what Diana Trilling once called, in a high-toned phrase describing the vocation of their New York intellectual circle, "the life of significant contention."

And so Trilling's considerable weaknesses—whether in his personal or intellectual life—notwithstanding, I still find it inspiring that he made so much of his abilities and preoccupations. His arguably coterie stance, his predominant focus on nineteenth-century Britain, his near-exclusive interest in cultural criticism—and now his family conflicts and alleged psychological disorder—all issued forth in rich insight and finally lend him even the appearance of rare openness and breadth. For me, an awareness of his limitations somehow humanizes him. I think of Trilling's own exhilarating perception of George Orwell's severe limitations as a writer and man: "He is not a genius—what a relief! What an encouragement. For he communicates the sense to us that what he has done, any one of us could do."

And yet, my "speculation" about Trilling's standing in the future represents much more a hope than a prophecy. It is, moreover, contingent upon a possibility fast receding: that he will be thoughtfully read and pondered by future intellectuals. Perhaps he will not be.

And let me close on that somber possibility. For, as I have already suggested, the existence of other, less comforting parallels to George Orwell makes me wonder if Trilling is also destined to become "the American Orwell" in this ironic, trivialized sense. One ponders the emerging resemblances between the two men's posthumous fates: the skirmishes over their mantles, the relentless preoccupation with their personalities, the obsessive interest in their private lives—all of this at the expense of attention to their serious work. Little of it has to do with higher ideas; almost all of it reflects (and spices) the higher gossip. The ravenous maw of intellectual celebrity devours everything and exists only to engorge more;[9] the personality cult controversies and grave-robbing disputes do not return readers to the artists' writings: they displace them.

Like Orwell, Trilling is now honored in the breach: cited yet often unread, brandished yet seldom engaged. Like Orwell too, Trilling has become as important to many intellectuals for his iconic status as for his literary achievement. Their inflation into icons has resulted in their deflation as thinkers and writers. Indeed, even the openly admiring attitudes toward Trilling of Wieseltier and Himmelfarb may inadvertently contribute to such a deflation. For they speak of him in religious language. Wieseltier's "lofty" mystical-spiritual conception of the intellectual vocation, and Himmelfarb's allusion to Rabbi Eliezer in Micah (one notes that Trilling is often cast as a secular rabbi) demonstrate that the secular intellectual world possesses an unacknowledged religious sensibility. And just as in formal religions, the intellectual community has its icons. Trilling, if on a lower altar than Orwell, has become one of them.

So the last decade has opened another new stage in Lionel Trilling's reputation. Following upon Diana Trilling's sharp criticism of her husband in *The Beginning of the Journey*, James Trilling's *American Scholar* essay has focused attention on his father's family life and personality. That leaves us with a larger historical question about the zeitgeist: Does Lionel Trilling's posthumous "case" history of intellectual mantle-snatching and familial psychologizing merely define the present moment? Or does it represent his future significance?

It is still too early to say. And yet, given four decades of posthumous controversies about Trilling's legacy and the swerve of critical attention inward toward the private man, it seems sadly possible that his legacy will chiefly exemplify what might be ironically termed "the afterlife of significant contention."

The editorial board of *Partisan Review*, 1940: (*from left, standing*) G. L. K. Morris, Philip Rahv, and Dwight Macdonald; (*seated*) F. W. Dupee and William Phillips.

CHAPTER 2

"Dear Dwight,"
or "The American Orwell" (II)

A half century ago, Dwight Macdonald was periodically touted as "the American Orwell." Indeed the historian John Lukacs honored him in the Jesuit magazine *America* with that phrase,[1] and Orwell's widow, Sonia, considered commissioning Macdonald to write Orwell's biography.[2]

Macdonald and Orwell did have a good deal in common. Both came from the similar bourgeois backgrounds of Phillips Exeter Academy and Eton, somewhat comparable boarding schools. Macdonald developed a much closer personal relationship to Orwell during his lifetime than did any of the other *Partisan Review* (*PR*) writers.[3] He reviewed both Orwell's first collection of essays, *Inside the Whale* (1940), and his patriotic wartime manifesto, *The Lion and the Unicorn* (1941), in *PR*'s pages. Orwell corresponded frequently with Macdonald throughout the 1940s and contributed to the journal *politics*. (Macdonald proudly and defiantly lowercased the title, much as Orwell always referred to his "democratic Socialism" with the noun capitalized.) After Orwell's death, Macdonald lauded the first American edition of *The Road to Wigan Pier* (1958) in the *New Yorker*, championing Orwell as the author of "the best sociological reporting I know," a man who "lived the life of the people he wrote about." Like Orwell, Macdonald pioneered a distinctive sociological approach to contemporary popular and mass culture, what Orwell once called "semi-sociological literary criticism."[4] Macdonald and Orwell were also contrarians, though Orwell was a more serious-minded writer and more of a political pragmatist than the gadfly Macdonald. Nonetheless, it was precisely this shared contrarian spirit that led John Lukacs, who later became a friend of Macdonald's, to call him "the American Orwell" for his spirit of independence and defiant outspokenness—his capacity to go "against the American grain," the phrase of Macdonald's 1962 essay collection of that title.

But there the resemblances between Orwell and Macdonald end: their divergent careers owe much less to the quality of their talents than to the nature, depth, and fulfillment of their commitments.

I

Unlike George Orwell, whose centennial in 2003 was the object of myriad news articles, op-ed columns, magazine cover stories, and even radio and TV broadcasts, Dwight Macdonald's centenary three years later provoked barely a whisper, even among American intellectuals who had known him well or in periodicals that had frequently published his essays and reviews.[5] Moreover, even unlike his friend and intellectual contemporary Lionel Trilling, whose centenary in June 2005 was commemorated widely in the United States—via national academic conferences as well as articles in the *New York Times* and leading literary magazines—Macdonald's centennial several months later on March 24 went generally unnoticed.[6] Nor did the twenty-fifth anniversary of his death in December 2007 occasion much response from the cultural world.

Nonetheless, Dwight Macdonald once had the (perhaps questionable) distinction of being cast—along with several other leading members of the *Partisan Review* circle—as the "typical New York Intellectual." Yet he is probably the most unusual candidate within their group for that dubious honor. Educated at Phillips Exeter and Yale University, Macdonald was an upper-middle-class suburban WASP—unlike the other leading figures of the New York Intellectuals, a mostly Jewish, inner-city group. Another notable exception in this regard—in fact, even more so as a female member of their circle—was Mary McCarthy, who became one of Macdonald's closest friends.[7] Macdonald served as the model for McCarthy's essay "Portrait of the Intellectual as a Yale Man." (Indeed,

If the Mantle Fits . . .

I might also have titled this chapter "Portrait of the [New York] Intellectual as a Yale Man.") Mary McCarthy also drew on Macdonald for the endearing character of Macdougal Macdermott in her early postwar satirical novel, *The Oasis*.[8] In a less flattering light, Macdonald was also the object of Saul Bellow's biting satire in *Humboldt's Gift*, appearing as the figure of Orlando Higgins, the lightweight nudist intellectual.

As for Macdonald the man and writer, life was indeed just as strange and wondrous as fiction. His political pilgrimage represented a public drama that unfolded by leaps and lurches. After graduating from Yale in 1927, Macdonald worked for a year as a Macy's salesman and then joined the fledgling publishing enterprise of his fellow Yale alumnus Henry Luce as a staff writer for *Fortune* in 1929. Macdonald stayed with the magazine for seven years. He finally resigned when he felt that he was being politically stifled as he began to move leftward and embrace Marxism, a journey catalyzed by his 1934 marriage to Nancy Rodman and the influence of her wide circle of radical friends.[9] Macdonald became a self-declared Trotskyist in 1936.

Yet it was also true that, like many intellectuals, he became associated in the mid-1930s with the Communist Party because it seemed to represent the only decent alternative to what he judged the inexorable outcome of capitalism: imperialism, fascism, and economic depression. The Soviet purges of 1935–1938 deepened Macdonald's commitment to Trotskyism and induced him in July 1939 to join the Socialist Workers Party (SWP), the main political sect of Trotsky's American followers. Macdonald did so with the fervor of a newborn convert, but also with the retained critical faculties of someone who was no quacking ideologue or Communist stooge. Macdonald flirted with various left-wing factions besides the SWP during the late 1930s and early 1940s, ambivalently remaining within the Trotskyist fold until the middle of World War II, partly due to his enduring personal admiration for Trotsky throughout this period: Macdonald considered him an exemplary instance of the man of action and the man of reflection combined for a worthy radical purpose.

Inevitably, Macdonald's falling-out with the SWP was just a matter of time. It finally occurred when Trotsky decided that regardless of the USSR's actions, such as the Nazi-Soviet Nonaggression Pact of 1939 or Stalin's attack on Finland in the fall of that year, Soviet Russia had to be supported because it was a "worker's state," albeit a "degenerated" one.[10] This decision appalled Macdonald, who split with the SWP, helped form the breakaway Workers Party (WP) in 1940, and publicly began to criticize Trotsky's views, both in WP-sponsored organs and in the non-Trotskyist press. As a result, the WP began to demand that Macdonald submit all his writings to the Party leadership before publishing them. That was too much for Macdonald, who resigned from the WP in spring 1941 and later concluded that such strict Party control showed that Trotskyism "was merely a variant of Stalinism." Macdonald's recalcitrance and skepticism toward American Trotskyist leaders, and even Trotsky himself, did not please the "Old Man." "Everyone has the right to be stupid, but Comrade Macdonald abuses the privilege!" groused Trotsky.[11]

This zinger has been much quoted, though Macdonald's biographer Michael Wreszin speculates that it may be apocryphal (and Dwight's clever invention).[12] But what is clearly established is that one of Trotsky's last acts before he was assassinated in 1940 was a reply to Macdonald. Macdonald had castigated Trotsky for his brutal suppression of the Kronstadt uprising and execution of the defeated rebels, which Trotsky never repudiated, let alone expressed remorse or contrition. (Even today, orthodox Trotskyists tend to downplay the whole brutal incident in much the same dismissive tones as orthodox Communists do about later Soviet atrocities.)

Certainly Macdonald was temperamentally and socially unsuited to the SWP or WP. For instance, in full conspiratorial mode, most members took secret Party names. But in his inveterately puckish, nose-tweaking spirit of bemused defiance, Macdonald adopted "James Joyce." Could anyone have been more antithetical to the passionately committed ideological stances of Lenin and Trotsky than the ingenious ludic artist who authored *Finnegans Wake?*[13]

Already by this time Macdonald had become affiliated with a likeminded group of radical intellectuals who also exhibited the audacity to buck party discipline and think for themselves. In May 1937, Macdonald joined the editorial board of the newly refounded *Partisan Review,* working with editors Philip Rahv and William Phillips to shift it from a Communist Party organ to an independent left-wing quarterly ("Partisansky Review," in Edmund Wilson's sobriquet, mocking the Jewish co-editors who had shortened and anglicized their East European immigrant names).[14]

For a brief interval of a year or two, Macdonald was jubilant: he felt at home among this group of predominantly Jewish Trotskyists, an intellectual coterie that slaked his thirst for informed debate about politics and avant-garde sophistication in culture. And despite his subsequent dissatisfactions with most of his *PR* colleagues over their positions on World War II, McCarthyism, and the New Left, Macdonald's encounter

During the Democratic primary season in 1968, Macdonald sported on his lapel a "McCarthy for President" button, which replaced his traditional "Rosa Luxemburg" pin. A strong supporter of Eugene McCarthy's antiwar stance, Macdonald campaigned for the senator during the primaries.

with this like-minded literary species also furnished him with his vocation: for the rest of his life he would be a journalist, critic, editor, and commentator for various magazines, including the *New Yorker*, the *New Republic*, *Esquire*, and *Encounter*, to mention just a few.

Macdonald's years with *PR* (1937–1943) were formative ones. He completed much of his political education at this time, though Rahv and Phillips always regarded him as an intellectual popinjay and a political naïf. Because of the dizzying divagations of his political course occasioned by his numerous, abrupt ideological about-faces, Macdonald frequently was taken to have a frivolous political mind and was regarded as an impulsive jester. As we shall see, however, the simple truth is that such matters as theoretical coherence or even consistency were of secondary concern to Macdonald: in essence he was a rebel and gadfly, a member of the (sometimes-)loyal opposition, a thinker who exemplified the classic conception of the modern intellectual as a critic of the powers-that-be. Yet he was also a critic-from-within, a critic of the intelligentsia and of his own side, however temporary his alliance with that side might be.

"Dear Dwight"

Like most of his colleagues among the New York Intellectuals, Macdonald was highly critical of the liberalism of the New Dealers and of the illiberal liberalism of the Stalinists. He considered the nineteenth-century liberal mind to be outdated in the modern world. According to Macdonald, liberal philosophers such as John Dewey and William James, along with contemporary liberals such as Lewis Mumford and Arthur Schlesinger, were ill-equipped to understand the threats posed by mass man and the highly unstable economic conditions of the mid-twentieth century. During his Trotskyist phase, Macdonald saw them as blind to the fact that some kind of Stalinist, undemocratic, quasi-authoritarian system such as communism or fascism would be needed to achieve an egalitarian, ordered, law-abiding society.[15] The independent, liberal-Left positions advocated by socialists such as his wife Nancy's brother, Selden Rodman, editor of *Common Sense*, seemed to Macdonald utterly naïve, since they blithely assumed that "sweet reason alone" could transform monopoly capitalism into a decent socialism. For all his hatred of dictators such as Hitler, Stalin, and Mussolini, as Michael Wreszin persuasively argues in his excellent biography, Macdonald harbored a veiled admiration for them as men of power who did not shrink from the exercise of ruthless force to achieve their ends.

For a short time, Macdonald was able to reconcile his SWP/WP allegiance with his freethinking *PR* affiliation. As we have seen, when Macdonald joined *Partisan Review*, it was being transformed by editors Rahv and Phillips from a Communist Party tract into an independent Marxist organ sympathetic to Trotsky, then in exile in Mexico. The journal was designed to blend Marxist theory with serious commentary on art and culture, and Macdonald fit in well—at least intellectually. He had read Marx and admired Trotskyism because, in his words, it "was the most revolutionary of the sizeable leftwing groups . . . and, above all . . . it was led by Trotsky, whose career showed that intellectuals, too, could make history."[16]

In the September-October 1940 issue of *PR*, Macdonald published an extended obituary of Trotsky: "Trotsky Is Dead." Here he argued that in his last years Trotsky "had understood so much and yet did not understand enough; he probed boldly and deeply and yet did not go deep enough." Echoing the intra-party critique of Trotsky by ex-SWP member Max Shachtman, who had recently broken with the SWP to form his own dissident Trotskyist sect—the WP—Macdonald insisted that Trotsky had failed to understand the full significance of developments in Stalin's Russia and Hitler's Germany in the 1930s. While Stalin was certainly not taking Russia in a socialist direction, neither was

If the Mantle Fits . . .

he restoring capitalism. Instead, he "has created a new form of class exploitation—call it 'bureaucratic collectivism' for lack of a better term [the Italian Bruno Rizzi is usually credited with this coinage]—and only on this basis can the development of the USSR in the last ten years be understood."[17] Similarly, while Trotsky had provided a marvelous commentary on the Nazis' rise to power in Germany, he had failed to see that Hitler's regime had also set about building a new type of exploitative class society that was converging with Stalin's Russia.

II

Macdonald was by predilection and preference an adamant contrarian who could not resist tweaking noses and puncturing pretensions. He could not long abide "smelly little orthodoxies" (an Orwell phrase that he liked) and quickly became a rebel within any group that he joined, as he noted in his two essay collections recounting the early postwar era, *Memoirs of a Revolutionist* (1957) and *Against the American Grain* (1962).[18] He resigned from the SWP in October 1940 after only fifteen months as a member because the leadership demanded strict adherence to the party line;[19] soon he would also break with his *PR* associates over their support for the Allies in World War II.

Macdonald's pacifist-isolationist stance toward the war rankled most of his fellow *PR* editors and led to acrimonious, divisive debates. Macdonald had to fight to get his fellow editors to agree to publish his pacifist rejoinders to George Orwell, *PR*'s London correspondent, that appeared in the autumn of 1942. Indeed, his Marxist and secular Jewish colleagues at *PR* considered him hopelessly confused as a political thinker and much more of a moralist than a socialist, acridly predicting in one published editorial dispute that Macdonald's ethical impulse—exemplified by his intense esteem for Catholic writers such as Simone Weil and Dorothy Day—might soon lead him to join the Church. In reply, Macdonald readily admitted that moral and ethical considerations governed his ideological outlook, though he never exhibited, as he also noted, the slightest interest in religion or God.

The situation came to a head in mid-1943 when Macdonald attempted to take control of the magazine. With the intention of changing *PR* from a literary to a political review with a strong antiwar stance, he published (with junior editor Clement Greenberg) "Ten Propositions on the War," a feisty manifesto that vehemently castigated the war effort and its supporters. Finally, under pressure from Rahv and Phillips, Macdon-

"Dear Dwight"

ald resigned from the editorial board of *PR* in July 1943. Soon he set about founding his own magazine, which he launched with his wife's family inheritance.

Macdonald named his journal *politics*. He wanted it to be more political than *PR*, which steered away from controversial positions during the war out of fear of censorship.[20] For five years (1944–1949), largely as a one-man labor of love, *politics* voiced a radical, contrarian view toward the most popular war in American history. Often strident, unbalanced, and wide of the mark, it nevertheless exhibited a facet of Macdonald that remains of enduring value: his plain-speaking temerity as a voice in the wilderness and his bedrock human decency in the face of jingoistic fervor.

The intellectual historian Gregory D. Sumner has noted that Macdonald's *politics* "occupies a special, almost legendary place in the history of American radicalism" because it offered "a communitarian alternative to both Marxian socialism and cold war liberalism."[21] Its contributors included numerous leading European intellectuals such as George Orwell, Nicola Chiaromonte, Victor Serge, Simone Weil, and Albert Camus, along with expatriate intellectuals such as Bruno Bettelheim, Lewis Coser, and Hannah Arendt.[22] Sumner adds that Macdonald and the *politics* circle advanced ideas in the 1940s that foreshadowed "the experiments in 'participatory democracy' associated with the New Left two decades later, and they also anticipate current debates about the need for an independent sphere of civil society initiated by dissidents from the former Soviet bloc."[23]

I agree. Full of verve and wit, *politics* showcased Macdonald's remarkable ability—which he had honed at *PR*—to go against not just the American grain (like most progressives), but also against the ideological consensus of his cohort or immediate reference group of intellectuals (like today's neoconservatives). A case in point was Macdonald's hilarious critique of the hard Left in the magazine's May-June 1947 issue. In a vituperative piece on Stalin sympathizer Henry Wallace and his tortuous speechifying on behalf of the USSR, Macdonald lashed out at former vice president Wallace, who had been dumped from the Democratic Party ticket as FDR's running mate in 1944. Later collected in *Memoirs of a Revolutionist*, the piece was titled "A Note on Wallese":

Wallaceland is the mental habitat of Henry Wallace plus a few hundred thousand regular readers of the *New Republic*, the *Nation*, and *PM*. It is a region of perpetual fogs, caused by the warm winds of the liberal Gulf Stream coming in contact with the Soviet glacier. Its natives speak "Wallese," a debased provincial dialect.

Wallese is as rigidly formalized as Mandarin Chinese. The Good people are described by ritualistic adjectives: "forward-looking," "freedom-loving," "clear-thinking," and, of course, "democratic" and "progressive." The Bad people are always "reactionaries" or "red-baiters."[24]

This jaunty, punchy style characterized *politics* from the start. In the inaugural issue in February 1944, Macdonald announced that while his journal had no "party" line, it did have an editorial policy: "The magazine's political tendency will be democratic socialist. Its predominant intellectual approach will be Marxist, in the sense of a method of analysis, not a body of dogma. . . . It will be partisan to those at the bottom of society—the Negroes, the colonial peoples, and the vast majority of common people everywhere, including the Soviet Union."[25] (Here we see how *politics* anticipated both the black civil rights campaign of the 1950s and the dissident, anti-Soviet protest movement in Eastern Europe of the 1980s.) As for the USSR, Macdonald reaffirmed his revolutionary opposition to the war and reiterated his belief that the USSR represented a model of "bureaucratic collectivism": "Russia is a new form of class society based on collective ownership of the means of production by the ruling bureaucracy."[26]

III

At the time of *politics'* inauguration in 1944, Macdonald's position was still that of a heretical Trotskyist. But he soon embraced a stance that can best be described as "anarcho-pacifism." During the last months of World War II, *politics* was unambiguously pacifist-anarchist, an unpopular stance in the midst of what became known as "the Good War." But Macdonald never saw it as "good"—or even as a necessary evil, especially during its closing months. He was outraged by the massive Allied bombings and their terrible civilian casualties, a disgust that reached new levels when the United States used atomic bombs against Japan.

Convinced that mass movements in the modern world ineluctably lead in the direction of violence and ultimately totalitarianism, Macdonald formally abandoned Marxism in early 1946. He gave up all hope of socialist revolution in favor of the notion of individual witness. His break with Marxism was announced with the publication of "The Root Is Man,"[27] an ambitious essay that appeared in two parts in the March and April 1946 issues of *politics*. Despairing in political activity altogether and trusting only the integrity of the single individual, Macdonald insisted that political responsibility finally rested with the single individual: "the root is man."

Why did this sharp turn in his politics occur? The reality is that it was actually much less abrupt and sudden than Macdonald's harshest critics have allowed. It had in fact been developing for more than a decade. Macdonald always had an interest in the behemoth of the modern state.

During his honeymoon with Nancy in Majorca in 1934, he spent most of his time studying the rise of dictators and the dangers posed by the excessive concentration of centralized power. Macdonald's belligerent antiwar stance fed both his deepening hatred of statism and his idealistic insistence on an ethical approach to political life, and his growing pacifism was compatible with the anti-imperialist war position of the Trotskyists, all of which culminated in the mid-1940s in a full-blown anarcho-pacifism. As Michael Wreszin has observed: "As the fear of another war approached, Macdonald became obsessed with the power of the state to lead people into war."[28]

Thus Macdonald's sharp turn away from Trotskyism and toward anarchism, pacifism, and individualism reflected and fit well with his anathema toward Stalinism and the Soviet state. But Macdonald's embrace of anarcho-pacifism was not merely a response to historical and political developments; there were also personal and intellectual influences at work. Chief among them were two religious women who exemplified the committed intellectual for Macdonald: Simone Weil and Dorothy Day. (He later wrote flattering *New Yorker* profiles of both of them in the 1950s.) Weil was writing for *politics* as Macdonald was formulating the basic ideas of "The Root Is Man," and she became for him, in Wreszin's words, "a saint of individualistic activism." In particular, her *politics* essay on Homer's *Iliad* in November 1945 convinced Macdonald that the exercise of force or coercion eventually enslaves those who employ it.[29]

As for Dorothy Day, Macdonald occasionally spoke at her invitation at the regular Friday night forums of the Catholic Worker groups in New York, and he once told William Shawn, editor of the *New Yorker*, that he was "greatly impressed by Dorothy Day and her colleagues," who are "absolute pacifists, ardent pro-unionists, politically extreme radicals, distinguishable from Trotskyists only by their anarchistic bent, and they live lives of voluntary poverty. Helping the poor and the under-dog is their main activity."[30] It is significant that Macdonald's profiles of Weil and Day form the two closing chapters of *Memoirs of a Revolutionist*. Unlike Weil or Day, however, Macdonald never moved toward a religious foundation for his radical values. The basis for his outlook always remained an individualistic secular morality. It is also true that this stance fit best with his own temperamental bent toward individualism and rebelliousness, as his decision to launch *politics* as a one-man operation also testified.[31]

Macdonald's linkage of mass art and cultural forms of totalitarianism also reinforced his belief in anarchic individualism: all forms of central-ized authority and bureaucracy seemed to him evil. While his critics de-rided him as having succumbed to the depoliticization of American in-tellectuals and the turn toward quietism in the 1950s, Macdonald viewed his anarcho-pacifist stance as an example of authentic critical dissent and the assumption of full individual responsibility for revolutionary change or reform. Throughout the 1950s he continued to call for a revival of the American anarchistic tradition (he often wore a button endorsing Emma Goldman), and it was revealing that he was asked to speak on "the rel-evance of anarchism" at the first national convention of Students for a Democratic Society (SDS) held in New York in June 1960.[32]

Macdonald termed his form of pacifism "friendly resistance," and in the mid-1940s he became an active member of the War Resisters League and the Militant Peacemakers. Macdonald defended resistance to the draft and the public burning of draft cards. He corresponded with mili-tant pacifists and with jailed conscientious objectors, and he also com-missioned articles from anarchists and pacifists living in communes. His biographer Wreszin concludes: "He was drawn to [anarcho-pacifism] for ways to live his own life, to find more personal fulfillment, to escape the pressures, the lack of time for reflection in the rat race of urban existence."

By this time Macdonald had completely shed his Marxist past. Marx had been his Baedeker to the radical world, he said, but he was no lon-ger interested in the Marxist approach to political questions. Macdonald also wrote that by 1948 he had lost his faith "in any general and radi-cal improvement in modern society, whether Marxist socialism or by pacifist persuasion and ethical example." Socialism and pacifism, he claimed, "were quite bad for people" because they underestimated the threat from Stalin's perversion of communism.

These dramatic shifts in opinion resulted in Macdonald being dis-missed by many of his intellectual colleagues as a political buffoon, a

"Dear Dwight"

jokester more in love with a good quip than with serious analysis. To Irving Howe, Macdonald possessed a "table-hopping mind." Daniel Bell mocked him as "the floating kidney on the left." Indeed, Macdonald could decimate intellectual fashions, but his own mercurial political enthusiasms rivaled the rise and fall of women's hemlines.[33]

Consistency never was Macdonald's strong suit. Yet it is also true that he was not taken seriously—especially by pure political types such as Sidney Hook and Philip Rahv—because his sense of humor was unusual in the rarified atmosphere of the *Partisan Review* crowd, where comedy was considered something for the borscht belt. By the late 1940s he was in danger of being marginalized. His fellow *PR* editor William Barrett issued the ultimate verdict from their intellectual community when he later wrote: "For him, every venture into politics was a leap toward the Absolute. . . . He was a kind of Don Quixote or Galahad, alternately tilting at windmills in quest of the Holy Grail."[34]

What in fact remained constant throughout the early postwar era was Macdonald's hostility toward communism. The Stalinist takeover in Czechoslovakia in March 1948, succeeded by the Berlin blockade, transformed Macdonald into a cold warrior. With the outbreak of the Korean War in June 1950, his liberal anticommunism deepened and led to his temporarily becoming a fierce anti-Stalinist rallying to the defense of America against Soviet aggression. (Fifteen years later, he was to return to the radical camp by publicly opposing the Vietnam War.)

So Macdonald, once a disciple of Trotsky, was an antiwar Marxist until the war's end and then gravitated toward anarchism. He remained a pacifist until the Berlin Blockade in 1947–1948, when he reluctantly accepted that the United States was the "lesser evil." His critical support for the United States against the rising threat of Soviet imperialism culminated in his controversial declaration of "I Choose the West," voiced during a 1952 debate with Norman Mailer at Mount Holyoke, which Macdonald published as an essay of that title a few years later (also collected in *Memoirs of a Revolutionist*).

IV

From 1944 until 1947 Macdonald published *politics* as a monthly, but afterward only sporadically. When his enthusiasm for *politics* and Nancy's funds both exhausted themselves in early 1949, Macdonald closed down the magazine. During the 1950s, Macdonald never fully lost his interest in political topics relating to domestic and

If the Mantle Fits . . .

foreign policy. But his best work addressed cultural politics and the arts. While he thought of himself as a defender of the traditional canon, he concentrated his efforts on a critique of the middlebrow literature that thrived at midcentury—and that he despised. Although he continued to contribute political pieces occasionally to the "little" magazines and literary-intellectual quarterlies, Macdonald wrote increasingly for commercial publications such as *Esquire* and the *New Yorker*, whose staff he joined in early 1952. His feisty criticism in their pages amounted to a running commentary on what he regarded as the shallow, complacent "midcult" of the Eisenhower years.

The decade and a half following the disbanding of *politics* in 1949 marked Macdonald's most creative period. These years would also see him rise from a fringe political journalist to the status of one of America's most influential cultural arbiters. However consciously, Macdonald in the 1950s and early '60s sought in many ways to emulate the role that Orwell had played in England as the unpredictable, sometimes cantankerous, brutally honest observer of the national cultural scene. Convincingly or not, Macdonald in the 1950s did indeed aspire to become "the American Orwell."

What distinguished Macdonald in these years was an almost uncanny ability to expose the cultural fads and intellectual frauds of the day. It was a role perfectly suited to the withering ad hominem prose style that he had mastered in the 1930s and '40s from his battles in intellectual New York, where he had become a specialist in literary abuse. Once he turned to cultural criticism, Macdonald's judgments took on a new self-confidence. His positions on culture and art were firm and witnessed no sharp reversals. His cultural criticism never succumbed to the "grass-hopper" tendency that entered his political writings, which often zig-zagged due to his contrarian's anathema toward Party groupthink and any ideological "line." (That penchant had led to his being dismissed by his colleagues as "the Peter Pan of the Left.") Characteristically written with passion, authority, and certitude, Macdonald's cultural criticism reveals his conservative side as well as his misgivings about the judgment of the middle-class, midcult taste of the American public.

In the 1950s Macdonald was preoccupied with cultural politics, especially the widening gap between "high culture" and "mass culture." The major result of this interest was his landmark essay "Masscult and Midcult," published in *Partisan Review* in 1960. This essay was "high concept," a challenging "think" piece arguing that high culture was being aped and vulgarized by the insidious forces of mass taste into coffee-table "midcult," which inevitably catered to the lowest common denominator. It was the most important cultural essay that Macdonald ever penned, and it exerted great influence on debates in popular cultural studies, both intellectual and scholarly, during the 1960s and '70s. (Today, in an age when literary criticism is dominated by postcolonialism and deemed unsophisticated without some acknowledgement of academic, technical theories such as deconstruction and multiculturalism, "Masscult and Midcult" is often—and unjustly—neglected.)

For all his negativity about the corrupting influence of midcult and how it impersonated and undermined high culture, Macdonald's cultural criticism of the 1950s was the finest work of his lifetime. Once again, just as he had shown in his political commentary in *PR* and *politics* a decade earlier, his forté was always battling against the cultural consensus. Typical was Macdonald's proud, sharp letter of protest to the editor of *Twentieth Century* in December 1958. Macdonald wrote to contest the editorial introduction to his essay "America! America!" which had appeared in the previous issue. The editors of this British magazine had written that they "would not publish Dwight Macdonald's spirited and witty comment on American life" if Macdonald himself were not "a good American." Macdonald wrote in reply that "patriotism has never been my strong point." He continued: "I don't know as I'd call myself A Good American. I'm certainly A Critical American, and I prefer your country, morally and culturally, to my own."[35]

Macdonald's keenest cultural essays in the 1950s and '60s invariably fulminated against the tawdry artifacts of midcult and mass culture, because "democracy" in the Eisenhower era, Macdonald contended, had come to mean "dumbing down." Here is an excerpt from his caustic mockery of the "Revisers" who modernized the language of the revised standard version of the Bible:

> Reading their work is like walking through an old city that has just been given, if not a saturation bombing, a thorough going-over. One looks about anxiously. Is this gone? Does that still survive? Surely they might have spared that! And even though many of the big landmarks are left—their fabric weakened by the Revisers' policy of modernizing the grammatical usage—so many of the lesser structures have been razed that the whole feel of the place is different. In Cologne, in 1950, the cathedral still stood, alone and strange, in the midst of miles of rubble.[36]

Serious essays on Ernest Hemingway, Mark Twain, and James Agee show Macdonald becoming more and more disenchanted as the 1950s advanced. His pessimism deepened because he could find no repository for his hope: political affairs had turned sour for him, seeming futile and boring, and he found little to cheer in the world of literature.

V

Radical by conviction, Macdonald was conservative in temperament and taste, and this made him a traditionalist and even a curmudgeonly elitist in his later years. He came to hate avant-garde art and lashed out at both the action painting of artist Jackson Pollock, and Beat poets such as Allen Ginsberg and Jack Kerouac. Macdonald took special pleasure in puncturing what he considered critically inflated works, such as Colin Wilson's much-hyped pseudo-philosophical treatise of 1950s existentialism, *The Outsider*. (Macdonald's savaging of Wilson in 1957 was unusual in one sense. As his aforementioned letter to the editor of *Twentieth Century* attests, Macdonald was otherwise an Anglophile and prized the English literary scene over the American.) His last significant literary-political accomplishment was his championing of Michael Harrington's *The Other America* in the *New Yorker* in January 1963. Harrington's book had appeared nine months earlier and sold poorly; Macdonald's feature story brought it to President Kennedy's attention and thus helped launch the War on Poverty in the 1960s.

Macdonald also gave vent to his curmudgeonly side throughout these years in his expression of a mild anti-Semitism quite common among his classmates at Phillips Exeter and Yale. Macdonald had, in fact, harbored a WASP-ish condescension and even antipathy toward Jews during his teens, once writing to a Jewish girl that he "disliked rather violently the Jews as a race." His early anti-Semitic attitudes had much to do with his rearing, especially with his mother's negative social attitudes toward minorities and immigrants. By his late twenties, when he participated in the predominantly Jewish community of intellectuals associated with *Partisan Review*, he had outgrown most of these early attitudes. Nonetheless, Macdonald was suspected by some Jewish colleagues of being anti-Semitic, though most of them concluded that he simply relished argument and meant no personal offense in his highly critical attitudes about Israel, Palestine, Zionism, and most then-reigning interpretations of the circumstances of the Holocaust.[37]

Although Macdonald's anti-Semitic rearing was reinforced at Phillips Exeter and Yale, Wreszin notes that "Macdonald's entry in the 1930s to the *Partisan Review* circle soon led him to conclude that an intel-

"Dear Dwight"

lectual's identity had to be grounded in a cosmopolitanism that repudiated national chauvinism."[38] Macdonald sometimes called himself "a non-Jewish Jew," even proclaiming himself on occasion "an honorary Jew"; he declared proudly that "Red Rosa [Luxemburg] has long been my favorite revolutionist." Nonetheless, of course, he recognized that he was not Jewish, and as a result he often felt "alienated" (a signature term of the New York Intellectuals) as an outsider among the New York Jews. He condemned explicit displays of anti-Semitism, but he also castigated what he perceived in the early postwar era to be Israel's mistreatment of Arab refugees. Macdonald's exuberant intellectual jousting in defense of such positions, conducted in an impersonal yet aggressively charged tone, could easily be mistaken for hostile anti-Semitic remarks by those not well acquainted with him.[39]

Macdonald thus adopted the values and culture of a group of secular intellectuals who had largely ignored or shrugged off their Judaism and embraced socialism. The New York Intellectuals were cosmopolitan, broadly assimilative, and only marginally ethnic. They were proud to defend modernist literature and to deride cultural philistinism. Preferring the European cultural tradition emerging from the Enlightenment to their own Jewish cultural heritage, they did not return to their Jewishness until the 1950s, in the aftermath of the Holocaust. By the late 1950s and early '60s the theme of Jewishness began to be of greater importance to many members of the group—and to American Jews generally—than liberal anticommunism.

Unlike most of the New York Intellectuals, Macdonald supported the awarding of the Bollingen Prize for Poetry to Ezra Pound for his *Pisan Cantos* in 1948. Macdonald condemned the poetry for its anti-Semitism, but he praised the judging panel for having made the award on the basis of their estimate of the literary quality of Pound's poetry, leaving aside all political considerations, including the fact that Pound was accused of treason for his participation in Italian fascist propaganda against the Allies during World War II. Macdonald noted approvingly that no such state-supported award that honored the autonomy of art could possibly be given in a fascist or communist country.

Fifteen years later, adopting a stance that set him further apart from his *PR* colleagues and once again demonstrated his inveterate inclination to go against the grain of his reference group, Macdonald also joined the minority among the New York Intellectuals, such as Mary McCarthy, who defended Hannah Arendt's book *Eichmann in Jerusalem: A Report on the Banality of Evil* (1963), which set off a fusillade of protests by its claims that European Jews collaborated in their own destruction dur-

If the Mantle Fits . . .

Dwight Macdonald speaking at the "countercommencement" at Columbia University. The alternative, student-sponsored graduation ceremony was held on June 4, 1968.

ing the Holocaust. The book triggered fierce exchanges and mutual recriminations from its critics and advocates within the New York Jewish community. Macdonald was a close friend of Arendt, and he defended her as a fellow cosmopolitan who disavowed the ethnic partisanship of her Jewish intellectual critics. Echoing his position on the Pound controversy, Macdonald admired Arendt for maintaining an allegiance to independent, internationalist values that were opposed to patriotism and jingoism of all types.[40] (Macdonald always claimed that he was an anti-Zionist because of his anti-statist, anarchistic convictions.)

VI

Having largely abandoned political commentary after *politics* folded and immersed himself during the 1950s in cultural criticism, which he published in the *New Yorker* and other magazines, Macdonald began to write film reviews for *Esquire* in 1960; soon he also rediscovered his left-wing political convictions and enthusiastically supported the new radical movements. He was atypical of his generation of

"Dear Dwight"

intellectuals in his embrace during the 1960s of the counterculture, the New Left, and the antiwar movement. Most of his leftist contemporaries from the 1930s went in exactly the opposite political direction, and not only those who had turned to the right: for instance, Irving Howe remained a socialist yet wrote numerous scathing attacks on the New Left. So this new political turn by Macdonald witnessed him not only moving against the grain of his own drift away from political engagement, but also cutting against the grain of his own generation's attitude toward the New Left and the antiwar movement.

Yet there were also other factors governing his political radicalization at this time—issues associated with Macdonald's complex personal psychology. In 1967 he participated in the March on the Pentagon, lamenting only that he didn't get arrested. But he was in fact "arrested" in another, tragic sense: his once-prolific pen was frozen. The sad fact is that, though Macdonald was living out a second youth in the 1960s, he really marched in the streets because he could not sit still in his study. He became permanently depressed and morose, burdened by a severe writer's block that lasted the rest of his life and was exacerbated by heavy drinking.

Drawn back into political action in the mid-1960s by the Vietnam antiwar movement and student protests against the universities, Macdonald recaptured the radical self of his Trotskyist and *politics* years—walking picket lines, protesting against military recruitment, and denouncing the Johnson administration's conduct of the war. Unlike numerous gray-haired leftists of the decade, he was not living out a romantic radical dream that he had missed out on during his youth: Macdonald was always a proto-New Leftist. He was unlike other New Left enthusiasts of his generation such as Philip Rahv, who became at times a virtual parody of his old 1930s self as he wished he might have been. But the continuity of Macdonald's outlook and behavior in the 1960s with his core values during his Trotskyist and anarcho-pacifist periods, which ranged from his late twenties to mid-forties, is striking. The connection between Macdonald's attitudes of the 1960s and during the *politics* years is especially apparent: the unwavering stance of *politics* was moralistic, independent, and anti-institutional—in essence, very much like the New Left.

Nonetheless, what Macdonald could not recapture was his fluid pen, and he tortured himself for this failure with endless self-recriminations. By the early 1970s, Macdonald found it impossible to compose even an essay or book review. He spent his last decade distracting himself from his misery. Macdonald led a peripatetic existence as an intellectual gypsy, lecturing at various US colleges and universities, trying vainly to recharge his intellectual batteries by becoming an academic circuit rider and playing the role of the radical elder. Urged by friends to write his autobiography, which might have represented a history of American intellectual life in the mid-twentieth century, his literary impotence and drinking bouts stopped him. Macdonald died in December 1982 at the age of seventy-six, one of the last of the great critics of his generation.

VII

"Dwight" (strangers, in fact even adversaries, addressed him so, and rather fondly) was an inspired visionary and a creative, off-beat thinker with many friends and few enemies—despite his acid pen. Mary McCarthy's line about Macdougal Macdermott in *The Oasis* applied fully to Dwight Macdonald too: "The targets of his satire could never truly dislike Macdermott, for they found themselves endowed by it with a larger and more fabulous life."[41]

Indeed Macdonald was a gifted writer. He certainly had the talent to be "the American Orwell." Why did he fail to realize his potential? Why did he waste his prodigious energies on editing, on occasional journalism, and on peripatetic culture chat in his numerous rounds of college gigs?

In hindsight, Macdonald's abrupt turns, sudden manias, and intellectual "table-hopping" gave his work brio and color at the cost of significance and enduring impact. Orwell was a much steadier figure, both temperamentally and artistically, and he evolved politically and culturally, whereas Macdonald lurched from Luce to Lenin on his way to Lennon and popcult—in the process depleting his prodigious energies (and genuine enthusiasm) for both political and cultural criticism, and ultimately leaving him without any commitments or vision to affirm. In the face of his terminal case of writer's block and numerous incomplete projects, Macdonald berated himself mercilessly. As his addictions filled the vacuum left by his retreating talent, his only (quite inadequate) "out" was the bottle.

The fact is that Macdonald suffered from what could be called a gluttony for life experience. He could be a charming fellow, indeed a raconteur. ("He's all Dwight," Hannah Arendt once fittingly titled an affectionate portrait of Macdonald.)[42] "Dwight" loved the whole fabulous whirlwind of life—in fact, he loved to talk and always treated people, including his college students, as intellectual peers (even when he ripped apart their ideas).[43] His calendar was usually full, and he liked it that way. Excitement and variety were important to him rather than comfort and playing it safe. At his best he was playful and positive, imaginative and inventive. Yet he was also easily bored and tended to overvalue spontaneity and thus new beginnings. When it came to meeting people, designing projects, and immersing himself in the nitty-gritty of passing political and cultural events, he could have benefited from a large dose of sobriety.

Macdonald also found it excruciatingly difficult to remain steadfast during what felt like confining, painful phases of commitment. To limit himself often seemed like a form of death—but moderation and concentrated effort were precisely what he needed. When he was healthy, he was focused and purposeful and fully gratified to contribute something valuable to American criticism and culture. At his worst he became unproductive and stymied, preoccupied with ways of entertaining and distracting himself. His creativity became supplanted by anxiety, impatience, and a passion to consume—and the fatal outcome was a myriad of partially completed projects and protracted periods of ennui and frustration. He strenuously avoided dealing with his frustration, but he was too alert to repress his awareness of it. Ashamed that he was squandering his great potential, both his frequent expression of exasperation and his cutting, often condescending attitude toward rival opinions masked his own disgust with himself.

Macdonald in overdrive was thus an intellectual thrill-seeker, reckless in pursuit of charged encounters, looking for highly stimulating sources of cultural entertainment yet quickly becoming jaded by them. It was in this more subtle sense, beyond the alcoholic binges, that he burned out and damaged himself by his excesses. These tendencies wearied him and proved wearing on others as well. Although he was already a proto-New Leftist two decades earlier, it is also true that the playful energy of the counterculture powerfully attracted the *puer* in "Dwight." In other words, one of the reasons that the New Left and the student movement captured his interest is that he could not stand being bored—and both the antiwar protests and the counterculture felt refreshingly new and different to him, an adventure for which he had longed. (Part of the reason Macdonald turned to movies was also that they were a new form of "serious" art for young intellectuals of the '60s, whose passion for them also gave Macdonald the feeling of recapturing his youth.)[44]

Yet his vain attempts to force himself to concentrate only exacerbated his cerebral circus; he really needed to quiet his mind and embrace the work of writing as a mundane, often laborious task of sentence-by-

If the Mantle Fits . . .

sentence composition—and also to accept the anxiety that inevitably surfaces when the words will not come.[45] By the late 1970s, Macdonald lacked the concentration to write at all. It was primarily the damming up of his literary energies that led him to take a string of one-year appointments at several universities. When the teaching stints ceased to come, he fell into a deep depression, which is precisely what his frenetic pace of activity had been staving off. Deprived of his manic-depressive defense as a university instructor, he deteriorated from dilettante to escapist, and his form of escape was alcohol. Macdonald had maintained a hungry anticipation of the future until his old age, but now he turned negative and wallowed in his misery as his health deteriorated and his writer's block paralyzed him.

VIII

Yes, all this was tragic. And yet: the tragedy of Dwight Macdonald's final years ought not to receive undue weight. Above all, it must not be permitted to overshadow his record of notable achievement during the prime of his life: his three decades of both distinguished commentary and impassioned engagement in the leading political and cultural events of his time.

What legacy does Macdonald leave us today? One of his own remarks about himself may point us toward an answer: "When I say 'no' I'm always right and when I say 'yes' I'm almost always wrong." He was correct.[46] His most lasting accomplishment was not his political essays, which have dated badly, but the cultural criticism he penned in the 1950s. The best of it, however, was negative. His eye for "the phony" (to use a 1950s word) was sharp, and his finest work was demolishing the work of the intellectually pretentious. Unfortunately, most of his positive criticism, such as "Masscult and Midcult," seems antiquated. His onetime fellow *Partisan Review* editor, the poet Delmore Schwartz, once rightly said of him: "Yes, antagonism for its own sake is his appetite and neurosis, and none of his political predictions come true, but he is a master of expository prose."

True enough, but Macdonald's enthusiasms for a cause blunted his skeptical edge, first as a Trotskyist in the Socialist Workers Party and then again in the 1960s. The man who had been famous for spotting the intellectually fraudulent was taken in by the likes of Eldridge Cleaver, the Black Panthers, and even lightweights such as Abbie Hoffman. Barbara Garson's tendentious play *MacBird!* (1967), which cast President

Johnson as a Macbeth who murders John F. Kennedy, was puffed up by Macdonald into a great work of art.

Yet all these errors and embarrassments are of secondary importance. The greatest misfortune is that Macdonald grew ashamed of not just his literary impotence generally, but of his incapacity to write a large work that might have had lasting value. Macdonald is seldom quoted nowadays, though he is occasionally cited as a significant literary figure of the past. One must especially lament his failure to write his own full-scale "Life and Times" autobiography, a project that his friend John Lukacs urged him to pursue in numerous letters and conversations. No one was better equipped to write an intellectual portrait of America at midcentury than Dwight Macdonald. He had the requisite personal experience, along with talent galore, but he lacked the staying power. This was ultimately his own verdict on himself; he judged himself by a book standard, indeed by the standard of a magnum opus. He could not fully accept that he had excelled in the form of the topical and occasional essay, like the other New York Intellectuals of his generation, many of whom had become skilled in intellectual journalism and critical polemic during their early Marxist training in dialectics and disputation.

And this severe judgment on himself finally did come to bear much truth: unlike the achievements of his colleagues and friends who wrote books that are still read today, such as Trilling, Howe, Mary McCarthy, Harold Rosenberg, and others—let alone Orwell—the wretched truth is that Macdonald squandered his brilliant literary gifts and authentic political passions in polemics, in ephemeral reportage and book reviews, in political fashions, and ultimately in alcohol. Not a single major literary project of Macdonald's ever got off the ground: his long-announced major critique of Big Steel, his analysis of the political economy of fascism, his historical study of the labor movement, his manifesto for anarcho-pacifism, his book-length treatise on mass culture, his critical appreciation of Edgar Allan Poe. For most of them, he never did more than assemble some of his notes. Macdonald published eleven books, but not one is still in print. Three of them were editions of other writers (Herzen, Poe, and the art of parody), while the other eight were collections of magazine pieces, some of which he reprinted three or four times.

Here, above all, the distance between Orwell and Macdonald is incommensurable. Orwell penned two of the most important works of political fiction of the twentieth century. Macdonald edited a magazine that exerted political influence on the American Left for two or three years. Whereas Orwell wrote at least three classics—*Homage to Catalonia*, *Animal Farm*, and *Nineteen Eighty-Four*—Macdonald never produced anything that commanded more than temporary notoriety. His lone essay of short-lived significance, "Masscult and Midcult," is now largely forgotten.

In hindsight, Macdonald himself would probably lament that he repeatedly "sold out"—to Luce, to sectarian politics, to middlebrowism, to Hollywood and television. Especially in this respect—to return to the nominations of Macdonald as "the American Orwell"—the divergence from Orwell is notable. Refusing to write full time for the Beaverbrook Press, Orwell had the courage and fortitude to become a *writer*, while Macdonald went to work full time for Luce, spent time as an editor, and later invested his energies in movie assignments, reviews, and other occasional pieces for *Fortune*, the *New Yorker*, and *Esquire* rather than sacrificing the glamour and income in order to pen substantial and lasting books. Whereas Macdonald became a prominent intellectual journalist by the early 1960s, Orwell became one of the leading fiction and nonfiction writers of the twentieth century, arguably its most important political intellectual, and a guiding light of both the intellectual Left and Right.

Today, if Macdonald is compared to Orwell, he seems less like "the American Orwell" than "the American Orwell *manqué*." Forgotten is the fact that both men were courageous nondoctrinaire radicals who shared much in common—a hatred of communism, an appreciation of good literature, and sympathy for the downtrodden. Unlike Orwell, however, Macdonald and his work have fallen into partly undeserved neglect since his death because so much of his energy was directed at topical issues that mean little to most people today. His virtual invisibility on the current national scene testifies that intellectual reputations seldom endure unless one produces one or two major works—and makes them sufficiently interesting and challenging to scholars that they are taken up within an academic field and enshrined as landmarks or curricular touchstones. Here too, one notices the vast difference from Orwell, who wrote at least two books—*Animal Farm* and *Nineteen Eighty-Four*—which are admired not only by students of British literature but also by political and literary intellectuals of both the Left and the Right.

All of these factors in toto have problematized Dwight Macdonald's heritage. He has suffered a fate common to personalities in politics who are frequently cited in the media: their visibility and influence decline steeply over time. Such a downturn tends to occur even more fully for someone without political power in his own right, such as Macdonald, whose public profile depended on access to literary organs with cultural power such as the *New Yorker* and *Esquire*.[47]

51   *"Dear Dwight"*

Three decades after his death, Macdonald is a forgotten man—unjustly so. True, he was wrong about many of the biggest events and issues of his lifetime, ranging from his positions on the New Deal and World War II to his ill-considered ardor for the Black Panthers and the Yippies. But Macdonald's genius was to "go to the root" and work through such wrongheaded positions to emerge with an original vision that reflected deeply held values and spoke to the main issues of his time, whether it was his quintessential American reformulation of anarchism in the 1940s or his stellar cultural criticism of the 1950s. As I indicated earlier, despite his reputation as an unserious "Peter Pan" thinker who caromed from ideology to ideology, Macdonald was actually quite consistent in his political and cultural outlook after breaking with the SWP, the WP, and then *Partisan Review* around the beginning of World War II. He remained during his last three decades a firm egalitarian and libertarian in politics, a fervent anti-statist and antiwar activist, and an elitist and traditionalist in art and culture—and he remained a radical humanist from beginning to end.

Macdonald sought to live a life of intellectual integrity and, despite his many mistakes and failures, I would insist that he did so. As he once wrote of Orwell in a 1958 essay reprinted in his last collection, *Discriminations* (1974), he was "tougher on himself and his own side."[48] Czeslaw Milosz spoke about the pertinence of "Macdonaldism," not just for Eastern Europeans but for the future of humankind. "They are surely able to appreciate his betting on slow processes in the human mass, and his belief that one man counts, or if we are lucky, three or four men linked by friendship. Macdonald seems to have pinned his hopes on the fermentation sealed beneath the surface, which is not automatic and to which everyone can contribute."[49]

Macdonald did indeed pin his ultimate hopes on a trust in the prospect of human maturation, a faith which he sustained across the decades through an old-fashioned communitarian vision of mutual aid in the anarchist spirit. And that is a political legacy worth not only honoring but also reinvigorating. A renewed appreciation of Dwight Macdonald's work, especially his trenchant critiques in *politics* of both liberalism and totalitarianism, is crucial to the task of revitalizing both political liberalism and radicalism in the twenty-first century.

The relevance of Macdonald's heritage for the renewal of the mainstream American tradition of liberal thought warrants a final mention. Like Lionel Trilling, Macdonald was a fierce critic of the "liberal imagination" of progressives; unlike Trilling, however, he maintained no vision of an ideal liberalism against which he measured the shortcomings of the liberal imagination. Like Trilling, Macdonald lamented that liberalism was the dominant, if not the sole, intellectual tradition at midcentury in the United States. Unlike Trilling, he did not believe that liberalism needed to be recalled "to its first essential imagination of variousness and possibility, which implies the awareness of difficulty and complexity," but rather that intellectuals needed to "go to the root" to embrace an authentic radical tradition. Macdonald rejected any notion of liberalism as advanced by most rationalists: a belief in human perfectibility, an optimistic faith in progress, and the correction of wrong by human reason. To Macdonald, these were shibboleths. In reality, according to Macdonald, twentieth-century liberalism consisted of progressive clichés, imprisoning systems of political machination, and systematic if benevolent discrimination based on complacent acceptance of social conditions. Stalinist fellow-traveling was his most glaring example of misguided liberalism during the 1930s, but Macdonald insisted that Marxism was not alone responsible for the deficiencies of liberalism.

And yet, in another sense, again like Trilling as well as Orwell, Macdonald was a liberal critic of liberalism, the critic of the Left from within its own ranks. He would have cherished receiving kudos like the frequent tribute to Orwell as "the conscience of his generation."[50] Macdonald agreed with Trilling's praise in *The Liberal Imagination* of Hawthorne's "dissent from the orthodoxies of dissent." And as the orthodoxies of dissent rapidly changed in the mid-twentieth century, Macdonald's positions changed with them. His radical, anticapitalist stance never altered, but his specific positions often seemed, as one sympathetic critic expressed it, "more numerous than the *Kama Sutra*."[51] Macdonald shifted course as the cultural and political winds demanded; always excitable and irresponsibly responsive to life, he was not just a rebel with a cause, but rather one with many (and often short-lived) causes. Amidst all his turns and gyrations, however, he remained throughout his career a passionate political skeptic and a defender of high cultural standards.

"Dwight" did always go "against the grain." As he himself once put it, he certainly was "A Critical American." Milosz once called him "a totally American phenomenon" in the tradition of Thoreau, Whitman, and Melville—"the completely free man, capable of making decisions at all times and about all things, strictly on the basis of his personal moral judgment."[52]

Regrettably, whatever our assessment of whether Macdonald was an "American Orwell"—*manqué* or not—there is nobody like him on the current intellectual scene. There are many anarchists, pacifists, and cultural mandarins today, but no intellectual has forged a political and cultural vision to compare with the scope and comprehensiveness of Macdonald's work during his prime. One can point to various writers and intellectuals who resemble him in different respects: Christopher Hitchens, the British expatriate writer and a vocal Macdonald admirer, is certainly the most prominent, and he shares both Macdonald's contrarian and even Trotskyist orientation as well as his cultural elitism.[53]

So Macdonald casts a long shadow, and his absence leaves a large hole in American intellectual life. In fact, I believe that "Macdonaldism" can help not only to revivify American liberalism, but also to keep radical discourse alive in this country. One man does count—and he (or she), if inspired with a sufficiently compelling vision, can draw together three or four or many more. Macdonald himself did that, not just in forming a community around *politics* but also through his voluminous writings over the course of a long and productive career. If much of his political journalism has become rather dated, both his example and his insouciant, soaringly irreverent prose style still shine forth and have lost none of their relevance.

And that is why he is worth remembering.

If the Mantle Fits . . .

CHAPTER 3

"St. Irving"?
or "The American Orwell" (III)

n *Achieving Our Country*, Richard Rorty lauded Irving Howe's "incredible energy and exceptional honesty," "making him virtually "a warrior-saint" who "came to play the role in many people's lives that Orwell did in his."[1] The historian Josephine Woll recalled in *Dissent* after Howe's death, in a comparison that many of his friends would have endorsed, "For Irving, Orwell was the model of a writer; for me, Irving was."[2]

Such paeans have struck most neoconservatives as deplorable. "Preparations are apparently under way to make [Howe] into the American Orwell," lamented Joseph Epstein, who dismissed Howe's radicalism as evidence of a politically immature and insecure thinker, indeed of a card-carrying lifetime member of "the Old People's Socialist League." Hilton Kramer has agreed, castigating Howe's principled refusal to renounce socialism as fashionable leftism and hopelessly maudlin utopianism. More than that, Kramer has pronounced all of Howe's political writings—including his work on the political novel and other literary essays written from an explicitly left-oriented perspective—to be "worthless."[3]

Yes, Irving Howe (1920–1993) had his admirers—and his detractors. Neoconservatives are not alone in refusing to canonize Howe as "St. Ir-

Irving Howe, editor of *Dissent*, late 1950s.

ving."[4] In a memorial column on Howe in the *Nation*, Alexander Cockburn derided Howe as "an assiduous foot soldier" in the campaign to "discredit vibrant political currents electrifying America and supporting liberation movements in the Third World," a lapsed radical whose "prime function in the last thirty years of his life was that of policing the Left on behalf of the powers that be."[5]

For these diverse reasons, ranging from the literary and political to the temperamental, a perpetually embattled "St. Irving" came to identify passionately with "St. George." A major influence and near-constant presence for almost a half century in Irving Howe's life, Orwell became for Howe an "intellectual hero."[6] Already in the mid-1950s, Howe viewed Orwell not just as a literary guide but as a model of the radical writer. By 1968, Howe was even allowing himself to imagine that "if he had lived," Orwell would have steered a course similar to his own, lambasting both Establishment politicians and apocalyptic populists:

For a whole generation—mine—Orwell was an intellectual hero. He stormed against those English writers who were ready to yield to Hitler; he fought almost single-handed against those who blinded them-

If the Mantle Fits . . .

selves to the evils of Stalin. More than any other English intellectual of our age, he embodied the values of personal independence and a fiercely democratic radicalism. Yet, just because for years I have intensely admired him, I hesitated to return to him. One learns to fear the disappointment of fallen heroes and lapsed enthusiasms. I was wrong to hesitate . . .

It is depressing to think that, if he had lived, he would today be no more than sixty-five years old. How much we have missed in those two decades! Imagine Orwell ripping into one of Harold Wilson's mealy speeches, imagine him examining the thought of Spiro Agnew, imagine him dissecting the ideology of Tom Hayden, imagine him casting a frosty eye on the current wave of irrationalism in Western culture!

The loss seems enormous. . . . He was one of the few heroes of our younger years who remains untarnished. Having to live in a rotten time was made just a little more bearable by his presence.[7]

Looking back on the late 1960s, Howe acknowledged the crucial role that Orwell had played in those years as a beacon that steadied his gaze on radical ideals—yet that also illuminated social realities with a clear-sightedness that enabled a necessary measure of detachment. "I bridled at the notion that the literary life was inherently more noble than the life of politics," Howe recalls. "I bridled because acknowledging this could have been politically disabling at a time when politics remained essential, but also because I knew that it held a portion of obvious truth—otherwise, how explain my inner divisions?"[8] Striving for literary excellence and yet to keep alive what he termed socialism's "animating ethic,"[9] Howe found in Orwell the political self that he believed, fairly, Lionel Trilling and the *Partisan Review* ex-radicals had forsaken. Howe wanted "instances of that poise which enables a writer to engage the passions of the moment yet keep a distancing skepticism." Trilling "spoke for part of what I wanted, yet another, perhaps larger, part of me had to speak against him."[10] Trilling spoke for the skeptical Howe, Orwell for the passionate Howe. "I saw Orwell," Howe recalls, "as a fellow spirit—a radical and engaged writer."[11]

As Howe had acknowledged in *Partisan Review* with a mixture of outrage and regret more than a decade earlier, Trilling would not have described Orwell this way. Nor as a "revolutionary" personality. Nor, given his valuation of Orwell's respect for "the familial commonplace" and the "stupidity of things,"[12] as a rebel against middle-class life. But Howe regarded an Orwell hemmed in by the conventional bourgeois

57 *"St. Irving"?*

pattern as "empty," politically "harmless." "Dangerous" was "better": only a recognizably radical image could truly "challenge" and "trouble us."[13]

With the neoconservative embrace of Orwell in 1983–1984, Howe reassumed the role of defender of "his" Orwell, the radical Orwell. The neocons' open, blatant heist of Orwell exercised Howe far more than did the neoliberals' courtly canonization in the 1950s. "Kidnapping Our Hero": that was how an indignant Howe characterized Norman Podhoretz's bold claim to Orwell as a "forerunner" of neoconservatism in a *Harper's* cover story titled "If Orwell Were Alive Today." Howe disputed Podhoretz's contention, insisting that "to the end of his life Orwell remained a writer on the Left."[14]

Howe also continued to identify passionately—and perhaps even unconsciously—with Orwell as a stylist. Howe's convictions about prose style, voiced in the preface to the third edition of *Politics and the Novel*—reissued just months before his death in 1993—resound with a direct, if unacknowledged, echo of Orwell's famous aspiration to write "prose like a window pane." Howe wrote: "Now, especially at a time when critical writing is marked by jargon and obscurantism, my inclination is to care most about lucidity. The writer of expository prose, I now feel, should strive for that most difficult of styles: a prose so direct, so clear, so transparent, that the act of reading comes to seem like looking through a glass."

During this last decade of his life, Howe came to cherish his public identification as "the American Orwell." Orwell is one of "the writers who have meant most to me," one of "the crucial witnesses," Howe says at the close of his intellectual autobiography, *A Margin of Hope* (1982). "It is with their witness that, along the margin, I want to identify," a witness to witnesses. The 1984 "countdown," which pushed Orwell into the incessant glare of the international media, also solidified the perception of Howe—at least on the liberal left—as the American successor to his "intellectual hero."[15] Indeed some left-liberals explicitly honored Howe as "the American Orwell" of his generation. For instance, Sanford Pinsker saw Howe as a "moral conscience," a tribute that echoed V. S. Pritchett's famous declaration of Orwell as "the conscience of his generation":

The passion of his argument, by turns fiercely moral and scrupulously fair; the clarity of his prose; a voice that speaks with authority, and powers that grew more refined, more subtle, even as they retained a kinship with the sheer exuberance of those times, those places . . . :

If the Mantle Fits . . .

Howe retains a position as a moral conscience, almost unparalleled in contemporary letters."[16]

Or as Lewis Coser, Howe's old friend and former *Dissent* co-editor, memorialized him:

Lionel Trilling once told how he had been looking for an appropriate word to characterize George Orwell, whom he had wished to eulogize. It finally seemed to him that a very old-fashioned word was most appropriate, the word "virtue." This word seems to me also most appropriate to characterize Irving Howe. He was a virtuous man, one who tried to live up to self-imposed moral standards and moral duties. George Orwell, Ignazio Silone, and a few contemporary and near-contemporary writers who stood very high in Irving Howe's pantheon won his admiration not solely because of their sheer literary merits but also, perhaps above all, because they provided guidelines of how to behave in a dismal world with virtuous commitment to moral standards.[17]

I

"Irving made a lot of enemies in his lifetime," recalled Robert Boyers, an intellectual and friend on the Left. Here again, the comparison with Orwell is apt. A case could be made that Orwell and Howe were the two Old Left intellectuals most hated by the New Left during the 1960s. (Howe was fond of William Dean Howells's remark that anyone could *make* enemies, but the real test was to keep them. By that criterion, both he and Orwell succeeded well.) Orwell was, however, arguably better at reconciliations. In Howe's case, though he occasionally reconciled after falling out (with a few writer-intellectuals, such as Lionel Trilling and Ralph Ellison, and a few New Leftists, such as Jack Newfield, Carl Oglesby, and Todd Gitlin), Howe made and kept an impressive number of enemies.[18]

Howe's chief enemies and most severe critics included onetime friends and colleagues in his New York circle who had moved to the right in the late 1960s and '70s: Hilton Kramer, Norman Podhoretz, Saul Bellow, Midge Decter, and Sidney Hook. But other harsh critics stayed on the political or cultural left—and disapproved of Howe's moderate socialism—or moved even further left, such as Alexander Cockburn, Philip Rahv, and the majority of those New Left leaders whom Howe had excoriated in *Dissent*'s pages. Still other opponents, such as Richard Kostelanetz and Philip Roth, were literary or aesthetic rather than explicitly political adversaries.

For instance, Bellow dismissed Howe as "an old-fashioned lady."[19] Roth, upset over Howe's attack on *Portnoy's Complaint* as reinforcing Jewish stereotypes, parodied him as Milton Appel, a "sententious bastard. . . . A head wasn't enough for Appel; he tore you limb from limb."[20]

Other foes attacked Howe as a critic-shark who patrolled New York's cultural currents. During the late 1960s, when acrimonious differences over the Vietnam War and the counterculture split American intellectuals into rival camps, the poet Robert Lowell lambasted Howe as the archetypal "New York Intellectual,"[21] an elitist radical looking down on humankind. Lowell wrote in his sardonic poem, "The New York Intellectual" (1967):

> Did Irving really want three hundred words? . . .
> How often one would choose the poorman's provincial
> out of town West Side intellectual
> for the great brazen rhetorical serpent
> swimming the current with his iron smile![22]

In the early 1970s, Philip Nobile mocked Howe as "the Lou Gehrig of the Old Left," "who is always there when you need him with a clutch position paper on the Cold War, Vietnam, Eugene McCarthy, confrontation or sexual politics." Nobile added that Howe often assumed a gatekeeping or moderator's role, "serv[ing] as the left's chief of protocol, correcting the manners of apocalypticians and calling for coalitions always and everywhere."[23] To Lowell and Nobile, Howe was an American commissar imbued with the joy of sects, an intellectual iron man whose pen never ran dry. Or, as Nobile once remarked of Howe's circle: "They must be New York intellectuals. See how they loathe one another."[24]

By contrast, some of Howe's neoconservative critics—such as his first biographer, Edward Alexander—value his literary criticism and his work on Yiddish literature; they confine their ire largely to his political writing, which they consider naïve or ideologically blinkered and unable to change with the times.[25] Alexander and other Jewish neoconservative critics have been especially hard on Howe for his positions on Israel, particularly his support of the Israeli Labor Party and left-oriented organizations associated with the peace camp, such as American Friends for Peace Now.[26] Neoconservative opponents have also castigated Howe's

If the Mantle Fits . . .

sectarian articles for the Trotskyist group to which he belonged in the early 1940s, pieces that Howe wrote in his early to mid-twenties and never reprinted—and for which he felt rather apologetic in later years.[27] A few neoconservative critics seem determined to haunt him with them.

But the celebrations of Howe's political acumen, intellectual range, and particularly his Jewish cultural criticism and collections of Yiddish literature vastly outnumber the attacks. Already by the mid-1960s, recalled Kenneth Libo, Howe's graduate student at Hunter College and later his research assistant and collaborator on *World of Our Fathers*, Howe "had become a hero of sorts to many liberal-minded academics of my generation." Upon publication of *World of Our Fathers* in 1976, notes one literary historian, Howe "was greeted as a cultural hero" within the American Jewish community.[28] Reviewing *World of Our Fathers* that year, the Catholic priest-sociologist Andrew Greeley exclaimed that "us Irish, we should be so lucky to have an Irving Howe." In 1977, the editors of *Moment* published a poll in which ten renowned American Jews listed the ten "most formative books of the Judaic world, representing all times, all places." *World of Our Fathers* was the only book on American Jewish history to make any of the lists—alongside the Bible, the Talmud, the Passover Haggadah, and the daily prayer book.[29]

Frustrated by what he regarded as the universal hallucination bedeviling the New York literary community, such praise of Howe drove Nathan Zuckerman (a.k.a. Philip Roth) to exclaim about "Milton Appel" in *The Anatomy Lesson*: "When literary Manhattan spoke of Appel, it seemed to Zuckerman that the name Milton was intoned with unusual warmth and respect. He couldn't turn up anyone who had it in for the bastard. He fished and found nothing. In Manhattan. Incredible."[30]

If anything, the celebrations have only intensified since Howe's death. "A kind of moral hero," wrote Mitchell Cohen in *Dissent*. "One of the steadiest minds in modern American life, and one of the most steadying, . . . the splendid voice of social democracy," eulogized *The New Republic*, alluding to Howe's essay collection of the mid-1960s, *Steady Work*. "A monument to a range and a depth almost impossible to imagine in one human being, combined with a quiet decency," Robert Kuttner rhapsodized. Leon Wieseltier went, if anything, even further. "A great-souled man," he called Howe in the *New York Times Book Review*, "the man who, more than any American intellectual of his generation, by his work and by his example, conferred greatness upon the homeliest of qualities, . . . the quality that mattered most to Orwell and Silone: the quality of decency."[31]

The intense admiration continues to the present day. *"World of Our*

Fathers WAS my ethnic revival," recalled Matthew Frye Jacobson. "There is no doubting that Howe was among the spiritual authors of my most deeply held scholarly and civic conviction."[32] In 2003, Joseph Dorman called Howe "a true intellectual hero of the Left."[33] Even Ronald Radosh—a former adversary within the New Left who had moved far to Howe's right—pronounced him "undoubtedly one of our country's most eminent intellectuals, a man of passion and intelligence."[34] Edward Alexander concurred, memorializing Howe in his biography as "one of the most original, principled, and independent minds of twentieth-century America."[35]

II

However much Howe's "enemies" may ridicule comparisons portraying him as "the American Orwell,"[36] one cannot deny that the ongoing controversy about Howe's heritage does indeed resemble—as we also saw in a rather different way in the case of Lionel Trilling's embattled legacy—the cultural politics of Orwell's reputation.[37] In fact, apart from such exceptions as Noam Chomsky and Howard Zinn, probably no American socialist thinker of his generation has provoked more disagreement within the Left and aroused more vitriol among neoconservatives than Irving Howe. And I would argue further that Howe, like Orwell before him, became the "conscience" of his generation and, ultimately, of even our nation's intelligentsia. As a result, the stakes involved in disputes about Howe's legacy are high. For to elevate or denigrate Howe—as has long been similarly the case in Britain with Orwell—is to affirm or assault nothing less than the recent history of the American liberal-Left, the status of the radical dissenting tradition, and the relevance of social democracy or democratic socialism to the American polity.

To understand how Irving Howe has come to occupy such a cultural role—and how he himself understood that role—let us recall the literary-political legacy that Howe embraced as his own. And let us do so by way of a quartet of intellectuals dear to Howe's heart, and who formed the intellectual-moral center of his critical outlook. For a leitmotif of this chapter, which is quite evident in the critical responses already quoted, is the (contested) perception of him as a literary-political hero. I believe that Howe aspired to a kind of intellectual heroism[38]—very much like the writers with whom he identified, the figures who came to figure prominently in his imaginative and emotional life. As we shall see, Howe's choice of literary-political models furnishes insight into his much-disputed legacy as well as his impressive achievement.

Howe exalted four near-contemporary figures that inspired him from his youth onwards: Trotsky, Orwell, Ignazio Silone, and Edmund Wilson. Orwell was his most durable and all-encompassing admiration, but the other three were also long-standing objects of his esteem and even wonder. Frequently Howe's identifications with them were so deep and intense that they amount to self-portraits. Above all, Howe held Orwell and Silone in high regard. He prized them, as Lewis Coser noted in his already-quoted memorial tribute, not so much because of their "sheer literary merits"—for they are not the greatest literary artists—but rather "because they provided guidelines of how to behave in a dismal world with virtuous commitment to moral standards."

Howe's first great hero of History was Leon Trotsky, the man whose political orientation Howe embraced as a young teen when he entered the Trotskyist youth organization, the Young People's Socialist League. Howe's enduring fascination with Trotsky's leadership skills—and indeed his esteem for Trotsky the man and writer as a "figure of heroic magnitude"—is well known.[39] Trotsky's personal example and writings helped draw Howe into and sustain him in the Trotskyist movement. Howe remained a committed Trotskyist for more than a dozen years, from the age of fourteen to his late twenties.

Even after officially withdrawing from his Trotskyist sect, the Shachtmanites (led by Max Shachtman), in October 1953 at the age of 33, Howe continued to include Trotsky among his culture heroes, his only explicitly political figure (except perhaps for Norman Thomas).[40] Howe's biographical study *Leon Trotsky* (1977) makes clear his youthful veneration of Trotsky: "How intransigent he remained in defeat! To have come even briefly under his influence during the 1930s was to learn a lesson in moral courage, was to learn the satisfaction of standing firm by one's convictions, to realize that life offers far worse things than being in a minority."[41] On the final page Howe concludes:

A good portion of the writings of this extraordinary man is likely to survive and the example of his energy and heroism is likely to grip the imaginations of generations to come. . . . Trotsky embodied the modern historical crisis with an intensity of consciousness and a gift for heroic response which few of his contemporaries could match. Leon Trotsky in his power and his fall is one of the Titans of our century.[42]

"St. Irving"?

Howe retained a passionate, conflicted, yet lifelong identification with Trotsky for his "moral courage" and ability to stand alone.[43] (Some critics have argued that Howe whitewashed Trotsky and downplayed his moral as well as political crimes.)[44]

Howe's great esteem for Orwell, whom he repeatedly acknowledged as his "intellectual hero," is well known. And this time Howe chose well: Orwell's skepticism toward ideology countered the influence of Trotsky's allegiance to Marxist abstraction and will to the god of System.

Moreover, Howe rightly intuited that he and Orwell shared significant literary affinities—in the main, a similar kind of rhetorical, inventive (rather than creative or purely literary) imagination. Like Orwell, who was the twentieth-century master craftsman of trenchant catchwords and enduring neologisms, Howe carved lapidary formulations in powerfully, and sometimes beautifully, chiseled language, whereby he too added phrases to the cultural zeitgeist. Howe especially admired those passages in which an author wrote "clenched" prose—a favorite Howe epithet—and his own best writing possesses a rigorous, taut dynamism. Indeed, one could say that the prose gifts of both writers crossed from the rhetorical to the journalistic. Like Orwell's catch phrases, Howe's coinages were often polemical—and directed at explicitly political targets: "this age of conformity" (his swipe at the intelligentsia's conservative turn in the 1950s), "socialism is the name of our desire" (adapted from Tolstoy's famous assertion about God), "the New York Intellectuals" (a phrase that he gave wide currency, if not invented, to characterize his *Partisan Review* circle), "guerrillas with tenure" (perhaps his sharpest cut at the New Left's guru scholars),[45] "a world more attractive" (a little-known phrase of Trotsky expressing love for art over politics), "confrontation politics" (what Howe characterized as the New Left's negotiating style), and "craft elitism" (how arcane literary theory, exemplified by poststructuralism, exploits jargon to exclude the nonspecialist reader), among other phrases.[46]

Orwell did not hesitate to borrow words and phrases for his own purposes and to reinscribe them—and neither did Howe. This is apparent in Howe's book titles, such as his volume of literary criticism, *A World More Attractive*, which recalls Trotsky's phrase but transmutes a political expression to foreground aesthetic principles. But it is also evident in Howe's edited volumes, such as *The Radical Imagination* and *The Radical Papers*, which nod to Trilling's celebrated *The Liberal Imagination* and to the Pentagon Papers, respectively.

Ignazio Silone was, for Howe, a literary-political hero much like Orwell, another writer and radical about whom Howe felt no ambivalence—

"My favorite living writer," Howe once called him.[47] And perhaps Howe felt a closer fraternal proximity to Silone than to Orwell, as if Silone were merely a slightly elder intellectual big brother. (It is also notable that Silone was the only member of Howe's pantheon who ever published in *Dissent*.)

In his essay on Silone, originally published in 1956, Howe acknowledged him as an exemplar of the conscientious, responsible, outspoken dissident intellectual living on "an intellectual margin."[48] (I believe this phrase served as the germ for the title of Howe's autobiography, *A Margin of Hope*.)[49] Indeed Howe came to see himself as a kind of Jewish-American Silone: "The man who will not conform," Howe wrote about Silone, "is a dissenter." Howe elaborated in terms that suggest veiled autobiography: "His own attitude toward socialism was to retain the values, even if he could not retain the doctrine. Silone's demand, at once imperious and relaxed, was that others would share with him a belief in the recurrent possibility of goodness."[50]

Howe calls Silone "a luminous example" of "a patient writer, one who has the most acute sense of the difference between what he is and what he wishes."[51] Howe proceeds in terms that suggest Silone's heroes—and their author himself—represent a level of heroic living that Howe longs to reach in his moments of utopian yearning:

> The hero of Silone's fiction feels that what is now needed is not programs, even the best Marxist programs, but examples, a pilgrimage of good deeds. Men must be healed. They must be stirred to heroism rather than exhorted and converted. Unwilling to stake anything on the future, he insists that the only way to realize the good life, no matter what the circumstances, is to live it. The duality between the two heroes, between the necessity for action and the necessity for contemplation, between the urge to power and the urge to purity is reflected in Silone's own experience as novelist and political leader. In his own practices as an Italian socialist, he is forced to recognize that the vexatious problem of means and ends involves a constant tension between morality and expediency.[52]

Furthermore, Howe agreed with Silone that heroism is "a condition of readiness, a talent for waiting, a gift for stubbornness." Howe admired Silone's resolution and steadfastness despite the fatiguing labor of striving for a more virtuous social order, what Howe called Silone's "heroism of tiredness." Howe aspired to such a heroism himself.[53] Ultimately he realized that patience, alertness, and waiting had to be his way, too—and

65   *"St. Irving"?*

the way of all those who would hold fast to the ideals of socialism. And so Orwell became for Howe a model of "the intellectual hero," Silone "the hero of tiredness."[54]

Edmund Wilson was the only American member of Howe's heroic quartet. Yet young Howe prized Wilson partly for his mastery of the European literary and political traditions. For an aspiring cosmopolitan writer-critic such as Howe, at *Partisan Review*, the American outpost of European culture in the mid-1940s—indeed the premier cultural magazine of the American intellectual world from the 1930s through the 1950s—Wilson represented European intellectual sophistication on native ground. He stood before Howe as an *engagé* intellectual (like Orwell and Trotsky) who had never succumbed to the coarseness of ideology (unlike Trotsky—and unlike the youthful Trotskyist Howe). Of course, Wilson was also the only member on this high stage of Howe's literary pantheon connected with Howe's intellectual orbit in New York, a fact that obviously rendered him a figure in even closer proximity (physically, if not fraternally or ideologically) to young Howe than Silone. Howe could (and did) get to know Wilson personally.[55] Ultimately he granted Wilson too a measure of heroism—and Wilson's literary stamina, indeed superhuman energy, matched Howe's own. Unlike Silone, Wilson was a hero of tirelessness:

> Writers and critics looked up to him, both those for whom he served as a mentor and those ambitious enough to have him as a model. . . . His career took on a heroic shape, the curve of the writer who attains magisterial lucidity in middle age and then in the years of decline struggles ferociously to keep his powers. One doesn't customarily think of writers as heroes; nor are heroes always likeable. But in Wilson's determination to live out the idea of the man of letters in his glowing eagerness before the literatures of mankind and in his stubborn insistence on speaking his own mind, there is a trace of the heroic.[56]

These remarks of Howe on Edmund Wilson came to apply to Irving Howe himself. In *A Margin of Hope*, Howe cited Wilson as his chief literary model (along with Orwell).[57] Here again, as with Howe's other literary heroes, one discerns a resemblance to Wilson in Howe's own "magisterial lucidity" and "stubborn insistence on speaking his own mind"—and also a "trace of the heroic."

If the Mantle Fits . . .

III

The animating idea of one of Wilson's critical studies, which Howe much admired, could serve as an alternate title for this chapter: "the triple thinker." I mean it to apply here both in the sense of Howe's immersion in and mastery of three worlds—literary, political, and Jewish—as well as in Wilson's sense. "The artist should be triply (to the nth degree) a thinker," wrote Wilson in *The Triple Thinkers* (1938), which set forth Wilson's ideal of the writer's relationship to society and reflected his disillusionment with Marxism as a way of reforming society or even adequately describing it.[58]

Wilson's triple thinkers—above all, Pushkin, James, Shaw, and Flaubert, from whom Wilson borrowed the phrase—are unwilling to renounce responsibility either to themselves or to their society.[59] They refuse to dwell in a private garden of self-cultivation or to turn themselves into political hacks or social do-gooders. Instead, they seek meaning in the tensions between their inner and outer worlds. These tensions stimulate intellectual leaps, indeed imaginative triple jumps. The triple jumper of the mind soars dialectically to the triple thought: art functions as an existential guide. Aestheticism—art for art's sake—is the single thought. Its antithesis, the double thought, arises from the realization that beauty does not exist as a transcendent, eternal abstraction but rather arises from social circumstances. This insight, if it loses dialectical fluidity and ossifies beyond conviction to dogma, becomes the doctrine that art must promote social reform. The triple thought is the recognition that art is all this and much more, indeed that the work of art can enlarge our awareness, ennoble our inner lives, and enrich the human condition. This level of thought distinguished the best work of Trilling—and perhaps characterizes the ethos for the New York Intellectuals in their heyday, and the way they blended art and politics while resisting ideology.

I regard Irving Howe as a Flaubertian—or Wilsonian—"triple thinker." Although Wilson's exemplary thinkers were nineteenth-century literary men par excellence, triple thinking is not associated with a particular epoch, form, genre, or style.[60] It envisions new relationships, connects the real to the ideal, interweaves the social and artistic planes—and generates disturbance.

Irving Howe certainly was a thinker ("to the nth degree") who generated a lot of disturbance. And I would argue that he moved far beyond the double thought (and sometimes doublethink) of his youthful Trotskyist dialectics to become a mature "triple thinker," one of our

"St. Irving"?

Howe, early 1980s, around the time of the publication of his intellectual autobiography, *A Margin of Hope*.

most sophisticated critics, possessed of a rare gift to appreciate art as an existential guide—like his models Orwell, Silone, and Wilson himself.

Moreover, as I have already suggested, Howe's thinking was also "triple" in another sense: he was fluently trilingual in three domains. Howe lived concurrently in three overlapping, interacting worlds: American socialism, humanistic criticism, and Yiddish culture—and he commuted constantly among them. They were his three great loves, and he witnessed all of them grow pale and frail in his own lifetime.[61]

Howe's lifetime of faithful commitment to politics, literature, and Jewish culture formed the center of his mature thought. First (at least in his public life) came Howe's politics: Howe the activist, the editor of *Dissent*, the radical humanist and committed writer. Then there was Howe the literary and cultural critic, especially Howe the prose stylist and lover of language. The last (yet perhaps also first) love concerns Howe the Jew, the East Side boy, the faithful steward of *Yiddishkeit*, the author of *World of Our Fathers*.

IV

Not just Howe the socialist, critic, and Jew—but also Howe the man—is my concern in this chapter. So: what kind of man was he?

If the Mantle Fits . . .

Howe not only popularized the phrase "New York Intellectuals" in his brilliant 1968 essay of that title; he also came to personify, as both his admirers and adversaries have recognized, some distinctive features of the species.[62] The personal memoirs of friends and colleagues invariably address his complex personality and intellectual temperament. Most of Howe's acquaintances speak with affection and gratitude about both his mentoring role in their intellectual lives and his comradely companionship on their political and professional journeys. The colleagues of Howe with whom I've talked invariably also speak of him as intense, an indefatigable worker, a man who strove relentlessly toward his goals, a man capable of single-minded effort, a man of strong moral principles who would not rest until the job was done and done right, a man whose opinions and beliefs on any subject were neither held lightly nor separated from his personal relations.

I spoke with Irving Howe on only two occasions: at an Orwell conference in 1983, when I interviewed him, and during his visit in 1986 to the University of Virginia, when he lectured on the American Renaissance from sections of *The American Newness* (1986).[63] He had just retired from the City University of New York, where he had held the title of Distinguished Professor of English and was on the verge of receiving a MacArthur Foundation fellowship in 1987.

I noticed Howe's intensity, but I was also impressed by how his work became more reflective (and autobiographical) with the years. When I shared that perception with Howe's friends, they described to me his mellowing, his growing capacity to relax, his increasing ability to transcend partisanship. The mature Howe knew there was also a time for frivolity and lightness—and so he learned in later life to open himself to new pleasures, such as the ballet.[64] He didn't let his purposefulness degenerate into anxiety about achieving a goal. As Daniel Bell put it in his tribute to Howe in *Dissent*: "Irving changed not only his opinions but the way he held them."[65]

For me, it is not just the critic and intellectual, but Howe the man, and the man within the writings, who proves compelling. It is a quality of human presence, and indeed of presence in the word, especially the modulation and rhythm of his discerning, composed, often poignant literary voice that stays with me. What inspires me above all is the trajectory of his career, Howe's wherewithal to change—less his political outlook than his personal manner. When I met and corresponded with him during his last decade, he had already begun to exhibit a patient trust in the slow work of dialogue, in the slow work of time; that is, he was applying

"St. Irving"?

his convictions about the need for "steady work" not just to his political vision but to his personal values—the true mark of a Wilsonian "triple thinker."

Howe himself recognized all this. "Looking back at my disillusionment with political ideology," he wrote in 1982, "it would be more correct to say that my politics changed because I became, I like to think, more humane, tolerant, and broadminded. If I'm right in using those adjectives, then it became easier for me to acknowledge things that a rigid ideology would deny."[66] As he grew older, he became more flexible, more open to the alternative views and differing gifts of others—as well as more practical and nuanced in his daily politics.

But if Howe mellowed, he did not become lukewarm. He always ran hot on both justice and equality, the polestars of his radical humanism; he stayed cool—nay, cold—to neoconservative celebrations of capitalism, far-left diatribes against "Amerika," and academic jargon of all kinds. In short: Irving Howe stuck to his convictions. Opposition only served to fortify his dogged determination. He could be abrupt and flinty when confronted with what he regarded as stupidity. Or when he encountered intellectual complacency or smugness—especially if it rested on academic credentials. (He was proud that he had become a chaired professor without ever bothering to get a PhD.)[67] He usually found the most effective way of doing things in the least amount of time and could be irritated by people who he felt were wasting time by questioning his method or his rationale. He was unusually sensitive to criticism because he subjected himself to very high intellectual standards that included sharp self-criticism, so that further negative feedback rarely seemed to him necessary. All of which is to say: he may have relaxed his manner, but never his standards.[68]

Talking to his friends, I also became more aware of Howe's rare capacity to hold together the big picture with the fine points. He always had a mind for facts, categories, and technical detail that nonetheless did not lose sight of larger questions. And in his later years, his great self-discipline seldom deteriorated into grim determination, even though he maintained his impassioned sense of mission that led him to want to improve the world. As Leon Wieseltier observed in his memorial address on Howe: "He saw the end of socialism. He saw literature mauled by second-rate deconstructionists and third-rate socialists of race, class, and gender. And he saw the world of Yiddish disappear. But he never surrendered to nostalgia. He remained almost diabolically engaged with the politics and culture of his time."[69]

Although Howe was astonishingly erudite, he did not disdain the

If the Mantle Fits . . .

dirty work of politics, the necessary efforts to bring about the reforms he believed in. He was willing to get into the trenches and bring about the changes he advocated. But there were times—such as during the Vietnam War in 1966–1967, when he wrote *Thomas Hardy*—when he also sought to go "far from the madding crowd" and immerse himself in literature in a quiet natural setting.[70] He enjoyed the give and take of political involvement less and less in his last two decades, though he remained politically active.[71] Most of all, as his friends confided to me, he improved his ability to talk *to* others rather than *at* others.

Howe became more tolerant; he did not become permissive. He never granted that people could just do whatever they liked. Rather, he developed the talent of the tolerant man to respect differences of opinion, never believing that everything was equal and nothing made a difference. He learned to drop debating points—and in doing so he became far more accepting of others without ever simply becoming indifferent. He remained upright while becoming less self-righteous.

Howe's hunger for social justice could go beyond moral seriousness to almost messianic longing. In *World of Our Fathers* Howe exalted *menshlikhkayt* [humaneness], calling it "that root sense of obligation which the mere fact of being human imposes upon us." It is a "persuasion that human existence is a deeply serious matter for which all of us are finally accountable. . . . We cannot be our fathers, we cannot live like our mothers, but we may look to their experience for images of rectitude and purities of devotion."[72]

Again that "seriousness." But also "rectitude" and "purity": These attributes too were central both to Howe's literary sensibility and his commitment to socialism. A man of principle, he maintained a "purity of devotion" to the ethos of socialism—and referred to himself as a "radical humanist," even after *Dissent* dropped its masthead motto ("a socialist quarterly") that had explicitly identified the magazine with socialism in the late 1950s.[73]

V

Howe's son, Nicholas, relates that the phrase "It's like the crumb" became an endearing shorthand joke between Howe and his friends to describe a wonderful, gratuitous detail in a work of fiction—which, as detail evolved into story, assumed the form of an anecdote.[74]

Especially at his memorial service and in the memorial issue of *Dissent* (Fall 1993), his family, friends, and colleagues sprinkled delicious *shtiklakh* (morsels) about Howe's foibles and eccentricities. Everyone spoke about "Irving."

These first-person reminiscences, composed of striking details and revealing anecdotes, vividly evoked the man—and make vivid reading for us today. The crumbs abound: Irving at the baseball game reminiscing with beer-guzzling fans about having seen Babe Ruth play in Yankee Stadium, Irving brusquely ending a phone conversation by hanging up the phone before a friend would say goodbye, Irving leading a *Dissent* editorial meeting with a mixture of benevolence and argumentativeness. Some recollections consist of choice *shtiklakh*, while others are less edible or digestible to his friends. Nonetheless: the crumbs on his coat are there.

One crumb often passed around among his friends was the joke that Irving Howe was the last nineteenth-century Russian writer. In fact, Howe does seem made in the image of the Russian intellectual of that era: a utopian, an idealist, a radical reformer, an impassioned advocate. Morris Dickstein once called him "a counter-puncher who tended to dissent from the prevailing orthodoxy of the moment, whether left or right, though he himself was certainly a man of the Left. . . . Whatever way the herd was going, he went in the opposite direction." And these attributes were not confined to his political or cultural criticism. They manifested themselves in his prose style. As Nicholas Howe observed, Irving had "a utopian faith in the reader."[75]

Unsurprisingly, Howe also deeply identified with—and ever more so as he grew older—the greatest nineteenth-century Russian writer, utopian, and reformer/revolutionary: Leo Tolstoy.

I have already discussed Howe's four literary-political models from the generation immediately preceding his own. But he honored literary and political figures from other generations too. Let us also attend here briefly to another diverse quartet of inspirational—and cautionary—influences on Irving Howe.

One of them was Tolstoy, who also induced him to hold the looking glass up to himself. Howe's comments on Tolstoy are transparently self-reflexive: "I love the old magician in the way that Chekhov and Gorky loved him—for his relentlessness of mind, his unquestionable desires. Of course he succumbs to moral crankiness, to intemperate demands for temperance, but stubborn and even perverse, he remains faithful to the contradictions of his sensibility."[76]

And there is more: "Tolstoy keeps groping for some stable position between the esthetic and the ethical. He never quite finds it, but he can write as if indeed he had found it." All this mirrors Howe—with his love of the ballet and the polemic, his affinity for literary criticism and poli-

If the Mantle Fits . . .

tics, his tense balance between poetical sensibility and ideological conviction. As if to supplement Tolstoy's *Confessions* by voicing his own, Howe adds this (self-)criticism of his moral passion: "In a few instances, Tolstoy's ethical imperiousness does overwhelm his esthetic pattern."[77]

Yes, Howe's own vulnerability to self-righteousness and godlike Final Judgment must also be conceded—and they never vanished completely. But he largely avoided the fate of another epic Russian author, one of the greatest twentieth-century writers, Aleksandr Solzhenitsyn. "What has happened to Solzhenitsyn?" Howe asked in 1989. "The answer is that his zealotry has brought about a hardening of spirit. . . ."[78] Solzhenitsyn lacked what Howe often referred to as "moral poise," which he defined as a sense of "ease in a world of excess." Instead Howe himself heeded the example of the Yiddish writers whom he cherished for their wondrous balance amidst adversity, above all Sholem Aleichem, the "dominant quality" of whose literary imagination "is his sense of moral poise. I can't resist a few more words on the matter of 'moral poise.' . . . [Y]ou see how balanced, at once stringent and tender, severe and loving is his sense of life."[79]

Howe also aspired to such "moral poise," and that is why Sholem Aleichem was ultimately also a literary (and political) model for him. And Howe himself could indeed be a stringent and severe man. That was the form that his tender sense of life sometimes assumed, the means whereby he maintained a poised balance amid all the demands of his triple loves. The balance did sometimes have something of the tenseness—the "intemperate temperance"—of the aged Tolstoy. That was the price that his friends—and above all Howe himself—paid his daimon for his extraordinary intensity, concentration, and passion.

One is reminded that Howe began his career with a study of another intemperately temperate man. In his first book, *The UAW and Walter Reuther* (1949), co-authored with B. J. Widick, the twenty-nine-year-old Howe wrote that Reuther, a left-wing anticommunist labor leader whom young Howe much admired, was *"an unfinished personality"* battling to reconcile the pursuit of power and the call to a nobler vision. Which would be stronger, mused Howe, the drivenness or the dream?[80]

Howe too remained an unfinished personality. But then—who doesn't?

Irving Howe—skeptical dreamer, chastened revolutionary, driven reformer, and reluctant anti-utopian animated by utopian longings—held these oppositions in coiled (or "clenched"), productive tension to the unfinished finish, still yearning, still striving, still steadily working toward his vision of a better world.[81]

73　　*"St. Irving"?*

VI

Irving Howe was not only a vocal radical humanist and the most influential American socialist intellectual of his generation. Howe was also, in my view, the last major American public intellectual who commanded recognition and respect both within cultural and academic circles and across a broad ideological spectrum—certainly the last of the Old Left. Not only was he prolific—he wrote eighteen books, edited twenty-five more, penned dozens of articles and reviews, and edited *Dissent* for forty years—but he was competent and more often brilliant in virtually every literary endeavor of his mature years. While some readers may find his work on the relationship between politics and literature to be most valuable, I believe that his contributions to the study of Yiddish literature and Jewish immigrant history are most likely to last.[82]

Indeed, it is quite possible that Howe's work will endure longer than that of the elder generation of New York Intellectuals in whose shadow

Howe in the early 1990s, not long before his death in May 1993.

If the Mantle Fits . . .

he sometimes found himself.[83] Not only is much of his rich oeuvre of literary and political criticism still in print, but *Dissent*, which Howe faithfully edited for four decades, celebrated its fiftieth year of publication in 2004. Woody Allen's joke two decades ago in *Annie Hall* that the magazine should merge with the neoconservative journal *Commentary* and be renamed *Dysentery* elicits today no more than a smile from serious readers. Allen's movie has become a period piece, whereas *Dissent* continues to represent the distinctive voice of American social democracy and radical humanism.

And yet—always an "and yet"—Howe's undying voice often seems to murmur: "Not enough ... all is lost—*already* lost." Or as Howe phrased it in his last collection of short pieces: "Should anyone remember?" The question almost wafts up from the grave, for it appears in the closing lines of Howe's posthumously published *A Critic's Notebook* (1994). Ever the devil's advocate of his own positions, Howe was speaking here in the voice of a young skeptic who doubts that his elders' experience holds any lessons pertinent to the present—yet who also remains resolutely sanguine about the future: "And isn't it wonderful," he observes, "that we have survived all these catastrophes?" After a pause, the senex Howe—the old man of the Old Left—replies. His response echoes today as though the ghost Howe had arisen to answer: "Yes, it's wonderful, but our hearts also sink before the ravages of time. ..."[84] And many who remember Irving Howe also feel regret about the man's death, which reminds us of the inevitable human fate that we all succumb ultimately to the ravages of time.

But the spirit of a true calling does not succumb; it endures. As Howe declared in his landmark essay "This Age of Conformity," published a half century ago, in 1954: "What is most alarming is not that a number of intellectuals have abandoned the posture of iconoclasm of the Zeitgeist. Give them a jog and they will again be radical, all too radical. What is most alarming is that the whole idea of intellectual vocation has gradually lost its allure."[85]

It never lost its allure for Irving Howe. He remained a model of the humanist intellectual, and he impresses me as such today. So let Howe himself have the last word:

> The most glorious vision of the intellectual life is still that which is called humanist: the idea of a mind committed, yet dispassionate, ready to stand alone, curious eager, skeptical. The banner of critical independence, ragged and torn though it may be, is still the best we have.[86]

"St. Irving"?

Christopher Hitchens in his thirties, as he began to make a name for himself in the United States as an expatriate political journalist and cultural critic.

CHAPTER 4

Fellow Contrarians?
or "The (Anglo-)American Orwell" (IV)

C hristopher Hitchens (1949–) is one of our most prominent and controversial public intellectuals, and numerous cultural critics have compared him—favorably or
unfavorably—to George Orwell. In an October 2005 Internet poll conducted among its readers by *Prospect* to discover the world's leading
public intellectuals, Hitchens ranked fifth.[1] His international status as a
major intellectual is a post-9/11 development. In fact, rather like Orwell
before the success of *Animal Farm*, Hitchens was relatively little-known
outside intellectual circles until the mid-1990s,[2] when he became a
much-quoted and -interviewed critic of the Clinton administration from
the Left, especially during the Monica Lewinsky scandal and impeach-
ment proceedings.[3]

Hitchens began to ascend to his present level of international visibility in September 2001, when he defiantly—and soon definitively—
parted ideological company with the Left.[4] Here again, observers have
been quick to draw a comparison with Orwell.[5] Just as Orwell became a
national figure once he equated Stalinism with rule by pigs in his best-
selling beast fable, *Animal Farm*, so too did Hitchens rise to prominence
for his outspoken, rhetorically incisive criticism of the Left following the

9/11 terrorist attacks. Supporting the administration of George W. Bush, Hitchens defended Bush's "war against terrorism" (Hitchens branded the enemy as "Islamo-fascism") and condemned the Left for opposing military intervention to halt terrorists and tyrants such as Osama bin Laden and Saddam Hussein. Hitchens's positions rankled many socialists (Alexander Cockburn accused him of becoming "just another conservative porker"), and the ensuing row ultimately led Hitchens to resign his post as a contributing editor and regular columnist with the *Nation*.

It was this gesture that catapulted him to the center of political controversy and raised his public profile both in the United States and abroad. In an acrid farewell published in the *Washington Post* ("So Long, Fellow Travelers"), he came out foursquare against the antiwar Left and in favor of a preemptive strike on Iraq. Hitchens thus gave up his fortnightly column, "Minority Report," in the *Nation*, quitting the Left's leading journal of opinion in September 2002 (after a twenty-year stint) with the claim that its post-9/11 "paleoliberal" politics marked a sharp sea change. Since he had started writing for the *Nation*, argued Hitchens, it had turned into "the echo chamber of those who truly believe that John Ashcroft is a greater menace than Osama bin Laden."[6]

Of course, Orwell was not alone among radicals in his early condemnation of Soviet communism and his "Left patriot" stance in the 1930s—nor was Hitchens the only leftist to advocate strong military measures against bin Laden's al-Qaeda and Saddam's Iraq. But Hitchens and Orwell expressed themselves unequivocally and in arresting phrases that commanded attention and provoked bitter quarrels. For his part, Hitchens seemed to see his break with the *Nation* as comparable to Orwell's estrangement from the *New Statesman and Nation* (after editor Kingsley Martin rejected Orwell's dispatches from Spain about the machinations of the Stalin-affiliated International Brigades).[7]

While Hitchens's break with the *Nation* triggered a new round of criticism from the Left, liberals and centrists who were reformulating their political stances leapt to his defense. Some allies immediately compared Hitchens to Orwell—long before the publication in late 2002 of his book *Orwell's Victory* (American title: *Why Orwell Matters*).[8] For example, former *New Republic* editor Andrew Sullivan made the Orwell connection explicit. A fellow British expatriate also residing in the United States and bearing complicated ideological coordinates, Sullivan wrote in *The Times* of London: "[L]ike Orwell, he quit. Not for the Right, not for social status, not for the 15 minutes of infamy every

Hitchens emigrated to the United States in 1980 and was branded a renegade two decades later by his colleagues on the Left after he supported the U.S.-led invasions of Afghanistan and Iraq. A strong admirer of Orwell, and the author of *Why Orwell Matters* (2003), Hitchens became an American citizen in 2007.

turncoat gets. He quit for the possibility of thinking outside any political loyalties at a time when such loyalties are as trivial as they are corrupting. And one day, the Left will come to realise his point."[9] Going several steps further than Sullivan, Ron Rosenbaum of the *New York Observer*, commenting on Hitchens's support for the war in Afghanistan, referred to him as "a George Orwell for our time."[10]

Is he? Is Christopher Hitchens the Orwell of *his* generation, of the aging New Left, the baby boom generation that came of age in the 1960s—and that, arguably, came to political maturity after 9/11? Is he "the (Anglo-)American Orwell" of our day? (Hitchens, whose wife and daughter are American citizens, acquired American citizenship in April 2007.)

There are in fact some broad similarities: Both Orwell and Hitchens are public school graduates and brilliant prose stylists. Like Orwell, Hitchens is first a moralist and second a political and cultural critic. For instance, like Orwell, Hitchens—though much less fervently (or publicly)—has reservations about abortion and contraception.[11] Moreover, Orwell was, and remained to his death, a self-avowed man of the Left and anti-Stalinist, as well as an uncompromising atheist,[12] an anti-imperialist, and an anti-Zionist.[13] In each of these respects, Hitchens can be said to resemble Orwell, even though Hitchens has abandoned the self-description "socialist" (though not "leftist"). What remains disputable, however, is whether the ex-Trotskyist Hitchens—who even today harbors not only lingering affection but also guarded admiration for Trotsky (the "Old Man")[14]—has ever been, like Orwell, an anticommunist (as opposed to being merely an anti-Stalinist).[15] Of course, the obvious literary differences also bear noting: unlike Orwell, Hitchens is no novelist or fabulist; he limits himself to journalism, reportage, and essays. But within those nonfiction limits, his productivity and range of topics easily match, if not exceed, that of Orwell.

Not surprisingly, Hitchens's ex-comrades on the Left blanch at the thought of likening him to Orwell. Quite apart from any comparison according to genre or subject matter, they consider Hitchens, at least since September 2001, no "leftist" or radical whatsoever. To them, his recent trajectory represents a rightward lurch far removed from Orwell's "critic within the Left" stance. Moreover, they hold that simply in terms of temperament and class attitude, Hitchens lacks Orwell's human warmth and deep feeling for the common man.[16] Vilified as an ex-leftist, renegade, turncoat, and traitor ever since his vocal support for the US-led invasions of Afghanistan and Iraq in 2002-2003, Hitchens's numerous radical critics view him not as "Orwell's successor" but rather as Paul Johnson's successor. (Johnson is the ex-leftist editor of the *New Statesman* who has turned sharply rightward, becoming a leading conservative intellectual and Tory pundit.)

My own judgment is that Hitchens is a radical who possesses what Conor Cruise O'Brien called Orwell's "Tory growl." His contrariness resembles Orwell's so-called antinomianism—and Hitchens is equally hard to place ideologically.[17] For example, he writes in *Letters to a Young Contrarian*:

> I have not, since you asked, abandoned all the tenets of the Left. I still find that the materialist conception of history has not been surpassed as a means of analyzing matters; I still think that there are opposing class interests; I still think that the monopoly of capitalism can and should be distinguished from the free market and that it had certain fatal tendencies in both the short and long term.[18]

If the Mantle Fits . . .

I

Having immigrated to the United States in 1980, Hitchens rose from his respected standing as a talented British expatriate journalist in the late 1980s and early 1990s to become an internationally recognized essayist and commentator on a wide range of political and cultural issues, especially after the events of September 11, 2001. Although a series of attacks on Mother Teresa, Bill Clinton, and Henry Kissinger first established his radical credentials in the United States, as well as his gadfly status on the Left, he is now best known for his messy split with the antiwar Left over the war in Bosnia and the US invasions of and occupation policies in Afghanistan and Iraq—particularly his vocal (yet not uncritical) support of the War on Terror conducted by the Bush administration. And it is these associations that prompt some observers—mostly admirers, yet also a few severe critics (such as Alexander Cockburn)—to propose him as "a George Orwell for our time."

Hitchens is the author of a volume of autobiography, *Hitch-22: A Memoir*. He has also written *Love, Poverty, and War* (2005), *A Long Short War: The Postponed Liberation of Iraq* (2004), *Orwell's Victory* (2002), and *Letters to a Young Contrarian* (2001), among numerous other books. Some of his work reflects his impassioned opposition to theocracy, organized religion, and indeed religious belief. *God Is Not Great: The Case Against Religion* (2007) argues that religion does more harm than good in the world and that society would benefit if faith were kept out of the public square.

On the evening that I interviewed Hitchens, he was still partially recovering from a festive late night event with his Iraqi friend Ahmad Chalabi. The party, which included more than a hundred guests, was hosted by Hitchens in his Washington, DC, apartment and did not break up until 4 a.m. Hitchens is a zealous defender of Chalabi and his associates, whom Hitchens regards as Iraqi democrats deserving thanks for the welcome fact that Saddam and his Baathist supporters are no longer in power in Iraq. Hitchens dismisses those who charge that Chalabi sent fabricators into the arms of US intelligence and also ducked responsibility for helping to push the United States into war on the basis of misinformation (or disinformation). Before the interview, Hitchens told me that he considers it preposterous that a lone voice such as Chalabi's deceived the entire Bush administration and the rest of Washington into launching the Iraqi invasion in 2003. Moreover, Hitchens regards it as laughable that Chalabi's Iraqi National Congress (INC) persuaded the

US Senate to pass the Iraqi Liberation Act in 1998 and then again to vote for the Bush administration's joint resolution in October 2002 that authorized the use of force in Iraq—and even more ludicrous that the INC was able to manipulate the combined intelligence services of Britain, France, and Germany, as well as the CIA and other US intelligence agencies.

In the conversation that follows, Hitchens reaffirms his break with the Left even as he refuses to join sides, in more than a tactical sense, with the Right. Here again he demonstrates himself to be an intellectual gadfly or "contrarian," very much in the spirited tradition of his hero Orwell. At times, however, Hitchens is perhaps open to the charge that he does not so much promote a dissenter's position as revel in his contrariness, perversely insistent on opting out of both the liberal and conservative camps. However, with respect to the frequently heard charge from the Left that Hitchens has become a neoconservative, I have my doubts. Yes, he has turned rightward, but only slightly. For example, his chief criticism of Bill Clinton is that he betrayed liberalism (and seduced the Left); his criticism of Islamo-fascism is that it is far more unjust and dangerous than was the Bush administration to international peace.

To put it another way, though he no longer refers to himself as a socialist (to the satisfaction of many radicals) and still identifies himself with the Left (to the consternation of many leftists), Hitchens has become less ideologically motivated and more of an issue-oriented thinker. He follows what he regards as his own conscience and neither seeks nor expects support from any intellectual coterie.

Hitchens does not discuss Orwell in the following interview except to mention him in passing. And yet, given the frequent comparisons between Hitchens and Orwell—which multiplied in the wake of Hitchens's 2002 bestseller, *Orwell's Victory*—the interview provokes one to wonder about the question repeatedly voiced by intellectuals, W.W.G.O.D. (What Would George Orwell Do?). As we shall see, the interview captures a crucial moment in Hitchens's political evolution and possesses biographical and political importance, not mere chronological value. For it showcases Hitchens's positions on both the American-led invasion of Iraq in the spring of 2003 and its occupation since that time.[19] Hitchens also discusses the Bush administration's War on Terror and related matters.

The conversation took place in Hitchens's Washington, DC, apartment on November 14, 2005.

If the Mantle Fits...

JR: *It is well known that you opposed the first Gulf War in 1991 and cas-tigated the administration of George H. W. Bush. Yet you supported the 2003 Iraqi war conducted by George W. Bush. The reasons for your about-face are not well understood by many observers. Could you elaborate on them?*

CH: Well, the first Gulf War was not a regime-change war. What I criti-cized about it—apart from the shady origins of the question as to whether or not there had been some kind of prearrangement to cobble up Kuwait—which I still think is an open question—is that the conflict arose against the background of a president who was up to his thorax in the Iran-Contra racketeering. The Gulf War was designed to restore the status quo ante, aimed in other words at the retention of Saddam Hussein, the restoration of the Kuwaiti royal house, and so forth. On that basis, I didn't feel there was any valid and moral pro-war position to take. I did not rid myself of that rather fatuous position of approximate moral equivalence until the very end of the war when I realized that, if it had not been prosecuted, Saddam Hus-sein would have been allowed to keep Kuwait.

Events soon persuaded me that I should criticize Bush Sr. for not run-ning a tougher war, for not making it into a regime-change war. So my dif-ferences were not abolished, but their ground was altered. Once I decided all that and had seen the evidence for it, and then once I had—after Bush Sr. left office—visited Bosnia-Herzegovina during the Soviet attempt to erase Bosnia and then Bosnian Muslim life and culture, I became one of those who believes it not profane to say that American intervention can be a good and indeed overdue thing.

JR: *In thinking about the war on Iraq, wasn't it reasonable to suppose that the government of President Bush would not seriously wish to reconstruct and build a democratic Iraq so much as to win control of Iraq's oil reserves and to enrich those who have in fact been enriched by lucrative, government-sponsored contracts over the course of the last two years? The fact that this is a scenario predictably associated with the American radical Left should not entirely discredit this scenario, should it?*

CH: Those who want to examine the relationship between cynical corporate interest and American conquest should know that I've written quite a number of books pointing out the consequences in Iran, Chile, and South Africa and elsewhere flowing from precisely that kind of political conjunction.

A number of people are very determined to oppose the regime-change policy of this administration. In regards to this subject, US policy has not been linked to the usual calculus of business and corporate interest. Bush decided to take the risk of a democratic revolution. The oil robbers, and the Saudi Arabian government that are their main patron, were entirely opposed to the government of Saddam Hussein. A fool on the order of George Monbiot[20] or Michael Moore would say that the United States went to Afghanistan in order to build a pipeline across the country of Iraq.

The tone of this question, which I very well recognize, is the refusal by people to realize a new situation when they see one, or a new policy, and instead to fall back into usual customary propaganda.

JR: *If we bracket the question of whether the current Bush administration was right in its early decision to remove Saddam by military force, what about its conduct of the occupation? What has gone right, and what opportunities have been missed? In hindsight, what do you wish had been handled differently with regard to the conduct of the war and the occupation of Iraq?*

CH: Well, to answer those points in reverse order, I would say that the human, material, economic, and political costs would have been much higher if the removal of Saddam Hussein were postponed longer. We were looking at an imploded, disordered, disintegrated Iraq, which would have invited opportunistic interventions—actually invasions—from Turkey, Iran, Saudi Arabia, in each case sponsoring the most extreme fundamentalist forces, and the ultimate result would have been the devastation of Iraqi society by a combination of sanctions plus fascism.

The only real criticism to make of intervention in 2003 would be that it was too long of a span to wait since the first Gulf War and was the less good alternative to completing the job in 1991. By the way, the inquest arguments about Iraq should begin no later than 1991–1992 with the decision not just to confirm Saddam Hussein in Iraq, but actually to, in a sense, underwrite that position. With that proviso, I'm absolutely in favor of a press inquiry into what went wrong in 2003 and afterward.

JR: *Does the considerable achievement of deposing and capturing Saddam justify the political, financial, and human costs to the United States that have thus far accrued—and which promise to mount much higher before the job is done or abandoned?*

CH: We will know it when we see it—presuming that we exclude, as it might be we must, any proposal to abandon our responsibilities to Iraq, which extend back over many decades. We have incurred an inescapable responsibility to that country and have made a number of very solemn promises that we are not entitled to renege on. Those who want to walk away from responsibility show that they do so by the selfish arguments that they use.

If the Mantle Fits . . .

So assuming we exclude that option, two things remain to be done: one is to inflict an annihilating military defeat on the forces of jihadism: we must prove that this can be done. To demonstrate in practice that it can be done would be a gigantic gain in itself.

How long that would take? I don't know. That it will be done, I have no doubt. It's not just a matter of the overwhelming military superiority that we can exercise, nor is it a matter of the moral superiority that we can deploy. The fact is that we know that we are facing the scum of the earth in the form of a fascist minority within an ethnic minority of an ethnic minority, a sect which enjoys support from despots themselves in doubt of long-term survival in the region, particularly Saudi Arabia and Syria.

That is the most overwhelming task, the one that decides everything else: to prove to everybody that jihadism cannot take a country as its victim and keep the people enslaved. The parallel responsibility is to create a federal system responsive to democratic consensual procedure rather than force and cruelty. It might be that the longer these things take, the better, because the more decisive their outcome will be. I'm not in a hurry.

JR: *If there is a civil war in Iraq, and it grows, would you favor more or less immediate American withdrawal, on the grounds, perhaps, that our continued presence can only make things in the country even worse?*

CH: I believe that the United States is right in insisting that Iraq remain a state. There is nothing holy or sacred about the borders of Iraq or its constitution as Muslim. It is a very approximate idea of a state, not a country; nonetheless, I think that it is correct for the United States to insist that it be a federal and democratic state, which is the only alternative either to the rule of all Iraqis by minorities, which has been tried and failed already, or a civil war in partition. I think the chances of civil war have been immeasurably diminished by the regime change, in comparison to its likelihood if Saddam would have kept himself in power.

I fear, and I will repeat this again as a general answer to all your questions, that the intervention was too late. I believe it should have taken place thirteen years earlier than it did. Still, I believe that we have responsibilities to the Iraqi people. And one of these, very importantly, is that we do not abandon our promise to the Kurdish people, not just in Iraq, but also other regions—so that they will enjoy a form of self-determination in their turn. From that pledge we had no right to withdraw, and if Iraq is to fail as a society, which might happen due to blows delivered to it mainly by the Sunni Muslim extremists, then at least that much can be salvaged.

With that said I have never yet met an Iraqi who self-identifies entirely as Sunni, Shiite, or Kurd.

85

Fellow Contrarians?

JR: *Do you agree that capitalism does not in fact need democracy to function effectively and that the notion that it does has been used as a convenient cover for the profoundly undemocratic impulses of regimes typically favored by American administrations?*

CH: Well, historically, capitalism hasn't exactly required democracy—the collaboration of the large monopolies in Germany, for example, with the Nazi party is very well known. They preferred dictatorship to democracy. They felt it to be more the case that capitalism was compatible with dictatorship. Capitalism is compatible in its monopoly-cartel form with apartheid in South Africa and with Communist Party rule in China.

Capitalism led by governments such as the United States has its versatility, or if you prefer to say, its immorality. I mentioned the cartel and the monopolistic forms of it for a reason. It can probably be said about capitalism now that it may not require democracy, but it does seem at its best with it, in an open society, because it's so much based on the ability to transmit and receive and process advanced information. It doesn't work very well in a closed society.

JR: *Should it matter to those who support American policies in places like Iraq that Halliburton pays about $15 million in taxes each year when its appropriate tax bill should total about $250 million, which it manages not to pay by moving its assets offshore and thus demonstrating that it has not the slightest allegiance to the United States or to American democracy?*

CH: The difficulty for those who stress questions like this is that it is impossible for them to show that Iraq could have been any more "privatized" than it already was—in other words, an entire state, its treasury, and its economy and its resources were the private property of a psychopathic crime family. That was the case with Saddam's group. Even the worst, most sheep-like of corporate intellectuals would have seen that as a horror. And if Halliburton is found to be overcharging or underpaying or underbidding, all those responsible should go to jail.

This has no bearing at all on either the justice or necessity of the case for regime change. And I would remind you that, in 1991, Saddam Hussein, on evacuating Kuwait, set fire to the oil fields and flooded the gulf with oil, incidentally destroying all marine life and ecology in the area, just as an act of fascistic vindictiveness. It was thought at one point that those fires might go on burning until the end of the last century. But most of those fires were put out in a cleanup that took about two years.

JR: *Benjamin Barber writes in* Jihad vs. McWorld: *"Terrorism turns out to be a depraved version of globalization; no less wedded to anarchist dis-*

order than are speculators; no less averse to violence, when it serves their ends, than marketers are averse to inequality and injustice when they are conceptualized as the costs of doing business." Is this a plausible way of thinking about the present situation?

CH: Well, I would like to think that Professor Barber has a lot of jokes in him. If Professor Barber thinks that marketing shoes is the equivalent to suicide bombing, he is entirely welcome to his own opinion. I hope that he is relatively alone with it. But he should have worked a lot harder on this. It is the sort of thing that isn't appropriate for a serious discussion at a serious time. This is not the time to be dicking around. I don't mind people being wrong or saying that I am wrong, because the stakes are very high and one must attempt great exactitude for real clarity. What is increasingly not forgivable is flippancy and frivolity at the level of Professor Barber's comments.

It is not because of the West, or because of its consumers, that Muhammad al-Gadafi is the ruler of Libya. The two are completely unconnected. Libya needs more globalization, not less. The aspiration of all Libyans, when they have been allowed to express their opinion, is precisely that.

JR: *Much has been made in recent years of the Bush administration's disregard for the sort of multilateralism once thought to underwrite American foreign policy. In your view, is the current administration's tendency to scoff at international treaties and to display frequent contempt for the UN simply the sign of a newfound realism and refreshing candor?*

CH: The United States, in common with most Arab and Muslim societies, is a signatory to the international agreement propagated by the United Nations, and we don't have the right to resign from the position that our signature represents, nor do they. That's the short answer. Let me elaborate. The United States had to act as if it were the United Nations in 2003, because it alone was prepared to enforce the many dozens of disregarded resolutions with respect to Iraq. If there had been a will on the part of the United Nations—suppose it had decided to enforce them—the United States would have been given the job of doing so. That would have also been the case if the United Nations, for example, had decided to do anything more than nothing about Bosnia or Rwanda or Somalia. It would have been the United States that drew the job of providing the heavy transport planes and the enforcement on the ground and the military relief and the rest of it.

So this is just to restate the problem in a different way. One of the overwhelming and positive outcomes of the international disagreement over

Fellow Contrarians?

Iraq has been to expose the hollowness of the United Nations, and to make it evident to everybody that no one can rely upon it at any moment of physical or moral crisis. The easiest way to support that, I suppose, or at least the quickest, is to point this out: in April 2003, if he had still been president of Iraq, Saddam Hussein would have been appointed the chairman of the United Nations Special Committee on Disarmament. At that point, a line of absurdity would have been crossed that can't be crossed again. That's a lot more ridiculous even than Iraq having been a member of the Human Rights Committee.

The second answer is that the United States was not acting in a culturally imperialistic way when it helped the people of Afghanistan to write the constitution that reserves 25 percent of seats in the parliament for women. I don't think that is in any way contrary to the teachings of the Koran. For this reason, I'm very opposed to the compromise made by the US government in its negotiations in Afghanistan or Iraq with those party members who might wish limitations based on religion or designed to enshrine any one religion. I am very critical of the weirdness of some American negotiators to allow the establishment of any religion by name, or religion in general, into any constitutional document. Iraq is not a Muslim country. There is no such thing as a Muslim country.

JR: *Let me approach some of the foregoing issues from a different angle. Numerous critics of US foreign policy maintain that American credibility abroad has suffered enormously in the Bush years. They argue that the United States is seen throughout the world not as a country that supports democracy, plurality, and tolerance, but as one that simply supports American business interests, pretending all the while that it is defending civilization. Why should people all over the world regard the United States this way if in fact there is more to be said for US policy, including its design in the Middle East?*

CH: I don't accept either of the underlying assumptions of the question. In the first place, when it is said that American credibility has suffered, I want to know with whom. Is that with Mr. Chirac? Why is it assumed that these people's opinions should count, or even that they do count? There appears to be a feedback loop involved. If they say we don't find the United States as credible as we used to, do we take their word for it? Do we have any reason to do so? That's the first point.

Second, even supposing that the United States openly favored vast international economic inequalities, would that disqualify the United States from enforcing United Nations resolutions on Iraq? I don't see how the two things are connected in any way.

Suppose the United States was, as it used to be, the patron of military

If the Mantle Fits . . .

protection in South America. Would that mean that it had no right to enforce the decisions of the UN? I don't think so, even in that case. I would prefer it to be otherwise, but there is nothing that makes the one contingent upon the other.

The redistribution of resources within Iraq is already quite impressive. If peace could be established and if the oil industry could be revived, there would possibly result two very positive events. First is instituting the proposal made by Dr. Ahmed Chalabi, among others, that all Iraqis be paid—as Alaskan citizens are, for example—a certain rent from the oil revenues, that everyone be given a share. Second is that peace and a revival of the oil industry might undercut the existing, outrageous, and inefficient monopolies in Iran and Saudi Arabia, both of whom dread the revival of the oil wealth of Iraq.

It's certainly true, for example, in the Kurdish areas of northern Iraq that quite a lot of progress has been made, really quite considerable prosperity. Large projects of development and innovation are being made. I don't know whether those who want more equitable distribution have reported on this, but until they have, I distrust them. I'm not sure I trust their good faith, in other words, on redistribution, equity, protectionism, or agrarianism, the latter of which I believe they secretly prefer, which is more of an equality of backwardness.

JR: *Often it is said that Americans are notoriously bad at processing even the elementary facts and information presented to them, so that ignorance about basic realities—the fact that Iraq was not directly responsible for the attacks of 9/11, the fact that those in the Bush administration who really did think there were WMDs in Iraq only supposed this because they knew that we had supplied them, et cetera—seems so permanent and deep that virtually nothing can affect it. Your view of this?*

CH: Nobody who travels around the United States lecturing or debating, or who appears on call-in shows on radio or television, can be anything other than alarmed at the extraordinary depth and extent of ignorance in this country. I don't know that it's worse here than elsewhere, but I know that it is more important because American voters are asked to make decisions very often for other countries too.

Yet the instances you give are not the persuasive ones. The instinct of the American public, if it was only an instinct, to identify Saddam Hussein's regime with the concealment of weapons of mass destruction is a sound instinct based on solid fact. And so is its view that there is a connection between the pseudo-secular fascistic regime of Saddam Hussein and the jihad system.

Fellow Contrarians?

All this was sounder than the views of most American intellectuals, who continue to insist that the Saddam regime had proclaimed secularism and therefore by definition could have had nothing to do with Islamic jihad, in other words not that it didn't, but that *it couldn't*. This view is so stupid that, as an author whom we both admire once said: "Only an intellectual could be dumb enough to believe that. No ordinary person would be such a fool." [The reference is to George Orwell, a loose version of a line from his wartime essay "Notes on Nationalism."]

JR: *What prospect is there that so-called moderates will, within the next ten or twenty years, take gradual control of Islamic societies?*

CH: The one word that we should not use, whether they are actual or potential allies, is the word "moderate." That word used to be applied to, for example, the Saudi Arabian ruling family, because it appeared not to be inimical to American interests. That used to be the working definition of "moderate." If you remember, "moderate" was the description of the Iranian Revolution when it was prepared to accept American weapons—i.e., if they were to accept the American weapons, they must be "moderate" by definition.

So the word is suspect. For example, the Sunni Muslims were fighting against Saddam Hussein before we were. They were a genuine people's army struggling for national liberation. I think that the word "moderate" would not be very relevant to them; I would say "revolutionary." Of those in Turkey who wish to have their country enter into the European Union, I think the word would be "democratic" or "secularist." You might call those in Indonesia who wish to see their country not destroyed by nihilistic attacks "pragmatists."

But all these cases turn on circumstance. The one word that must *not* be applied is "moderate."

If you want to ask yourself what the Islamists have in store for us, you have only to see what they have done to Afghanistan or are trying to do to Iraq. Those who put their lives on the line every day in Afghanistan and Iraq to fight against them deserve a better fight than we are modeling. But a victory of the Muslims, since you ask me about that, is in my opinion impossible. First, it is unthinkable, and second, it is actually not possible to restore that kind of thing or to put the Muslim world back to the desert conditions that gave birth to it. The effort to do so can be enormously damaging. It simply cannot be successful. It's defeated already by its own ideology, it's defeated by its own method, and it's not at all by coincidence that its method is principally identified with suicide and with the supposedly bold affirmation that death is preferred to life and valued more highly. This

If the Mantle Fits . . .

attitude is exactly what is so self-destructive, pornographic, and sadomas-
ochistic that it allows me to describe it as fascistic.

And fascism was defeated mainly because of its own infatuation. It has a
death wish.

JR: *Edward Said wrote more than a decade ago about the destruction of
the university in the Middle East, exemplified by the absence of critical thinking among students and teachers. Although Martha Nussbaum and others
have noted that the university under the leadership of Sari Nusseibeh in East
Jerusalem has made real efforts to turn things around, is it your impression
that much progress has been made or that in fact things have grown even
worse since Said wrote his report?*

CH: No. The general state of the universities is well known for combin-
ing the worst qualities exemplified by their leaders.

But again I am referring to the Arab universities. More books are translated and published in foreign languages in Athens every year, even though
Greece is a small and poor country, than in the whole Arab world combined.
The Middle Eastern countries are dealing with a growing population of un-
educated young people, especially young men. That, and that alone, is the
supposed "root cause" everyone looks for. Terrorism is not the root cause
of it, but enjoys a very warm and fetid relationship with those things. There
isn't anything even remotely corresponding to education, or to anything
that approximates to enlightenment or open-mindedness.

So yes, the answer must be that it is worse for simple reasons of population. The reverse is the case in Iraq, where there are now six television
stations and twenty-one independent newspapers in a country where until
three years ago, it would have been death for you and your family to have
a satellite dish, or to have any contact with a foreign journalist, or to access outside information. I think that the renaissance has come to the Arab
world through the opening of schools, universities, bookshops, and other
cultural institutions. A revival in Iraq is already well under way.

JR: *Is it fair to say that Israel is no longer a key element in the politics of
Middle Eastern countries dominated by Islamist radicalism? Or will Israel
remain central no matter what steps are taken by its leaders to dismantle the
settlements and reach a modest accommodation with a figure such as [Pales-
tinian leader] President [Mahmoud] Abbas?*

CH: If only symbolically, Israel represents to many Arabs, including
secular ones, a reminder of defeat and humiliation, given that the Arab Palestinian population lives under a regime which it had no part in framing.
In other words, they are not under a government by consent, and that is an

outrage in my view. It's a mistake to imagine that we should appease this outrage—it treats the entire Palestinian population with contempt. Nothing is more fascist than to have their national claims ignored as we conduct the struggle against terrorism. I think these two matters—the war on terrorism and a Palestinian state—are entirely separate.

JR: *Most theories of just war proceed from the conviction that the weapons used in a just war must discriminate between combatants and noncombatants. In your view, is this a tenable proposition for belligerents like the United States to observe in proceeding with operations directed against so-called terrorist states?*

CH: Arguments about just war have very little to say about weaponry traditionally because weaponry was what it was. Just war theory has to do with necessity, with the proof that all other alternatives have been exhausted. It's merely wishful thinking to say that one hopes to minimize our death count. Who would not say that?

This form of argument has proceeded in very practical terms in the recent past in the United Nations. A regime can be removed if it can be done without doing much damage to the population. And then you factor in, as I think one must, those who would have died in any case either by violence, neglect, famine, disease, or other preventable causes of death had the regime been allowed to go on. We can actually now be able to make rather bold statements about what used to have to be accepted rather cynically.

I don't think that the [Bush] administration or the Defense Department has received enough credit in its effort to develop systems of weaponry that would minimize fatalities to noncombatants. That's one of the lessons that the United States armed forces did learn in Vietnam, where they were rightly accused of using barbaric methods of warfare, including chemical proliferation, napalm, phosphorus, high-level aerial carpet-bombing, and so forth.

I wasn't myself present at the fall of Kabul. I was on the border of Pakistan. But friends of mine that had the opportunity to be there play by play with the Northern Alliance—friends who had been seeing on the screens or hearing about the bombing—were astounded. They couldn't tell whether Kabul had been bombed at all; there was no sign of it having been bombed, so careful and specific were the targets that were being bombed.

I'm not sure that can be said in every case in Iraq. But we know now that there is a new standard by which commanders can be judged; they can report to the president as the commander-in-chief, in which he gives the order that an illegitimate government should fall and its population not suf-

If the Mantle Fits . . .

fer, with some reasonable expectation of accuracy. I think this puts us into a completely new era.

JR: *David Rieff and others have lately complicated our view of the effects of humanitarian intervention and assistance in developing countries. How have your own views of such intervention and assistance programs evolved in recent years?*

CH: I don't think that David Rieff's book is his best, but it may be his most heartfelt [*A Bed for the Night: Humanitarianism in Crisis* (2003)]. The whole idea always advanced by economic aid and development aid, which was that there is a danger of preventing people from finding solutions to problems that are endogenous to their own society or their own states, is true. It's true that aid programs may create a number of international wards.

But it seems to many of us that David was right the first time about Bosnia and about Kosovo. That there were certain outrages that couldn't be permitted to burn themselves out, or to run their course, because the precedent of committing ethnocide in a European country would not just be horrifying morally, but it would make us complicit as spectators—and almost participants, since we would be withholding resources that we might have devoted to help.

Second, this bad example could have rapidly spread, say to the Transylvania dispute between Hungary and Romania—to cite a single instance in the same region. It was something that ought to have been preemptively stopped for very good logical and moral reasons.

I think it must be for this reason that we have had such a bad conscience about Rwanda because it was known not only that we failed but that we did not try. Small efforts might have had a specific effect, and these measures were withheld. That is the awful madness we faced; we were just not interested. These examples always weigh more with me than with those who say: "Well, look at Kosovo now. There are so many people who depend on Western aid and on NGOs and UN presences." That may well be true. Which is why I continue to insist on a point that I've never heard addressed, let alone rebutted—or repeated by critics of Iraq. What did they think was going to happen to Iraq, or what had been left of it, under the stewardship of Saddam? Can't they see that there would have been a Congo or a Rwanda in Iraq? An outcome that would have ended the idea of opportunistic intervention in Muslim countries, an outcome exacerbating all the conditions of strife and greed leading to bankruptcy, famine, disease, and dissipation?

Fellow Contrarians?

All these things would be occurring in Iraq with multiplied force in the face of neglect or indifference.

JR: *What about the international sanctions? Many critics of US policy point to UN and other reports that the invasion was outrageous and unnecessary because the sanctions were working. Or they argue that the sanctions themselves were not just outrageous but ineffective—except in the horrible effects that they inflicted on millions of Iraqi children.*

CH: Let's take the critics of the administration's policy at their own face value. It was said by those who didn't like the invasion that the international sanctions, which were keeping Saddam in his box, were killing about 100,000 Iraqi children a year. I never thought those figures were absolutely certified, but let's say a very large number of preventable deaths among the most vulnerable section of population.

We turned to them and said these sanctions are imposed on a criminal regime in a failing state. We can lift the sanctions but we will have to get rid of the regime. Sanctions on Saddam make life acceptable.

But that is bad faith, John. Now we have lifted the sanctions on Iraq, which is one of the reasons the lights don't go on in Baghdad and why there are terrible traffic jams. Everyone is loading as many electrical devices as they possibly can at home (and thus overloading the electrical systems), as well as choking the streets with millions of new imported cars.

The combinations of the sanctions on Saddam, and his efforts to circumvent the sanctions, while inducing him to stir up hatred and use divide-and-rule tactics in order to keep his regime in power, would have led to an implosion. Which is what we were looking at—and, as far as I could see, was walking toward us.

Those twelve years should have never been allowed to occur in Iraq, but they were allowed, and if we had waited fifteen years it would have been horrific. Do they favor the Bush Sr. policy of confirming Saddam in power after the victory in Kuwait? If they do, they have to accept the possibility of what fails.

If they don't, they would not say that the inquiry into what happened in Iraq should have begun in 2003. Well, the other two dates I've suggested would be: 1979, when the Nobel Prize winner Jimmy Carter gave Saddam Hussein permission (and some say encouragement) to invade Iran. Certainly from that date a great deal of later misery and warfare originate. Or I might want to start the inquiry many years earlier with the role of the Central Intelligence Agency in helping both the Iranian and Iraqi dictatorships come to power, that being one of the uncounted costs of the Cold War. Well, that might be going back a little too far.

In other words, we must understand that we have a long responsibility for what's happened to the Iraqi people and cannot pretend otherwise. Those who want to have an inquiry only as part of a military withdrawal convict themselves.

JR: *Many liberal-leftists admire your case against Islamo-fascism, yet they believe you undermine your argument by supporting Bush and the neo-conservative agenda in Iraq. These liberals, such as Paul Berman, propose a Third Force between the anti-American, neo-isolationist Left and the neo-conservatives. They usually see you as a potential ally, but you seem to have repeatedly declined their invitation to join them in a liberal-Left interventionist coalition. Why?*

CH: I suppose I can say that I'm very proud that they agreed with me about Islamo-fascism—as being fascism with an Islamic face, as I put it. I didn't support Bush when I coined that.

Furthermore, obviously I can see the charm of that invitation, but I can also see the temptation of it. In other words, if I said yes, of course I would then rather have a third way between Michael Moore and George Bush. And so then, whatever form we might like the fight against Saddam and the Taliban soldiers to take, we could be sure it wouldn't be run like it was by the former governor of Texas.

I don't see such a Third Force forming that would constitute the preferred element here. I would rather say that what I want is for the US administration and the American citizenry to commit firmly to resist, regardless of who is serving as president. That does not involve twisting the alignments with which I am involved.

JR: *Would you agree that the press in the United States has been less than committed to truth-telling in the years since 9/11? And would you suggest ways that might be effective for getting the American press to do its job better and, for example, to acknowledge that most embedded reporters can't be expected to tell any complex truths about their experience?*

CH: I have two answers for that. One is: I became a journalist so I wouldn't have to rely on the press for information. I don't read it any more than I absolutely have to, and when I do so it's in order to find out what other people think the story is. I usually get my information from other sources. I don't watch any television at all. So that either qualifies me or disqualifies me.

As to a herd mentality in the press, I've seen that for many years now. I've known these people my whole life, and I see how they behave at a press conference. There was a herd mentality in Sarajevo, with which I happened to agree, although generally I have never liked the consensual pack of the press corps.

The press corps mentality on Iraq has for a long time been united that the situation is a "quagmire." That's [acquired the status of a] fact; they decided a long time ago that "quagmire" was the best option and it really shows.

JR: *Let me close with a different kind of question that is prompted by the Left's scorn for your positions on Iraq, terrorism, and so on. Which of the many ad hominem attacks, delivered largely from the Left, bother you the most? There's the "he's a ranting drunkard" charge, the "ex-socialist-turned-neocon-sellout" indictment, and the "money-grubbing and sensationalistic faux Orwell" putdown, among many other taunts and affronts.*

CH: None of those charges bother me; I'm indifferent to all of them. They don't really touch me. Most of them are so palpably untrue that it's easy for me to ignore them. I'm perfectly capable of having a social drink and simply stopping with that, and the others aren't even hard-hitting. You have to understand that, in most of these cases, I started it myself. I got personal with my critics, and they are simply returning the fire in kind. I don't believe the character of a person is irrelevant to the positions that he adopts on moral and political events. It's all relevant, and so our temperaments and personal habits are available for scrutiny too.

JR: *Which of your contrarian opinions—on the Iraq War, Bush, Paul Wolfowitz, Michael Moore, Bosnia, Clinton, Sidney Blumenthal, or any other—bothers your critics the most, do you think? Which of these has burned bridges that the Left will never allow to be rebuilt?*

CH: Undoubtedly, it's my position on the war. Those other names and issues are more or less passing phenomena, but this is here to stay. I hate the antiwar Left for the wave of anti-Americanism they've unleashed around the world today, and I'll never forgive them for their casual disregard for the suffering of the Iraqi people. Things are much, much worse than before 9/11 and it's because of the antiwar people.

If the Mantle Fits . . .

CHAPTER 5

"True Patriot and Traditionalist,"
or the (Hungarian-)American Orwell (V)

L
ike his close friend and fellow gadfly intellectual Dwight Macdonald,[1] the historian John Lukacs is a resolute iconoclast, an adamant antinomian, and a great admirer of Orwell. Above all, Lukacs values Orwell's distinction between patriotism and nationalism. Following Orwell, Lukacs notes that patriotism is "defensive," while nationalism is "aggressive." Whereas patriotism is linked to one's homestead and to the particularity of place, nationalism derives from "the myth of a people."[2] For Lukacs, "patriotism is traditionalist, nationalism is populist." This formulation underscores Lukacs's distrust of charismatic leaders and "the masses," for "populism" represents for him the most vile and insidious force in modernity, and Lukacs relentlessly attacks it throughout his work. Moreover, in a sense Lukacs admires Orwell for his "growth" toward a figure resembling— well—John Lukacs. As Lukacs puts it in "The Legacy of Orwell": "Orwell advanced in his thinking from consciousness of class to consciousness of nation. He advanced from his principal preoccupation with social justice to a preoccupation with language and truth. From being a radical revolutionary he advanced to being a traditionalist."[3]

Lukacs added that Mussolini was also a "post-Marxist thinker" who

John Lukacs, the distinguished historian of World War II and biographer of Churchill and Hitler. Lukacs was a close friend of Dwight Macdonald's and a fellow admirer of Orwell.

understood that "nation" was more important to the populace than class. Mussolini emphasized that he was an Italian first and a socialist "only second." Lukacs argued that Mussolini's "recognition" paralleled "the discovery Orwell was also to make in his own way."[4] It was a discovery that Lukacs—also a post-Marxist (or post-ideological) thinker—had made at an early age as a result of living in occupied wartime and postwar Hungary under Nazi and Stalinist domination.[5] One senses that Lukacs cherishes Orwell for having struggled to perceive and give voice to the same hard-won truths that Lukacs himself champions. He prizes, as it were, the Lukacsian features that he discerns in (or projects into) the Orwell physiognomy. It is these which make Orwell "a great man"—a phrase that Lukacs the historian reserves for the leading figures in his pantheon, such as Tocqueville, DeGaulle, and above all Churchill and Pope John Paul II:

> Orwell was a great man because he refused to blind himself to realities which others refused to see; and he was able time after time to change his mind on critical issues. Gradually, slowly, he changed his mind

on the question of bourgeois values, on the relationship between totalitarianism and capitalism, on the future of Spain, and so on. What
Orwell learned in the course of his development was that some of
the best qualities of the English working class were really bourgeois
values. The tremendous desire of the working class that Marx had
completely ignored was for a kind of respectability which Orwell was
not embarrassed to associate with such bourgeois virtues as decency
and probity.[6]

An equally treasured aspect of Orwell for Lukacs, as I have already
suggested, is that Orwell understood the importance of "nation over
class"—and yet resisted the lure of "nationalism." Orwell was a true
"patriot," which owed to his "traditionalism," his "realism," and his fundamentally bourgeois outlook:

> Important in any account of Orwell is his discovery in 1940 that he
> was a patriot—not a nationalist, as Hitler had called himself, but a
> patriot. Orwell's conclusion was the opposite of Hitler's as it was op-
> posed to the views of contemporary neo-conservatives and Reagan-
> ites who had tried to claim Orwell as their own. This is a part of a
> verminous lie which has been told again and again in discussions of
> Orwell (who belongs no more with the neo-conservatives than with
> American intellectuals who remain committed to the Marxist mode).
> No traditionalist—and Orwell had become a traditionalist by 1940—
> can have wanted to make common cause with people who have no use
> for the kind of political and historical realism he had made his own.[7]

That last sentence witnesses Lukacs crossing the line from admiration of
Orwell to self-projection: Orwell "the traditionalist" of 1940 was in fact
the committed socialist who was completing *The Lion and the Unicorn*,
in which he called for a full-scale revolution in England, including abolition of the House of Lords, an institution that had existed for more than
seven centuries.

Lukacs refers to Orwell liberally through his oeuvre, demonstrating
his acquaintance with even the less well-known works of Orwell, such
as his essay on Tolstoy and his oft-forgotten early novels *A Clergyman's
Daughter* and *Keep the Aspidistra Flying*.[8] (Lukacs even alludes to Orwell's "critique" of how history is mistaught in *A Clergyman's Daughter*.)[9] Despite Lukacs's fervent commitment to Catholicism, including a
spirited defense of Franco and the fascists of the Spanish Civil War, he

expresses high esteem for Orwell's *Homage to Catalonia*, even though he also admires the reactionary Catholic and pro-Franco writer Georges Bernanos (author of *The Diary of a Country Priest*). Both Orwell and Bernanos (and also another of Lukacs's great loves, Simone Weil, a supporter of the Spanish Republicans) were "patriots."[10] Lukacs even compares the closing lines of *The Lion and the Unicorn*—in which Orwell voices a deeply felt, even sentimental love of England and its countryside—to Lukacs's own Philadelphia homestead:

> What George Orwell wrote about England during the welter of the last world war applied to Philadelphia perhaps more than to any other city in America: no matter how things would change, it would not lose all its peculiar flavor: the gentleness, the hypocrisy, the thoughtlessness, the respect for law would remain; like England after 1941, Philadelphia during the last half of the American century would still be Philadelphia, "an everlasting animal stretching into the future and the past and, like all living things, having the power to change out of recognition and yet remain the same."[11]

Again and again, Lukacs bemoans that "most American conservatives" have remained "unaware of the crucial difference" that Orwell draws in "Notes on Nationalism": the distinction between "the ideological nationalist and the true patriot." Whereas the former hungers to "extend the power of his nation," the latter is motivated by "love of his country." According to Lukacs, nationalism is primarily evil because it is a rival religion. Both the Nazis and most American conservatives "put their nationalism above their religion, their nationalism *was* their religion."[12]

I

These salty, grandly generalized opinions are vintage Lukacs: he possesses a quirkiness, a skepticism, and above all a critical independence that distinguishes him among contemporary intellectuals. As the editors of *Remembered Past* (2005), a comprehensive collection of his work, write in their preface: "Independence is the hallmark of Lukacs's mind and character, from whence arise both the originality of his thought and the obscurity of his reputation."[13] Or as Lukacs himself has written, responding to an academic historian who speaks of "the impossibility of reconciling the critical independence usually cherished by intellectuals with participation in politics":

If the Mantle Fits . . .

Very few intellectuals seriously cherish their own or anyone else's critical independence. The more important consideration for most intellectuals interested in public life is the achievement of position. In one of Evelyn Waugh's later, not very good books, there's a wonderful passage which reads, "In a democracy, men do not seek authority so that they may impose a policy; they seek a policy so that they may impose authority."[14]

Lukacs's own critical independence is exemplified by an unusual aspect of two essays that he wrote within a span of a little more than six months during 1980–1981, both of which addressed the future of the Solidarity movement in Poland. The articles were controversial and proved prophetic: he argued that the Soviet system was near collapse in Eastern Europe and that communism as an idea was intellectually bankrupt.

What makes these two articles so unusual, however, was that they appeared in the leading liberal and conservative journals in America: the *New Republic* and *National Review*.[15] Is there any other American intellectual in the last three decades of whom one can say the same?

The articles are not just prescient but self-revealing, indeed in a broader cultural sense: they disclose the place that John Lukacs occupies on the American intellectual scene. His psychological makeup bears striking affinity with Orwell's own, and he is equally hard to categorize politically or ideologically. Conservative by temperament, radical in intellect, reactionary by conviction, Lukacs is that rare intellectual creature: one who almost always runs against—and locks horns with—his fellow intellectuals, the "herd of independent minds," in Harold Rosenberg's sardonic phrase.

Lukacs is a scholar-intellectual of indisputable gifts and impressive achievement, yet he is almost impossible to classify. Intellectual nonpareil, historian *sui generis*, he defiantly and gloriously represents an extinct species: the gadfly as a man of letters. In a career that spans more than sixty years, he is among the most prolific scholars writing about modern history, dealing with topics as diverse as World War II, atomic physics and the epistemology of historical knowledge, the rise of American democracy and the accompanying spectre of demagogic populism, and—arguably his most important and original domain—the art of historiography and the nature of historical consciousness.

It is in fact the extraordinary range and diversity of Lukacs's scholarship that partly accounts for why he has never been properly understood by his intellectual contemporaries—and also why he has never acquired a circle of protégés or a school of followers, whether of aspiring intellectuals or junior historians. Nonetheless, his admirers comprise a diverse group that includes some of the keenest, most original minds that twentieth-century America has witnessed: for example, the leftist intellectual historian H. Stuart Hughes, the political columnist and commentator George Will, the cultural historian and social critic Jacques Barzun, and the legendary scholar-diplomat George Kennan. Still, even these distinguished figures have reflected patterns of thinking and position-taking that lend themselves to some definite taxonomies: none of them has espoused an outlook so idiosyncratic, or *Weltanschauung* so singular, as to risk incomprehension, dismissal, or mockery. None of them has adopted stances so rebellious, nor pursued a path so unorthodox as Lukacs.

II

John Lukacs was born into a bourgeois family in Budapest on January 31, 1924. His father was Roman Catholic; his mother was Jewish. Raised in the Catholic faith, he nonetheless retained a deep affection for his mother after his parents divorced. She was an Anglophile and saw that Lukacs learned English and gained an appreciation for British culture.[16]

Lukacs was largely untouched by World War II until 1944, when he was sent to a labor battalion in the Hungarian army during the last stages of the German occupation of Hungary. In the spring of 1945, he evaded arrest by the Nazis, but he had no doubts about his likely fate at the hands of the Soviet liberators. Already an Anglophile like his mother, Lukacs established contact with American and British military observers after the Russians liberated Hungary in 1945. At the war's close, he resumed his studies. By the spring of 1946, when he attained his PhD in European diplomatic history at the University of Budapest, Lukacs had become convinced that the Russians would install a communist puppet regime. Through one of his American contacts, Admiral William F. Dietrich, he fled Hungary for the United States that summer. (The story is related in Lukacs's masterful book on the fateful year of 1945, *Year Zero* [1978], in which Lukacs includes a memoir of his Hungarian youth before his escape to the West.)

A year after arriving in America, Lukacs settled in Philadelphia. In 1948, at the age of twenty-four, he secured a job teaching history at Chestnut Hill College, a small liberal arts college for Catholic girls. He taught for almost fifty years there and at another small Catholic institution in the Philadelphia area, La Salle College. Despite periodic offers in later years to teach at larger, more prestigious institutions, he remained there until his retirement in 1993. He did, however, teach as a visiting professor at some of the most distinguished American research universities, among them Columbia, Johns Hopkins, the Fletcher School of Diplomacy at Tufts University, Princeton, and the University of Pennsylvania. Among his visiting professorships were appointments at the University of Toulouse in 1964–1965 and the University of Budapest in 1992.

When Lukacs left Hungary for the shores of the United States, the Cold War was just beginning. Having witnessed the brutality and inhumanity of the Soviet occupation of his native land, Lukacs harbored no illusions about the "noble intentions" of the Soviet Union, as did so many on the American Left. So he was first pegged as a member of the political Right because of his anticommunism. In reality, however, he was never more than a fellow traveler of the Right. Lukacs viewed the obsession with anticommunism of most American conservatives as foolishly "immature." In 1957 he wrote, in a characteristic barb, that "except for a few aged Marxists huddled in New York, there are few truly international Communists left."[17] In his essay "The American Conservatives" (1984), Lukacs summed up his attitude toward early postwar liberalism and conservatism: "The liberals were senile while the conservatives were immature."[18] Still, determined to interpret Lukacs as nonetheless favoring their side, some conservative critics were quick to respond: you can outgrow immaturity, but there is only one dire end for senility.

During a robust literary career of more than a half century, Lukacs has expressed these convictions in an oeuvre both diverse and far-reaching. He has published more than two dozen books, along with hundreds of articles, essays, and reviews. One of his most recent books, *George Kennan: A Portrait* (2007), recounts his friendship with the eminent diplomat-scholar.[19] Another is the compelling story behind one of Winston Churchill's greatest speeches, the "Blood, Toil, Tears, and Sweat" address of May 13, 1940.[20]

III

Lukacs has never achieved the academic recognition that the breadth and innovativeness of his scholarship warrant. The reasons are both personal and intellectual. Never a careerist—in fact, he believes that teaching undergraduates has helped hone his literary style and taught him to "describe things simply but not superficially"[21]—he

"True Patriot and Traditionalist"

has neither cultivated a coterie of dissertation students nor attended (i.e., schmoozed at) academic conferences. First and last, he has been a historian and an undergraduate teacher: the "historical profession" and the academic mill have exerted no attraction. He has prized the undergraduate classroom experience, contending that it has made his writing more accessible to the literate general audience whom he wants to reach.[22]

Lukacs strongly believes that history should not be a form of communication between academic historians. His commitment to writing absorbing narrative history has also made him—despite his interest in historiography—wary of grand theory and system-building. With a nod to Orwell, he refers to academic historians and other gatekeepers of historiography as the "many Experts with Degrees from Institutes and Ministries of Truth:"

> They are processing words, answering machines, and computing very selective data. The year 1984 is now well behind us. Our world is not, as Orwell wrote it might have become, one of political totalitarianism. Nor is it reactionary (in *1984* Orwell wrote that science and technology would decay under totalitarianism) . . . [What has occurred is] just the opposite: Newspeak and doublethink and untruth are "scientific" and "progressive." They are instruments of a new bureaucratic kind of tyranny that Tocqueville had envisaged though Orwell did not. Their main instrument is the computer, which is not a robot, since it is "programmed" by men. Whatever does not fit in it will remain unrecorded for posterity. It reduces life to a system. A system, by its very definition, is exclusionary. Whatever is not part of it must be discarded, forgotten, destroyed.[23]

Lukacs is also sharply critical of what he invidiously terms "historianship"—a form of insularity whereby historians are more interested in their standing in the academic profession than in the study of history itself. He insisted in one interview that these developments are "ruining [the practice of writing] history." There are too many historians, according to Lukacs, "whose main interest . . . is concentrated on such petty things as tenure, secretaries, parking spaces at the university, and so forth."[24] These convictions resonate with his commitment to accessible writing, his aspiration to reach a wide audience, and his appreciation of literary style in historical writing.[25] As he remarked in a 1994 interview in *Pennsylvania History*: "History has no language of its own. [It is] not only written, but spoken, taught and thought in everyday language. If history is not written well it means it's not thought out well."[26] Here again, Lukacs offers allegiance to the author of *Nineteen Eighty-Four*, noting Orwell's reverence for "The Word," exemplified by Orwell's own "prose like a windowpane" and his biting satire of language abuse and obfuscation. (Characteristically, Lukacs emphasizes that Orwell deplored the corruption of "traditional" language.) Lukacs elaborated on these thoughts in one of his most widely cited essays, "It's Halfway to 1984," published in 1966 in the *New York Times Magazine*:

> Orwell was frightened less by the prospects of censorship than by the potential falsification of history, and by the mechanization of speech. The first of these protracted practices would mean that the only possible basis for a comparison with conditions other than the present would disappear; the second, that the degeneration of traditional language would lead to new kind of mechanical talk and print which would destroy the meaning of private communications between persons. This prospect haunted Orwell throughout the last twelve years of his life. Some of his best essays dealt with this theme of falsifications of truth—even more than totalitarianism, this was his main concern.[27]

IV

What political tradition reflects Lukacs's cultural outlook and social criticism? Lukacs scoffs at any such label as "conservative" or "radical." With nose-tweaking exuberance, he insistently refers to himself as a "reactionary." Certainly we might provisionally call him a "traditionalist": he possesses a deep respect for the past, maintains a profound suspicion of the modern world, and exhibits immediate allergic reactions to all fads and most conventional wisdom.

All these features of Lukacs's literary personality are on prominent display in his combatively unapologetic apologia, *Confessions of an Original Sinner*, published in 1980. As the title of this feisty autobiography suggests, Lukacs is a pious Catholic believer, and it is this firm commitment to a traditional—indeed, pre–Vatican II "reactionary" Catholicism—that has induced many observers to brand him a "conservative."[28]

Certainly Lukacs is a cultural conservative. Although he possesses a deep temperamental disaffinity for close association with political

"True Patriot and Traditionalist"

groups or intellectual circles, he is on especially cordial terms with the so-called paleoconservatives (e.g., with the Intercollegiate Studies Institute, whose press has published several of Lukacs's books).

These friendly relations notwithstanding, Lukacs has never embraced any such group designations as "conservative" or "paleoconservative." Both in academic and intellectual terms, he defies categorization. This bracing independence of mind, unequivocal contempt for ideological sects, and hypervigilant wariness toward intellectual coteries has endeared him to his most loyal readers, though it has certainly limited and complicated—and, quite arguably, thoroughly confused—his wider reputation.

Throughout his long career, Lukacs has never subscribed to the standard anticommunist *Weltanschauung*. Unlike many conservatives (including a large number of paleoconservatives, such as William F. Buckley) during the early postwar era, Lukacs regarded Senator Joseph McCarthy as an opportunistic thug. For Lukacs, McCarthy represented the crudest, most threatening expression of a populist nationalism, a phenomenon that Lukacs regarded (and still regards) as the most dangerous trend of the twentieth century.

Lukacs's stance toward anticommunism has been nuanced. He scorned communism's success in winning converts and sympathizers among soft-minded American leftists, never doubting (for example) that Alger Hiss was guilty of treason for political espionage. Yet Lukacs also viewed the American Right's obsession with communism as self-defeating, because communism was ultimately a doomed, outdated nineteenth-century concept, and the Soviet Union represented no ideological threat to the West.[29] Lukacs trumpeted the argument that the USSR was dangerous because of its military power, not its ideological profile—an argument that he advanced as long ago as 1961 in his first popular success, *A History of the Cold War*.

It warrants mention here that Lukacs's concerns with the Cold War induced him to turn his sharp eye to the great historical event that shaped it, World War II. Beginning with *The Last European War* (1976), a study of the first two years of World War II, Lukacs has written several historical accounts about the significance and consequences of the Second World War that combine narrative and analytical methods. Lukacs structured his 1976 monograph via an approach that he first developed in *A History of the Cold War*. The book is divided into two unequal sections, a brief "Main Events" followed by a much longer analytical section on the "Main Movement."

The Last European War was followed by *The Duel: 10 May–31 July*

If the Mantle Fits . . .

1940: The Eighty-Day Struggle Between Hitler and Churchill (1991) and *Five Days in London, May 1940* (1999), rendering these works a fascinating, if informal, trilogy in which Lukacs repeatedly explores and speculates just how close Hitler came to winning the war in 1940.[30]

Lukacs makes no apologies for the popular success of either these narrative histories of World War II or his biographies of Churchill and Hitler, though he maintains that his scholarship is impeccable and can easily stand comparison with that of academic historians. Indeed he is especially proud of his biographies, and it was Lukacs's absorbing preoccupation with the crucial opening years of World War II that drew him to study its two key architects, Hitler and Churchill.

According to Lukacs, Hitler was the greatest revolutionary of the twentieth century—more significant than Lenin or Stalin—because his rhetoric and the Nazi mass movement wove together the four most potent forces of the modern era: nationalism, populism, socialism, and anti-Semitism. In his ground-breaking historiographical study, *The Hitler of History* (1997), Lukacs follows an approach suggested by the English historian Herbert Butterfield to "not cover periods but deal with problems."[31] Lukacs portrays Hitler as cunning and rational—and not at all the madman of popular histories. With regard to Hitler's anti-Semitism, Lukacs contends that its roots are not in pre-World War I Vienna (as Hitler claims in *Mein Kampf*), but rather arose from his experiences in Munich following the November Revolution after the war and especially during the brief leftist-communist regime in Bavaria in 1918–1919. Once the Depression had taken hold, Hitler cleverly exploited Germans' antipathy toward the Jews. But Lukacs believes that it was Hitler's anticommunism, not his anti-Semitism, that enabled him to appeal to the middle classes as well as to the German working class.

Lukacs's engagement with World War II and Hitler induced him to study the career of the Führer's foe and the war's hero, Winston Churchill. In a series of closely reasoned yet also impassioned books, culminating in an incisive assessment of the British prime minister's entire career, *Churchill: Visionary, Statesman, Historian* (2002), Lukacs argues that Churchill was ultimately the savior of Western civilization. Without Churchill's refusal to make a separate peace in the summer of 1940, Lukacs believes, Hitler would have won the war. In his World War II trilogy, especially *Five Days in London, May 1940*, Lukacs describes the intense pressure on Churchill to make a deal with Germany and how adroitly he outmaneuvered those (such as Lord Halifax, the British foreign secretary) who favored a brokered peace with Nazi Germany.

Lukacs believes that Churchill as statesman excelled the other major

"True Patriot and Traditionalist"

Allied leaders, Roosevelt and Stalin, and was superior to another of Lukacs's personal favorites, Charles de Gaulle. Recognizing that Nazi Germany posed the graver threat to the West, Churchill was willing to forge an alliance with Stalin's Russia. The choice was agonizing yet brutally straightforward: better half of Europe under Soviet rule than the entire continent dominated by the Nazis.

Lukacs is less impressed by Churchill's role as the rallying voice of anticommunism after World War II. Lukacs holds that anticommunism became an obsession, particularly in the United States, where it skewed political life for a generation. In a review essay of the Eisenhower-Churchill correspondence, Lukacs insists that the American public's virulent anticommunism tragically resulted in a missed opportunity to resolve the Cold War in the months after Stalin's death in March 1953. Few historians share this view, maintaining instead that the USSR's post-Stalin leadership was too weak and divided to enter into any serious negotiations or a rapprochement.

V

Lukacs's views of the 1950s are also rare (and unpopular) among conservatives in other ways. For instance, he has also voiced a low opinion of Dwight D. Eisenhower, a conservative icon of the 1950s. According to Lukacs, Eisenhower was a shallow, superficial president whose administration was an abject failure. This critique has put Lukacs at odds with most presidential scholars, who have ranked Eisenhower among the ten greatest American presidents.[32] Not surprisingly, Lukacs bristles when conservatives cite such self-congratulatory rankings.

Not only is Lukacs critical of Eisenhower, but he also looks dimly on the Republican Party of the 1950s, arguing that after World War II it promoted and exploited the populist nationalism that he regards as so perilous to the modern world. As an example of its misguided nationalism, Lukacs often cites a plank from the 1956 Republican Party platform calling for the establishment of military bases around the world. Lukacs's reactive temperament induces him to draw attention to such obscure, oft-forgotten statements in order to chasten conservatives and heave a counterweight against their ready replies that it was the Democrats, not the Republicans, who took the United States into Vietnam, the most divisive war in American history.

Nonetheless, the undaunted, convinced conservative might retort: the most extreme expression of populist nationalism in the form of a proud

If the Mantle Fits . . .

American exceptionalism was uttered by John F. Kennedy. In his famous inaugural address of January 1961, he promised to "bear any burden and fight any foe" of freedom around the globe. Indeed, from the standpoint of populist nationalism, it would be interesting to compare Kennedy's inaugural with Eisenhower's farewell speech, in which Ike warned against the militarization of society in general and the "military-industrial complex" in particular. The two speeches were delivered within weeks of each other. In any case, it is indisputable that Kennedy's successor as president, Lyndon B. Johnson—the most ambitious domestic reformer since FDR—irreversibly plunged the nation into the morass of Vietnam soon after JFK's death by sending 500,000 troops there. Moreover, it is worth noting that a Republican president, the much-maligned Richard Nixon, eventually withdrew the United States from the seemingly inextricable Vietnam quagmire.

VI

Lukacs is also a fierce critic of the 1960s. Here again, however, he deviates from the conventional view of the 1960s as the era that reshaped modern American history. Lukacs argues instead that the decade is largely continuous with the 1950s. "It is a great error to believe that the Sixties amounted to a radical break with the Fifties," Lukacs has written. "There is plenty of evidence that the puerility of the 1960s (for that is what it was) existed already in the 1950s: the increasing influence of the pictorial imagination, for instance—especially embodied in television—or what happened to popular music."

If nothing else, the originality, or sheer orneriness, of such pronouncements gained Lukacs broader recognition—and entry into the mainstream press—by the early 1960s. His articles began appearing not only in scholarly journals but also in such prominent mass-circulation publications as the *New York Times Magazine*, *Horizon*, and *Esquire*. Yet because of his unorthodox opinions, he was never consistently identified as an adherent of any particular intellectual group or school of thought. Lacking support from any intellectual circle or literary network that might have promoted his work and defended his positions, Lukacs won no more than a handful of discerning, enthusiastic readers: his audience was limited by his intellectual temerity and outsider status. This was especially the case within the American literary academy and among academic historians, who neither appreciated nor accepted his work. They tended to dismiss his theoretical writings as irrelevant to the craft of historical writing, and to denigrate his brilliant narrative histories of World War II, along with his absorbing biographies of figures such as Winston Churchill and Adolf Hitler, as "popular" rather than scholarly history, indeed as little better than literary journalism. Such dismissals go far to explain Lukacs's own deep disdain for both the American intelligentsia and the historical profession.

From the mid-1960s to the early 1970s, both the radicalization of America in response to the Vietnam War and the violence and anti-intellectualism of the student protest movements further complicated Lukacs's political stance. He now castigated the Left as infantile and boorish, just as the Right had been during the McCarthy era. Largely because of his dismissal of communist ideology, Lukacs became associated at this time with the rising conservative movement in the United States. In the course of time, the protest movement and counterculture prompted Lukacs to redefine his political views. Although he wrote extensively for William F. Buckley's *National Review* and R. Emmett Tyrell's *American Spectator* from the mid-1970s to the early 1980s,[33] Lukacs began at this time to reject, explicitly and vociferously, the label "conservative" and instead began to call himself a reactionary, a self-identification that he reiterated with perverse glee in *Confessions of an Original Sinner*.

Characteristically, however, he is a reactionary of a quite original sort—a respectable "bourgeois reactionary." (He proudly served in his neighborhood planning association outside Philadelphia for more than three decades.) Such a reactionary is paradoxical because it is normally understood that a conservative may be bourgeois, but a reactionary is definitely antibourgeois. (For instance, Dostoevsky was a reactionary, but never a conservative.) A reactionary emphasizes the corruption of modern society and its economic system, while conservatives who are bourgeois make their peace with capitalism.

The great reactionaries are always great romantics. Even though they hanker after a more organic society that has no possibility of political realization, this does not prevent them from expressing their nostalgia for the past in beautiful art or brilliant works of scholarship and imagination. One might argue that Lukacs exemplifies the reactionary historian in this particular sense. Reactionaries are less susceptible to the vulgarities that typify the conservative bourgeois. Like those on the radical Left, they tend to abhor bourgeois life. What is odd about Lukacs, of course, is that he is in many respects quintessentially bourgeois.

So Lukacs has worn the label "reactionary" lightly—no more than any other term or stance has it defined him in any predictable, circumscribed way: his politics and social criticism elude such shorthand summaries. He remains difficult to categorize, even if his autobiography has handily provided readers with an arresting label. In hindsight it is as if Lukacs adopted the term "reactionary" as a shock tactic. It could unfailingly function to push people's buttons. By "speaking the unspeakable" ("A reactionary!" gasped the literati), Lukacs could thumb his nose at the cultural trendiness and radical chic of the modern age, especially the de rigeur "hip" '50s and "groovy," "with-it" '60s.

To the extent that this may have been Lukacs's motive for embracing and enshrining the "reactionary" label as his own, it fit well and reflected the same rationale as his unfashionable, indeed antediluvian self-designation as an "original sinner." After all, who in the modern world nowadays speaks about "sin," let alone calls himself "an original sinner"? Who else, in penning his *Confessions*, bypasses the secularist Rousseau and goes all the way back to one of the first fathers of the Church, Augustine?

Here again, one suspects that "traditionalist," or even more so "neo-traditionalist," did not strike Lukacs as sufficiently provocative to jangle the chains of the liberal-radical intelligentsia—nor arresting enough to challenge the secular, modernist pieties of the cultural elite. Yet to "confess" himself to be an "original sinner" in his morals and a "reactionary" in his politics and social views? Yes, *that* might hit the nerve of contemporary culture.[34]

This is not to say that Lukacs is not serious about the term "reactionary." It does apply to him, and he means it to be taken in earnest. And the same is true for his self-identification as an "original sinner." Lukacs enjoys "bourgeois" pleasures; he is no ascetic and does not regard himself as a saint. As we have suggested, however, neither these terms nor any others have served as a fixed identification that has restricted Lukacs's range of positions or made him immediately understandable to his audiences. Unlike most reactionaries, he has never revolted against or detested the bourgeoisie. In fact, Lukacs has lived a bourgeois life in an older suburb of Philadelphia. During his three decades of service on his neighborhood planning association, the "reactionary" Lukacs waged a long battle against commercial overdevelopment in the area.

Lukacs's self-definition as a reactionary is, therefore, quite plausible. He means that he is a patriot (not a nationalist) and a skeptic regarding the American dream of progress. Of the American Right today, Lukacs declared in an interview: "They're not conservatives. They're not traditionalists."[35] He is especially dubious about the role of technology in modern society. American conservatism, he holds, has been weakened by its ferocious anticommunism, by its belief in science and progress,

"True Patriot and Traditionalist"

and by what he considers an aura of "sourness." Modern conservatives, particularly the neoconservatives, have contributed to the besetting evil of the age: the degeneration of American democracy into a crude form of populism.

In two portraits of the recent past, *Outgrowing Democracy: A History of the United States in the Twentieth Century* (1984) and *The End of the Twentieth Century and the End of the Modern Age* (1993), Lukacs argues that democracy has been corrupted and is now threatened by what he calls "the populist Right," a term he associates with contemporary conservative pundits (such as the neo-isolationist Pat Buchanan) and with past political figures (such as Huey Long, though one could retort that Long was a classic left-wing populist and never a rightist).

VII

As the 1980s unfolded, Lukacs drifted further away from any sort of mainstream conservatism. As already noted, he wrote extensively for *National Review* in the 1970s. In fact, Lukacs was even interviewed by William F. Buckley on his popular *Firing Line* television program. Lukacs's antagonism toward American conservatives, however, intensified as their political fortunes prospered in the late 1970s, reaching a peak with the election of their standard bearer, Ronald Reagan, as president in 1980. Lukacs voted for Reagan in 1980 largely out of disgust with the feebleness of Jimmy Carter's presidency. But Reagan soon became Lukacs's bête noire, a genial nullity who represented everything wrong with American conservatism.

Lukacs viewed Reagan as a political lightweight, the product of shrewd public relations. Here was a Hollywood B-actor turned Commander-in-Chief: a nightmarish fulfillment of the Peter Principle of ever-ascending, maximized incompetence. For Lukacs, Reagan represented the triumph of American demagogic populism. The spectre that Lukacs had warned against for decades had thereby become reality—and in the deceptively benign, quintessentially American form of the General Electric host and genial "aw-shucks" California cowboy as absurd occupant of the Oval Office.

What exercised Lukacs above all about the new president was Reagan's simplistic view of the world as if it were a Warner Brothers studio set depicting an earlier era—as if the subtleties of international geopolitics were indeed reducible to good guys wearing white hats battling bad guys in black hats. Worst in Lukacs's eyes was Reagan's crazed anticom-

If the Mantle Fits...

munist convictions even into the late 1980s, which Lukacs regarded as hopelessly outdated. When Reagan was credited in the 1990s by conservatives (and much of the mainstream press) with bringing about the collapse of communism, Lukacs would have none of it. Instead he attributed the defeat of communism to the courage of the peoples of Eastern Europe, particularly the Poles and Hungarians, along with the dramatic role of Lukacs's sole contemporary hero, Pope John Paul II. By contrast, Reagan exemplified the populist nationalism that Lukacs regarded as the curse of the age, and Lukacs's derision of Reagan soon led to chilly relations with the administration's supporters. By mutual consent, Lukacs disappeared from the pages of *National Review* and the *American Spectator* in the early 1980s.

In "The Legacy of Orwell," Lukacs heaped scorn on the "Orwellian" abuses of language practiced by Reagan and many of his right-wing supporters:

> What would Orwell have thought about a president who calls a nuclear rocket a "peacemaker"? About another president whose spokesman called a lie a "non-operational fact"? What would he have thought of the machine worshipers who are now to be found on the right, not on the left? What would he have thought about the world of NASA and Star Wars, of the canned commentary of the *National Review*, of William Buckley, Kingsley Amis, Tom Wolfe? He would have despised them all. As a traditional English intellectual, not an ideologue with an orthodoxy to defend at all costs, he continued to think the beginning and the end of all things [was] the word itself. Everything he learned in the course of his development was consistent with this insight that you can't know the truth if you do not pay attention to abuses of the word.[36]

During the Reagan era, a note of pessimism about the future of the West in general and the United States in particular also crept into Lukacs's writings. The passive response of "the West"—i.e., the United States, above all—to the Hungarian Revolution of 1956 had initially led Lukacs to wonder if Western civilization was decaying. In later years—in the wake of the West's tepid response to Czechoslovakia's Prague Spring in 1968 and Poland's Solidarity movement in the early 1980s—Lukacs concluded that the West had lost confidence in its own culture, a phenomenon that worsened as the decades passed. By the mid-1990s, his doomsaying cultural pronouncements resembled those of a communist refugee newly arrived to America's shores: Aleksandr Solzhenitsyn.

"True Patriot and Traditionalist"

Not unlike Solzhenitsyn,[37] Lukacs argued both in *Outgrowing Democracy* and *The End of the Twentieth Century* that the West had lost its dynamism, with the United States falling hostage to an elective monarchy (the so-called imperial presidency) debased by public relations and political polling.[38]

Responding in an interview to a question about his major literary-historical achievement, Lukacs pondered his voluminous writings across more than five decades and declared his work in historiography as his proudest accomplishment. He regards *Historical Consciousness; or, The Remembered Past* (1968) to be his enduring contribution to the study of history.[39] He is deeply chagrined that his conceptual writings on the metaphysics and epistemology of history have been "ignored by the very people whose work is in historiography," as he expressed it to historian Patrick Allitt.[40] When he discovered that the leading journal of international historiography, *History and Theory*, had not only failed to commission a review of his landmark work in that field, *Historical Consciousness*, but even to include it in an exhaustive bibliography, he sent "a short, angry letter to the editors" that concluded with an accusation of their "Orwellian" motives: "By having tried to render my work into an UNBOOK, you have not succeeded in making me an UNPERSON."[41]

VIII

Lukacs's literary output has remained impressive throughout the last three decades. Since the 1980s, Lukacs has published significant works on Philadelphia, on fin de siècle Budapest, on Winston Churchill's rivalry with Hitler, and on the career of George Kennan—along with two volumes of autobiography and an unorthodox amalgam of history and fiction (*The Thread of Years* [1998]). The latter is perhaps the most original work of Lukacs's enormous oeuvre.

The key to Lukacs's productivity is his tremendous personal drive and near-Herculean energy. His remarkable vitality, still undimmed in his late eighties, has been indispensable to his independence and feeling of invulnerability. He possesses a remarkable self-confidence that manifests itself in the form of a take-charge attitude and an inveterate willingness to go it alone whenever necessary. At the same time, Lukacs is also convivial and quite sociable, and he can be a very loyal friend and strong supporter—as intellectuals who differed with him in many respects, such as Dwight Macdonald, discovered to their joy.

But Lukacs is no team player, and—as we have seen—he is not afraid to cut his ties with his literary outlets (such as *National Review*) and powerful opinion makers (such as William F. Buckley). Strong-willed and forceful, Lukacs is ideally suited to the life of the freelance writer, the independent intellectual, the voice in the wilderness. Like Orwell—in fact, even more so than Orwell—he is the quintessential rebel and outsider. Or perhaps the more suitable word to describe Lukacs, as in the case of Christopher Hitchens, is "contrarian," which also connotes that one is a rebel for rebellion's sake. For better or worse, that is often true for both of these otherwise utterly different Orwell admirers, Hitchens the heterodox ex-Trotskyist atheist and Lukacs the orthodox Catholic reactionary.

This willingness reflects Lukacs's personal courage and chutzpah. But it also can make him a difficult man to deal with, because getting his own way is important to him—even at the cost of intellectual influence or financial sacrifice. Because Lukacs's self-assertive modus operandi sometimes predisposes him toward conflict and strife, he can fall prey to a tendency to "bite the hand that feeds him" and perceive divergences of outlook as slights and insults that may not exist at all, or might be easily reconciled with good will.

Lukacs's background as a survivor of Hitlerism and Stalinism goes some distance toward explaining these attitudes: he is a survivor above all. He has experienced the world in terms of struggle and endurance, and he has continuously tested his mettle against the political environment— and prevailed. Knowing what it takes to survive, he has developed a powerful style of self-assertion, and because this mode of self-expression has led to such favorable results in terms of his productivity and ability to thrive independently, he has developed a steely self-determination.

Blessed with a very strong ego, Lukacs's capacity to execute projects that he envisions is unrivaled: once his ego fuses with a vision that he develops for a project or idea, he can readily bring that vision to life, presenting it convincingly and with dramatic power. Ultimately, Lukacs's confidence in his gifts extends to the conviction that he can and will emerge victorious in the end. Even if his literary and intellectual achievements are undervalued by the present generation of scholars and intellectuals, posterity will vindicate him. Lukacs is willing to take the long view. That orientation also fits with his "reactionary" outlook, his love of the past as a historian, and his trust in the future as a Catholic believer.

Indeed, in light of his personal temperament and convictions, Lukacs's faith functions as a kind of countervailing force: his Catholicism, with its emphasis on self-surrender, impedes and limits his impulse toward self-assertion. It also has endowed him with a spiritual humility that enables him to relinquish his willfulness in order to serve something greater than his own ambitions, whether that cause is his neighborhood planning association or the work of a friend such as Macdonald.

Both in his writing and in his personal relations, Lukacs is willing to take on battles for the sake of ideas he believes in, people who matter to him, and causes he espouses. He is not "needy"—he does not "need" supporters or allies. He welcomes them, and he is a big-hearted, jovial spirit when he socializes with them. His willingness to go it alone extends to a belief, however reluctant, that he may not be able to rely on anyone or anything outside himself. Having grown up in an Eastern Europe in which he had to be sufficiently resilient to meet whatever challenge might come up, he has had to develop a tough, aggressive shell, a form of character armor that remains fortified unless he is quite secure among friends. Probably the only American leader in recent memory for whom he has had much respect or affection is Harry S. Truman, whose signature phrase could also serve as Lukacs's own: "The buck stops here."

Lukacs is not afraid to take a stand, even—or especially—an unpopular one. However accurate the impression that he is first and last an Eastern European immigrant intellectual, Lukacs is also a classic "rugged individualist" in the nineteenth-century American style. He is hardworking and often businesslike in his approach toward his intellectual projects and his interactions with colleagues and editors. One reason why he has published so much and so widely is that Lukacs is an intellectual entrepreneur. Yet he is by no means a literary hustler who trims his sail in order to ingratiate himself with influential editors or publications. His intellectual integrity and a bedrock self-confidence free him from the temptation to such compromises.

As we have seen, however, neither these uncommon virtues nor Lukacs's prolific output has gained him a large audience or high esteem in American intellectual circles. Although many of his books have received enthusiastic reviews and have sold well (e.g., the last volume of his trilogy on World War II, *Five Days in London: May 1940*, which benefited from a boost from New York City mayor Rudy Giuliani after the 9/11 crisis), Lukacs remains an outsider, ever alienated from the intellectual world in which he lives. Likewise, in the eyes of the members of the historical profession, Lukacs is a "non-person," in the word of distinguished historian Eugene Genovese (if not, as Lukacs himself has expressed it, "an UNPERSON") a man ignored because his work accommodates no nice, neat intellectual category. For Lukacs, that has been the tribute exacted—and the renown withheld—for his "critical independence."

Unbowed and uncowed, John Lukacs simply will not chop himself down to fit into Procrustean beds—whether of the Left or Right, whether of the intelligentsia or the academic elite.

Part Two

Politics and the German Language

10 GEBOTE

für den neuen sozialistischen Menschen

1. DU SOLLST Dich stets für die internationale Solidarität der Arbeiterklasse und aller Werktätigen sowie für die unverbrüchliche Verbundenheit aller sozialistischen Länder einsetzen.

2. DU SOLLST Dein Vaterland lieben und stets bereit sein, Deine ganze Kraft und Fähigkeit für die Verteidigung der Arbeiter-und-Bauern-Macht einzusetzen.

3. DU SOLLST helfen, die Ausbeutung des Menschen durch den Menschen zu beseitigen.

4. DU SOLLST gute Taten für den Sozialismus vollbringen, denn der Sozialismus führt zu einem besseren Leben für alle Werktätigen.

5. DU SOLLST beim Aufbau des Sozialismus im Geiste der gegenseitigen Hilfe und der kameradschaftlichen Zusammenarbeit handeln, das Kollektiv achten und seine Kritik beherzigen.

6. DU SOLLST das Volkseigentum schützen und mehren.

7. DU SOLLST stets nach Verbesserung Deiner Leistungen streben, sparsam sein und die sozialistische Arbeitsdisziplin festigen.

8. DU SOLLST Deine Kinder im Geiste des Friedens und des Sozialismus zu allseitig gebildeten, charakterfesten und körperlich gestählten Menschen erziehen.

9. DU SOLLST sauber und anständig leben und Deine Familie achten.

10. DU SOLLST Solidarität mit den um ihre nationale Befreiung kämpfenden und den ihre nationale Unabhängigkeit verteidigenden Völkern üben.

WALTER ULBRICHT AUF DEM V. PARTEITAG DER SED AM 10. JULI 1958 IN BERLIN

Issued by the Central Committee of the East German Communist Party in July 1958, the "Ten Commandments of Socialist Morality," as they were termed, specified the political duties of GDR citizenship and aimed to form "the new socialist human being." Some of the commandments reflect a surprisingly Protestant (and indeed capitalist) work ethic. For instance, the seventh commandment might have been written by Ben Franklin in *Poor Richard's Almanac*: "You should strive to improve your performance at work, be thrifty, and develop socialist work discipline."

CHAPTER 6

The (Un-rosy) State of
Orwellian Unlearning

A famous Herblock cartoon from the early postwar era shows a Moscow schoolboy slinking home from class, his shoulders drooping, his head bent. From behind the Party newspaper, whose front page features the usual headlines about Comrade Stalin's heroic exploits, the boy's father puffs stolidly on his pipe and asks: "Well now! And what have we unlearned today?"

Almost seven decades later, the joke and its Orwellian idiom have regained their relevance; ever since the collapse of several East European communist governments in the late 1980s and the breakup of the Soviet Union in 1991, parents in formerly communist nations have asked the question of their own children.

After the fall of the Berlin Wall in 1989, the question possessed a special urgency in the former East Germany—in no small part because its recurrence evoked previous cataclysms of commotion in eastern German schools. In fact, with adjustments to its newspaper headlines, the cartoon could have illustrated German education in the Third Reich or even during the Weimar Republic of the 1920s. Indeed, the practice of rewriting history à la George Orwell's *Nineteen Eighty-Four* is one of the few constants in modern German education. From the majesty to the disaster of Prussian monarchy, from the wisdom to the folly of Weimar republican democracy, from the glory to the horror of National Socialism, and from the greatness to the abomination of "Red" communism, German lessons are swiftly learned and "unlearned."

And now the curtain has risen on yet another era.

The history of this spasmodic process—the more than sixty years of successive waves of unlearning and relearning that have swept through eastern German classrooms since 1945—is a complicated story of repeated attempts to reform an educational system and foster a new Fatherland.

I

This chapter possesses not only a historical but also a personal dimension. It addresses the consequences of the nation's current round of educational renewal in the newest "New Germany," and it also ponders the possible lessons (or Orwellian "unlessons") for us Americans, especially American educators like myself. More than two decades since the fall of the Berlin Wall, the erstwhile "New" Germany is the region of the former East Germany or GDR, rechristened after national reunification in October 1990 as "the new federal states" of the Bundesrepublik, or BRD (Federal Republic of Germany). The "former" GDR, the "new" states: the names alone suggest the dimensions of the identity crisis in the post-reunification era in eastern Germany, a traumatized land dubbed by one western German "a kind of halfway house for ideologically abused adults."[1]

Our attention in the following pages will thus concern not the agonized transition from brown to Red or the so-called *Stunde Null* ("zero hour") of 1945. Rather, we focus here on the evolution from Red to black/red/gold, an often un-rosy process to be sure, associated with the sometimes convulsive, still-ongoing, so-called *Wende* ("turn") of 1989–1990.

As we shall see, to speak of the frenzied, headlong changes that have occurred in the eastern German educational system as "reform" is to choose a prosaic characterization, but the breadth of the term suggestively embraces the range of controversy involved in the region's turbulent transition from communism to capitalism. Outraged, resigned, assertive, and confident voices have variously called the current transition a *Wessi* (western German) occupation-style reconstruction, a con-

Politics and the German Language

servative restoration or even retrogression, a Teutonic regeneration, or a democratic renewal. Whatever their views, however, few *Ossi* (eastern German) families have been untouched by the most recent *Wende*, especially as it has transformed the educational system, which mutated overnight from a centralized bureaucracy within a communist state into a federalized bureaucracy within a capitalist one.

Americans and others in the West have followed with interest the dramatic economic and political upheavals since 1989/90 in the former GDR: its severe unemployment, its deeply ingrained *Ausländerfeindlichkeit* (xenophobia), its serious neo-Nazi violence. But we have scarcely noticed the sea change in its educational system; no comprehensive English-language study of the history of the GDR educational system has ever appeared, either before or after the latest *Wende*.[2] Most Germans, however, consider educational reform one of the long-term issues facing eastern Germany, perhaps even a key both for coping with the region's social crises and for shaping the future of united Germany in the twenty-first century.

II

So once again, eastern Germany has undergone a round of re-education. Rapidly and inexorably, the little Red schoolhouse has been freshly repainted. Then again—depending on your perspective—perhaps it's been razed and completely rebuilt, this time incorporating all the structural flaws of western, "imperialist" social problems. Or maybe neither: Numerous eastern Germans victimized under the *ancien régime* claim that high Communist Party officials and *Stasi* (secret police) informers have managed to retain their responsible positions in the educational bureaucracy, hardly punished under federal republic law. Antagonized by what they consider a new politics of injustice, these vocal critics see Comrade *Wessi* as little better than Comrade Stalin; indeed it seems like the communist epoch all over again. Big Brother, *noch einmal*: Eastern schools haven't been repainted, let alone stripped for a new coat—just whitewashed.

So if eastern German schools are in fact helping to foster a new Fatherland, the unquiet doubts still resound: How new? And of what sort? Two decades after the fall of the Wall, what clues from the past do we have about the future of the "New Germany"? Is reunified Germany the precursor of a Fourth Reich? Or a throwback to the last united German republic—the struggling, unstable, prewar state of the Weimar era? Or

The (Un-rosy) State of Orwellian Unlearning

an affluent, powerful, and peaceful member of the European Union? Or something else entirely?

Many commentators look to the German past for the answers—and specifically to Germany's last encounter with "re-education." For talk of eastern German "educational reform" has often been euphemistic for "political re-education"—itself a deliberate euphemism for the Allied policy of de-Nazification and democratization during the 1945–1949 occupation. That program applied to peacetime conditions what Allied intelligence had otherwise called "psychological warfare." In a word: propaganda. For occupation authorities judged that the punitive measures dictated to the Germans after World War I, as defined by the 1918 Treaty of Versailles, had failed disastrously. In the three western zones, as well as in the Soviet zone in the east, the Allies decided to embark upon a different strategy this second time: to win German hearts and minds.[3]

The onset of the Cold War in 1947 cut short re-education programs in the western zones, which united to become the Bundesrepublik in May 1949. But anti-Nazi re-education in the schools of the Soviet zone was thoroughgoing—if also thoroughly pro-Soviet. Whatever their view of events since 1989, easterners have agreed the similarities between Allied "re-education" of the 1940s and western "re-education" in the 1990s were uncanny. Eastern Germans witnessed more than educational "reform" or partial "de-communization"; they experienced political re-education in its classic form. Their hearts and minds—first and foremost through the schools but also through advertising, the media, and other institutions—were wooed to western democracy, capitalism, and consumerism. Throughout the 1990s, as well as sixty-five years ago, it was fitting to speak not just of *Umerziehung* (re-education) but what could be termed in Orwellian language *Un-erziehung* (un-education)— or more familiarly, *Verlernen* (unlearning).

Is "re-education" even possible? Or is it inevitably just propagandizing in a new direction—that is, from Nazism to communism, or from communism to capitalism? Eastern Germans have been unlearning socialism and communism. They have been unlearning the virtues of centralized planning and the vices of world capitalism, and learning the wonders of the marketplace and the joys of competitiveness. Among the "young revolutionaries" turned young consumers, socialist faith has proven just as obsolete as GDR products. As older Germans often said before the euro was introduced, "It has become D-marks *über* Karl Marx."

"All history," wrote Orwell in *Nineteen Eighty-Four*, "was a palimp-

Politics and the German Language

sest, scraped clean and reinscribed exactly as often as was necessary." The rewriting of history: in Germany, it has been the Orwellian "mutability of the past" all over again. Like Winston Smith, "tutored" in Room 101 by the schoolmasterly re-educator O'Brien, another generation of eastern Germans has been, once again, unlearning—or re-learning?— that 2 + 2 = 5.

III

German history and *Nineteen Eighty-Four* share more than a casual relationship; indeed the association is bizarre and schizophrenic. In West Germany, Orwell stood for years as an English prose model for older *Gymnasium* pupils and as an intellectual hero for liberal writers such as Heinrich Boll and Günter Grass. But even as *Nineteen Eighty-Four* topped *Der Spiegel*'s best-seller list for almost two years running during 1982–1984, Deputy Culture Minister Klaus Höpcke was declaring in the Party's leading theoretical organ that *Nineteen Eighty-Four* addressed "the characteristic features of capitalist reality," "the multinational firms and their bloodhounds." Höpcke's reading of the novel—which had been banned with the rest of Orwell's oeuvre since the GDR's inception—put Party functionaries in the curious position, much like Winston Smith, of falsifying history even as they discussed a book about the falsification of history—indeed, as they discussed an officially banned book that GDR citizens could not admit they had read.[4]

Within a few years, however, the situation was almost reversed—ironically, not so much because of the passing of 1984 as of the arrival of 1989. Even as the toppling of neo-Stalinist regimes and the discrediting of totalitarian ideologies threatened to render Orwell's novel of the future a historical curio for western readers, the reading of Orwell—persona non grata throughout the existence of the GDR—became part of the much-discussed eastern German *Nachholbedarf* (need to catch up)—and easterners, especially students, began reading *Nineteen Eighty-Four* voraciously.[5]

Written in the wake of World War II and published in 1949, *Nineteen Eighty-Four* depicts a world of three totalitarian superpowers that have arisen in the aftermath of an atomic war, a scenario roughly corresponding to the western "free" world, the communist world, and the Third World (led by the People's Republic of China). During the early postwar era, when the separate states of

The (Un-rosy) State of Orwellian Unlearning

partitioned Germany came to embody the opposing ideological divisions between the capitalist West and communist East, Germany occupied the front line of the bipolar Cold War. Attacked in East Germany as anti-Stalinist propaganda and promoted in West Germany as anti-Stalinist warning, *Nineteen Eighty-Four* came to represent for many Germans a horrifying prophecy not only of what the Reich might have been—but of what the GDR, as a Soviet satellite, had actually become.

It was in this context of what one historian has called the Germans' "fascination" with *Nineteen Eighty-Four* that I began to explore German history.[6] My encounter with Orwell's work a quarter century ago had established my first visceral connection to postwar socialism, anti-totalitarianism, and European cultural politics.[7] It was precisely the convergences between the worlds of *Nineteen Eighty-Four* and divided Germany, and most especially the Orwellian flavor of GDR life—with its Newspeak, its Party-line rectifications, its ideology of "All animals are equal, but some [Party] animals are more equal than others," and above all its mutable past belched from versificators and sucked down memory holes—that originally drew me to study Germany's cultural politics. I devoted the 1980s—*Orwell's Jahrzehnt* (Orwell's decade), in Günter Grass's phrase—to writing a scholarly book on the checkered afterlife of the socialist Orwell, the most influential English-language anticommunist writer. One chapter in that book dealt with reception of *Nineteen Eighty-Four* in postwar West Germany—where Orwell is the best-selling English-language writer of the century. I also wrote a piece on *Nineteen Eighty-Four* as "prophecy and warning" for a Leipzig journal (courageously accepted, the editor proudly reminded me on our first meeting, even before the fall of the Wall).[8]

In the course of my research during the 1980s, I became electrified by my conversations with several middle-aged eastern Europeans and East Germans who told me how they had procured copies of *Nineteen Eighty-Four* in the 1960s—in *samizdat*, since reading the novel was strictly illegal. Devouring the book overnight, they passed it on through the dissident underground, knowing they faced imprisonment if caught with it. The East Germans described the eerie experience of already having known Orwell's catchphrases—e.g., *der Grosse Bruder, Zweidenken* and *Doppelzüngigkeit* (doublethink), *die Gedankenpolizei* (Thought Police), *Gedankenverbrechen* (thought-crime), *Neusprech* (Newspeak), *Krieg ist Friede, Freiheit bedeutet Sklaverei, Unwissenheit ist Stärke* (War Is Peace, Freedom Is Slavery, Ignorance Is Strength)—through Western as well as GDR news sources.[9] They recalled their astonishment that an Englishman who had never lived under a dictatorship could describe with such accuracy the regime of terror that they had experienced as young people in rebellion against the state. For them, *Nineteen Eighty-Four* crossed the line from dystopian fiction to living nightmare.

By 1990, it was no longer enough for me just to read about the GDR's Communist Party, the SED (*Sozialistische Einheitspartei*, Socialist Unity Party). I wanted to experience it—or at least its demise—firsthand. The Orwell connection led me to spend twenty months during 1990–1995 in the "New Germany" and to visit eastern Germany's schools, universities, and cultural institutions. And to ask: What did East German students learn? What are they now unlearning? For some aspects of their *Umerziehung*, or *Un-erziehung*, strike me as special forms of doublethink, which entails "holding two contradictory beliefs in one's mind simultaneously, and accepting both of them." The Party hack—a.k.a. the "doubleplusgood duckspeaker"—knows in which direction the Party wishes his or her views to be altered, writes Orwell, and thus "knows he is playing tricks with reality." Yet, Orwell adds, "by exercise of doublethink he also satisfies himself that reality is not violated."

So I wanted to know: How Orwellian was—and is—eastern German life? How are eastern Germans confronting the waves of new revelations about their own Nazi and Stalinist collaborations? And is the ongoing political re-education of eastern Germans—into (among other transformations) good consumers—just another form of thought control?

Again and again in our interviews, my East German dissident acquaintances gave me a starting point for the answers: All of them affirmed that the communist campaign to win minds began on the "cultural front" with my own profession of teaching. The offensive commenced in the schools. Youth and education formed the two pillars of the GDR utopia. As the old SED slogans trumpeted:

> *WER DIE JUGEND HAT, HAT DIE ZUKUNFT!*
> [Who has the youth, has the future!]
> *MAN MUSS DIE MENSCHEN NUR GEBÜHREND*
> *SCHULEN—DANN WERDEN SIE SCHON*
> *RICHTIG LEBEN!*
> [You need only to school people properly—then
> they'll live right!]

The (Un-rosy) State of Orwellian Unlearning

Some of my East German acquaintances reenacted, often with mock-serious voices and gestures, the ceaseless, ritualistic SED sloganeering; their descriptions of their own GDR school days—especially when leavened with vivid accounts of Nazi catchwords and youth activities—eerily evoked for me the climate of *Nineteen Eighty-Four*. Indeed SED Newspeak—or *Ostspeak*—was ubiquitous in the former GDR. The Party had a slogan for everything, because so-called DIAMAT (dialectical materialism) claimed to be a comprehensive Marxist-Leninist *Weltanschauung* that explained everything: a claim promoted by the title of a standard book gift for youths of the 1950s, *Weltall, Erde, Mensch* (Cosmos, Earth, Human Being).

For East German youth above all, SED Ostspeak became the public mother tongue. In school and through the national media, the SED droned and drummed and dinned Party duckspeak into schoolchildren, even preschoolers. Following Stalin, SED leaders built their collectivist chimera on an ideological campaign based on thought control: in education and of youth. "*Stürmt die Festung Wissenschaft*" ran the old Party slogan. "Storm the citadel of learning!" Marshal Stalin himself had issued the marching orders, declaring educational institutions "the citadel of learning" that "we must capture at any price. This citadel must be taken by our youth, if they wish to take the place of the old guard." The Soviets called the campaign *vospitanie* (moral-social development); the East Germans termed it *weltanschauliche Erziehung* (education for a world outlook). Whatever the name, the intent was the same: creating the new socialist *Mensch*. Ideology and character-building were the content; civic training was the method.

It was too late to convert most of the old-timers, the SED agreed. But certainly young people could be persuaded of the validity and inevitability of communism, even if demonstration of its superiority entailed a dialectical sleight-of-hand, what Orwell in *The Road to Wigan Pier* called "that pea-and-thimble trick with those three mysterious entities, thesis, antithesis, synthesis." The Kremlin had long known how to play DIAMAT. "Marxism is omnipotent," Lenin proclaimed, "because it is true!" Stalin advanced the corollary: "Marxism is true, because it is omnipotent!" Countless duckspeaking SED leaders, quacking DIAMAT logic, affirmed both propositions, and bannered the triumphant conclusion in GDR schools for decades: "*Der Sozialismus siegt!*" "Socialism is winning!"

The children could be "persuaded." Stalin himself, lionized in SED meetings as "the world's greatest teacher and scholar," had promised:

"Give me four years to teach the children, and the seed I have planted will never be uprooted!" Comrade Josef Vissarionovich, of course, was himself extirpated from Soviet and GDR life soon after Khrushchev denounced his big-brotherly "cult of personality" at the Twentieth Congress of the Communist Party of the USSR in 1956. But Stalin's seed found fertile soil in the progeny of Party pedagogues. Through school and youth programs, post-Stalinist GDR and Soviet bureaucrats tirelessly propagandized—or re-educated—the young. For to remake humanity, to form the "new socialist human being," demanded seizure of the "citadel of learning."

IV

There are two citadels to be captured, however, just as there are two sorts of eastern German un-learning. The first fortress is the citadel of the knowable and ascertainable. Its seizure entails the unlearning of facts and dates, of sacrosanct dogmas and doctrines, the knowledge of what was and what is. This is unlearning as faith-stealing. Reality becomes an ideological shell game whereby State propagandists replace one citadel with another, so that only a spectral citadel remains: the Ministry of Truth. Now the command economy of the mind prevails: You unlearn and relearn to hold two contradictory ideas in mind at once. And believe both—on command. Classic Orwellian doublethink: $2 + 2 = 5$.

IGNORANCE IS STRENGTH!

But there is also unlearning to dream, to wonder about what yet might be. This second fortress of the self is the citadel of the imaginable. You unlearn to hope, to aspire to a different and radically better future. You undergo the de-illusioning that spirals downward into disillusion—and ultimately into cynicism or nihilism.

How Orwellian was—and is—eastern German life? Its Orwellian dimension since 1989 has consisted not just in the incessant, relentless, systematic unlearning of Party lies and the "rectification" of historical falsehoods, but in dream killing, in the unlearning of utopian possibilities. As one elderly woman in Weimar, daughter of an SS soldier and herself an SED member, cried to me at the close of a six-hour conversation:

The (Un-rosy) State of Orwellian Unlearning

Now? Now I believe in nothing! Nothing and nobody! Except my family. Church, state, Party, nation—they've no meaning for me. . . . They [the Nazis and SED] robbed me of my innocence, cheated me of my youth, duped me of my ideals.[10]

We in capitalist America have never had to unlearn our ideals, the ideals of liberal democracy, in so radical a fashion. So we sometimes forget that, for hundreds of millions of people, communism once was— and for many millions still remains—a dream of justice and equality. "A spectre is haunting Europe—the spectre of Communism," wrote Marx and Engels in *The Communist Manifesto*, and for postwar Americans that apparition became the totalitarian terror of *Nineteen Eighty-Four*. "Better dead than Red," we told ourselves through wave after wave of "the Red scare." Witness the terms "Iron Curtain," "the Wall," "the Evil Empire": decade after decade, "communism" has meant to us the abolition of freedoms, confiscation of property, overthrow of governments, and revolutionary violence. We often fail to appreciate that, for the citizens of many countries, "communism" has long signified a utopian dream, not a hellish nightmare:

> . . . [I]t was a dream that gave it birth
> Not a dream that will dissolve in mist by day
> But one that was also Lenin's:
> "Thunder! Strike! But also dream!"
> Our songs are quaked from anger
> From beautiful words, careful tones . . .
> We have lived every syllable
> Every note is written with blood . . .[11]

Today, most younger eastern Germans have learned to "think like westerners," especially Americans, and to equate Leninist dreams with Orwellian nightmares. Several older generations of eastern Germans— and their counterparts throughout the European continent—share the existential despair of my acquaintance from Weimar, a melancholy not limited to a handful of disaffected intellectuals, but rather a mass phenomenon.

This mass experience, especially as it relates to the imagined world of *Nineteen Eighty-Four*, is a theme of a university course I once regularly taught in the history of utopian thinking. Titled "The Quest for Community," it traces a dream (or chimera?) whose pursuit cast a long

Politics and the German Language

shadow across the twentieth century. Now, as did their grandparents in the wake of the collapsed Nazi "utopia," a new generation of Germans is mercilessly unlearning to dream about the best of all possible worlds, or even to trust in ideals at all.

In 1991 I lectured at Leipzig University on Orwell and *Nineteen Eighty-Four*. The parallels between the world of the novel and the police states of Nazi Germany and Stalinist Russia are obvious and well known, and I myself had already written about them. But in a post-lecture discussion, I listened as Leipzig students—not all of whom had read *Nineteen Eighty-Four*—immediately drew detailed analogies between Orwell's Oceania and the GDR. "*Big Brother*'s little twin!" one student called the former GDR. Indeed the GDR and *Nineteen Eighty-Four* entered the world together in 1949, another noted; several remarked, contemptuously, that the closest approximation in Eastern Europe to stultifying Oceania turned out to be their own tiny land located on the Elbe. Warming to their task, they elaborated: the Party in *Nineteen Eighty-Four* was the SED; the Thought Police was the *Stasi*; Goldstein and his Brotherhood were the GDR dissidents; the child Spies (*Späher*, Scouts) were the JP (*Junge Pioniere*, Young Pioneers) and FDJ (*Freie Deutsche Jugend*, Free German Youth); and Newspeak was the Party mumbo-jumbo (*Parteirotwelsch*) at SED meetings. Even Orwell's Two-Minute Hates and Hate Week had their analogues in Party slogans, youth rallies, and school programs. *Tragt den Hass in jedes Herz!* (Carry Hatred in Your Heart!) ran one slogan, which could often be heard during the GDR's mandatory "antifascist" "defense education" sessions, including school rifle practice and military drills for fifteen-year-olds. And on and on and on.[12]

As in 1945, so too in the 1990s in eastern Germany: the promise of collectivist utopia gave way to the fear of Orwellian anti-utopia. Ideals can be perverted, idealists can go too far. Idealism is the utopiate of the apparatchik. The Stalinist reaction to the horrific Nazi utopia led to a communist police state itself not so different from the empire of Oceania in *Nineteen Eighty-Four*. And the lessons of anti-utopian thinking have penetrated deeply into eastern German minds. Today, capitalism seems to be teaching *Ossis*, however belatedly, that you must reject utopianism in toto as dangerous and deluded idealism. You must face the hard limits of what human nature and the here-and-now make possible. You must make the best of the actual choices presented by reality, rather than pursue a communitarian dream.

The (Un-rosy) State of Orwellian Unlearning

V

The unlearning proceeds apace. Not that most GDR adults had grand illusions, at least by the late 1980s, about the virtues of the much-heralded *Erste Deutsche Arbeiter-und-Bauernstaat* (First German Workers' and Peasants' State). But many of the children did—and so did some of the educators themselves, who created and distributed the propaganda in which they partly believed. Moreover, as one Party functionary in Leipzig told me, even the skeptics had believed more than they thought they had: "Sure, I knew that not much work got done. And I knew the estimates of GDR emigration. But I had no idea that the Party was so corrupt, and that the system was so moribund and decrepit. I had only a vague idea of the yawning gap between the propaganda and the truth."

No generation of Germans in this century has possessed more opportunities than the present one of the new millennium: no war from which to recover, no dictatorship to endure, no hyperinflation. Yet many eastern Germans have felt less like proud victors in a peaceful revolution—free at last to rejoin their long-lost family members in the West—than gullible victims and war-weary losers faced with occupation by a smug, alien power. For many eastern Germans have felt deprived of everything they knew. Now, it is *all* untrue; now they're radical skeptics or revolutionary nihilists. As one teenage FDJ member in Berlin, in his final year of high school, told me in 1990: "Everything we learned was a lie! And now—now?!—we're going to get the TRUTH?! C'mon! Gimme a break!"

"*Die Partei, die Partei! Die hat immer recht!*" went the old song: "The Party, the Party! It's always right!"

> It gave us everything
> Sun and wind
> And was never miserly.
> And what it was
> Was Life
> And what we are
> We are through it.
> It never abandoned us.
> When the world almost froze over
> We stayed warm.
> This Mother of the Masses
> Fed us and cradled us

Politics and the German Language

In her mighty arm.
The Party, the Party,
It's always right!

When "it"—Life itself—no longer *is*, what then? When the Mother of the Masses ups and leaves? When the world does in fact freeze over?

What happens when it comes to this? The notion that you can know *anything* is undermined, that you can trust in *anything* is subverted, that you can believe in or hope for *anything* is crushed. At that moment of shattering revelation, Orwellian unpersonhood and Nietzschean nihilism pass into Kafkaesque despair.

Until something or someone comes along to fill the vacuum. Then $2 + 2 = 5$, if Big Brother says so.

VI

A battle of re-education versus reaction has been scourging eastern Germans' souls. At the heart of their struggle is the traumatic legacy left by an educational system that was and is no more. But I do not thereby refer merely to education in the narrow Anglo-Saxon sense— which focuses exclusively on schools and universities—but also on re-education; that is, on *weltanschauliche Erziehung* as the re-formation of national identity, as the historical-cultural process of a people repeatedly reconceiving themselves. Perhaps a better term is that far-reaching German concept *Bildung* (education, culture, self-development)—by which I also mean to include the extracurricular educational/cultural institutions and the general ideological climate in which GDR youths were "bred" to be "young revolutionaries." *Bildung* in terms of GDR "education" referred variously to schooling, acculturation, and agitprop. It included the relationships between GDR youth culture and Western popular culture, especially the roles of music, sport, national heroes, and the Party youth organizations. In fact, a discussion of *Bildung* in the GDR and the post-reunification east could also be titled "A History of Eastern German Education and Re-Education." That is a bit unwieldy, but the added phrase underscores that a history of eastern German education is necessarily also a history of eastern German re-education.

Mine is admittedly an eastern Germany seen through American eyes, indeed through American academic eyes. And so my reflections also mirror back, however intermittently, an American academy refracted through eastern German eyes. I went to the eastern German schools to grasp more fully how ordinary people participate in epoch-making History, how it bears on and unfolds in their lives, how they assimilate and incorporate it into their self-images. I traveled there to comprehend more clearly how a people copes with a failed revolutionary dream—in fact, with two dashed dreams: socialism and fascism both. And I emerged with dual insight: first, and primarily, into that uniquely eastern German burden. But second, and unexpectedly, my intimate encounter with the extreme example of an educational system run on ideology has sensitized me to the subtler case of its American counterpart. My extensive contact with eastern Germany has vouchsafed me a more concrete and nuanced understanding of my own immediate world—of the ideological character of American schooling, of the dangers of excessively politicizing the American academy, and of the trade-offs between excellence and equality—or between elitism and egalitarianism—inherent in the American educational experiment.

Thus I found that I could make sense of the communist experience generally and the GDR educational and cultural apparatus in particular only by acknowledging my own—quite unscholarly—urge to share my personal meeting of East and West. And so my journey to the ex-communist east has testified also to a profound personal education—and to my own unlessons. From a process of back-and-forth movement between two radically different educational systems, I unlearned lessons about utopianism, the state, and education: lessons not easily relinquished, lessons that I could not have unlearned in any other way.

And to unlearn can be more than a loss; it can also be to learn something invaluable.

CHAPTER 7

Books That Led
to Miniluv

n August 2003 I met several victims of human rights crimes under the dictatorship of the former German Democratic Republic (GDR) at the international George Orwell Centennial Conference held at the Haus der Zukunft in Berlin. Titled *Bücher, die ins Zuchthaus führten* (Books That Led to Jail), the conference featured the harrowing, Orwellian stories of several East Germans who became unacknowledged, if nonetheless genuine, martyrs of communist injustice in the GDR. Their stories moved and humbled me, so much so that I subsequently accompanied several of these former inmates of GDR prisons to visit one of East Germany's most notorious centers of interrogation and incarceration, the infamous "Camp X" in Hohenschönhausen in eastern Berlin. Because these men generously vouchsafed me the privilege of seeing the prison and its torture chambers through their own eyes and hearts and memories—a searing experience that I will never forget—I remained in contact with them and even solicited their painful stories for this volume.

Two men who co-organized the Orwell symposium, Baldur Haase and Bernd Lippmann, defied the GDR proscription on reading authors officially declared "hostile to socialism," such as George Orwell. For

On the occasion of the centennial of George Orwell's birth in 2003, the Haus der Zukunft sponsored a conference devoted to the relationship between Orwell's vision and GDR history, with particular emphasis on the topic of "forbidden books," such as *Animal Farm* and *Nineteen Eighty-Four*. This leaflet (which announced the conference's title) reads: "Books That Led to Jail: George Orwell Through the Eyes of the Communist Secret Service. A Colloquium on His 100th Birthday." Beneath the title is depicted the image of the Haus der Zukunft, a western Berlin organization which had served throughout the Cold War as a historical institute that conducted research on East-West relations.

George Orwell
1903/ 2003

Bücher, die ins Zuchthaus führten

George Orwell im Visier der kommunistischen Geheimdienste

Colloquium zum
100. Geburtstag

Berlin, 15./16.August 2003

LEFT: Baldur Haase, who was imprisoned for three years in an East German jail for the crime of reading Orwell's *Nineteen Eighty-Four*, published the story of his suffering in *Orwells DDR*. The memoir consists of a poignant account of his years in prison (1958–1961) and his critique of East Germany as "Little Brother."
RIGHT: Baldur Haase at twenty-two, shortly after his release from prison in May 1961, just three months before construction of the Berlin Wall.

their teenage temerity, exemplified by their reading *Nineteen Eighty-Four* and *Animal Farm*, respectively, they were punished with jail sentences that not only robbed them of their youth but also have shadowed and darkened the decades that followed. They suffered persecution as a result of reading "subversive" literature in the GDR, the self-proclaimed "Land of Reading," a.k.a. the "Land of Little Brother." I was appalled by the ill treatment to which Lippmann and Haase were subjected, from bogus trials to imprisonment in isolated cells to simple ridicule and sadistic mind games. (Herr Haase, a self-described GDR "thought criminal," titled his horrifying memoir about his imprisonment for procuring *Nineteen Eighty-Four* after the novel's author: *Orwells DDR*.) Like the other participants in the Orwell conference, these two men were locked away in GDR jails for political "crimes against the state." They were not subjected to physical torture by the secret police, but rather to interrogation methods and forms of psychoterror that scar the mind.[1]

Books That Led to Miniluv

Baldur Haase in Jena, in his late sxties, 2008.

Bernd Lippmann in Berlin, in his late fifties, 2009.

Hans-Eberhardt Zahn in Berlin, in his early eighties, August 2006.

Their stories, which serve as GDR counterparts to that of Winston Smith, were only two of the tragic tales of violated human rights that I heard at the Orwell conference in Berlin. All of the victims who shared their stories agreed that *Nineteen Eighty-Four* was an astonishingly accurate vision of the totalitarian state in which they themselves had lived and that Orwell's conceptualization in his novel of the relevant issues—such as political persecution, privacy invasion, groupthink, and state censorship—resonated powerfully for them when they read it decades ago, as it still does for readers today.

"The GDR slipped comfortably and eagerly into the mantle that Orwell had held up before it," stated Hans-Eberhardt Zahn. A Berlin psychiatrist who sat seven years in GDR jails, including the secret police's brutal Camp X, Zahn experienced many of the brainwashing and torture techniques that the GDR experimented with during the 1950s and '60s. Camp X's techniques focused on mental manipulation rather than physical torture. Indeed, there was even a swimming pool and a well-stocked library. Zahn, who had just come from the decrepit, understaffed prison at Bautzen, was amazed at the luxury and at first believed that he was in a special facility for prisoners about to be released. Soon he learned about the underside of Camp X: the ceaseless interrogations and subtle psychoterror, the spies planted everywhere who sought to befriend him, the incessant efforts to tempt him and bait him to provide information and denounce other prisoners. Zahn realized that Camp X was an intensified version of the GDR itself: "Camp X was indeed a microcosm of the GDR." When he proved to be largely unresponsive to these brainwashing techniques, he was transferred back to Bautzen—and, to his surprise, was relieved and extremely grateful.

Other speakers at the Orwell symposium addressed GDR state policy toward dissidents. For instance, Hans-Jürgen Grasemann of Braunschweig discussed how Article 27 of the GDR state constitution dealt with freedom of speech and expression in the GDR: "Every citizen of the GDR has the right to express his opinion freely and publicly within the scope of the laws of this constitution." That latter clause—"within the scope of the laws of this constitution"—proved to be a qualification that so compromised the assertion of freedom as to overwhelm it. This formulation was strategically employed against everything that did not safely conform to the dictatorship's narrow conception of state socialism. Article 27 proved to be a perfectly ironic statement of one of the tenets of Big Brother and Oceania: "FREEDOM IS SLAVERY."

A Polish participant in the George Orwell Centennial Conference compared Kafka's *The Trial* to Orwell's *Nineteen Eighty-Four*, noting that the totalitarian panopticon really has no need to keep track of "proles" and may reserve its scrutiny for well-placed Party members. "The power apparatus of the totalitarian state," argued Karol Sauerland of Warsaw, "regards the individual as merely a statistic. He or she is much like an insect or an animal—and can be safely left unattended. No spies are really necessary to keep an eye on him." Sauerland says that during the years of Communist Party rule in Poland, he was often asked secretly how many spies were required in order to spread angst and mistrust within a populace. He estimated that one spy per one thousand citizens sufficed to maintain the climate of fear on which a totalitarian system depends to intimidate its populace into submission.[2]

In my own talk, I aimed to present the perspective on Orwell held by Americans in the English-speaking world to a German audience that saw him primarily as a Cold Warrior, a view held partly because the first two books by Orwell that appeared in German translation were *Animal Farm* and *Nineteen Eighty-Four*. As a result, Orwell became chiefly known to Germans during the early Cold War era as the leading literary Cold Warrior of the West.

I

The past is indeed a foreign country, and many of the Orwell symposium participants lamented the fact that a younger generation of Germans and eastern Europeans know virtually nothing about the sufferings endured by thousands of their neighbors during the GDR dictatorship.

That ignorance reduces empathy and blocks genuine historical and political understanding. I myself can confirm how difficult it is to understand a historical period on the basis of written documents alone. It was invaluable for me to meet and converse with these former political prisoners in order to experience "lived history," for it was my encounters with these men and women that brought their oft-forgotten experiences to life for me.

My decision to befriend these ordinary eastern Germans—all of whom I interviewed during my travels since 1990 throughout the five eastern states—owes to the fact that I could not work through my own experience of the SED dictatorship, even at a distance of thousands of miles and decades of history, without hearing the fates of these unforgettable people. Their stories constitute a small and easily forgotten record in the annals of injustice in modern history. Depicting the efforts made by these men and women to come to terms with their traumatic pasts and lead productive lives, the stories also offer us an important opportunity: to see how dissenting truths can triumph over even the worst state dogmas and dialectical manipulations—and thereby contribute to preventing their repetition in the future.

And Orwell's *Nineteen Eighty-Four* represents a major contributing factor—in a most ironic sense—toward their prevention, my interviewees agreed. Several of them expressed to me that (thankfully!) Orwell ultimately "failed" as a political prophet—the nightmarish future that he envisioned has not come to pass—precisely because his warning proved so prescient and powerful. Yet they also emphasized that his warning nonetheless remains current and compelling. Moreover, they voiced concern that, as the number of witnesses to Germany's two twentieth-century dictatorships dwindles with the passing years, the political indifference of young people to their elders' hardships and sufferings may prove impossible to overcome. For that reason, it is even more important to hear and honor the stories of these witnesses—and to record their narratives, while time still remains.

II

Although they were not heroes in a grand sense, several of my interview subjects exhibited real bravery merely by publicly stepping out of line. Again and again, I found myself asking them—and myself—the following questions:

- How did these recalcitrant dissenters cope with what George Orwell referred to as "that pea-and-thimble trick with those mysterious entities of thesis, antithesis and synthesis,"[3] a sleight-of-mind integral to Marxist-Leninist dogmatics and dialectics?
- Did these victims possess exceptional moral and political qualities?
- What forces within them formed their wellsprings of resistance?[4]
- Looking back, how do these victims make sense of their suffering?

I was struck by the differences in people's reactions. Some suffered greatly and are bitter and angry. Others suffered, yet still somehow look back fondly on the GDR—often simply because it symbolizes the days of their youth or prime of life, and sometimes just because they once admired (and today grieve) its lost ideals of equality and justice for all.

Whatever their present attitude, I can report from my lengthy conversations with them that virtually all of my interviewees view themselves as utterly ordinary citizens who found themselves in extraordinary circumstances and felt compelled to speak and act. They are certainly not in the habit of regarding themselves as models of outspokenness and bravery. It was with some degree of astonishment that they listened patiently as I insisted that their stories deserved to be communicated to English-speaking readers with no experience of dictatorship who need desperately to comprehend: "It can happen here, too." For we too need concrete reminders as to how human rights abuses of all kinds are perpetrated and where they lead—and how the victims can and do respond.

I also confess that my more distant, perhaps fanciful, hope is that the victims may help heal their traumas by talking or writing about them.[5] That aspiration is linked to an even greater one: Could the airing of such individual experience help heal our communities? If talking about one's personal traumas can lead to healing for an individual, then a discussion of trauma by an important public figure may also contribute to a society's collective healing.[6]

I was most gratified to learn that the Orwell conference's co-organizers, Bernd Lippmann and Baldur Haase, maintain that hope. When they planned the George Orwell Centennial Conference, they invited to our sessions not only other victims of human rights abuse under the GDR regime, but also the general public.[7] These two men—like numerous other GDR victims—have also published memoirs and scholarly works about the GDR's human rights violations. Moreover, Herr Haase has both designed an elaborate website about his years in a GDR jail and conducted several tours of German schools during 2002–2010, speaking to thousands of high school pupils about his anguish and misery as an "inmate" in "Orwell's Reich."

As Susanne Vees-Gulani writes, "Trauma often causes silence that can only be overcome by some kind of testimony or witnessing or confession. Silence for a long time, then witnessing (or testimony or some kind of therapeutic situation—narration or story-telling), then a kind of healing through the process of narration itself, or perhaps also through the understanding and sympathy of the addressee, the listener, or the reader."[8]

Can empathy and understanding of suffering heal victims of abuse? Can they even help heal readers, and possibly even heal a society?

Perhaps.

CHAPTER 8

$2 + 2 = 5$?

"W hen you see how they [East German educators] twisted even arithmetic exercises for first-graders into ideological lessons," a retired professor of mathematics in the former German Democratic Republic (GDR) once said to me, "You know they were serious about inculcating the tenets of M-L [Marxism-Leninism]." He showed me a couple of East German textbooks from the 1960s, and I immediately saw what he meant. GDR educators' approach to mathematics ultimately resulted in a math curriculum more ideological than even that of the Nazis. And for a simple reason very much connected with simple arithmetic: more decades available to propagandize. Nazi educators had fewer than a dozen years to develop their curriculum, whereas East German policymakers had more than four decades to refine "M-L math," not to mention the advantage of drawing on Soviet scholarship since 1917 as well as a distinguished radical German and European legacy stretching back long before Marx and Engels. As we will see, GDR educators fully exploited math's didactic, indeed Orwellian possibilities, using it to promote socialist patriotism, Marxist class consciousness, specific communist doctrines, and hostility toward the "imperialist" West. *"Newnumb"*: So might the appendix to *Nine-*

"M-L Math": the evolution of class relations under capitalism only increases the gap between the rich and poor, contends this textbook cartoon. The four frames show the movement from colonialism to mercantilism to imperialism to the advanced capitalism of the 1970s, in each stage of which the rich "multiply" their wealth. The caption reads: "Capitalist Development."

teen Eighty-Four have termed the progressivist math in GDR textbooks. Let us therefore examine the mathematics textbooks themselves, proceeding grade by grade to analyze their ideological content and strong attempts to legitimate GDR cultural and military policy. It warrants emphasis that no more than one-fifth of units in GDR math textbooks bear direct ideological traces. Still, as in the case of school subjects such as biology and chemistry, SED (East German Communist Party) educators did not hesitate to exploit "M-L math" whenever it might serve Party goals: to strengthen solidarity with the working class, promote socialist patriotism and internationalism, and deepen hatred of Western imperialism and militarism. Of course, these agitprop goals are hardly surprising—and certainly had their (much milder) Cold War counterpart in Western (and particularly American) math textbooks. This chapter conveys the extraordinary scope of the SED's pedagogical agenda, however,

Politics and the German Language

as it addresses in detail these ideological uses. Their scrutiny via diverse examples yields important, still relevant lessons, even though the communist state that inculcated them is now defunct.

The main lesson is a simple one, and it serves as a cautionary warning for educational policymakers everywhere, including the United States.[1] And the warning is this: Education that becomes political "re-education"—an attempt to "make over" human beings according to the requirements of an ideology— undermines the freedom and dignity of the individual. That, in turn, ultimately undermines both the ideology and the state that champions such a policy. Such "education" loses touch with what it means to be human—and miseducation is the result.

I

Except for German language and literature, mathematics was the only subject taught in all grades of the GDR school system. The math curriculum ran as follows:

Grades 1–3: arithmetic
Grades 4–7: arithmetic, geometry, algebra
Grades 8–9: geometry, algebra
Grades 10–12: geometry, calculus, advanced mathematics

The typical method of fostering "socialist personalities" in GDR math class was via workbook problems, which sometimes functioned as subliminal indoctrination. Alongside exercises on magnitude, on the relations between figures and forms, and on quantities expressed symbolically, there would suddenly appear a multiplication problem on GDR brown coal exports, a decimal problem on Soviet space records, a geometry problem on the potato yield from a Czech collective farm, or an algebra problem on American arms expenditures. As in the case of German grammar and spelling exercises, a sampler of such math problems furnishes insight into the ideological convictions that SED educators felt most important to inculcate at different ages.

Consider, for instance, the following second-grade problems. Pupils are asked to compute something more than just whole numbers; the problems introduce work-related topics relevant to school field trips and to the child's immediate experience. A typical exercise involves this field trip to a model socialist factory site in the week before the GDR's national holiday of Worker's Day:

145
$2 + 2 = 5$

1. *Multiplication and division with the number 9:*

a. In the days before May 1, the best pupils of the school visited workers in their factories. At the factory entrance, they were divided into groups of 9. How many pupils formed 5 groups?

b. Every group was introduced by members of the factory's brigade sponsor: 2 groups visited the factory carpentry room, 3 groups went to workers in the foundry. How many guests did the workers in the factory carpentry room and foundry have?[2]

The math problems in fourth through seventh grades cover a wider ideological territory, including GDR industry and world socialism versus imperialism.

1. Workers in the GDR water industry presented 10 water pumps, valued at 40,000 East German marks, to the Democratic Republic of Vietnam, so that the irrigation lines destroyed by US bombers could be repaired. *What was the total value of this gift?*

2. At a solidarity meeting, three apprentices gave 1.35 marks in October. In November, each of them gave 65 Pf [Pfennige = pennies] more than in October. In December, each of them gave 10 Pf less than in November. *How much did the three apprentices give in November all together?*

3. The number of residents in a city in the Soviet Union was 2,150,000. It rose 200,000. *How big is the population total of this city?*[3]

4. An NVA [National People's Army] jet fighter flew 18 km in 1 minute. *How far would it travel in a half-hour flight?*

5. A supersonic plane of the NVA flew 25 km in 1 minute. How far would it travel in 15 minutes?

6. A tractor driver harvests potatoes. In a shift he harvested 6.09 hectares and needed 5.9 liters of fuel. The projected production norm is 5.85 hectares and 6.3 liters per shift. *What percent of the acreage of his norm did the tractor driver fulfill? How many liters of fuel did the tractor driver save with an acreage completion of 6.09?*

The fourth-grade teaching guide for math expressly notes that "especially good possibilities are available" to select textbook problems that demonstrate "the great success of our socialist reconstruction. . . . It is, therefore, an essential task of the teacher, both in the [selection of] material and in his presentation, *to actualize with full effectiveness its potential for socialist education.*"[4]

The middle-grade math texts offer numerous examples of this "potential," of what might be thought of as "progressivist arithmetic," or "the higher math, GDR-style." A pattern is not hard to detect here:

1. In 1950, the GDR had a total of 75,000 cars. After 10 years, the number had quadrupled. In 1970, the total was already above one million cars. In comparison with 1960, the number of cars had increased by 1,500,000! *Calculate the number of cars in 1970!* [The ubiquitous exclamation points in GDR math problems are in the original.]

2. In 1960, the GDR had 500,000 mopeds. After 10 years, this number had tripled. In 1974, there were 2 million mopeds. In comparison with 1970, the number by 1975 was up 600,000. *Calculate the number for 1975!*

3. The production of whole milk rose 500,000 tons between 1960 and 1975. In 1960, it was 1,000,000 tons. *Calculate the production of whole milk for 1975!*

4. The time required to produce electrical ovens has been reduced $1/6$ since 1955. *How long does it take to make ovens that had required 552 hours in 1955?*

5. By means of a new experiment, a brigade of VEB [People's Own Firms, or state-owned companies] raised its performance of cable production threefold. It had been 780 meters. *How many meters more of cable were produced? How many meters of cable did the brigade produce altogether?*[5]

6. The petroleum refinery at Schwedt delivered 300,000 filled-up wagons. Each wagon is 10 meters long. *How long would the line be, if one placed these wagons next to one another?*[6]

7. An LPG [state-owned agricultural cooperative] raised its acreage results in rye from 2200 tons to 2500 tons through better cultivation of the ground, good fertilizer, and timely pruning. In the previous year, 74 hectares were harvested; this year it is 81 hectares. *How many tons more were harvested?*[7]

8. A factory raises its production annually by 8 percent. *How high is the production increase at the end of 1970 compared with the beginning of 1965?*[8]

Some arithmetic problems seem designed to accompany the well-known GDR song of the 1950s and '60s, "My Friend: The Plan":

1. The fulfillment of the three-month plan and an over-fulfillment

2 + 2 = 5

of the plan resulted in a production total of 15,000 bicycle covers in these three months. *How many covers were produced in one month?*

2. The fulfillment of the six-month plan and an over-fulfillment of the plan by 30,000 bicycle pumps resulted in a production of 270,000 pumps in these six months. *How many pumps were produced in one month?*

3. A factory delivered 18,000 tons of cement per month over five months. The half-year plan expects 100,000 tons. *How many tons of cement are still to be delivered to fulfill the plan?*

4. A factory delivered 15,000 tons of industrial limestone monthly. The half-year plan demands 80,000 tons of limestone. *How many tons of limestone are still to be delivered to fulfill the plan?*[9]

Whatever else may be said about such exercises, there is a noticeable dearth of problems illustrating production losses or the under-fulfillment of GDR norms.

The fourth-grade teaching guide offers special exercises to supplement the textbook problems. Their themes also exemplify the guide's concern with realizing math's "potential for socialist education." As in the case of the grammar exercises in elementary school German schoolbooks, military themes are especially popular.

1. Three classes of a grade are competing in the donation drive "Help for Vietnam." Class 4A collected 33.75 marks. By collecting old clothes, Class 4B reached four times the total amount of Class 4A. Class 4C only collected $^1/_3$ the amount of Class 4A. *How many more marks did Class 4A donate than Class 4C? How many marks did the three classes together donate?*

2. An NVA [National People's Army] unit conducts a practice march. It leaves its barracks at 06.00 and heads back at 13.30. The average tempo of the soldiers was 5 km per hour. *How long is the length of the march on a map designed with a ratio of 1:100,000, if one considers that a half-hour break was taken during the march?*

3. The LPGs "Peace," "Unity," and "Solidarity" agree to become a larger farm cooperative. The LPG "Peace" possesses 684 acres of land, the LPG "Unity" has half as much, and the LPG "Solidarity" has three times as much as the LPG "Peace." *Calculate how many total acres of land the newly found agricultural cooperative possesses!*[10]

II

Upper-grade middle school and high school [EOS] math was linked to *Wehrerziehung*, the defense education class that included rifle practice and grenade throwing. This course began in the ninth grade and was closely coordinated with math classes in linear and nonlinear algebra. Upper-grade math textbooks contain a higher percentage of ideologically oriented problems—and more prominently displayed, often with illustrations—on topics central to the scientific-technical revolution such as computers, electronics, and electrical energy. Many such exercises contain "agit-prop bites" inserted in the middle, rendering them into a form of what might be termed "army algebra." For instance:

> Because of the rapid development of the GDR People's Economy, the demand for electrical energy rose from year to year. Our Republic is today one of the leading countries in the world in the per capita production of electrical energy.
>
> In 1960, the production of electrical energy was roughly
> $$W = (40) * (10k) * W_h.$$
> Given an average annual growth rate of 5 percent, the development of electrical energy production from 1960 to 1980 can be described as $W_n = W_o * 1.05n$ (n e V; O = n = 20). That means that the production of electrical energy—in order to keep pace with the level of 1960—must rise by more than 2½ times above its present level.[11]

Most conspicuous in the upper-grade math textbooks is the appearance of increasingly more NVA soldiers, missiles, warships, and tanks. All of these changes aimed "to prove once again that the socialist social order is superior to the capitalist."[12] This problem on the 1988 EOS graduation exam for mathematics—which doubtless would have given Euclid pause—is exemplary:

> At a practice session of the missile unit of the NVA, a flying object at Point P (-6, 9, 7) is pinpointed. It is cruising at a constant speed of S_1. Twenty seconds later it is identified at Point Q (2, 1, 11).
>
> At Point A, a defensive missile rocket is launched. It flies in the direction of the vector:
> $$M = i + 2j + 5k$$
> The cruising speed S_2 of this rocket is straight. The defensive mis-

2 + 2 = 5

sile meets the flying object at Point S. *Calculate the average speed of the rocket if its launch at A followed 2 seconds after its pinpointing at Point Q.*

Mathematik 9 offers a variety of other examples of such "M-L math." Indeed, this textbook is a stunning reading experience for the Western reader. Bannered on the front cover of the 1979 edition is Lenin's celebrated quotation—often cited in GDR textbooks—that abstract science leads one "not further from the truth, but nearer to it. . . . [A]ll scientific abstractions reflect Nature more deeply, more truly, more completely."

The placement and content of this quotation suggest how important SED educators regarded math's potential contribution to the Marxist-Leninist *Weltanschauung*. Perhaps the decision was made—in the wake of the introduction of *Wehrerziehung* into GDR schools in the fall of 1978—to feature the Lenin quote even more prominently than in previous editions. (The 1967 edition of *Mathematik 9* used the same quota-

Of politics and numbers: the following textbook illustration for Bertolt Brecht's "Song of the Class Enemy" exemplifies the GDR program *Erziehung zum Hass* (education for hatred), as it depicts a worker who is inflamed with righteous class hatred. The caption includes a stanza from Brecht's song: "What I also keep on learning / which is an equation just as simple as $1 \times 1 = 1$: / I have never had anything in common / with the interests of my class enemy."

UND WAS IMMER ICH AUCH NOCH LERNE,
DAS BLEIBT DAS EINMALEINS:
NICHTS HABE ICH JEMALS GEMEINSAM
MIT DER SACHE DES KLASSENFEINDS.

Politics and the German Language

tion as its epigraph, placed on the cover before the title page. The text added the obvious: "These thoughts of Lenin also apply to the highest levels of abstraction—to the formal speech of mathematics" [p. 3].)

Mathematik 9 is often startling in its abrupt shift from standard algebra formulae to M-L exercises in "Politics and Numbers." Repeatedly, after a series of polynomials with complex coefficients, or in between routine problems on sets and vectors, comes an exercise such as "Calculate the flight path of six NVA rockets."

Consider, for instance, the following three passages that introduce chapters in *Mathematik 9*. The first passage leads off a unit titled "Quadratic Functions and Quadratic Equations," which is illustrated by three NVA jet bombers:

> The socialist camp is equipped with the best defensive weapons. These modern fighter bombers of the NVA can fly with the speed of supersonic planes. A higher altitude and more energy are therefore required.... One can calculate the movement of a body with the help of the equation $W = (m/2)*(v/2)$.
>
> The kinetic energy of a body grows with constant mass given a rising arc of speed. This physical law is an example of a quadratic function.[13]

A second unit, titled "Powers and Functions," begins with a photograph of a platoon of NVA soldiers firing tank shells. Above it appear the words:

> After they are fired, shells move in a ballistic curve whose width and height depend on the trajectory of the firing, among other things. If air resistance doesn't influence the flight, the path will be a parabola. The pictures of special exponential functions are, therefore, parabolas. Paths of firings can, with the help of mathematical functions, be measured and the site of firing also calculated.[14]

A third unit, titled "Exponential Functions and Logarithms," portrays a Soviet nuclear ship. The text reads:

> The first nuclear-powered ice breaker, the "Lenin," entered into service in 1960 and belongs to the Soviet ice fleet. The nuclear material, Uranium 235, decays in the reactor of the icebreaker and releases warm energy. The decay of a radioactive element occurs according to the following law of decay: $n = f(t) = (n)*(e/2)$.

As happened in earlier grades with arithmetic and geometry, *Mathematik 9* also contains military-oriented problems for solution:

1. A tank of the National People's Army traveled a distance of 230 km. In its original fuel tank it still had 40 liters. If the fuel consumption per 100 km was reduced by 15 liters, this tank would have a mobile radius of 270 km. *How large is the capacity of the fuel storage tank? How much fuel is consumed in a distance of 100 km?*[15]

2. A transport column of National People's Army vehicles received the command to reach, at top speed, a point 120 km away. By raising their speed 10 km per hour, they reached the stated point 1 hour earlier than they would have by the original speed. *How much time did the column take to reach the stated goal, if one presumes that their advance remained constant?*[16]

III

How much time . . . ? That question was indeed the calculation that should have been on SED educators' minds by the late 1980s—the "higher calculus" of M-L, as it were—and it stands as a fitting note on which to close this chapter. As historical hindsight now makes clear, the policies of GDR leaders would soon run out of time to reach their stated goals and by November 1989, with the fall of the Berlin Wall, would instead fully delegitimize the GDR itself.

Yet the "socialist school" of the GDR left its ideological imprint upon millions of East German schoolchildren—who are now adult citizens. Its demise notwithstanding, they survive today. And while it is safe to say that GDR textbooks shaped schoolchildren's outlooks during the existence of the socialist state, the longer-term effects are more difficult to gauge.

Nonetheless, this much can be said: Textbooks did indeed form a cornerstone of the GDR school curriculum—though, as East Germany's defunct status doubtless suggests, their ultimate effectiveness is disputable. But the lessons that they sought to impart are indisputable. GDR primers and school readers told schoolchildren who and what to admire and abhor. Civics textbooks exalted a model of German socialist youth and instructed GDR pupils what to think about the West, especially the United States, and what to think about the Soviet Union. History textbooks shaped pupils' views about the major events of GDR and world history, whereas textbooks in the sciences and mathematics, as we have seen, reflected the doctrine of so-called DIAMAT (dialectital materialism).

Still, the question remains: How—and how effectively—did GDR textbooks fulfill their main task of creating "young comrades"?

The disinterested Western historian must answer that question cognizant of his own history yet as free as possible of ideological bias. And I must emphasize here my preference for capitalist democracy over state socialism, while also stressing that I have cited numerous examples of "politics and numbers" in this chapter in order to be thought-provoking rather than politically provocative. I do not mean to suggest that all GDR citizens were lock-step, ideologically benighted, card-carrying Communist Party functionaries—or even to imply that all lifelong Party supporters rigidly conformed to official GDR views. Rather, I have meant to convey that what we can term a "textbook mentality"—which equated citizens' critiques of the Party and GDR government with disloyalty and such bourgeois sins as individualism, negativism, and cosmopolitanism—imprinted itself deeply on generations of GDR pupils.

My research on eastern Germans' lives since German reunification in October 1990 establishes that those GDR citizens who broke free of such indoctrination still bear marks of its influence, even long after leaving school—and long after the GDR's collapse.

No book-length study has discussed how the East German textbook sought to shape the *Weltanschauung* of GDR youths and form the young citizens' mind. But the math textbooks well illustrate that if one wants to know what GDR students were told to think about their nation, their governing Party and its leaders, their so-called Soviet "friends," and their class enemy, no better source exists. For here we have the dogmas of the SED communicated in their most simplified form and manufactured in the millions for mass consumption.

It is perhaps impossible to reconstruct at this date what GDR citizens actually thought about their state and its place in the world. Few reliable records and no public opinion polls existed in the former GDR (at least none that were ever published in the West). Some demographic information and research data were available from the *Zentralinstitut für Jugendforschung* (Central Institute for Youth Research), yet for the most part Western scholars could only estimate or speculate about what GDR citizens actually thought. But specifically because of the scarcity of survey data, the East German textbooks are invaluable. For as the numerous math exercises in this chapter show in rich and vivid detail,

$2 + 2 = 5$

GDR textbooks powerfully reveal what citizens were once *supposed* to think.

"Do the math": Were elections in which a single slate of candidates—put forward by the State's ruling Party—received 99.7 percent of the vote "free and democratic"?

Jawohl! But how?

Add it up in Orwellian *Newnumb*: 2 + 2 = 5.

Politics and the German Language

Forward and never forget
wherein our strength resides!
Whether famished
or whether fed
Forward and never forget!
Solidarity!
BRECHT, "THE SOLIDARITY SONG" (1931)

CHAPTER 9

Behind the Wall, or How the Eurasian Reich *Viewed Oceania*

I have never forgotten a casual remark made to me by a Humboldt University student shortly after the fall of the Berlin Wall in November 1989 and before German reunification in October 1990. We were riding the subway in East Berlin and discussing his school days. He glanced out the window at a large clock face and said: "Every time I looked at the Tower of Nations clock"—which features a map of the world's time zones—"I was reminded that I couldn't travel."

During my visits to eastern German schools in 1989–1990, teachers and pupils told me much the same about geography class: for many of them, it had been a constant reminder, particularly when it covered the topic of "KA" ("alien capitalist territories," a.k.a. the West), of what they *couldn't* do. It reminded them that they might never be able to visit the *republikflüchtig* (illegally escaped) brother in West Germany or their relatives in America. It reminded them of the wonders of the world that they might never glimpse except on their television sets. And thus, like the East Berlin clock, it was cause for anger.

My recollection serves as a representative anecdote for this chapter about social studies education in the now-defunct GDR and, more spe-

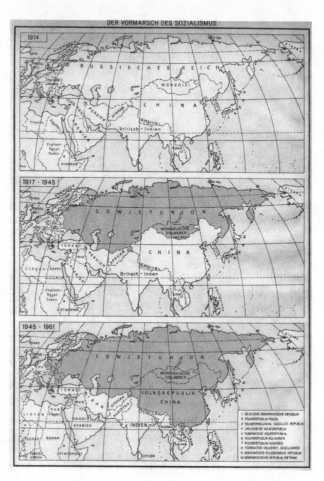

DER VORMARSCH DES SOZIALISMUS

1914

RUSSISCHES REICH
MONGOLEI
CHINA
Britisch-Indien

1917 - 1945

SOWJETUNION
MONGOLISCHE VOLKSREP.
CHINA
Britisch-Indien

1945 - 1961

SOWJETUNION
MONGOLISCHE VOLKSREP.
VOLKSREPUBLIK CHINA
INDIEN

1 DEUTSCHE DEMOKRATISCHE REPUBLIK
2 VOLKSREPUBLIK POLEN
3 TSCHECHOSLOWAK. SOZIALIST. REPUBLIK
4 UNGARISCHE VOLKSREPUBLIK
5 RUMÄNISCHE VOLKSREPUBLIK
6 VOLKSREPUBLIK BULGARIEN
7 VOLKSREPUBLIK ALBANIEN
8 FÖDERATIVE VOLKSREP. JUGOSLAWIEN
9 KOREANISCHE VOLKSDEMOKR. REPUBLIK
10 DEMOKRATISCHE REPUBLIK VIETNAM

Geography pupils of the 1960s through the 1980s studied from this atlas, which was used in all elementary grades in the GDR. First published in 1962, it highlights the expanding influence of communism in the early postwar era. The caption reads: "The Advance of Socialism."

cifically, for the way East German geography textbooks abridged citizens' freedom of travel, speech, and even thought.

How did GDR geography textbooks portray the world's physical horizons and thereby shape the mental horizons of its young readers? This is the key question that the following close analysis of East German geography textbooks is meant to answer, an inquiry that will repeatedly traverse the ideological crossroads of walls, classrooms, and stopped clocks.

But before proceeding to a scrutiny of the textbooks, a brief word both about my own standpoint as an American cultural historian and about the daunting rhetorical and political challenges faced by GDR textbook writers is appropriate.

My research into the ideological and militaristic aspects of East German geography texts has confronted me not only with the stark reality of communist propaganda efforts, but also with their forceful adversarial critique of the geopolitical intentions of the United States and the capitalist world. While I dispute that critique, I do not mean to imply that the Soviet Union (and Eastern Europe) constituted a black-and-white "evil Empire."[1] Nor do I deny the complexities of the Cold War (in which the United States also took self-compromising positions) or the validity of some aspects of the Marxist analysis (or of European scholars critical of American foreign policy).[2] Rather, I respect the seriousness of the GDR textbook authors' critiques by engaging their work seriously, indeed sometimes combatively, as I offer here a self-consciously Western (indeed American) response to their claims.

My second preliminary point has to do with the difficult task that faced the editors of GDR geography textbooks. When writing a geography textbook about capitalist nations—above all Europe, particularly West Germany—GDR educators of the post-Wall era (1961–1989) had, of course, an especially thorny problem. It was a problem that entered every young reader's mind, yet which the textbooks could not directly address: the frustrating irony of studying countries that you were forbidden to visit. (Several junior high school pupils whom I interviewed in 1990 were well aware of, and enraged by, the paradox. Even some socialist countries—especially countries outside Eastern Europe, such as Cuba—were nearly impossible to visit.) And yet nowhere do the GDR textbooks, nor even the teaching guides, ever breathe a word about travel restrictions. It was a topic just too hot to handle.

Still, the issue lurked in the shadows, above all in units that dealt with the German border and the Berlin Wall. Like the Wall, it was *there*. With pupils in the uncomfortable position of learning about numerous nations to which they could never travel until retirement age, the question that dared not speak its name crouched in catatonic anguish on the tip of even children's lips: Since we can't go anywhere, what do we need this subject *for*?

The agitprop in the geography teaching guides tried, of course, to head off that question; but in the units on the capitalist world, SED educators had to perform a virtuoso balancing act that camouflaged their violation of fundamental human rights. They had to justify the value of studying the capitalist world and yet condemn it too. They had to douse the desire to travel to the West by making the capitalist world seem not even worth visiting. And yet, the very treatment of the capitalist world fueled the GDR citizenry's obsession with it. As we shall see, however unsuccessfully, the textbooks attempted simply to annihilate the question by force of sheer invective.

Behind the Wall, or How the Eurasian Reich Viewed Oceania

II

Geography was one part of a comprehensive core curriculum of ideology in schools of the German Democratic Republic, from whose influence even the sciences and mathematics were not wholly free. Geography and *Staatsbürgerkunde* (civics) aggressively promoted the GDR and the *Bruderländer* ("brother lands," or fraternity of socialist nations). That was their main aim: to convince pupils that, when all was said and done, they were socialists and GDR citizens first and last. Right or wrong—no, left or wrong—the GDR was still their country, still their socialist Fatherland.

Geography succeeded *Heimatkunde* (local/regional studies cum folklore) in fifth grade. Known as *Erdkunde* ("earth studies," geography), it took up its topographical aspects, leaving overt agitprop for *Staatsbürgerkunde* (civics). But like GDR civics, geography was highly political. It served as one half of what might be termed "advanced socialist Fatherland education."[3]

GDR *Erdkunde* thus focused not merely, and often not chiefly, on the "green earth"—that is, the physical features of a region (climate, elevation, soil, vegetation, population, and land use—but rather on the rapidly expanding "red earth." What educators sometimes termed "socialist geography" frankly argued the superiority of socialist nations' use of the earth's resources—which postwar History was rapidly demonstrating by the spread of communism throughout the globe. Indeed the inside front cover of the standard middle school atlas of the 1950s through '70s gives graphic testimony to these aspirations: three maps covering Europe and Asia appear; they are dated 1914, 1917–1945, and 1945–1961, respectively. The first map contains no red; the next map is half covered in red, and the third is dominated by red. The title: "*Der Vormarsch des Sozialismus*" (The Advance of Socialism).[4] The military connotation of the subject noun seems deliberately chosen.

Yes, the message is graphic: *Der Sozialismus siegt!* "Socialism is winning!"

GDR *Erdkunde* was therefore frequently less concerned with the study of the earth than with the revolutionary advance of socialism upon it. And geography teachers were supposed not merely to describe that advance but to contribute to it. "Forward and never forget! / wherein our strength resides," as Brecht's "Solidarity Song" expressed it. Or as the familiar slogan, derived from a speech by Social Democratic Party leader Wilhelm Liebknecht in 1872, put it: "*Wer die Jugend hat, hat die Zukunft*" (Who has the youth, has the future).

Politics and the German Language

Geography possessed the same ideological orientation as *Heimat-kunde*. But its range and depth were greater, especially in the upper grades, where it addressed polytechnical educational issues as well as cultural and moral ones. In the introduction to *Geographie 5*, pupils received a glimpse of what lay in store in upcoming years:

> We already know from *Heimatkunde* a great deal about our home locale, our home *Kreis* [small region], our home *Bezirk* [district], and Berlin, the capital of the German Democratic Republic. We've also heard about the life of people in the Soviet Union and in other socialist nations. So we have already gained our first acquaintance with geography. But that isn't enough at all. . . .
>
> Many working people need geographical knowledge in their daily work. Construction workers and engineers and architects have to understand the layout of the ground when they build new houses. Farmer comrades must observe the contents of the soil exactly, in order to raise their agricultural production.[5]

Or as the geography teaching guide phrased it, in a unit entitled "The Significance of Geography Class in Fifth Grade and in the Following School Years":

> The material of 5th-grade geography is especially well-suited to further the acquisition of knowledge about the socialist Fatherland and a feeling of pride in [our] achievements and a feeling of solidarity with working people. In geography the preconditions for the educational effectiveness of [other subjects in] later grades is created, above all in the units treating other socialist states, especially the Soviet Union; here, and in the treatment of West Germany and other capitalist states, the pupil gains a partisan perspective. Beyond all this, the pupil should already in 5th grade acquire the foundations of a materialistic *Weltanschauung* and a socialistic way of behaving within his learning collective.[6]
>
> In these ways, geography class makes an essential *contribution to the formation of socialist personalities* who are being trained to adopt—ambitiously, critically, and independently—the task-oriented, socially necessary perspective.[7]

The geography syllabus for polytechnical middle school through high school proceeded in two phases. In the first stage (fifth through ninth grades), the emphasis—at least formally—was on physical geography.

Behind the Wall, or How the Eurasian Reich Viewed Oceania

The regions of the world were studied according to topographical and ideological categories; that is, by continent and hemisphere (and, secondarily, by political system—whether socialist or capitalist). In the second stage (ninth through twelfth grades), pupils also studied economic geography, especially "the socialist world system," concentrating chiefly on economic development. Upper-grade elementary school geography concerned itself more with Marxist-Leninist theory. But all grades celebrated the economic successes in the socialist camp (especially the Soviet Union and Eastern Europe, with West Germany's failures serving as counter-examples illustrating the weaknesses of capitalism).

The following two sections deal in depth with how these topics were presented in the first two years of the GDR curriculum.

III

The fifth-grade curriculum covered the physical geography of the GDR itself. Much attention is given in *Geographie 5* to its topographical distinctions: the plains and valleys of the north, the hills and mountains of the south. But the political dimension of such facts is never forgotten. For instance, the text repeatedly stresses that the GDR land mass is "tended with care" by socialist agriculture and industry. Unsurprisingly, no mention is made of the GDR's dying forests, poisoned rivers, and polluted air. The paragraph on socialist agriculture concludes: "The land is the most important natural foundation of agricultural production. In order that its bounty may be maintained and even increased, it is carefully tended in socialist society."[8]

Whereas GDR mathematics mixed politics with numbers, GDR geography mingled ideology with geology and topography. It made passing reference to the relation between the "laws" of physical science and scientific socialism; the teaching guide advises teachers to mention the "dialectical aspect" of physical geography, meaning how Marxist-Leninist doctrines and Nature share the same "general lawfulness."[9] But the teaching guide notes that this theme will be handled systematically in the upper grades and should remain in the background in fifth grade. Thus *Geographie 5* is less "ideology and geography" than a counterpart to Western political geography, though this de-emphasis on agitprop is more true of the texts in the 1970s and '80s than those of earlier decades.

While *Geographie 5* is divided into two parts based on GDR topography (the plains of the north and the mountains of the south), its subchapters are organized according to the GDR's administrative system of 15 *Berzirke*;[10] this allows for a political emphasis to the text, featuring local political achievements and economic geography. For instance, subchapter and unit titles include "The Development of Rostock," "Big Chemical Firms," and "The New Residential City of Eisenhüttenstadt."[11]

The first chapter of *Geographie 5*, "The GDR—A Socialist State," gives the flavor of the text. It presents a map of the *Berzirke* and an overview of the physical facts of the GDR: size, population, population density, major rivers, and so on. The opening paragraphs make clear, however, that a strong political emphasis in geography class is to be expected:

> Under the leadership of the Socialist Unity Party [SED, or Communist Party], the working class rules in the GDR. In alliance with the comrade farmers, the intelligentsia, and all other working people, the working class promotes the interests of the whole *Volk*.
>
> All the important means of production are the property of the *Volk* or Party. . . .
>
> The GDR is cordially allied with the Soviet Union and all other countries in the socialist community of nations. Many socialist countries cooperate closely in the RGW [*Rat für Gegenseitige Wirtschaftshilfe*, the Council for Mutual Economic Assistance, a.k.a. COMECON, the East European counterpart to the European Union]. In this way, people from the allied countries get to know and understand one another better and better.
>
> The GDR maintains diplomatic relations with almost all nations of the earth. It conducts peaceful trade with many nations and helps young national states with economic reconstruction.[12]

Featuring units entitled "The GDR—a Socialist State" and "Berlin—Capital of the German Democratic Republic," the chapter on East Berlin is the longest and most detailed in *Geographie 5*. East Berlin—always referred to simply as "Berlin" in official language (West Berlin was termed "Westberlin")—is described as "the political center of our Republic," "a modern socialist capital." In the style of the *Heimatkunde* textbooks—and anticipating the more extensive attention to the political history of modern Berlin in history class (tenth through twelfth grades)—the opening unit on Berlin gives a quick, five-paragraph overview of wartime and postwar Berlin.[13] For example:

Behind the Wall, or How the Eurasian Reich Viewed Oceania

In the Second World War, large parts of Berlin were destroyed. After the liberation of Berlin by the Soviet army, the city was occupied by troops from the Soviet Union, the USA, Great Britain, and France. A separate administration was introduced in the three western zones with the support of the western occupation powers. These measures destroyed the unity of the city. Berlin was split into two parts. . . .

The three former western sectors form the politically autonomous area of *Westberlin*. From this center the economy of the GDR was damaged year after year. Therefore, on August 13, 1961, our government decided on protective measures on the border of our Republic and *Westberlin*.[14]

The unit concludes: "Berlin, the capital of the GDR, is a major, modern socialist city. Working people from all *Berzirken* of our Republic cooperate to make the city ever more beautiful."[15]

The East Berlin chapter also spotlights the GDR's political structure, featuring photographs of the State Council headquarters and of "Red City Hall," the site of the municipal administration of Berlin that was built with reddish brick. The unit (1967 edition) begins:

Our capital Berlin is the site of the highest body of the People in the GDR, the *Volkskammer*. . . . Between the meetings of the *Volkskammer*, the direction of the state and society lies in the hands of the State Council. It is under the direction of *Walter Ulbricht*. . . . The leading party of our state is the party of the working class.[16]

This paragraph exemplifies how socialist educators determined that geography could make a contribution to the formation of the desired socialist *Weltanschauung*. The various regions of the GDR are primarily treated as occasions to present the state philosophy and structure of government of the GDR, as the end of the closing chapter of *Geographie 5* evinces:

The GDR is a socialist state. All measures of the Party and State are directed toward the constant improvement of citizens' lives. The economy is developed systematically, under the direction of the Party, in the interest of all citizens. . . . On account of their productive labor, all working people have a share in the development and execution of the plans [Five-Year Plans].[17]

IV

Elementary geography textbooks for sixth through eighth grades devoted roughly equal space to capitalist and socialist nations: sixth grade covered Western Europe and "the socialist countries of Europe"; seventh grade treated the USSR and Asia; eighth grade addressed North and South America, Africa, and Australia.

Geographie 6 is divided into two parts. The division is not geographic (west vs. east), however, but political: "Capitalist Countries of Europe" and "Socialist Countries of Europe." And the introduction ("Overview of Europe") signals that the textbook will be blending geography and ideology in order to develop a "partisan perspective." *Geographie 6* begins with a table that ranks the rivers of Europe according to length: the Volga and Donau are first and second; the table then skips to the Rhine, which comes in a poor ninth. (The Elbe is tenth.) The editors then state:

> One can order the states of Europe according to their geographical position. (See illustration 8 above.) All of Eastern Europe belongs to the European part of the Soviet Union. The entire Soviet Union is the biggest country in the world.
>
> If one divides the states of Europe according to their political organization, they belong partly to the socialist and partly to the capitalist countries. Until the end of the Second World War, the Soviet Union was the sole socialist country in Europe. Since then, the number of socialist countries in Europe has significantly grown.

The introduction concludes with the sentence: "The biggest part of the land mass of Europe is occupied by socialist countries."[18]

Given its division into east and west on the basis of political systems, Europe was the perfect setting for comparing the relative successes of socialism and capitalism—and, of course, of the two Germanys—and it is fascinating to see here how *Geographie 6* employs geographical facts, often in the form of charts or lists, to imply—without ever actually stating—that socialist nations are superior to capitalist ones. Nothing is falsified. But the impression of the overall superiority of socialism is effectively communicated. The fact that socialist nations occupy a greater land mass than the capitalist ones implies other sorts of superiority. That the USSR contains the biggest rivers (the Rhine is the only western European river even mentioned in the chart) and is the "biggest" country in the world geographically implies its greatness in other areas of interest.

Here again, however, the difficult problem arose for GDR educators of "studying" the West while at the same time stifling students' desire to *see* it. How could they make the West seem so bad that it was not even worth visiting? The solution, as we have already seen, was to condemn capitalist nations as—to borrow Ronald Reagan's notorious phrase about the Soviet Union and Eastern Europe—an "Evil Empire."

Consider, for instance, the presentation of West Germany and Great Britain in the chapter "Capitalist Countries of Europe" in *Geographie 6*. More than a third of Part 1 is devoted to West Germany. In the opening paragraphs, under the heading "The BRD [West Germany], a Capitalist Nation," which is accompanied by photographs of young workers on strike, we learn:

> As in all capitalist countries, the raw materials, industrial firms, and banks belong principally to private property owners, the capitalists. Even the land and terrain are, in largest part, private property. The capitalists represent only a small part of the population, but they govern the economic wealth of the state. The actual earnings of the working people are really received by them as profit . . .
>
> There is only one political party in the BRD that openly and fearlessly battles for a just order. That is the [West] German Communist Party (DKP).[19]

This text is followed by a lone unit question phrased as a command (complete with exclamation points):

> Contrast property and power relations in the BRD with those of the GDR! Prove why there cannot be any exploitation of people here![20]

The section on Britain is cast in similar terms:

> Great Britain is the *country where capitalism originated*. . . . Back then, the ruling classes of Great Britain governed the greatest merchant and war navy. They had conquered huge territories in Asia, Africa, and North America and had oppressed the peoples there. Such a subordinated and exploited country is called a colony.[21]

The summary for Part 1 opens:

> All capitalist countries possess these distinctive features:
>   1. The same property and power relations prevail in capitalist

Politics and the German Language

countries. Almost all the means of production, above all the industrial firms, belong to a small minority of the population. The great mass of the working people is exploited by the capitalists for their own profit. All essential measures of the government serve to maintain these capitalist relations.

2. The capitalist class is opposed to the working class. The workers battle for improved working and living conditions. They struggle for secure jobs, good educations for their children, and suitable medical insurance as well as a beautiful and natural environment. The capitalists ultimately have only one interest: the protection and increase of their profits.[22]

On the other hand, the chapters on the "Socialist Countries of Europe" in Part 2 are an inspiring story of progress, persistence, courage, and human dignity. After contrasting the distinctive features of *"socialist relations of production"* point for point with those of capitalism, the introduction explains the "developmental path" of Eastern Europe with a short historical overview. Interestingly—perhaps to heighten pride in the success and independence of the *Bruderländer*—any expression of gratitude to the USSR for its role in this history is omitted:

In the era of capitalism (until 1944–1945), Poland, Hungary, Romania, and Bulgaria—already industrialized Czechoslovkia was an exception—were among the most economically backward countries. . . . The need became even greater during the Second World War (1939–1945), when troops from fascist Germany invaded. . . .

With the liberation in 1944 and 1945, the Volk drew the correct conclusions from their experiences suffered during the capitalist era. They first altered the political relations. The Volk assumed rule. . . . Then property relations were altered. Against the bitter resistance of the capitalist exploiters, the exploiters were dispossessed of their firms, which were acquired by the Volk. Under great hardships, the Volk proceeded to overcome their war losses and develop the young socialist countries from backward rural countries into modern industrial countries with sophisticated agricultural production. In all this, they have proven that workers and peasants are able to govern a state successfully and to develop its economy for the welfare of all.[23]

Geographie 6 stresses that, despite this awful past, socialist countries are committed to peaceful cooperation with their capitalist neighbors and can rest confident in their superiority. Class conflicts will continue under capitalism; under socialism, all conflicts are resolved in comradely fashion. The future belongs to the socialist nations because the laws of History are on their side. As the summary for Part 2 notes:

> With the Great Socialist October Revolution, the lawful transition from capitalism to socialism began. The Soviet Union forged ahead on this path as the first country. . . . [Under socialism], emergent difficulties and problems are overcome and dissolved in the common socialist interest and in comradely character. . . .
>
> The socialist countries of Europe decisively campaign, in the interests of their peaceful reconstruction, for cooperation between socialist and capitalist nations.[24]

Similar arguments and modes of presentation are also found in seventh-grade geography, which covers the USSR and Asia. Unlike other texts, however, *Geographie 7* lionizes the USSR explicitly and in unrestrained language:

> Everywhere in the Soviet Union, modern science and technology are used. . . . For the first time in the history of Humanity, affairs are decided by working people. . . . The successes since the Great Socialist October Revolution show that no other social order can produce such achievements. . . . The socialist world order has become the decisive force of the present. . . .
>
> A close friendship exists between the Soviet Union and our Republic. . . . The working people in the Soviet Union and in our Republic pursue common goals: Under the direction of the Party of the working class, they both are building a future that offers peace, security, prosperity, and happiness for all people. That's why the citizens of our Republic have such heartfelt feelings of friendship toward the Soviet Union.[25]

As the seventh-grade teaching guide notes, the emphasis should be on "socialist ideological education":

> In the foreground is the goal of making the pupils aware of the political significance and economic strength of the first and most important socialist country of the world. . . .
>
> In the sense of proletarian internationalism, the conviction should be deepened that the Soviet Union pursues consistently a peace poli-

tics and stands as a model for the further development of socialist states, and also that close friendship exists between other socialist states and the USSR. These educational goals constitute the leitmotifs in the entire handling of the Soviet Union.[26]

The seventh-grade units focus on the leading nations in socialist Asia: China, Korea, and Vietnam. The "educational emphasis" when discussing the "historical-geographical" dimension of China, according to the teaching guide, should be "Education for hatred against the oppression and plundering of peoples by the imperialists."[27] The opening paragraph of the unit on the Democratic Republic of Korea (North Korea) runs: "Korea was divided by the imperialists. The attempt of the USA to annihilate the Democratic Republic of Korea failed."[28] The Vietnam unit is titled, "The War of Independence of the Vietnamese Volk." "Education for hatred" against US imperialism and "solidarity" with the Vietnamese *Volk* is highlighted as the "educational emphasis" in all editions of the teaching guide.[29]

> Pupils recognize especially in the portrait of the criminal war of aggression by the US that imperialistic nations are not above even making war in order to halt Asian progress. But their wars are opposed by aid for economic reconstruction from the Soviet Union and other socialist countries. . . . The victory of the Vietnamese Volk should be especially honored [1978].[30]
>
> The heroic struggle that the Vietnamese Volk have carried on for years against the aggression of US imperialism is the focus in the treatment of the Democratic Republic of Vietnam. The portrait of the development of this battle for liberation serves, on the one hand, as an example for the national liberation movements in Southeast Asia, and on the other hand, characterizes the brutality of imperialism, which violates human rights and sovereignty in the service of its interests.
> . . .
> The pupils must gain the conviction that US imperialism, which has taken over the positions of the earlier colonial powers, tries with all its means to halt the independent and progressive development of peoples, but that in Asia too, developments are increasingly defined by the growing strength of the socialist world system. . . .
> The pupils can establish with emotionally effective and current press clippings that the US is conducting a barbaric war of aggression in Southeast Asia. . . . [1968][31]

This textbook cartoon shows the capitalist West dominating both the communist and Third World (frame 1) until the communist rises up against the capitalist (frame 2), and the Third World also then rebels, at which point the imperialist powers fall (frame 3)—and the world belongs to the communists and the developing countries. The caption reads: "The Modern Era."

Geographie 8 focuses on Africa and the Americas, particularly the United States.[32] The opening paragraph on Africa heralds the liberation movement that has led to "50 independent nations" in the postwar era, concluding with the question: "How has it happened that the African independence movement has achieved success and imperialistic colonialism has almost collapsed?" The answer is not hard to fathom:

> The cornerstone for this development was laid with the Great Socialist October Revolution. For the first time, in a sixth of the globe, capitalism was overcome and workers and peasants began to erect the first socialist state, the Soviet Union. . . . With the victory of the workers and peasants in the Soviet Union began *the epoch of the world-wide transition from capitalism to socialism*. A characteristic of this epoch is the independence movement among the colonially enslaved peoples of Asia, Africa, and Latin America.[33]

Geographie 8 extensively discusses neocolonialism in Africa, which is described as a continuation by the capitalists of the old imperialistic aims of the colonial powers. "The imperialist powers exploit toward these ends their *monopolies* and the *dependence on exports and imports*

Politics and the German Language

of the African states."[34] Teaching guides advise referring to "so-called 'economic aid'" from "the imperialistic states."[35] Special attention is given in *Geographie 8* to the "Suez aggression" of 1956 and the "Israeli aggression" of 1967. The text spotlights model socialist states such as Zaire, which gained independence in 1960 and, under the socialist government of Mobuto, nationalized the mining industry in 1967.[36] Pupils encounter the following unit questions:

1. Review: a) In what form and under what conditions do the monopolies draw their profits from Africa? b) What possibilities do the imperialistic states exploit in order to gain influence over the developing countries?

2. Explain via the example of the historical development of the Republic of Zaire the features of colonialism and neocolonialism!

3. Report on the penetration of BRD monopolies in Africa! Take a position![37]

Recognizing that identification with the continent of Africa is hard for GDR pupils, the teaching guide on the Africa units issues classroom instructors a challenge: "Educational success will essentially turn on the partisan position of the teacher."[38]

V

Of greatest interest to an American reader, of course, is the treatment of the United States in *Geographie 8*. Not surprisingly, the picture is wholly negative, buttressed by quotations from observers such as "V. I. Lenin, who studied the US intensively."[39] Following Lenin's remarks, the text organizes its discussion of the United States into the "industrialized North," the "formerly slave-holding South," and the "colonized West." Lenin's approach testifies to the truth of the "dialectical-materialist *Weltanschauung*," for it proves that "social relations, not Nature, are the decisive factors" in economic development.[40]

Indeed each unit in *Geographie 8*, as the teaching guide makes clear, is meant to convey an ideological point. "Pupils should grasp societal oppositions" when studying New York; life in Appalachia teaches that "monopolies only lead to the striving for maximum profit"; the iron ore and steel industries in Detroit, Chicago, and Pittsburgh reveal how "automation, under capitalist conditions, has negative consequences for the workers (greater danger of unemployment)"; the wealthy petrochemical

Behind the Wall, or How the Eurasian Reich *Viewed Oceania*

industry in Texas, Louisiana, and Tennessee instructs how the American "oil monopoly" gets "high profits" from nations such as Venezuela; American agriculture shows the "contradiction between the possibilities of productive means and the inhibiting role of [capitalist] productive relations."[41]

According to *Geographie 8*, racial discrimination and nationwide poverty dominate the American scene. No positive aspects of "the American way of life" are depicted, nor are US advances toward racial tolerance, equality, and economic well-being noted. Photographs of protest demonstrations against racial discrimination and Mississippi tenant huts accompany passages such as the following, which are representative:

> The contempt for human beings of the ruling classes shows itself especially in the treatment of the *Negro population*, who are only assigned subordinate work and receive only a percentage of the wages that white workers—who had to fight hard labor battles—receive.[42]
>
> The obsessive struggle for profit produces horrible misery, crime, and immorality.... The country has 256 hunger areas, above all in the South....
>
> That is the US today. While the ruling classes, year after year, could pay out $30 billion for the criminal Vietnam War, there reigned in their own country mass misery, crime, and immorality. A horrible indictment against the capitalist system![43]

The unit questions reinforce this unrelievedly dark portrait, often inviting students to draw on knowledge gained either from history class or from geography units on other continents:

> 1. Explain, given your knowledge from history class, how the United States developed into a monopoly state and into the most powerful capitalistic and imperialistic country!
>
> 2. With which countries have you already become acquainted in which US monopolies occupy a ruling position?
>
> 3. Name the reasons why the US monopolies are compelled, in spite of their high profits in their own land, to exploit the raw materials of other countries![44]

The summary both approaches US imperialism from a "socialist world system" perspective and examines its domestic consequences.

The Soviet Union, the leading state of the socialist world system, has

This textbook cartoon portrays racial discrimination against minorities and their poverty in the United States in the 1960s. The caption reads: "Would you like to fly to the moon, Joe?" The starving companion answers: "Why? Is there work there?"

melted the earlier great [economic] lead of the US as a result of the former's lightning development. . . .

US monopolies control more than four-fifths of the industries in Western Europe making calculating machines, a considerable part of the auto, oil and chemical industries, airplane construction, and other decisive industrial branches. . . .

Just as the US undermines progressive forces throughout the world, so too do the reactionary powers-that-be within the US, in order to bolster their exploitative position, move against the progressive movement in their own country using the cruelest methods. They even kill politicians on their own side, as the example of the murdered Kennedy brothers shows in terrifying fashion. The leaders of the Negroes have suffered and still suffer the same fate on racial grounds, as happened to Dr. Martin Luther King.[45]

The teaching guide reflects these same priorities, and indeed functions as a kind of keyword index to GDR agitprop against the United States:

> The treatment of the political divisions in America is meant to emphasize that the USA is the most aggressive imperialistic state. It constantly tries to expand its spheres of influence and to influence the countries of Latin America politically and economically. This fact should be a leitmotif throughout the entire treatment of the following sections of the syllabus.[46]
>
> [Highlights to] elaborate: USA, the most powerful, but also most aggressive imperialistic country; leading power of NATO; rejection by the population (also the colored peoples) of its imperialistic politics; its racial discrimination; its rule of power (murder of Dr. Martin Luther King, Ku Klux Klan); demonstrations against the Vietnam War; colored medal winners in [1972] Olympics admit membership in Black Power movement and are expelled from US team.[47]

All this should be contrasted with the revised, post-Wall *Geographie 8*, which was issued in late 1990/early 1991. The editorial closing date (*Redaktionsschluss*) is listed as 2 July 1990, so the book was written right in the middle of the accelerating breakdown of the GDR system just months before German reunification in October 1990. Among the most notable changes are that the back cover of the new *Geographie 8* depicts an African American couple . . . and they smile! In GDR textbooks from the '70s and '80s, all Africans and South Americans look stern and/or unhappy, even (or especially?) if they are portrayed as class-conscious freedom fighters for socialism. (Indeed, before 1990, all "natives" in GDR textbooks [Native Americans in the US, Africans in Africa, Asians in Asia, or Latins in South America] were shown either as suffering or working together "in solidarity" with aid workers from the Eastern Bloc.) But now they have apparently rejoined (as eastern Germans will soon do?) a larger, nonpartisan, geographical family that includes their former enemies. So now they comprise one big happy and smiling clan.

Another significant change in the post-Wall *Geographie 8* is that questions marked with an asterisk (*) are ones for "stronger and more intelligent pupils"; one never saw such "elitist," "bourgeois" questions in the GDR's "uniform polytechnical" schoolbooks before 1990. (Likewise, in the source reference section, page 3 has been revised: Odo Marquard and other Western sources are being used, along with traditional M-L sources.) The eastern German gymnasium graduate who sent me a photocopy of his *Geographie 8* textbook for 1990–1991 wrote about still another change that continued to impress him years later:

> One thing you can't see from the copy is the remarkable change in the printing quality compared to our old textbooks. Whereas the old ones were made of cheap paper, the new one came in a very good printing quality (soft and heavy paper). Also the design surprised all of us. I remember that in the first lesson we just flicked through the book and (the boys especially) were amazed at the pictorial content of the book: there were pictures of skyscrapers, American cars, a picture of a truck in the chapter on Canada (like the ones we saw on TV in American series like *Knight Rider*, etc.). I even cut out some of the pictures and pasted them in my notebook just because I liked the colourful pictures of the "New World."[48]

VI

Although the previous two school years focused increasingly on economic geography, ninth-grade pupils also received a global overview of physical geography that stressed "above all the great possibilities under socialistic relations for the transformation of agriculture."[49] It is noteworthy that environmental pollution is never addressed except in relation to the abuses of imperialism. Indeed the ninth-grade syllabus found it easy to reconcile the GDR's scientific-technical revolution and ecological concerns. "Socialist society is convinced that the structure and lawfulness of the geosphere will be ever more comprehensively understood and that socialist productive processes should constantly use the environment better and intervene in the processes of the geosphere systematically and more strongly."[50]

Economic geography in ninth through twelfth grades treated the relation of physical and economic relations to the production of raw materials and their manufacture into finished products. Textbooks were divided into units on industry, agriculture, and economic relations (within "the socialist community," with "imperialist" nations, and with "young nation-states"). The ninth-grade curriculum focused on the USSR and the socialist countries of Eastern Europe (especially Czechoslovakia and Poland);[51] the tenth-grade curriculum covered the same ground and included the GDR (and, until the 1970s, the BRD).[52] Units on subjects such as the economic development and socialist transformation of

Cottbus are common, followed by unit questions such as "Compare the present state of economic development in the Cottbus Bezirk with that of 1945!"[53]

The following passage from *Geographie 10* serves as a touchstone of economic geography in the POS (elementary school):

> In 1976, the People's Republic of Bulgaria constructed in Varna a bridge 2 km long and 48 meters high over the passageway from the Black Sea to the Varna Sea. Since then, ships weighing up to 100,000 tons can travel within 20 km away from the coast, where the chemical firm Devnya lies. In the direct vicinity of the firm, they can dock in a new harbor or be loaded up. Therefore they need not repeatedly load and unload coal imported from the Soviet Union or dung, cement and other products slated for export. Now many workers can be transferred to other areas of the People's economy. The total economic advantage justifies the extraordinary high costs of the bridge construction. Moreover, the construction work has made shorter travel times possible for ships that want to leave Varna toward the south. The bridge is part of a future *Autobahn* from Varna to Burgas.

The passage concludes by stressing the dialectical "unity" between the economy and the Volk under socialist planning: "The use of land in socialist countries must proceed in unity with the further improvement of the working and living conditions of the population."[54]

Much of ninth- and tenth-grade economic geography is devoted to the analysis of "economic laws" of Marxism-Leninism that define the modes and relations of production. Attention is given to such concepts as socialist economic integration (the law of economic cooperation of socialist nations in the RGW) versus imperialist market competition (Common Market rivalries and inconsistent policies). (Unit question: "Prove that the countries of the RGW constitute the most stable and dynamic economic region of the world!")[55] The text also addresses goals such as systematic socialist economic development (the law of equal or proportional development of all socialist regions), a policy that contrasts with the haphazard and unequal economic development of capitalism (e.g., nations versus colonies, wealthy neighborhoods versus slums, the boom-bust cycle of prosperity and recession). Pupils also study neo-colonialism more rigorously and are informed about the differences between mutual aid among socialist nations and exploitative "developmental aid" from imperialists.

Geography in the upper grades is not meant to dwell on theory; the teaching guides stress the "dialectical unity" of theory and praxis. Indeed the Varna bridge project serves as an example of socialist economic integration, which is a "lawful, long-range process" and a precondition for the optimal use of a region's resources. The principle of socialist economic integration also reflects COMECON's commitment to equal socialist economic development, which gives witness to how the USSR aids the *Bruderländer* to achieve a living standard equal to (or even better than) its own. Teachers are also urged to pose practical questions derived from socialist theories of economic geography such as the following: "What must we do in order to raise our living standard even more?" "Why does the systematic use of land contribute to the increase of worker productivity and to the improvement of our life?" "How do socialist countries achieve better use of the social and natural resources of their land, so that a rise in worker productivity is made possible?" "Why are the centers of great American cities deteriorating?" (The guide proposes that pupils' class reports take Detroit or St. Louis as examples, though "for variation" Tokyo and Yokohama are also suggested.) Pupils "must gain the conviction," concludes the teaching guide, that problems such as "traffic chaos, bad living conditions in slums, minimal opportunities for recreation in city centers, and unemployment are part of the essence of capitalism, and that it is not possible in capitalism for all working people to be guaranteed a high material and cultural living standard."[56]

Senior high school (EOS) pupils also studied both physical and economic geography. But the curriculum differed in two ways: EOS geography emphasized specific industries (chemical, steel, iron ore) and their relation to the "socialist world system," and it focused almost exclusively on socialist nations, even giving substantial attention to smaller socialist countries such as Hungary (whose prairie region of Hortobagy is featured in and pictured on the back cover of *Geographie 11* [2nd ed., 1983]).[57] In physical geography, this socialist focus meant excluding or limiting discussion of certain topographies and climates (such as tundras and tropics) since few or no socialist nations could illustrate them. Economic geography in eleventh and twelfth grades reviewed many regions that earlier grades addressed, developing the extant "partisan perspective" via newly gained Marxist-Leninist theories on topics such as socialist economic development and neocolonialism.[58] Especially in earlier textbook editions, the partisanship is often quite aggressive. And, in hindsight, it is sometimes ironic, as when modest productivity increases are claimed to signal the impending "triumph of socialism in the economic competition between the socialist and capitalist systems."[59]

VII

Like the "higher calculus" of official GDR math, however, SED geography did not require "positivist" evidence to support such claims. Hard evidence or none, "dialectical unity" or not, Marxist-Leninist theory was to guide the young revolutionary's spirit. Fostering the new fatherland by creating "little comrades"—textbook Reds—would fulfill the oft-trumpeted slogan of Party duckspeakers: "*Wer die Jugend hat, hat die Zukunft!*" (Who has the youth, has the future!) Young revolutionaries were to be imbued with the progressive faith encapsulated in the refrain of Brecht's "Solidarity Song," cited at the outset of this chapter:

> Forward and never forget!
> Solidarity!

Yes, however long the march might require, however slow and halting the fulfillment of History's "laws," M-L theory insisted: *terra rosso is the future.*

And the present?

To sustain the socialist believer in the present, Party "goodthink" (a.k.a. socialist "conviction") was all:

> Die Partei,
> die Partei,
> die hat immer recht.

CHAPTER 10

Revenge of the
Thought Police

Leipzig is the so-called *Heldenstadt* (City of Heroes), as the bumper stickers on a few cars remind me. These are the streets where hundreds, and later thousands, of protestors marched through the streets with candles in their hands throughout the fall of 1989 in defiance of the East German government. Their bravery led to the opening of the Berlin Wall that November and the toppling of the SED regime a few months later—and ultimately to Germany's reunification in October 1990.

Five years later, the streets in the smoggy city center are nearly empty. It's a warm mid-September afternoon in 1994. Ute, twenty-three and a first-year student in German literature at Leipzig University (formerly Karl Marx University in the GDR), enters and greets me. In the GDR days, she had enjoyed special state benefits unavailable to Winston and Julia in *Nineteen Eighty-Four*—that is, as a prospective member of the SED's "Inner Party." As a teen she was an accomplished figure skater in a top *Sportschule* (sports school); indeed, at sixteen, a young *Privilegierte* (privileged one) on her way to joining the elite traveling *Sportkader* (sports cadre).

Still slim and athletic, Ute has come to tell me about her expulsion

JOHANNES R. BECHER

Der Staat

Ein Staat, geboren aus des Volkes Not,
und von dem Volk zu seinem Schutz gegründet –
Ein Staat, der mit dem Geiste sich verbündet
und ist des Volkes bestes Aufgebot –

Ein Staat, gestaltend sich zu einer Macht,
die Frieden will und Frieden kann erzwingen –
Ein Staat, auf aller Wohlergehn bedacht
und Raum für jeden, Großes zu vollbringen –

Ein solcher Staat ist höchster Ehre wert,
und mit dem Herzen stimmt das Volk dafür,
denn solch ein Staat dient ihm mit Rat und Tat –

Ein Staat, der so geliebt ist und geehrt,
ist unser Staat, und dieser Staat sind Wir:
Ein Reich des Menschen und ein Menschen-Staat.

To a much greater degree than pupils attending the standard polytechnical elementary school in the GDR, athletes in East Germany's *Sportschulen* were drilled in socialist ideology. Poems such as *"Der Staat"* (The State) formed a significant part of the elementary school German literature textbook, as in the case of *Unser Lesebuch* for seventh grade. The last two stanzas read as follows:

Such a state warrants the highest honor,
and the People vote for it with their hearts,
for such a state serves them in word and deed—

The state so beloved and honored
is our state, and we are this state
an empire of human beings and a human state.

The poem was composed by the erstwhile German expressionist Johannes R. Becher, who was the GDR's most prominent state poet and served as its Minister of Culture during the 1950s.

almost a decade ago from the elect Red circle, the causes of which, she told me on the phone, "I have lately been brooding about incessantly." She did not elaborate. I know only that the Orwellian saga of her youthful rebellion against the State and her struggle to leave the GDR in 1988–1989 had begun soon thereafter.

Reared in Weissenfels, a town near Leipzig, Ute was born into a family of athletes. In the 1950s her father competed on the GDR national ice hockey team and her mother was a top handball player and member of the GDR national championship squad; Ute's older brother, Dieter, played on the regional championship soccer team. Sports was the family's joy and preoccupation. Like Oceania's Julia, Ute was unpolitical and little interested in affairs outside their immediate circle; her family turned to sports as a respite or even escape from Cold War agitprop and the ideological trench warfare between the early postwar GDR and West Germany. Ute adds that her parents were also "completely unpolitical people."

"My parents simply wanted to live in peace," Ute says in a tired voice. She takes out a cigarette and lights up. "They never spoke for or against the State. They were never much interested in Party pronouncements." Ute's father joined the Liberal Democrat Party, which, like the other noncommunist parties, existed merely to provide an appearance of a democratic political process. In reality, it served the interests of the ruling Communist Party elite; it had no real power whatsoever. Ute remembers that her father had very little to do with his political party. "Perhaps that's why he was willing to enter it," she says.

Ute's father, who died in 1987, had led an unusual life of relative independence. Upon gaining his high school diploma in the early 1950s, he could have gone on to higher education, but his own father had owned a small grocery store, and the State, after nationalizing the property, permitted the son and his wife to administer it under the auspices of the HO (*Handels-organisation*, state business organization) as *selbstständige Kaufleute* (independent businesspeople).

Ute attended the local school in Weissenfels and participated in afterschool activities, especially sports, on the grounds of the local Pioneer House, where the Young Pioneers and older Thälmann Pioneers played after school. Strongly influenced by her father, and with his coaching, Ute entered competitive skating at the tender age of seven, first in roller skating and then in ice skating. Despite the fact that her legs were of unequal length, which necessitated inserting a special right heel to even her leg length, creating an enormous strain on her young body, Ute dominated her rivals. Along with the other skater "prospects" in her school, Ute trained every day, often traveling to other regions to compete. Skating was a passion that consumed all her free time and won her wide recognition; she became her class's "Sport Representative" in the Thälmann Pioneers.

Over the years, Ute watched, enviously, as friends left their regular schools to enter *Sportschulen*; potential athletic stars started professional training at different ages, depending upon the State's determination of when intensive practice and expert coaching was advisable. Gymnasts started in fourth grade, swimmers in fifth grade; figure skaters, whose talents usually mature somewhat later, typically did not enter a *Sportschule* until seventh or eighth grade.

Ute's own career began at the age of twelve. At the state competition for figure skating, Ute performed a triple Salchow expertly, earning one of the top scores. She and her parents were thrilled when she received a *Berufungsurkunde* (certificate of calling) to attend the major district *Sportschule* in Erfurt, even if it was sixty miles from home. The invitation's language evinced the GDR's determination to endow this honor with the prestige of tradition; in 1981, like a distinguished scholar "called" to a chaired professorship at a leading German university, Ute, along with a dozen other young female skaters from her region, was "called" or "nominated" to the Max Norgler KJS (*Kinder- und Jugendschule*), a *Sportschule* named after a Communist Party member and athlete who had died in a Nazi concentration camp.

The Erfurt *Sportschule*, which trained nine hundred students in eighth through tenth grades for all the major Olympic sports, was essentially an elite *Turnschule*, a boarding school for athletes. Faculty and staff lived "on campus." Regular subjects were also taught, but these were secondary; the coaches usually doubled as teachers and considered the former role primary. Each athlete kept a *Gesundheitsbuch* (health journal) and received a full checkup every month at the health center on the premises; the medical care was the best that the State had to offer. Athletes trained year-round; in the off-season, Ute's group of six skaters ran fifteen kilometers per day. Parental visits were limited to an occasional weekend; students could return home for just two weeks in the summer, during which they were also assigned workouts.

The daily regimen was strict:

- 6 a.m.: Reveille. (Ute still remembers with distaste the shrill female voice "brightly urging us to 'Rise to a new day'!"—which uncannily evokes for me the morning warm-up drill instructress from Orwell's *Nineteen Eighty-Four*.)

- 6:30–9 a.m.: Ice training.
- 9 a.m.–1 p.m.: School.
- 2–6 p.m.: Ice training.
- 7–10 p.m.: Study hall.
- 10 p.m.: Lights out.

"I soon noticed that academics meant very little," Ute recalls. Every athlete had to belong to the FDJ (a Communist youth organization); "study hall" was often given over to FDJ meetings. Teachers, all of them Party members, would lead the daily political discussions. Topics included freedom fighting in *Bruderländer* (brother countries) such as Nicaragua, Western imperialism in El Salvador, and the American invasion of Grenada.

"Sometimes I felt like disagreeing just because of the arrogant attitudes of some of the discussion leaders," Ute says. "But I never said anything in public—it was pointless to say anything. It would just turn into a headache." Ute judged that it was better just to keep quiet and say little; silence was usually interpreted as agreement, and that would end a meeting sooner. Besides, nobody really cared all that much about ideological attitudes. The school cared about sports performances; only the older athletes had to support the State publicly. At sixteen, Ute couldn't say anything against the State, she says, "But I could be more or less indifferent and not get into any trouble at all. That was my father's approach—and my own."

Ute says that Western TV was forbidden in the *Sportschule*; social activities were almost nil, limited to a film or a dance every other week in the cafeteria.

"Nobody, as far as I recall, ever said, 'I want to watch Western TV like other kids,'" Ute says. "I don't remember anybody ever having a Western bent at all. Not that any of us ever said that *Der Rote Oktober* [Red October]"—which specialized in ideological rock—"was our favorite group either! Their music was too political. But the Pudhys, Silly, and Pankow—I liked them, and so did many others.

"Nobody ever complained. We all knew why we were there. To become *Hochleistungssportkader* (top performance athletes). People like Katharina Witt, the 'ice princess,' were national celebrities. We watched them on TV. The coaches knew her; they held up athletes like her as a model. 'Socialism with a beautiful face,' my brother Dieter and his friends called her."

The joke about Witt, delivered in a cynical tone, alludes to Dubček's

Revenge of the Thought Police

famous remark during the "Prague Spring" of 1968 that he sought to build "socialism with a human face." This term was widely (though privately) mocked in East Germany at that time because official East German propaganda proclaimed that East European socialism was already fully "humanized" and thus had no need for Dubček's so-called democratic reforms. The mockery exposed the gulf between the GDR's propagandistic claim to embody "real existing socialism" (or Marxism) and the socialist reality of the GDR. And the mockery turned to cynical, barely suppressed outrage when, in late August 1968, East Germans learned that GDR troops were being sent in to crush the Prague Spring—the first time that German troops had been deployed in Czechoslovakia since the Nazi years.

Ute pauses and folds her hands.

"We knew what the rewards were," Ute concludes. "And we wanted them. The coaches and teachers reminded us every week that we were the *Privilegierten*. Even if we didn't always feel so 'privileged,' we believed we were the elite."

The peak moment in Ute's athletic career came when she made the semifinals in her age group in the GDR's 1984 youth *Spartakiad*, held every other year in Leipzig. Then came the kind of injury endemic to high-performance athletes. Attending a two-week training camp in Nordhausen with other top athletes, Ute trained harder than ever and injured her comparatively weak right leg. But her "perspective"—the word used in GDR sports jargon for one's *Sportkader* prospects—was still "good"; her coaches told her to rest. After several weeks, when her condition had still not improved, surgeons operated on her leg. The operation was successful; her hospital physician informed her that she could resume training within two months.

When she returned to the *Sportschule*, she began light training, hobbling around on her cast. But soon Ute's idyll was shattered. One day the head of the figure skating department called her in to see him. Her injury, he said, and her less-than-stellar though strong performance had forced him, reluctantly, to make an unpleasant decision: she had "no perspective anymore"; she would be dropped from her skater group and put in the tenth grade "exit class" for six months, after which she would be discharged to a regular high school. And so, not long after the February 1984 winter Olympics in Sarajevo, in which the lissome eighteen-year-old skater Katharina Witt won her first gold medal, Ute was out.

I

Ute was shattered. At sixteen, she felt she had "no perspective" anymore in life itself; all that she had worked toward, for almost a decade, had suddenly dissolved.

Why? Ute asked herself again and again. Why?! Just a few months ago, her "perspective" had appeared rosy. Why now?!

She couldn't come up with a good answer.

But her father arrived a few days later with the probable one: Dieter, twenty, already in trouble for expressing public criticism of GDR life, had officially joined the Lutheran Church, had been confirmed in the faith, and (as an act of solidarity with several friends jailed on political grounds) had applied the previous month to emigrate. (Both Lutheran and Catholic dioceses could sponsor a limited number of emigrants from the GDR on religious grounds.)

GDR *Kader* had to come from families unswervingly loyal to the state and had to be without relatives in capitalist countries. Ute was being punished for her brother's defiance.

Ute was *orientierungslos* (adrift). Having finished the ten years of required schooling, she vaguely thought of getting a job near her parents in Weissenfels. She also applied, however, to an advanced high school in Leipzig, known as one of the best—and "Reddest"—schools in the region. Under ordinary circumstances, she should have been denied admission to this high school because of her brother, but she had applied there shortly after her brother applied for emigration, and she guesses, in hindsight, that the Leipzig school simply failed to contact the *Sportschule* for her updated records after accepting her for admission. So, upon receiving her letter of acceptance for eleventh grade, Ute decided to pursue her studies for two more years and gain her high school diploma, which would improve her job prospects.

Her acceptance into this elite "Red" school was one of those inexplicable screw-ups so characteristic of bureaucracy—and of totalitarianism generally, where so much was being watched and recorded that accumulation far exceeded the capacity for assimilation and action: the inefficiency of paranoiac hypersurveillance.

Even now, Ute says, her memories of those first weeks in the new high school are tinged with anguish. Not only was she far behind her age group academically and socially, but she was having heart and circulatory problems, the result of the abrupt halt of her training regimen and a too-short tapering-off period in the *Sportschule* exit class. More-

Revenge of the Thought Police

over, when she thought of her old athletic acquaintances, most of whose "perspectives" were still bright, Ute felt pangs of envy for what might have been. Her Erfurt group of skaters would, in the next four years, produce an Olympic champion (Gunda Kleemann), a world champion, and a runner-up in the European Championship Games. And Ute had been at their level.

Still, to her surprise, she says that she discovered her first, main, and enduring feeling was simply one of relief: the *Leistungsdruck* (performance pressure) was now off; at last she had the freedom of other girls. "And the freedom to smoke a cigarette!" she adds with a satisfied smirk, exhaling a long stream of smoke. Her feeling of *Schwarzglück* (lucky misfortune) began after the GDR followed the USSR's dictates and refused to travel to Los Angeles for the 1984 Summer Olympics. She recalls how older sports acquaintances, a few of whom were already assured a place on the GDR Olympic team, were devastated by the Soviet-led boycott.

"All that sacrifice, all that training—for what?!" Ute says.

I didn't want that kind of restricted life anymore. But it's only in hindsight that I've realized what I missed by going to the *Sportschule*. I didn't have a normal youth at all. I didn't know how to relate to people outside sports, I didn't know how to relate except as a competitor! I never had a *Liebchen* [boyfriend]—I never even had a date!—until I was seventeen. When I was small, everyone was always saying, "Your school years will be the most beautiful time of your life." But, no, that wasn't so for me. I had to catch up in practically everything.

And she grew appalled as she understood better the scope and nature of the GDR drug program for athletes. She says that she herself never took drugs; GDR figure skaters did not receive hormones until after tenth grade. But she had noticed—without yet fully comprehending—the effects of drugs on other athletes at Erfurt.

"Although we ice skaters got only vitamins, I noticed right away that something was terribly wrong with the girl swimmers," Ute recalls.

At fourteen, they had shoulders as broad and muscular as adult men—and voices just as deep, which was doubtless why the coaches wouldn't allow most of them to give interviews. Before I left Erfurt, one older girl visiting an old teacher told me about how she was taking drugs to delay or advance her periods according to scheduled competitions. Later, I heard that most of the same things were occurring with the ice skaters. One girl even told me that the discus throwers

Politics and the German Language

and shot putters were instructed to get pregnant several weeks before an international track meet to increase their weight and strength—and thereby their throwing capacity. And then, of course, as soon as the track meet was over, they got abortions.

Ute falls silent. She stubs out her cigarette. She shakes her head. She then proceeds to tell me about the Soviet and East European policy of manipulating pregnancies and abortions to enhance female athletic performance, a practice whispered about among the athletes yet largely unknown among ordinary citizens, let alone in the West, until after the fall of the Berlin Wall. The best-known athlete to admit that she had conceived and aborted a pregnancy to improve her sports performance has been Olga Kovalenko, a USSR gold medalist in gymnastics at the 1968 Olympics, but Scandinavian physicians told the *Sunday Times* of London in 1994 that "the practice was commonplace for athletes in what was then East Germany" (November 27).

"Unimaginable, isn't it?" Ute asks. "And I never heard, either at Erfurt or afterwards, of any athlete refusing the abortions, drugs or other coaching orders."

I'm glad I didn't have to face that. At sixteen, I wanted to win just as badly as anyone else. According to the swimmers, the coaches told you it was necessary for top performance. Whether it was vitamins or hormones, you took them. You didn't question anything at that age—or even later. The coaches and doctors were prescribing it, the Olympic stars were doing it. They were our mentors and our models.

Ute's adjustment to a normal life, however, was hampered by her concern for Dieter, who had emigrated to West Berlin in late spring 1984, just before Ute left the *Sportschule*. Even though she was no longer in training, the school would not allow her to see him off at the Leipzig railway station.

"Suddenly he was gone," Ute says. "I cried for weeks—I had hardly seen him since I was thirteen—and now, just as I was coming home and starting a new life, I thought I might never see him again."

She and her family did, but only in the face of strong opposition from the State—and even their own relatives. One of her mother's cousins was a Leipzig city councilman and a leading regional Party man; he warned them to cut off all contact with "that black sheep" in West Berlin. Another cousin taught history at a Dresden college and said the same. Both families broke off all contact with Ute's family.

It was only via elaborate subterfuges that she and her parents managed to visit Dieter—stratagems which, as their *Stasi* (secret police) file would later show, did not go unnoticed by the authorities. As it turned out, they were right to suspect that their incoming mail from the West was periodically read by *Stasi* agents. And even if their business phone was not closely monitored, they, like all GDR callers, had to register to phone West Berlin, and the wait often took a full day.

The conditions were difficult. Dieter could not return to the GDR—nor, of course, could his family visit him in West Berlin. But working through Czech acquaintances, Ute's parents arranged family get-togethers in Karlovy Vary—still known to Germans as Karlsbad, a famous Bohemian health spa town of 25,000 in the Sudetenland, which is located in the corner of Czechoslovakia closest to the GDR, less than two hours from Weissenfels. On the pretense of "taking a cure" or visiting friends who were taking one, many GDR families would rendezvous with their emigrant relatives in this region; the local Czechs specialized in discreet German-German contacts—and turned a tidy profit at it.

"Every spring and fall, and on a few other occasions, we would drive to Karlsbad, or nearby, to meet with Dieter," Ute says.

The border police were mean. They knew what was going on over there, even if they couldn't get the Czechs to do much about it and didn't know in each case when GDR families were meeting secretly. Police supervision at the border was draconian. I would always sit up front and flirt with them. Sometimes it worked. But sometimes it didn't—and on those occasions they would turn the car inside out, often for an hour or two, searching every nook and cranny, even our clothing. And searching for what? Nothing! And remember—we weren't even traveling to the West those times. Our destination was another "socialist Brotherland." They knew that they couldn't prevent us from traveling to Czechoslovakia, but they could make it so unpleasant that we'd think twice about going again.

Then, once we got there, the Czechs milked us good—DM 20 per day just for the rooms. You had to pay Western currency. My brother always brought the money and paid for all of us. We only stayed two or three days, Friday to Sunday—we didn't want to attract undue attention. My father had to be back to open the store, and I had school or work. A few times, though, given my brother's schedule, we could only see him on a weekend that conflicted with my round of duty in the FDJ harvest campaign, when my youth group had to gather potatoes or beets or something. But once I skipped it and saw him—

though if the authorities had known why I was absent, there would have been consequences.

A whole new world opened for Ute through her infrequent contacts with her brother. He enlightened her about Western music. He spoke authoritatively about Western books and dismissed most GDR literature as "Party trash." Although he had once been an excellent athlete himself, he now condemned GDR sports as blatant military education—though he did not defend NATO missiles or Western capitalism. Ute had never met anyone who was "against the State" before. For her, Dieter became a rebel hero.

After receiving her high school diploma from the EOS in 1986, Ute moved with a girlfriend to Leipzig and applied to study to become a skating coach at the renowned German College of Physical Culture, the leading center for sports research in Eastern Europe and the only state university in the world exclusively devoted to physical education and sports medicine. Despite excellent scores on her entrance exams, Ute was refused admission—even though a fellow high school classmate who applied with lower scores and no *Sportschule* background was admitted.

"That was it: that time I had no doubt that the reason was my brother," Ute says. "Before that, I was still willing to compromise with the State. That experience was my breakthrough—and the beginning of my break."

II

The combination of the meetings with Dieter and this latest rejection quickly radicalized Ute. At first her rebellion chiefly took aesthetic form. By day she worked in a "dead-end job" as a waitress near the university; on the weekends and at night she drew stares on the street, and sometimes hostile treatment from Leipzig police, for dressing in black with a fiery orange punk haircut: in the GDR of the mid-1980s, such a gesture was understood by everyone as not just a cultural statement, but a protest against the State. That was especially the case in Ute's circle, which included members of a subversive youth group that dubbed itself the *Geschwister Scholl* (Scholl Siblings), named after the dissenting Munich University students led by a brother and sister who were later executed by the Nazis.

By 1988, at twenty, Ute had decided: she too would emigrate, even though success would mean—as in the case of her brother—never seeing her friends and parents again except on brief, furtive visits to Czechoslovakia. She planned to expedite her emigration application via the same route that Dieter had taken: she too would cultivate church "sponsorship." But like her brother, Ute had no interest in Christianity as a religion and had never had any contact with it. The *Sportschule* generally prohibited Christians, and few Christians were accepted to the elite high schools. Although the ideology of Marxism-Leninism hadn't sunk in deeply, atheism had.

As had *Realpolitik*: Ute saw that the churches had some "free space"—and she realized that they were the way out. So she began attending discussion meetings at the St. Nicholas Church in Leipzig, and also the "Monday Circle" meetings during her visits to Weissenfels, both of which were attended by many nonbelievers and were devoted to nonreligious topics such as disarmament, ecology, and conscientious objection to military service. She expressed an interest in being confirmed in Weissenfels, as her brother had been.

To Ute's surprise, Dieter discouraged her, convinced that the maneuver wouldn't work a second time. Doubtless the *Stasi* kept some kind of tabs on him: the State, if not the Church, would balk this second time around. So Ute decided in late 1988 to pursue a different route to freedom, the only other way out short of going to jail and hoping that you would be *freigekauft* (bought free) by the West Germans. An old high school classmate had met and fallen in love with a West German visitor and had been allowed to emigrate; Ute now determined to do the same.

Waitressing at the restaurant, Ute relates with a grin, she would chat up single, male West German visitors—she was careful to ascertain their status—and explore whether her potential "rescuer" was truly "emigration material." The State generally assumed that sudden, grand German-German romances were bogus; Ute would have to meet a man willing to court her, write and telephone often, visit Leipzig regularly, and marry her. The longer and better documented the courtship, the better the odds of state approval for emigration. To leave the GDR by this route, Ute would have to fill out a lengthy questionnaire about the origin and course of their relationship, complete with detailed written proof of its authenticity (love letters, logs of phone calls, and so on). It was an invasive procedure that allowed the State into one's innermost private affairs, a bureaucratic nightmare designed to intimidate and to discourage the very thought of emigration. Ute would have to expose everything, which she knew she could do only if the relationship were a theatrical fabrication. But Ute was resolved. Belatedly, Dieter offered to

Politics and the German Language

find a partner among his West Berlin circle, but Ute declined the favor: She would conduct her "manhunt" herself.

And almost right away, she did meet her "rescuer": Heinz. Indeed the circumstances of the courtship surprised her—and tempered her growing cynicism about life.

Heinz was a German literature student in Göttingen. He lived just across the border in West Germany and was able to visit every month. She found herself, at the end of their first lengthy conversation, telling him the truth: She didn't want to share her life with him, she just wanted to emigrate.

"He was just so good," she recalls. "He said, 'I understand your situation. I just want to help you.' I loved him—and still love him—for that. She said he had met ex-GDR students in Göttingen. He was willing to phone and visit me every month—for years, if it meant that. We never slept together—he did it simply out of *Menschengefühl* [human feeling]."

At first, Ute says, she held back a great deal from Heinz—even worrying that he might be a spy. But she soon came to think of him as a "second brother." His charity and power of empathy, Ute acknowledges, was one of those *kleine Heldentaten* (small heroic acts) that eventually brought down the GDR regime.

As it turned out, the regime fell before the scheme of Ute and Heinz was put to the test. The couple had agreed to "date" at least a year before Ute submitted the emigration application. But before the year elapsed, indeed just as Ute was starting to collect all the materials for the application, candles began to light up the Leipzig night as thousands of marchers took control of the streets. And on October 9, 1989, Ute, along with some acquaintances from St. Nicholas Church with whom she had stayed in touch even after dropping her plans for confirmation, fell in among their ranks.

And then—still an unexpected development just days earlier—the Wall fell.

Ute was free at last. But now that she could visit her brother and even live in the West, she decided—perhaps paradoxically—to stay put after all. Now that she was free to travel, she didn't need to emigrate. Thousands of East Germans, including many of her friends and coworkers, were now migrating westward and enrolling in overcrowded western German universities. Along with two close friends, however, Ute applied to study German literature in Leipzig, rented a student apartment, and matriculated in September to the Karl-Marx Universität of Leipzig, today returned to its original name of Leipzig University.

Revenge of the Thought Police

"Maybe it's all been for the best," Ute says. "Now I can read and study any writer I want. If I had gone to university in the GDR days, it would have been so limiting. As a German literature student, I could have studied German classicism and remained somewhat outside politics, or I could have pursued socialist realism: there was nothing outside or between them."

III

A long pause. We smile together. The stub of Ute's cigarette glows in the twilight. As she starts to speak, a waitress places a small candle stand on our table.

"But it's not entirely a 'Happy End,'" Ute says abruptly, sharply accenting the English phrase. Her lips turn downward. She takes out a single piece of paper and turns it face down. Just this month, her brother—who now lives in eastern Berlin—received his *Stasi* file, which ran to more than two hundred pages. She has brought a page of it to show me. Even though her family had always assumed that the *Stasi* were keeping tabs on Dieter, they'd had no idea of the extent of the surveillance. But now they know. Friends and classmates had spied on Dieter; even the family next door in Weissenfels had reported on her family to the *Stasi*. Ute, of course, is also mentioned frequently in Dieter's file.

"They knew everything about Dieter's life in West Berlin!" Ute says angrily. "Everything! Our 'friends' told them about his whereabouts at every turn! They regarded him as a *Verbindungsmann* [go-between], a poisonous influence infecting the family back home with 'Western' values and attitudes."

Ute hands me the page. Peppered with grammatical and spelling errors, it is written in what Ute calls "proper socialist Deutsch." The file refers repeatedly to Dieter Engelhardt as "der E." I bend over the page and read silently:

Der E. was in Amsterdam last week with two of his mates. They met up with a couple of other expellees from the Republik. . . . Der E. is still working part-time in the [old age] home and at the theater. According to Stück [a cover name], der E. has broken off with Anke and now often spends nights with an actress in the company named Gisela. She is twenty-five, a student at the FU. According to Stück . . .

Ute takes a deep breath and exhales. "We know who Stück [drama, play] is," she says in an even voice. "A buddy of my brother from school in Leipzig, a *ganz labiler Mensch* [quite unstable fellow] who had psychological problems after his release from prison. We've known him for ten years. And he was just one of their informants."

At least fifty, possibly up to a hundred friends and acquaintances—including members of the church groups in which she and Dieter discussed sensitive political issues—informed on Ute's family over a seven-year period, she says. Some of them are easy to identify: they are listed by name in Dieter's *Stasi* file. Those listed by name were not, technically speaking, *Stasi* informants. They did not sign contracts; they merely reported occasionally to *Stasi* agents and received token payments or favors. Professional informants, or IM—such as Stück—received cover names, signed contracts specifying their services and responsibilities, and were well compensated. The *Stasi* employed more than 200,000 collaborators who carried various titles, known (according to status and function) by acronyms such as FIM (the IM supervisors)—and compensated accordingly.

Ute has applied for her own file. She has no doubt that it includes reports from her *Sportschule* and high school classmates and teachers. She talks about the terrible feelings of anger and rage that grip her and her brother, who confided in friends only to be deceived and betrayed by them.

"Can you possibly forgive them?" I ask.

"I don't know, I really don't know," Ute says in a low voice. She falls silent. The candle flame dances brightly as a soft breeze sweeps by.

She is lucky compared to some people, Ute says. We talk of *Stasi* victims such as dissident Heinz Eggert, a Lutheran minister spied on by his friends, falsely accused of child molestation, committed to mental asylums, and then pumped with drugs by a trusted doctor to disable his will. Perhaps even more unfortunate was peace activist Vera Wollenberger, imprisoned and then exiled from the GDR, and later a member of the Green Party in the Bundestag, who found out that her own husband had reported on her to the *Stasi* for more than a decade.

"I think I'd kill myself if I discovered something like that," Ute whispers.

IV

And we talk of the collaborators, among them leading political and literary figures such as former GDR premier Lothar de

Maziere; Brandenburg prime minister Manfred Stolpe; avant-garde poet Sascha Anderson; playwright Heiner Müller; and writer Christa Wolf. All of them had, as it were, secretly served East Germany's Thought Police—while pretending throughout the GDR years and beyond that they were fighting Big Brother as courageous, defiant members of the underground Brotherhood. I muse on the comparison. What gall they had. They weren't much different from Oceania's O'Brien. Or perhaps his junior associate, Mr. Charrington, the Thought Police agent masquerading as a bookshop proprietor. But Ute only murmurs about "how depressing it all is."

The news about Wolf hit Ute hardest. A graduate of Karl Marx University in the 1950s, Wolf had been one of Ute's heroines—until she admitted in January 1993 that she had worked as IM "Margarete" between 1959 and 1963, and then exiled herself in sunny Santa Monica as a guest of that wonderful socialist institution, the Getty Foundation. Ute had defended Wolf against critics until recently, she said. Now Ute feels confused. Her contempt is mingled with pity; the *Stasi* had also spied throughout the 1970s on Wolf and her husband, referring to the couple as "Forked Tongue." Does that even the scale? Ute feels embarrassed for having spoken so passionately about Wolf's integrity and has trouble even reading her anymore. Having always valued Wolf's "authenticity" (Wolf's signature term) and having approached her as a moralist and critic of Party orthodoxy, Ute now finds that knowledge of Wolf's early IM years acts like "a dirty filter that discolors everything I've read by her."

I mention the problem of how to conduct "de-Stasification." Ute sighs. She says she has no solutions—or even suggestions.

"What good does revenge do?" She can only speak personally, she says. "It's hard to trust, it's hard to believe anymore. Even now, I don't know how many . . . if any . . . of the friends with whom I'm still in touch betrayed me."

Ute pauses. She picks up the piece of paper and folds it gently.

"The past is not dead; it is not even past." Ute is quoting—the sentence, she says, is the first line of *Patterns of Childhood*, Christa Wolf's 1976 novel about her upbringing in Nazi Germany and her agonized struggle to work through it.

"Often I find myself speculating, spinning conspiracy theories out of innocent remarks," Ute says. "Or are they innocent? . . . I try to understand, but . . ."

Ute's voice trails off. "Take the example of my family's next-door neighbors in Weissenfels. I haven't seen them since we got the *Stasi* file.

Politics and the German Language

But my mother, who had been trying to hold it all inside, had an argument with the wife one day last month. She got so mad that she finally told the woman off and called her a 'slimy *Stasi* weasel.' The woman denied it indignantly. My mother went straight upstairs and came back down and showed the woman several pages of Dieter's file that cited her by name. The woman turned white. She and my mother haven't spoken since then. They catch each other's eye on the street occasionally and quickly look away.

"I don't know how I'll react when I see this woman. Her husband drinks, she has no children, she is utterly alone. I think she used to gossip with my mother for hours partly out of loneliness, not just to report to the *Stasi*. I think she wanted attention and recognition. That may be why she was open to the *Stasi*'s overtures. She wasn't a Party member— she wasn't political at all. It was exciting and flattering for her to meet young *Stasi* men, have them taking down her words, and giving her little favors in return."

Ute looks away.

The candle on our table flickers faintly in the dark.

"At my best," she says, "that's how I try to imagine it."

Part Three

The Un(der)examined Orwell

George Orwell, March 1945, around the time that he met Hemingway in Paris. It was probably a fleeting, unremarkable encounter that has been blown up in popular culture into a storied meeting between two literary titans.

CHAPTER 11

Did Papa Rescue
St. George?

A fter the Spanish Civil War broke out in July 1936, an English writer set off that December for the Catalan front to battle fascism. He wound up fighting for seven months with a minor, independent, left-wing, quasi-Trotskyist militia, and then published a memoir of his experience that was ignored and sold a grand total of fewer than nine hundred copies during his lifetime. The author was George Orwell, and the memoir was the now-famous *Homage to Catalonia* (1938), today regarded both in the English-speaking world and in Spain itself as the best work of reportage to emerge from that bitter conflict.

Orwell was, of course, neither the only literary man to go to Spain to fight the fascists, nor the only one to write about it after returning home. The Spanish Civil War (1936–1939) claimed more than one million lives in a nation of twenty-five million people, and it inspired an impressive body of literature. Probably the best-known novel, and the only work of fiction to rise to classic status, is Ernest Hemingway's last great novel, *For Whom the Bell Tolls* (1940). Like Orwell's nonfiction documentary, Hemingway's novel is written from a leftist stance. But Orwell's enemies on the Catalonia battlefront are the Stalinists as well as the fascist rebels. While some observers believe that Orwell romanticized the Spanish peasants and proletarians much as he did the English miners and working class in *The Road to Wigan Pier* (1937), *Homage to Catalonia* remains the definitive study of the betrayal of the Spanish revolution by the communists. By contrast, Hemingway's novel represents a considerable artistic achievement, but it lacks the political maturity of Orwell's narrative.

Several intriguing links exist between these two honored writers. Critics have sometimes drawn attention to the resemblances between their prose styles: the concrete language, the simple declarative sentences, the terse dialogue, the sense of artistic compression.[1] Moreover, some of Orwell's rules of good writing in his essay "Politics and the English Language," such as "never use a long word when a short one will do," recall Hemingway's prose—indeed Orwell could have cited Hemingway's taut, crisp style as an example of this rule. Each author—utterly in his own way yet with a similar emphasis on simplicity, clarity, and concision—changed the way that writers of English in the twentieth century used the language. Both men wrote outstanding books, but their greatest achievements lay with language.

Orwell and Hemingway were mutual admirers—though the esteem was much stronger on Hemingway's part for Orwell's work than the reverse. Hemingway was impressed not only by *Homage to Catalonia* but also with some of Orwell's fiction, especially *Burmese Days* and its critique of the evils of imperialism. Unlike his distinguished English contemporaries (such as Evelyn Waugh) who esteemed Hemingway's literary craftsmanship, Orwell was not much taken with Hemingway's early novels or short stories, regarding *For Whom the Bell Tolls* alone as a major literary achievement. Orwell tended to lump Hemingway with what he called the "tough-guy" American writers of the 1920s and 1930s, a genre that he wrongly predicted would soon become dated.[2]

Given these affinities between the two men, it is perhaps unsurprising that, as *Homage to Catalonia* was being posthumously published in the United States in February 1952, Hemingway would be approached to review the book. His friend Harvey Breit, editor of the *New York Times Book Review*, wrote to Hemingway and asked him to undertake the assignment. Hemingway voiced his deep respect for Orwell as both a man and writer, though he declined on the grounds that he was weary of politics and didn't want to write anything about a book so highly political. Hemingway also told Breit that he and Orwell had met—not in Spain, as it turned out, but rather several years later in recently liberated Paris, at the close of the great war to which the Spanish conflict was a mere run-

The Un(der)examined Orwell

up: the final weeks of the Second World War, shortly after the Battle of the Bulge.

So in the early spring of 1945, during the dying days of World War II, George Orwell—a left-wing London novelist-journalist and author of a still-unpublished little fable that had been making the rounds of the wartime publishing houses—met Ernest Hemingway, then at the height of his international glory as a man of letters and well on his way toward becoming the biggest American literary icon of the postwar era. Just the thought of such a transatlantic cultural event is enough to spark the dramatic imagination and excite lovers of literature, both the fan of "Papa" or "St. George" and the serious literary historian alike.

One wants to know all the details.

I

Or did it happen? Did one of the most colorful meetings of twentieth-century literary figures ever really occur? Was it in fact a meeting—or an "unmeeting"?

Hemingway himself is one source of the story (which he repeated in different versions). Orwell mentions it nowhere in his journals or letters, but one of his literary acolytes, Paul Potts, claimed the meeting happened and wrote about it. Their accounts vary—and Potts, despite penning memoirs and reviews about Orwell, mysteriously waited fifteen years before ever reporting such a significant encounter.

Beyond the testimony of these two men, no evidence exists. The silence on Orwell's part is notable since he wrote several letters from Paris and Cologne during his war correspondent stint in spring 1945. None of them mentions Hemingway, let alone any conversation with him.

Is it not odd that nowhere in Orwell's oeuvre (now collected in a monumental twenty-one volumes as *The Complete Works of George Orwell*) does Orwell himself—still a comparatively little known London writer at the time—relate even the mere fact of meeting the famous Hemingway? Indeed, it is as if by his reticence on the matter that Orwell "the Truthteller" (as *Time* profiled him in 1952) indicts from the grave both Hemingway and the publicity-hungry culture-chat acquaintances, journalists, and scholars on the make, all of whom were eager to cash in on the growing reputation of "St. George" Orwell.[3] By circulating the incident only after Orwell's death, they were in effect making sure that no one could question the story.

Doubts have occasionally surfaced among the two men's biographers

Did Papa Rescue St. George?

about the authenticity of this storied, virtually typecast encounter. It is true that both men were in Paris between February 15 and March 6, 1945. (Hemingway departed on that date for Cuba.) They also could have met either at the posh Hotel Ritz (where Hemingway may have been staying) or at the Hotel Scribe (where Orwell and most foreign journalists in Paris lodged). Yet questions arise because, quite apart from Orwell's deafening silence, the incident was never mentioned—let alone corroborated—by any of Orwell's or Hemingway's close friends. Years after its alleged occurrence, the details vary in different (and often second- or even third-hand accounts), and the pair who reported the supposed facts were notoriously prone to embroidery or outright invention. Moreover, as we shall see, key aspects of both accounts have an ex post facto ring about them.

So the word "supposed" about the facts of this widely disseminated story is used here advisedly. The reality is that this celebrated encounter may have never transpired—or, more likely, never occurred in any form resembling the tale as it stands today. A close examination of how the story grew across a half century from the tiny seed that Hemingway tossed out during Orwell's lifetime to the sprawling yarn that Hemingway's executor published posthumously (fittingly, in what Hemingway himself called a "fictional memoir" otherwise devoted to his safari adventures) proves instructive as a case history of how literary legends are made, not born. Furthermore, a comparative historical account of the two men's relative status at different moments pricks the ballooning story, all of which has broad implications for literary historiography and biography generally and the evaluation of sources and evidence in particular.

II

Let us consider the origins of the story further. Three sources have reported the alleged meeting. Written from Hemingway's Cuban home, Finca Vigía, the first is a long, chatty, still-unpublished letter in March 1948 to Cyril Connolly.[4] The letter is very warm and open, suggesting that Hemingway and Connolly have become good friends on the basis of their get-togethers in London and Paris over the previous two decades.[5] Hemingway raves about Connolly's most recent work of nonfiction, *The Unquiet Grave* ("one of the very best books I've ever read"), which Connolly had just finished when they last met in Paris in 1945.[6] Hemingway then expresses regret that he didn't contribute his

The Un(der)examined Orwell

promised "Cuban Letter" to the October 1947 issue of Connolly's *Horizon*, reports on the lengthy illness (and recovery) of his son Patrick, and invites the Connollys to stay at the Finca Vigía while the Hemingways are in Idaho to do a film shoot. As evidence of how close their relationship had become, the letter to Connolly warrants quoting at length. Hemingway writes:

How are you? I never wrote you how good the book [*The Unquiet Grave*] was.[7] I think it is one of the very best books I've ever read. I'm almost sure it will be a classic, whatever that means. It is a fine book. I can see why you were so happy when you had just written it when we met in Paris. I may have written you all this before, but I think what happened was I started the letter and never finished it. I'm very sorry never to have written a "Cuban Letter." I have written nothing except this damn novel and made a vow that I would do nothing until it was finished. Added to this, my boy Patrick was very ill for five months and almost died. He's alright now. But it [Patrick's illness] took five months out of my work and that was why I did not have any "Cuban Letter" to contribute to the American number of the review *Horizon*. I have not seen the number yet, as the Germans who lived in our house while we were away did not forward it to Idaho. (Some damn friend of his borrowed it, but he has promised to get it back.)

If you ever want to work anything out for getting away from England in the winter, such as letting me give you dollars and you give me pounds in England or in Africa, let me know. Also, you can use my house if it would be any good to you while we are shooting in Idaho in the fall and early winter. You are damned welcome to come here anytime we are here. The Cinco is one of the greatest anti-angst places there is, or at least that I have ever found. It is very lovely and you would like the food and the drinks.

I was so sorry that I was so ballsed up in the war [during] the times we were together in London and Paris. I always get involved in wars, but I admire the way that you did not. It would be wrong for me not to fight,[8] but it was many times righter for you to do exactly as you did. I am no good at saying this sort of thing, but I wanted you to know how strongly I felt it and to tell you how much the Palinurus book [*The Unquiet Grave*] meant to me.[9]

Cyril, we were born into almost the worst fucking time there has ever been, and yet we have had almost as much fun as anyone ever had. In any other time, I would have had fun, but I do not know how it could have been more fun. The day after we got into Paris, I was

Did Papa Rescue St. George?

happier than I thought I could ever be. I knew I had written as well as I could and eaten and drunk and fucked as well as I could and now I have fought as well as I could. And for once successfully. And we had taken the city I loved best in the world, and I was sleeping in the Ritz Hotel.

Fairy stories do not come out that well! Afterwards we had to go and meet the dragon. But after we met the dragon, I was still alive when I saw you. Now we have to die, of course, and all the inevitables. But I have had a lovely life.

Wish you could come here and see this place and country. I would much rather have you see it and write about it than me write a "Cuban Letter."

Every bit of journalism is part of what you should write [that has] gone to waste, even when you make it as easy as a letter. But once I get this damn thing done, I can afford to waste. When you can't waste, you ought to quit anyway, except with wives and with writing. Money you certainly should waste, and quite often.

Forgive this dopey letter, Cyril. I wish we could talk. I was so happy seeing you last time.

Hemingway closes the letter with a request that Connolly convey his regards to Orwell:

If you ever see Orwell, remember me to him, will you? I like him very much and it was a moment when I had no time when I met him.

This final pair of sentences, which seem to be rather an afterthought, are the full record of any mention by either Hemingway or Connolly (or anyone else) regarding a personal encounter between Hemingway and Orwell during the latter's lifetime. The last two sentences are matter-of-fact. Fully absent is the all-too-familiar tone of Hemingway swagger and vainglory. Moreover, unlike the preceding paragraphs written to Connolly, Hemingway's closing comment about Orwell is neither maudlin nor hackneyed.

So there is no reason to dispute the empirical fact that an uneventful encounter between the two men did occur. Although Hemingway's penchant for bluster and bravado was already well advanced by the spring of 1948, he had not yet become so hungry for applause and so prone to fabrication as he would by the 1950s. If Hemingway had intended to invent out of whole cloth a meeting between himself and Orwell, he certainly would not have limited himself to such a modest description.

The Un(der)examined Orwell

And what would have been gained? Orwell was a relatively little recognized writer in wartime London, whereas Hemingway was already a novelist celebrated worldwide. Even in March 1948, after the unexpected success of *Animal Farm* in Britain and the United States, Orwell's international stature was still modest in comparison to that of Hemingway. In fact, at least since September 1939, when Connolly founded *Horizon* and turned it into the leading British literary magazine of the decade, Connolly himself was a better-known figure than Orwell and thus a much more valuable contact for Hemingway. This would soon change as *Animal Farm*—which had just appeared in the United Kingdom in August 1945 and in the United States in August 1946—became a best seller and won literary kudos both at home and abroad. But the full impact of its success had not yet registered in early 1948, especially in intellectual circles on the continent. (Nor had Orwell yet published *Nineteen Eighty-Four*, which appeared in June 1949.) Beyond all this, Hemingway was well aware that Connolly and Orwell were close friends (as the letter implicitly acknowledges), and that Orwell would have immediately been in a position to refute any distorted claim about their meeting. Here again, the letter to Connolly furnishes no reason to doubt the genuineness of this plain-spoken account. One is left with the impression that the encounter was fleeting and forgettable; Connolly mentions it nowhere either in his extensive writings about Orwell or in his correspondence with Eileen Blair and Sonia Orwell.

Notice, however, how the description of the encounter alters in the following letter in mid-February 1952 (also still unpublished) from Hemingway to Harvey Breit.[10] Hemingway tells Breit: "Here's the pitch on Orwell. *Homage to Catalonia* is a first-rate book.[11] Orwell was a first-rate man too. You see it through the book. But he was fighting with a no-good outfit."[12] Hemingway suggests his old (and now ex-) friend John Dos Passos as a better choice to review *Homage to Catalonia* because "he admired the outfit Orwell served with very much . . ." (Dos Passos also apparently declined.)[13] Hemingway said he was "sick to death and hell of politics of every kind and I do not want to write a review of Orwell's book which no one can honestly write without going into politics."[14]

After that "pitch," Hemingway returns to his French connection with Orwell. Hemingway claims that he never even inquired during their meeting why Orwell—who had wartime press credentials to file reports for both the London *Observer* and the *Manchester Evening News*—had stopped in Paris. Instead, Hemingway informed Breit that the meeting had occurred in 1945 "after the Bulge fight. He was in civilian clothes and I did not ask him what he was doing, but [he] was probably accred-

Did Papa Rescue St. George?

Harvey Breit was a literary critic and writer whose book of portraits, *The Writer Observed* (1953), featured Hemingway and other postwar contemporaries interviewed by Breit in his capacity as an editor for the *New York Times Book Review*. A friendly acquaintance of Hemingway, Breit was the recipient of a letter from Hemingway about Hemingway's wartime encounter in Paris with Orwell. It is the only piece of evidence that establishes any basis in historical fact for the elaborate claims that Hemingway made about his meeting with Orwell.

HARVEY BREIT

The Writer Observed

THE WORLD PUBLISHING COMPANY

CLEVELAND AND NEW YORK

ited to the Embassy or had come over for the BBC or some information service."

At this point Hemingway's version begins to raise bigger doubts, featuring an anecdote that resounds with the familiar strains of Hemingway braggadocio. Hemingway writes that Orwell sought him out at his hotel[15] and "told me he was afraid he was going to be knocked off by the communists and he asked me to loan him a pistol. The only pistol that I had which was suitable for civilian clothes was a .32-caliber colt with a very short barrel. I don't think the pistol would have done Orwell much good as I had found that it was not a very effective weapon. But it may have made him feel better. He was fairly nervous and worried."[16]

A few years later, when he sat down to publish an account of his Orwell meeting, Hemingway would supply the "missing" dialogue and add

The Un(der)examined Orwell

other literary embellishments—and add entirely new elements. He began in the late 1950s to write a substantial memoir that included discussion of their meeting. But this "revised" version did not see the light of day in published form until the appearance of *True at First Light* (1998), which was largely devoted to Hemingway's last African safari, a misadventure that ended in two disastrous plane crashes in 1954. Interestingly, and quite revealingly, Hemingway subtitles the book "A Fictional Memoir." In this revised version, he supplements his account of meeting Orwell by emphasizing Orwell's inordinate fear of being assassinated by a mysterious "They." After retelling the basic 1952 version of the gun loan, Hemingway recounts that he dispatched a couple of friends to watch out for Orwell's safety. They reported back to Papa that no one was following him.[17] With a show of self-display characteristic of his yarns of the 1950s, Hemingway fleshes out his 1952 letter to Breit in *True at First Light* as follows:

[I] warned [Orwell] that if he shot someone with it they probably would die eventually, but that there might be a long interval. But a pistol was a pistol and he needed this more as a talisman than a weapon, I thought.

He was very gaunt and looked in bad shape and I asked him if he would not stay and eat. But he had to go. I told him I could give him a couple of people who would look after him if "They" were after him and that my characters were familiar with the local "They" who would never bother him nor intrude on him. He said no, that the pistol was all he needed. We asked about a few mutual friends and he left. I sent two characters to pick him up at the door and tail and check if anybody was after him. The next day their report was, "Papa, nobody is after him. He is a very chic type and he knows Paris very well. We checked with so and so's brother and he says no one pursued him. He is in touch with the British Embassy but he is not an operative. This is only hearsay. Do you want the timetable of his movements?"

"No. Did he amuse himself?"

"Yes, Papa."

"I'm happy. We will not worry about him. He has the pistol."

"That worthless pistol," one of the characters said. "But you warned him against it, Papa?"

"Perhaps he would have been happier with a stinger."

"No," the other character said. "A stinger is too compromising. He was happy with that pistol."

We let it go at that.

Did Papa Rescue St. George?

It is worth noting—as Orwell liked to say—that, like the 1952 letter, Hemingway's "fictional memoir" showcases a Hemingway who is strong, properly armed, and solicitous about the "very gaunt" Orwell, who is "in bad shape" and "needs" even a "worthless pistol"—indeed needs it "more as a talisman than a weapon," the worldly-wise Hemingway observes. The story lifts off and takes wings after Hemingway assures Orwell that "Papa" can "give him a couple of people" who will protect him. Hemingway's "people" become his "characters" as the story slides into a dialogue with "Papa." Evidently names and descriptions of his "characters" are quite unnecessary in this piece of "faction." Hemingway himself plays the role of a commanding officer to whom his recruits report—or perhaps better, an omniscient author to whom his pair of characters reports. They even ask him if he wants "the timetables of [Orwell's] movements." Generalissimo Hemingway is uninterested

Hemingway's posthumously published memoir, *True at First Light*, was edited by his son Patrick. Much of the book is probably not autobiographical. It contains some passages regarding his encounter with Orwell in Paris in 1945 that Hemingway embellished.

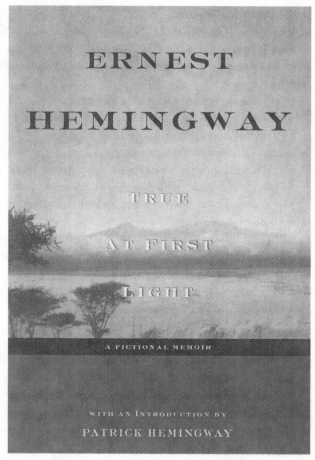

The Un(der)examined Orwell

in that, but he is happy that Orwell has managed to "amuse himself." Exuding manly confidence (and contradicting his earlier admission that the gun is not much of a weapon), he concludes: "We will not worry about him. He has the pistol." It is also interesting that here, Hemingway attributes the brevity of the meeting to Orwell, who had "to go" and therefore could not even "stay to eat." In the 1948 letter, the clear impression that Hemingway gives is that he himself was in a rush: "It was a moment when I had no time when I met him."[18]

The third source of the Hemingway-Orwell encounter is a fanciful tale by the poet Paul Potts (1911–1986), one of Orwell's impoverished bohemian friends. The story first appeared in Potts's memoir, *Dante Called You Beatrice* (1960).[19]

Whereas Hemingway's unpublished letter to Breit—an obviously firsthand account—lacks any literary touches and in fact any dialogue at all, Potts's story is a more detailed account—which, however, omits the gun anecdote. According to Potts, Orwell, who was staying at the Hotel Scribe in Paris, saw in the register of the Hotel Ritz that Hemingway was lodging there. Orwell went to Hemingway's room and knocked on the door. In Potts's version, Orwell did not introduce himself by his pen name, but rather—as if to diminish himself and as if he were not even a writer—by his birth name: "I'm Eric Blair."

Let us pause here for a moment and ponder the probability of such a scenario. How likely was it that Blair/Orwell would have introduced himself by a name totally unfamiliar to a stranger such as Hemingway rather than with the name by which any reader of *Partisan Review* might have known him? Moreover, how probable is it that Orwell would have searched out in a hotel registry the name of a famous writer like Hemingway and proceeded to knock unannounced on his door? In other comparable cases, ranging from T. S. Eliot to Parisian authors such as Malraux and Camus, Orwell wrote and introduced himself first (or asked his publisher to mail a copy of one of his books, such as *Animal Farm*).

Nonetheless, let us permit Potts to continue with his story. As Blair introduced himself, according to Potts, Hemingway was standing on the other side of the bed, on which there were two suitcases that he was packing. He looked up and saw that the man in the doorway was a licensed war correspondent and a British one at that. He bellowed, "Well, what the fucking hell do you want?" Orwell then softly replied: "I'm George Orwell." At once Hemingway became expansive. He pushed the suitcases to the end of the bed, knelt down, reached underneath it, and pulled out a bottle of Scotch. "Why the fucking hell didn't you say so?! Have a drink! Have a double! Straight, or with water, there's no soda."[20]

Paul Potts, a bohemian poet in the Fitzrovia section of London, sold his verse in broadsheets. Potts was a great fan of Orwell, who reciprocated Potts's affection with both friendship and financial support. In 1960, Potts published the first report of any encounter between Hemingway and Orwell in Paris in 1945, though most likely it was a highly exaggerated version of the real meeting. Like Hemingway's tall tale, Potts's rendition also mushroomed in a subsequent published version.

With that spirit-filled ending, Potts closes his vignette of the Hemingway-Orwell encounter. The story is surrounded by claims of Orwell's heroic virtue as a friend and of his genius as a writer. Dedicated to Richard Blair, Orwell's adopted son, the memoir is a soaring panegyric to the rebellious Orwell as "the man of independence." "He carried independence to such a length that it became sheer poetry," wrote Potts about his friend. "There indeed may be a Red Indian language somewhere on the northern borders of Manitoba in which the word for independence is George Orwell." Potts's essay is studded with flights of this sort:

> This always sick man made his typewriter take on the suggestion of a white steed. In his hand the biro he used for corrections could never quite help looking a bit like a drawn sword. . . . In his company a walk down the street became an adventure into the unknown. . . . In short his life was a duel fought against lies; the weapon he chose, the English language.

The Un(der)examined Orwell

On thinking of him a certain Don Quixote de la Mancha rides into mind on his horse Rosinante. . . . On him a tweed jacket wore the air of knightly armour. A cup of tea was wine before the battle. He carried no shield, used for a weapon plain facts loaded into simple English prose.

Potts seems to have considered his relationship with Orwell the single bright spot of his life. "The happiest years of my life were those during which I was a friend of his," recalled Potts. "I would have rather known him than have won the Nobel Prize." If there was little chance of the latter, Potts nevertheless did come to know Orwell as well as most literary friends in the late '40s. A penurious poet in the Fitzrovian literary world who was often mocked in wartime London intellectual circles, Potts was befriended by Orwell shortly after they met in 1944. Potts never forgot the act of kindness. His memories of Orwell, if expressed in flowery language, are nevertheless sincere and stirring.

It is transparently clear that Potts was smitten with Orwell, and that he was everlastingly thankful that such a great man had befriended him. Here again, however, we have no strong grounds on which to question the mere claim that some meeting between Hemingway and Orwell did occur, or even that Orwell told Potts that he had met Hemingway in Paris. (As we shall see, Potts would not have gotten the story from Connolly, let alone from Breit. He was not personally acquainted with Connolly and first wrote to him in mid-1956, when he had substantially completed the manuscript of *Dante Called You Beatrice*.)

III

Those are the "supposed" facts. In recent decades, one or another of the Potts or Hemingway versions of the story (and sometimes a hybrid composed of a mixture of their elements) has found a welcome home in the numerous biographies, literary portraits, and magazine fluff pieces written about Orwell and Hemingway. (For instance, Frances Stonor Saunders's *The Cultural Cold War*, which circulates a number of the sensational claims about both Orwell and his widow, Sonia, reports the story.)[21] It is easy to understand why. The letter to Breit features Hemingway's own voice and expressive, trademark slang in the service of his swelled ego. This Hemingway-Breit rendering appeared for the first time in Carlos Baker's *Ernest Hemingway: A Life Story* (1969) and has been widely cited and quoted ever since.

Did Papa Rescue St. George?

Potts's second-hand account (purportedly from personal conversations with Orwell) is also wonderful typecasting with its dose of Hemingway tough-guy talk and its appealing image of an unassuming Eric Blair bolstering his overall portrait of a diffident "Saint George." In either version, the tale not only adds a dash of color to any depiction of Orwell and casts Hemingway in a flattering light, but also (I can report firsthand) is greeted with delighted appreciation at literary dinner parties. Most secondary reports of the story have narrated it straight or related it as though it were a substantial encounter comparable to Orwell's other meetings with literary men in wartime Paris. Even biographers have done so. For instance, D. J. Taylor simply writes:

> Orwell, initially based in Paris, would spend a couple of months reporting on conditions in liberated France and, he hoped, following the Allied trail eastward in Germany. By the last week in February, he was installed in the Hotel Scribe, a popular resort for literary men in transit—where he met Ernest Hemingway, Harold Acton, and made his first acquaintance with the young philosopher A. J. Ayer—and was sending back dispatches on French public opinion and the political aims of the French resistance.[22]

However, a few Orwell scholars have, quite properly, arched their eyebrows in scoffing disbelief about the story's details—especially given Potts's well-known reputation in London for Pinocchio portraiture. Significantly, after its appearance in his memoir, Potts's version never surfaced in any article about Orwell (or Hemingway) until more than two decades after its original publication. It was first used in Sir Bernard Crick's excellent biography, *George Orwell: A Life* (1980).

Even those Orwell and Hemingway scholars who have cited some version of Potts's tale with a word of hesitation and qualification, however, have not inquired more deeply about its authenticity; none of them has bothered to interrogate or investigate it. One reason is that virtually all of them seem familiar with only one side of the story.[23] The Hemingway biographers invariably cite the Breit letter (and either avoid the Potts version or are not aware of it), occasionally pausing to wonder about the letter's veracity. Baker, for example, in his comprehensive, massively researched biography of Hemingway, reports the meeting as having taken place "with what truth it is impossible to say."[24] He leaves it at that. (Neither he nor any other Hemingway scholar seems aware of the 1948 Connolly letter.)

The Un(der)examined Orwell

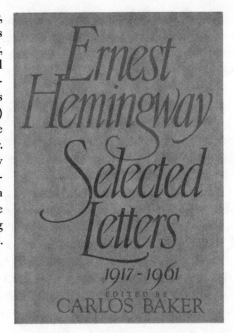

Carlos Baker, Hemingway's first biographer, edited several volumes (including Hemingway's correspondence) devoted to the American writer. Baker uncritically accepted Hemingway's version of his wartime Parisian meeting with Orwell.

Baker also notes in passing that Orwell and Hemingway first met in Barcelona during the Spanish Civil War. Where did he get that idea? He cites no source for it.[25] Such a meeting would have been highly unlikely. Orwell never mentioned the encounter in any of his voluminous writings about wartime Spain. Nor does Hemingway claim it happened—neither before nor after Orwell's death. (Baker is evidently confusing a nondescript encounter that Orwell had with John Dos Passos, both of whom developed strong friendships with literary anarchists and expressed sympathy for the anarchist cause.)[26]

Was Baker excessively credulous about Hemingway's claim to have offered Orwell hospitality in his private room and even loaned him a gun? Although Baker's monumental *Life* of Hemingway—the first biography of him ever written—was generally well received and remains the standard one cited, it is notably uncritical about Hemingway's legend-building. Baker has in fact sometimes been regarded as a fellow architect of Hemingway's mythmaking. Arguably, Baker's disinclination to investigate Hemingway's 1952 letter more thoroughly—in an otherwise exhaustive 652-page *Life*—makes him complicit in the entire episode of the Hemingway-Orwell tale. Having committed the last two decades of his distinguished literary career largely to Hemingway scholarship, Bak-

211

Did Papa Rescue St. George?

er seems to have developed a vested interest in accepting Hemingway's inflated reports about his activities, even though Hemingway was hopelessly prone late in life to telling tall tales to build up his public image and fortify his sagging ego. One critic of Baker's work argues:

> Baker chose not to question the Hemingway myth. . . . That Baker's biographical project was essentially concerned with the perpetuation of Hemingway's mythic persona has not escaped detection. Irving Howe . . . recognized what Baker had done (or rather what he had failed to do). So did Elizabeth Hardwick, who found "tiresome and displeasing . . . this fleshing out of the old Hemingway public persona." . . . Baker essentially shied away from any investigation, reinterpretation, or correction which did not "square" with the mythos. He criticized Hemingway only where Hemingway himself did so, or where Hemingway's well-publicized extremes of behavior would make his not doing so conspicuous. Baker's case is that, knowingly or not, his goal was not to de-mythologize: Rather, he undertook . . . to perpetuate Hemingway's mythic personality as historical reality and as objective truth.[27]

Also recounting the alleged story is Jeffrey Meyers, though he remains skeptical. Familiar with the minute details of both Hemingway's and Orwell's lives—he is the sole author to have written biographies of both men—Meyers is the scholar most qualified to corroborate or refute the story. Moreover, Meyers's *Orwell: Wintry Conscience of a Generation* (2000) benefits from the recent availability of Peter Davison's edition of *The Complete Works of George Orwell*. Meyers casts a cold eye on the conspicuous absence of reference to this meeting anywhere in Orwell's writings. He writes: "Orwell never mentioned their meeting and there is no record of their conversation." Yet even Meyers cites only the Potts version of the encounter and does not pursue the "supposed" facts any further in his biographies of either author.[28] (Nor does Meyers seem to know about the "record" of the conversation in the pages of *True at First Light*, which appeared in 1998, well before the publication of his Orwell biography.)

As we have noted, it is difficult to imagine Orwell not recording, either in his wartime dispatches or his correspondence with a wide circle of literary friends, any memorable contact with a writer as renowned as Ernest Hemingway.[29] For instance, if Orwell had shared drinks, exchanged stories, and borrowed a gun from Hemingway, would he not have mentioned it to friends such as Muggeridge and Anthony Powell, with whom he was lunching almost daily in 1945? It is difficult to believe that he would not have talked about such a meeting and that these two prolific letter writers and diarists would not have somewhere recorded the incident.

Moreover, would Orwell not have told his wife at the time, Eileen Blair? And would she in turn not have commented on it to Cyril Connolly, Orwell's close literary friend since his Eton days? In a letter of March 25, 1945, just three or four weeks after the presumed encounter between Orwell and Hemingway, Eileen Blair wrote to Connolly saying that "George is in Paris reporting for the *Observer*" and advises Connolly to forward any mail to her husband once Orwell reaches the press bureau location of his next assignment.

Beyond all this: as we have seen, Connolly himself was personally acquainted with Hemingway (they first met in Paris in 1929),[30] occasionally corresponded with him, and had recently met him in Paris, where they had discussed *The Unquiet Grave*. Would not Connolly have mentioned anywhere in their exchanges—or in his enormous body of journalism and reviews—a significant wartime Paris meeting between Hemingway and Orwell?

Again, the silence is deafening.

IV

So what does one make of all this? Did this meeting ever take place? Or was it from the beginning a "fictional memoir," largely a figment of Hemingway's Bunyanesque imagination?

A definitive answer is impossible: no incontrovertible evidence supporting or refuting the story has surfaced. As we have observed, however, three quite different versions of the encounter exist. In addition, even when the versions overlap, smaller, revealing differences in detail also prevail. For instance, Potts and Baker place the encounter at the Hotel Ritz.[31] But that is disputable. If it took place, the meeting could just as likely have occurred at the Hotel Scribe. Orwell was staying there in March 1945. Malcolm Muggeridge, in the second volume of his autobiography, says that he met a drunken Hemingway at the Hotel Scribe in the spring of 1945.[32] (Muggeridge does not say anything about a Hemingway-Orwell encounter.) Of course, Hemingway may have been simply drinking or dining at the Scribe, but foreign correspondents covering the war after the liberation commonly used the Hotel Scribe as their Parisian base. Potts's fanciful imagination may have invented the

Did Papa Rescue St. George?

Ritz—not only because it fit with his idealized version of Orwell (and with Hemingway's wealth), but also because he had probably never even heard of the Scribe. (Potts never visited France.)

Let us inquire further into the details. We can grant, on the basis of Hemingway's 1948 letter to Connolly, that the mere fact of a meeting is plausible. It is the protean *story* of the meeting that raises suspicion. Given that the three versions (two from Hemingway and one from Potts) of the expanded account originate in post-Orwell sources—the 1952 Hemingway to Breit letter and Potts's 1960 book chapter—how plausible are the "supposed" facts?

The Hemingway-Breit letter contains certain passages that are credible. The part about how much Hemingway admires Orwell's writing yet how he doesn't want to review *Homage to Catalonia* is not boastful. The section about meeting Orwell in his room, however, does sound like typical Hemingway big talk. Hemingway's claim about giving Orwell a gun also remains implausible.

With his connections in wartime England, Orwell surely could have secured a gun before his departure or during his Paris stay. (Hemingway was heavily armed before and after his war correspondent stint.) As a war reporter in Paris, how difficult would it have been for Orwell to find a gun? Crick also believes the gun story unlikely. On the other hand, a caveat must be entered: Orwell biographer Gordon Bowker discovered in the course of his research a fact that renders this portion of the story possibly valid. One of Orwell's London acquaintances, Rodney Philips,[33] sold Orwell a German luger pistol for five pounds in the summer of 1945—apparently because Orwell said that he needed to be armed since his enemies, especially the communists, might assassinate him.[34] The contention that Orwell feared assassination and that Hemingway supplied a snub-nosed .32 and arranged for friends to tail Orwell all come from Hemingway's letter to Breit.

As in the case of D. J. Taylor's biography, Bowker's acceptance of the Paris story and his uncritical attitude toward Hemingway seem rather ingenuous. Possibly, like many Orwell scholars and literary historians in Britain, they are unacquainted with Hemingway's tendencies toward megalomania and compensatory self-promotion during the last decade of his life. The fact is that Hemingway had a propensity toward fantasizing and grandstanding that became obvious (and worsened) as he grew older. Always something of a braggart, Hemingway indulged this weakness increasingly as the 1950s wore on. His third wife, Martha Gellhorn, once described him as the "biggest liar since Munchausen."[35] Heming-

The Un(der)examined Orwell

way himself virtually admitted as much—and considered it a reflection of his literary gifts:

> It is not unnatural that the best writers are liars. A major part of their trade is to lie or invent and they will lie when they are drunk, or to themselves, or to strangers. They often lie unconsciously and then remember their lies with deep remorse. If they knew all the other writers were liars too it would cheer them. . . . Lying to themselves is harmful but this is cleansed away by the writing of a true book which in its invention is truer than any true thing that ever happened.[36]

Certainly such an attitude would, at least in Hemingway's eyes, appear to fully justify his embroidery of the Orwell encounter within "a fictional memoir" such as *True at First Light*.

The timing alone of the story's first release in print in 1960 gives one pause (given the convenient fact that dead men tell no tales). The timing is not only significant because Orwell was not around to dispute the claim. After the publication of *Animal Farm* (1945), *Nineteen Eighty-Four* (1949), and two heralded essay collections (*Shooting an Elephant* [1950]; *Such, Such Were the Joys* [1952]), Orwell's reputation among the cultural elite (especially in New York and London) had come to eclipse Hemingway's own. And therein lies a motive.

The fact is that by the early 1950s, when Hemingway first began recounting the story, George Orwell was already dead, having passed away two years earlier at the age of forty-six, and his meteoric ascension to canonical status had raised his star among the literati above that of Hemingway. The latter's falling reputation as a creative writer was accelerating, braking only temporarily with the respectful critical response accorded *The Old Man and the Sea*, which was published in September 1952 (roughly four months after Hemingway's letter to Breit) and for which he won the 1953 Pulitzer Prize. At the same time public "Papalotry"[37] was reaching a crescendo: Hemingway's fame among the glitterati was approaching its high-water mark, soon to peak with his acceptance of the Nobel Prize in 1954—which some ungenerous critics attributed to fears among the Nobel Prize Committee members about the possibility of Hemingway's impending death after his near-fatal plane crashes that January.

Whatever their reasoning, Hemingway knew very well that the Nobel Prize for Literature honored his early achievements. So the capacity of the award to satisfy his raging ego was partial and temporary. As a result,

Did Papa Rescue St. George?

his macho lifestyle and headline-grabbing extra-literary activities intensified relentlessly as the 1950s advanced.[38] His psychic investment in this compensatory dynamic deepened and ultimately ruled his being in his last years,[39] as almost all of his newer writing, particularly his increasingly garrulous prose style, was mercilessly castigated and caricatured by literary critics worldwide.[40] The contrast between Hemingway's and Orwell's literary status in the 1950s—Hemingway's Nobel Prize notwithstanding—was widening. Whereas the Hemingway myth was becoming a bloated, self-inflated media spectacle without underpinnings in his art, and beginning to overshadow his literary identity, the Orwell legend was being viewed as founded on the perceived transparency between his life and work, thus burnishing his reputation. As Jeffrey Meyers notes: "Unlike Orwell, whose persona strengthened and confirmed the image of an upright man, Hemingway's legend swamped and destroyed the real artist."[41]

By the early 1950s, Hemingway was already veering out of control. He exaggerated, prevaricated, invented stories, contradicted himself, and was in general a very unlikable person and quite often a blowhard. All this must be entered in the docket against the tale. Once again, the meeting itself probably occurred—and was negligible, much like Orwell's brief encounters in Spain with Dos Passos or the young Willy Brandt; but the *story* of the meeting, even in its 1952 form (let alone the 1998 rendition), probably owes much to Hemingway's imagination, perhaps ironic proof that his literary gifts had not yet deserted him completely—or that his power of "artistic lying" was already fully available and ready for use.

Having argued that a declining Hemingway certainly had a motive to invent or embroider a story about meeting Orwell, we should also note that the period from 1948 to September 1952 was a literary low in Hemingway's career. He had just been crucified for *Across the River and Into the Trees* (1950)—including by Cyril Connolly—and had not yet published *The Old Man and the Sea*.[42] His weakness for braggadocio was at its peak, exemplified by his infamous, self-humiliating interview with Lillian Ross in the spring of 1950, in which he fully exposed himself as a Walter Mittyish fantasist.[43]

Was the Orwell tale Hemingway's attempt to connect himself to someone now taken more seriously than the author of *Across the River and Into the Trees*, which had been so roundly booed and even satirized by the critics?[44] Hemingway was in agony about its reception, and he was fast slipping into the permanent state of personal crisis that would lead to his suicide less than a decade later in 1961. At some level, he recognized that he had written nothing of consequence since *For Whom the*

The Un(der)examined Orwell

Bell Tolls (1940).[45] Edmund Wilson, once an admirer and friend, wrote in *The Wound and the Bow* (1941)—in a line that permanently bruised Hemingway's sensitive ego—that even before World War II Hemingway had already entered "into a phase where he is occupied with building up his public personality." Hemingway had created a persona that "is not only incredible but obnoxious. He is certainly his own worst-invented character."[46]

If not his worst character, the Hemingway persona of his last decade was certainly his most grandiose. Hemingway had morphed into the mythical "Papa" Hemingway of the newspapers and popular magazines: the full-bearded safari adventurer and big-game hunter, the hairy-chested brawler, the patron of saloon keepers, the literary hero of actors and actresses, the macho comrade of bullfighters and baseball players and boxers.[47] Dwight Macdonald's vicious parody of Hemingway reflected the verdict of the literary elite about Hemingway's own fall into self-parody and his deterioration as both a stylist and storyteller:

> He wrote a novel called *Across the River and Into the Trees*. It was not a good novel. It was a bad novel. It was so bad that all the critics were against it. Even the ones who had liked everything else. The trouble with critics is that you can't depend on them in a tight place and this was a very tight place indeed. They scare easy because their brains are where their *cojones* should be and because they have no loyalty and because they have never stopped a charging lion with a Mannlicher double-action .34 or done any of the other important things. The hell with them. Jack Dempsey thought *Across the River* was OK. So did Joe Di Maggio. The Kraut thought it was terrific. So did Toots Shor. But it was not OK and he knew it and there was absolutely nothing he could do about it.[48]

This context reframes our earlier question of Hemingway's motive pointedly: Was Hemingway desperately seeking to associate himself with Orwell, whose reputation in the 1950s as a writer was steadily climbing, in order to identify with a lost and squandered self?

Perhaps, and it is also plausible that Hemingway *was* quite embarrassed by his time in Spain—and declined Breit's reviewing request mainly for that reason. After all, Orwell's views of the Spanish Civil War had been vindicated, whereas Hemingway had been duped by the communists and their allies. (He never criticized the Stalinists or the USSR until long after the war.)[49] Probably one of the reasons that Hemingway didn't want to review *Homage to Catalonia* for Harvey Breit was

Did Papa Rescue St. George?

that such a review inevitably would have had to deal with how accurate politically Orwell had been about the war—and this would imply how wrong Hemingway was. Helping out Orwell in Paris could have helped Hemingway convince himself (if not others) that he too had been an outspoken critic of Stalin and the Stalinist intellectuals who visited Spain.[50] Furthermore, whereas Hemingway had gone to Spain to gather literary material, Orwell had gone to fight. While Hemingway fraternized with literary people, Orwell served as a soldier on the Aragon front—and even got a bullet through the windpipe for his trouble, temporarily rendering him voiceless and (even after he recovered) permanently weakening his vocal chords.

V

Such speculations aside, it bears repeated emphasis that neither of our two sources, Hemingway nor Potts, were known for being especially scrupulous or reliable with mundane facts. If the later Hemingway was a megalomaniacal self-advertiser, Paul Potts was a hopeless romancer. Each was a fabulist in his own way—and with his own particular reasons for promoting such a Paris legend. We have already addressed the issue of Hemingway's motives. What about Potts and his story?

FACING PAGE: As these magazine covers reflect, Hemingway became the subject of numerous feature stories in American magazines by the mid-twentieth century. Four of the covers reflect Hemingway's celebrity status in the 1950s and 1960s. After the publication of *Across the River and Into the Trees* (1950), Hemingway was derided by the critics as a has-been. Evelyn Waugh's "The Case of Mr. Hemingway" in *Commonweal* (*top left*) registered the critical consensus. Hemingway's stock rallied with the appearance of *The Old Man and the Sea*, which was printed in the September 1, 1952, issue of *Life* (*top, second from left*), taking up the entire issue and selling more than five million copies. Its phenomenal success led to Hemingway's reception of the 1954 Nobel Prize for Literature, an occasion that was overshadowed by two near-fatal plane crashes in Africa that summer—the tragic events that some critics have argued altered Hemingway's personality and reinforced his susceptibility to depression and suicide (*top right, middle left*). The next two *Life* cover stories (*middle right, bottom left*) indicate Hemingway's decline and fall. Despite his smiling visage adorning the cover of the September 5, 1960, issue, which celebrated the serialization of *The Dangerous Summer*, Hemingway was already suffering from severe psychological problems and convulsing in a sanatorium. Both the last *Life* cover story and the *Saturday Review* cover (*bottom right*) represent posthumous tributes to Hemingway, who committed suicide in July 1961.

Did Papa Rescue St. George?

Simply viewed as a literary artifact, Potts's tale is curious. He provides memorable details about the sudden appearance of a timid Blair in the doorway, Hemingway's suitcases on the bed, the Scotch stashed beneath it, the whiskey with no soda, and Hemingway's bravura greeting to Blair/Orwell. If Orwell had indeed told Potts all this, why does Potts stop there? Why does he exclude all detail of the topics the two writers actually talked about—which, after all, would have been the most interesting aspect of the meeting? Meyers suggests that inventing any further such dialogue was beyond Potts's limited literary skills.

Certainly Potts's version of the Orwell-Hemingway encounter should be doubted on the grounds of Potts's infamous reputation. A young Anglo-Irish Canadian, educated at Stonyhurst and a fervent ex-Catholic, Potts was ridiculed by much of literary London in the 1930s and '40s as "the People's Poet." His first book of poems was titled *Instead of a Sonnet* (1944), and many of his detractors joked that the title was ironically all-too-fitting, adding that both it and the rest of his oeuvre could well have been titled *Instead of a Poem*.[51] Perhaps Orwell empathized with him because, as Derek Stanford once remarked, Potts was "always odd-man out—a mostly unpaid, in-the-singular Opposition." From be-

FACING PAGE: Orwell also graced the covers of numerous magazines, though chiefly during the "countdown to 1984." Even in the 1950s, when his star ascended, Orwell's life was seldom the focus of interest in mass publications. In the popular press, Orwell's nightmarish vision and screaming catchwords in *Nineteen Eighty-Four* overshadowed interest in the man and writer. These four cover stories during 1984, however, show how the obsessive preoccupation in the media with Orwell's last novel spilled over into an insatiable urge to know more about the author of *Nineteen Eighty-Four* himself. Even audiences that weren't knowledgeable about Orwell's life celebrated him as a pioneering journalist, as in the case of the cover story in January 1984 that appeared in *The Quill* (*top left*). A November 1983 *Time* cover reflected a more typical view in mass culture of Orwell as "Big Brother's Father" (*top right*). In Britain, given the "Orwellmania" occasioned by all the hoopla and commercialism involved in the 1984 countdown, *Encounter* fairly asked, "Can Orwell Survive 1984?" (*bottom left*). A typical example of the cultural frenzy was the cover story of the *New Statesman* (*bottom right*) in its last issue for 1983. The magazine imagined a grand New Year's Eve party, in which it wished "doubleplusungood 1984 to all our readers." Among the guests greeting Orwell as he entered at the stroke of midnight are Queen Elizabeth, Ronald Reagan (sporting a button: "Ignorance is Strength"), Margaret Thatcher (wearing "Freedom is Slavery"), and other luminaries—all of them dressed in *de rigeur* Oceania uniforms of black overall trousers. Flanked throughout the room by Thought Police agents, they party under the watchful eye of Airstrip One telescreens.

The Un(der)examined Orwell

ing a supporter of Stalin in the 1930s, Potts broke away from Stalinism and affiliated himself with the London anarchists connected with Freedom Press (Orwell was also a member of that circle through his friends Vernon Richards and George Woodcock). Thereafter, Potts wrote intelligent appreciations of Ignazio Silone, Roy Campbell, and Ezra Pound, all of whom Orwell also admired for their literary talents, though he despised the fascist politics of the latter pair.

Potts was an itinerant poet notorious throughout London for hawking his broadsheet poems in pubs and on street corners. Incredibly dirty—

Did Papa Rescue St. George?

one friend described him as looking as if he had crawled out of a hole in the ground—Potts had a pathetic side, partly manifested in his puppy-dog veneration of Orwell. As Stephen Spender noted, Potts's memoir, *Dante Called You Beatrice,* "reads like the autobiography of a neurotic." The overriding impression left by the memoir is of a writer who has experienced excruciating suffering and wallows not infrequently in self-pity. Potts publicly identified himself as a failure—and not just a failure as a poet, but also as a husband, a family man, and a respectable bourgeois member of society. Potts exalted his failure as proof of his integrity; more than that, as Stanford suggested, he immersed himself in "the cult of failure." Perhaps Orwell also felt sympathy for Potts on this score. After all, in *Such, Such Were the Joys* Orwell also proclaimed himself a failure.

But, of course, Orwell never published that essay during his lifetime, and it dealt exclusively with the failure of Eric Blair, not George Orwell. Moreover, Orwell was a "failure" who became a great success. By contrast, Potts was a failure who became an ignominious failure—and proclaimed and indeed celebrated that "accomplishment" in the pages of his memoir. It must be conceded, however, that both men, to different degrees, quite identified with the cult of failure—and this shared predilection may also have disposed Orwell to empathize with or look kindly on the hapless Potts.[52]

Beyond all this, not only did the Potts tale not appear until a full decade after Orwell's death, but it also leaves an impression similar to *True at First Light* that it has been worked over and "factionalized." For the book chapter in *Dante Called You Beatrice* is virtually identical to Potts's rambling memoir about Orwell in the March 1957 issue of *London Magazine* ("Don Quixote on a Bicycle")—except that the magazine article omits entirely any mention of an Orwell-Hemingway meeting. Was this omission due to space limitations? Did Potts believe that the Hemingway encounter somehow didn't fit in? Or did Potts rather "remember" the story in all its picturesque detail only after 1957? Whatever one's verdict, the circumstantial evidence is not favorable to Potts.[53]

All such considerations aside, it bears noting that one of the most puzzling aspects of this running serial is why Orwell would have told his Hemingway encounter in such detail to Potts and no other member of his large group of friends. None of Orwell's closest friends—not Cyril Connolly, Sir Richard Rees, George Woodcock, Julian Symons, T. R. Fyvel, Powell, or Muggeridge —mentioned the story in their reminiscences about Orwell. Nor did Spender, a good friend of Orwell's, even allude to Potts's chapter on Orwell in his lengthy review of the

The Un(der)examined Orwell

memoir. Knowing Potts by reputation (and perhaps personally), one can only surmise that he and Orwell's other friends thought the whole thing a concoction of Potts's own quixotic imagination. Potts even wrote to Connolly during the mid-1950s to ask for help with publishing *Dante Called You Beatrice*, and it is likely either at that time or later that Connolly read the manuscript. Undoubtedly, he considered Potts such an unreliable source that he too never commented on Potts's version of the Orwell story.[54]

Connolly would, of course, have also been in a position to refute Hemingway's exaggerated story of his meeting with Orwell, and that is also possibly why Hemingway never published any version of the Orwell encounter. It is also intriguing that Connolly was on friendly terms with Harvey Breit, who could have passed on the details of Hemingway's 1952 letter to Connolly. The two critics corresponded and occasionally met when Breit was in London or Connolly was in New York, both men being cultural gatekeepers and clubbable intellectual journalists in their respective literary capitals.[55] There is no record of Breit ever telling anyone else about the Hemingway story, nor does any extant correspondence between Breit and Connolly relate to it. Here again, one must surmise that both critics dismissed the embroidered Hemingway account of 1952 as a typical act of Hemingway "faction."

Potts had a reputation for being a starry-eyed idealist, and he apotheosized Orwell in moral as well as literary terms. But the question remains: From whom did Potts get his information? Did Orwell ever mention to Potts a Paris meeting with Hemingway?

Yes, quite possibly so. Potts was unlikely to have gotten news of such an encounter from anyone else. Yet, of course, this does not exclude the possibility that Orwell also informed several of his other acquaintances about such a meeting. Why then didn't they ever write about it? Probably for a simple reason: it would have been much ado about nothing, because there was nothing to write about. It was a non-event not worth recording. Moreover, Connolly and Muggeridge (and possibly some of Orwell's other friends and acquaintances) had met Hemingway and his crowd themselves, and so they would not have been especially impressed about the mere fact that Orwell also had a brush with Hemingway for "a moment" in a Paris hotel.

Nonetheless, on the other side of the ledger, it should also be stressed: Potts did know Orwell personally. Apparently Orwell, whose circle of friends was wide and disparate, took a liking to (or took pity on) Potts, perhaps because he was shunned by so many people in the London literary scene. Potts spent time with Orwell in London and even visited

Did Papa Rescue St. George?

him on the isle of Jura, a sign of Orwell's favor. Crick quotes Potts's reminiscences extensively in his biography of Orwell. Crick calls Potts "a terrible liar and romancer," but he still regarded him as a useable source for Orwell's later life.[56] And not without good cause. For instance, unlike many of Orwell's closest friends, Crick noted, Potts knew that Orwell had written a never-published introduction to *Animal Farm* dealing with censorship that did not appear in print until 1972.

VI

If a final verdict cannot be delivered, we are nonetheless left with hunches and suspicions. Did Orwell and Hemingway meet as "Papa" recounts? Or was the encounter a product—wholly or in part—of Hemingway's desperate ego and Potts's urge to associate himself with a great man? And was Hemingway too perhaps seeking to associate himself with a writer whose fame was beginning to outstrip his own?

Ironically, Hemingway might indeed have met Eric Blair many years before his claimed encounter with Orwell in Paris. Until March 1928, Hemingway lived on the rue Férou in Paris, just a few blocks from Eric Blair. Just before Blair arrived there, perhaps Hemingway dined in the fashionable hotel on the rue de Rivoli where Orwell sweated out the day as a dishwasher. Surely Hemingway could have strolled many times past Hôpital Cochin, the pauper's hospital in the fourteenth arrondissment where Blair was treated for a sudden, potentially fatal outbreak of tuberculosis in early 1929. His experience there was the subject of his famous essay "How the Poor Die" (1946). Later, Orwell's first book, *Down and Out in Paris and London* (1933)—Orwell's own "fictional memoir"—recalled his months as a Parisian expatriate, a theme that Hemingway had memorably captured in *The Sun Also Rises* (1926)—and which he certainly lived out under conditions much different and more upscale than did Blair as an impoverished clochard.[57]

Ultimately lacking confirmation from other sources, we should remain wary: the evidence for the storied meeting is tenuous. Biographers and cultural historians should not report it uncritically and without comment. Although we cannot say with certitude that it did not take place, it leaves one with the impression of Hemingway and Potts as fellow colleagues of Winston Smith at the Ministry of Truth, happily engaged in "rectifying" the facts and rewriting literary history.

CHAPTER 12

Big Rock (Sugar)candy Mountain?

After Eric Blair returned from Paris in the spring of 1928, he began tramping that autumn through the metropolitan area of London and his native Southwold. Around that time, a traditional ballad that had been popular in the hobo world since the turn of the century received its first recording, sung by a hobo known as Haywire Mac, a.k.a. Harry McClintock. McClintock and other hobos in the United States and Europe had been singing the tune at least since the 1890s.[1] Originally, it described a child being recruited into hobo life by tales about "The Big Rock Candy Mountains." Such recruitment efforts, however amateurish, apparently did occur, with hobos enchanting poor children with fantastic "ghost tales" of wondrous adventures featuring hobo life.[2]

Did the future author of *Animal Farm* ever hear the song? Might its hobo vision have figured in Orwell's creation of Old Major's "Beasts of England" and Moses the raven's fraudulent Sugarcandy Mountain? This hobo ballad, which became known as "The Big Rock Candy Mountains"—even though the unsanitized version below was never published verbatim in any recordings[3]—runs as follows:

HARRY McCLINTOCK "Haywire Mac"

Recorded 1928-1931

The Great American Bum

One sunny day in the month of May,
A jocker he come hiking;
He come to a tree, and "Ah!" says he,
"This is just to my liking!"

Chorus:
"I'll show you the bees,
And the cigarette trees,
And the soda-water fountains,
And the lemonade springs
Where the bluebird sings
In the Big Rock Candy Mountains."

So they started away on the very same day,
The bum and the kid together,
To romp and to rove in the cigarette grove
In the land of sunny weather.

They dreamed and hiked for many days,
The mile posts they were countin',
But they never arrived at the lemonade tide
And the Big Rock Candy Mountains.

The Un(der)examined Orwell

The punk rolled up his big blue eyes
And said to the jocker, "Sandy,
I've hiked and hiked and wandered too,
But I ain't seen any candy.

I've hiked and hiked till my feet are sore
And I'll be damned if I hike any more
To be a homeguard with a lemonade card
In the Big Rock Candy Mountains."[4]

The lyrics of the last four stanzas in the best-known recorded version
of the ballad are as follows:[5]

In the Big Rock Candy Mountains there's a land
    that's fair and bright
Where the handouts grow on bushes and you sleep
    out every night
Where the boxcars are all empty and the sun shines
    every day
On the birds and the bees and the cigarette trees
In the lemonade springs where the bluebird sings
In the Big Rock Candy Mountains

In the Big Rock Candy Mountains all the cops have
    wooden legs
And the bulldogs all have rubber teeth and the hens
    lay soft-boiled eggs
The farmer's trees are full of fruit and the barns are
    full of hay
Oh, I'm bound to go where there ain't no snow
Where the rain don't fall and the wind don't blow
In the Big Rock Candy Mountains

In the Big Rock Candy Mountains you never change
    your socks
And the little streams of alcohol come a-trickling
    down the rocks
The brakemen have to tip their hats and the railroad
    bulls are blind
There's a lake of stew and of whiskey too
You can paddle all around 'em in a big canoe
In the Big Rock Candy Mountains

Big Rock (Sugar)candy Mountain?

In the Big Rock Candy Mountains the jails are made
    of tin
And you can walk right out again as soon as you are in
There ain't no short-handled shovels, no axes, saws
    or picks
I'm a-going to stay where you sleep all day
Where they hung the jerk that invented work
In the Big Rock Candy Mountains

The lyrics of "The Big Rock Candy Mountains" project a hobo's idea of utopia—a vagabond vision of paradise. The recorded song is a Depression-era vagrant's version of the medieval concept of Cockaigne, the land of milk and honey, for it speaks of trees on which cigarettes dangle like autumn leaves about to fall, of "streams of alcohol" trickling down through the rock crevices, and of a lake of whiskey which greets the always-parched pilgrim like an oasis amid a desert.

The vision of a "Big Rock Candy Mountain" does indeed sound like a contemporary analogue to the dream of a "land of cakes and ale" envisioned by the starving peasants of the Middle Ages. Cockaigne, which is often translated from Old English as the "Land of Cakes," featured rivers flowing with wine, streets paved with pastries, and houses built of sugarcane. As in a child's fairy tale, nothing in the shops of Cockaigne requires money to possess; everything is free. Even roasted geese waddle about in search of a welcoming human stomach eager to dine on them.

The homeless men who exchanged songs such as "The Big Rock Candy Mountains" lived in an epoch before the advent of social security or welfare programs. Their reveries about a land of milk and honey—or rather, a mountain ridge of whiskey and cigarettes—represented a form of shared fellowship, a dream of utopia where there would be rest and plenty for all. The song fit with their lifestyle and their street talk. They were accustomed to giving one another tips about the "way of the road" and exchanging tall tales. There was always news of the warmer shelter a few blocks away, the better soup kitchen down the street, or the more hospitable boarding house in the next town. So it was not such a leap for McClintock and others to rhapsodize about a hobo's Land of Oz just over the horizon, where handouts grew on bushes, luxurious railway cars traveled free of charge, and neither rain nor snow nor cold ever marred a hobo's day.

The Un(der)examined Orwell

Old Major, who represents a composite of Marx and Lenin in *Animal Farm*, had a "dream" of an animal paradise, whose description (in his animal hymn "Beasts of England") bears notable similarities with "The Big Rock Candy Mountains."

The most famous site dubbed "the Big Rock Candy Mountains" is located in Utah.

Big Rock (Sugar)candy Mountain?

I

Did Eric Blair ever hear the song "The Big Rock Candy Mountains" during his down-and-out days in 1928–1929? Or perhaps later? After all, he tramped intermittently in London's environs until October 1931. No trace of the song surfaces in his essays such as "Hop Picking" (1931) or in the published version of *Down and Out in Paris and London*, which appeared during the depths of the Depression in January 1933. Nor is there any mention in any of his correspondence that he heard it. His sole essay devoted to British music hall songs, which also refers to some American tunes, does not cite it.[6] Nor, finally, does Orwell's second literary notebook, which alludes to some American songs, refer to it.[7] Peter Davison observes: "As this was a personal notebook, an aide memoire, my guess is that had it served in any way as a source to 'Beasts of England,' it would have been listed."[8]

Nonetheless, as a cultural historian interested in Orwell's life and as a literary critic curious about the source material of his work, I've long wondered if he may indeed have known about the song and waited until the mid-1940s to find a place for it in his writings. Let us recall the ballad that Old Major teaches the barnyard animals shortly before his death, a venerable hymn which has been passed down through generations of pigs and which he calls "Beasts of England":

> Beasts of England, beasts of Ireland
> Beasts of every land and clime
> Hearken to my joyful tidings
> Of the golden future time.
>
> Soon or late the day is coming,
> Tyrant Man shall be o'erthrown,
> And the fruitful fields of England
> Shall be trod by beasts alone.
>
> Rings shall vanish from our noses,
> And the harness from our back,
> Bit and spur shall rust forever,
> Cruel whips no more shall crack.
>
> Riches more than mind can picture,
> Wheat and barley, oats and hay,
> Clover, beans, and mangel-wurzels
> Shall be ours upon that day.

The Un(der)examined Orwell

Bright will shine the fields of England,
Purer shall its waters be,
Sweeter yet shall blow its breezes
On the day that sets us free.

For that day we all must labour,
Though we die before its break;
Cows and horses, geese and turkeys,
All must toil for freedom's sake.

Beasts of England, beasts of Ireland,
Beasts of every land and clime,
Hearken well and spread my tidings
Of the golden future time.[9]

"Beasts of England" has a comical element apparent not just in its lyrics but also in its melody. Orwell writes that although Old Major's voice was "hoarse," the song possesses "a stirring tune, something between the 'Clementine' and 'La Cucaracha.'" But "Beasts of England" is also quite serious, and its seriousness is arguably heightened in a sense unknown in Orwell's day, when there were no worldwide animal rights' campaigns or ready accusations of "species-ism." "Beasts of England" is an animal's utopian "dream" of Cockaigne: "a dream of the earth as it will be when Man has vanished." As Old Major announces to the animals collectively assembled in Farmer Jones's barnyard:

And now, comrades, I will tell you about my dream of last night. I cannot describe that dream to you. It was a dream of the earth as it will be when Man has vanished. But it reminded me of something that I had long forgotten. Many years ago, when I was a little pig, my mother and the other sows used to sing an old song of which they knew only the tune and the first three words. I had known that tune in my infancy, but it had long since passed out of my mind. Last night, however, it came back to me in my dream. And what is more, the words of the song also came back—words, I am certain, which were sung by the animals of long ago and have been lost to memory for generations. I will sing you that song now, comrades.[10]

Big Rock (Sugar)candy Mountain?

To put my question quite pointedly: Is it possible that in the late 1920s or early 1930s Eric Blair was, as it were, "tramping toward *Animal Farm*"? Quite possibly so. After all, the name Sugarcandy Mountain seems rather transparently to echo Big Rock Candy Mountain. Is the near-repetition mere coincidence? Also notable is the punk's complaints, "I ain't seen any candy" and "I'll be damned if I'll hike any more," both of which lines recall the swindle[11] of religion as "pie in the sky" that Sugarcandy Mountain in *Animal Farm* signifies. Orwell is quite explicit that Sugarcandy Mountain, as preached incessantly by Moses the raven, is another false Cockaigne, another "golden future time," as it were, that merely serves to reconcile the barnyard animals to their dismal fate under the pigs. If the pigs' "Animalism," a.k.a. Marxism-Leninism, is a false secular religion, Moses's Sugarcandy Mountain represents ersatz religion itself.

We are told that Moses "would perch on a stump, flap his black wings, and talk by the hour to anyone who would listen." On Manor Farm, he was "hated" by the other animals because he was Jones's "especial pet," "did no work," and was known to be "a spy," "a tale bearer," and "a clever talker."[12] He has changed his masters but not his mien on Animal Farm. His hypocritical sermon never varies: "'Up there, comrades,' he would say solemnly, pointing to the sky with his large beak—'up there, just on the other side of that dark cloud that you can see—there it lies, Sugarcandy Mountain, that happy country where we poor animals shall rest forever from our labours!'"

Orwell notes that the pigs tolerate Moses—that is, the Church—because they realize how effectively religious belief can suppress rebellion and even discontent, just as Stalin permitted the public return of the Russian Orthodox clergy because he realized that he could exploit the Church for his own purposes.[13] (The name "Moses" is well-chosen, for it covers both the Russian Orthodox and Catholic churches [and Judaism as well]: the raven brings divine law to the animals just as the historical Moses delivered it to the Israelites.)[14] Orwell's satirical edge is sharp, with the allegorical correspondences between the barnyard events and Soviet history brilliantly inventive and cleverly formulated:[15]

In the middle of the summer Moses the raven suddenly reappeared on the farm, after an absence of several years. He was quite unchanged, still did no work, and talked in the same strain as ever about Sugarcandy Mountain. . . . He even claimed to have been there on one of his higher flights, and to have seen the everlasting fields of clover and linseed cake and lump sugar growing on the hedges. Many of the animals believed him. Their lives now, they reasoned, were hungry and laborious; was it not right and just that a better world should exist somewhere else? A thing that was difficult to determine was the attitude of the pigs toward Moses. They all declared contemptuously that his stories about Sugarcandy Mountain were lies, and yet they allowed him to remain on the farm, not working, with an allowance of a gill of beer a day.[16]

Obviously, "Beasts of England" and Sugarcandy Mountain were closely linked in Orwell's mind as secular and religious utopias, respectively. So it is unsurprising that reverberations from "The Big Rock Candy Mountains" are discernible in both of them. Sugarcandy Mountain is also an animal vision of heaven, that "happy country where we poor animals should rest forever from our labours!" It too is a vision of Cockaigne, blessed with "everlasting fields of clover." It too is a "Land of Cakes," consisting of "linseed cake and lump sugar growing on the hedges." Whereas "Beasts of England," the official hymn of "Animalism," is based on the stirring lyrics of "L'Internationale," Sugarcandy Mountain is the celestial paradise of the Russian Orthodox Church.[17] "Beasts of England" projects an animal vision of heaven, an "animaltopia" in which "all animals are equal." It is the utopia of "four legs good."

Of course, the verbal echo between "The Big Rock Candy Mountains" and Orwell's Sugarcandy Mountain is obvious and direct. Nonetheless, while it is plausible that Orwell borrowed from the title of the popular song—indeed, that he meant to draw a clear allusion to the ballad—neither circumstance would necessarily require him to have been familiar with an oral version from the hobo/tramp subculture. The folkloric motif of the Land of Plenty is so widespread that claims of one particular text directly influencing another are unsupportable without close, extensive parallels, which do not exist in this particular case.[18] Still, the foregoing analysis suggests that whereas Old Major's "dream" and Moses's "higher flights" ultimately derive from a vision of Cockaigne, "The Big Rock Candy Mountains" may represent an immediate source that furnishes some of their concrete imagery and motifs. (One English friend reminds me that in British English "sweets" = "candy." "Candy" is usually regarded as an Americanism for sugar-based confections, which would support the notion of an American source for the raven's ersatz Elysium.)[19]

Did Orwell, however deliberately or unconsciously, draw on "The

Big Rock (Sugar)candy Mountain?

Big Rock Candy Mountains" and freely distribute some of its details into the lines of both "Beasts of England" and Moses's speech? Perhaps. It is known that the endlessly quoted, culminating line in *Animal Farm* was a borrowing from a throwaway sentence in Philip Guedalla's "A Russian Fairy Tale," an anti-Soviet fable published in 1930. Guedalla wrote that there was a good Fairy "who believed that all fairies were equal before the law, but held strongly that some fairies were more equal than others."[20] Significantly, *Animal Farm* is subtitled "A Fairy Story." To cite these facts is not to discredit Orwell, but rather to note that he had no qualms about engaging in some casual borrowings and never mentioning it. So it's quite plausible that he may have done the same with McClintock's "The Big Rock Candy Mountains."

All this is, however, merely circumstantial evidence. Nowhere does Orwell explicitly acknowledge a source for Sugarcandy Mountain (or "Beasts of England"). This does not imply that Orwell plagiarized "The Big Rock Candy Mountains,"[21] or even that he "failed" to acknowledge his source—no more than in the case of his obvious debt to "L'Internationale," which also goes unmentioned throughout his oeuvre. Rather, it is simply to ask whether another one of the heretofore overlooked allegorical correspondences within Orwell's beast fable is "The Big Rock Candy Mountains." After all, Orwell's beast fable *is* an allegory. So even if we do not insist that "The Big Rock Candy Mountains" is a literary source for "Beasts of England" or Sugarcandy Mountain, we can draw attention to the similarities between the two because the parallels are certainly uncanny.

III

The fable is, yes, an "animallegory." But *is* it anything more than a case of uncanny parallels? Aside from these tantalizing tidbits—which consist of plausible biographical scenarios of Blair's tramping days, of lyrical resonances between McClintock's song and Old Major's beast hymn, of echoes between the hobo song and Moses's rhetorical flights, and of the obvious repetition of the "candy mountain" image—does any firm evidence exist that Blair/Orwell ever heard "The Big Rock Candy Mountains" or knew that McClintock's Vagabond Valhalla had, as it were, materialized in late 1928 in the hills of Utah?[22]

As it turns out, one obscure, buried remark in a forgotten book review suggests that Orwell probably did have the hobo song in mind. In a

The Un(der)examined Orwell

little-known, four-sentence review of *Corn on the Cob*, a book of popular American ballads edited by A. L. Lloyd,[23] Orwell writes:

> *Corn on the Cob* is unreasonably expensive but it is pleasant to be able to get hold of full versions of such half-known songs as "Frankie and Johnny" or "The Big Rock Candy Mountains."[24]

That single reference establishes that Orwell was familiar with "The Big Rock Candy Mountains" some time before the appearance of this brief notice in the *Manchester Evening News* in November 1945—that is, quite likely before *Animal Farm*'s publication in August 1945. Of course, in context the allusion is sardonic: Sugarcandy Mountain clearly represents religion as the "opiate of the masses." Given that the lyrics of "Beasts of England" also reverberate with the echoes of "The Big Rock Candy Mountains," Orwell was arguably contending that socialist utopianism is no less an opiate than religion: both promise "pie in the sky" at some indefinite future date, and both promises are empty. And that suggests that the satirical point of *Animal Farm* is not merely that the Soviets betrayed their own revolution, but that all revolutions are ultimately frauds.[25]

A. L. Lloyd was a pioneering figure in British folk music, both as a collector of lost or forgotten folksongs and as a performer in his own right. Lloyd was also a vocal Stalinist who was blacklisted by the BBC and other organizations, though he worked briefly at the BBC during World War II around the same time that Orwell was a broadcaster there. Apparently the two men never met, though they also shared a deep interest in the suffering of British coal miners.

Big Rock (Sugar)candy Mountain?

So perhaps Eric Blair *was* "tramping toward *Animal Farm*" in his late twenties. (Notably, the Paris section of *Down and Out* contains passages in which Orwell compares the *plongeur* to a caged animal.) Might we also then speak of "Beasts of Utah"?!

Maybe. All we can say with confidence is that there are striking similarities (verbal, functional, ideological) between the hobo ballad and the utopian visions of Old Major and Moses. The evidence is sufficiently strong to show that Orwell was aware of the existence of "The Big Rock Candy Mountains," but that fact does not establish that the song was definitely a source for the utopian images in Orwell's fable. Nor can we claim on the basis of firm evidence that the similarities between Old Major's and Moses's utopian visions can be traced back to a common source in the hobo song.

Nonetheless, we can be sure that Orwell was familiar with the ballad, a fact that makes the numerous parallels that we have been discussing not just interesting but quite compelling. The scope and richness of these parallels fall short of representing sufficient proof to support a case for the ballad as a key source in *Animal Farm*. Yet they do furnish us with intriguing evidence that reframes our perspective on parts of Orwell's fable; that is, they form the constituent parts of a new and hitherto unexplored context in which to explore the veiled biographical background of *Animal Farm* and, by implication, the relation between Blair's personal experience and Orwell's literary craft.

On that basis, we might inquire into other, more speculative possibilities about the relation between "The Big Rock Candy Mountains" and *Animal Farm*. For instance, might Orwell have heard the famous recording of the song released by Burl Ives in early 1949? Again, no evidence exists for the possibility, but the conjecture raises a number of other fascinating questions. Much admired for his genial style and gentle nature, Ives was a well-known musical film actor and folk singer already widely celebrated for his recording of "On Top of Old Smokey." He was a family entertainer who was quite popular with children.

So let us—with all the aforementioned caveats about premature conclusions and tenuous, speculative claims in mind—give our imaginations free rein for a moment. If the author of *Animal Farm* and *Down and Out* ever did hear Ives's recording of "The Big Rock Candy Mountains"— which was a hit tune frequently played on the radio in 1949–1950—he must have smiled. Orwell would have immediately recognized that Ives, as if he were a benign Squealer altering "The Seven Commandments of Animalism" with a few swabs of his paintbrush, proceeds to whitewash the hobo hymn of its racier street slang and hobo underworld coloration.

Burl Ives, beloved crooner of American songs. One of his biggest hits was his version of "The Big Rock Candy Mountains."

Ives, who had a seemly image of a homey, upright, simple-hearted folk singer to protect, released his "uncolorized" version of "The Big Rock Candy Mountains" in which the "cigarette trees" become peppermint trees, the "streams of alcohol" become streams of lemonade, the lake of gin goes unmentioned, and the "lake of stew and whiskey" becomes a lake of soda pop.[26]

Orwell had just completed *Nineteen Eighty-Four* in early 1949. If he chanced to hear Ives's rendition, surely he would have had a good chuckle about the way in which the original ballad of his tramping days had gone "down the memory hole." It had been "rectified" by the music industry, which realized that a wholesome entertainer such as Burl Ives would never succeed with a song that advocated "cigarette trees" and "streams of alcohol." The sanitized version of "The Big Rock Candy Mountains" would probably have struck Orwell as a tame analogue to Winston Smith's "rectifications" at "*Minitrue*"—or better, to Squealer's blasphemous tamperings with Animalism's commandments, culminating in his reconstruction of the Seventh Commandment: "All animals are equal, but some are more equal than others."

Given that during 1943–1945 Orwell was still serving as literary editor of *Tribune*, where he received review copies of dozens of books every week, it is also quite possible that he ran across Wallace Stegner's novel *The Big Rock Candy Mountain*, published in late 1943—just when Orwell was intensively working on *Animal Farm*. If so, perhaps the timing

Big Rock (Sugar)candy Mountain?

Wallace Stegner, the distinguished American writer, wrote *The Big Rock Candy Mountain* (1943), which Orwell may have come across during his editorship at *Tribune*. Stegner's novel also appeared in a special wartime edition for U.S. Army and Navy personnel.

The Un(der)examined Orwell

of Stegner's novel prompted Orwell to consider the name "Sugarcandy Mountain" or even influenced some of the lines in "Beasts of England." No evidence exists to support that possibility, no more so than for our conjecture that Orwell might have heard Burl Ives's version of the hobo song sometime during the lonely months when he lay in the hospital in 1949–1950. Significantly, however, Stegner's novel also describes a Cockaigne, the American West: a brave New World, a mecca of opportunity where people could remake their lives and discover gold mines. The novel both captured and contributed to the legend of the American West, a myth of boundless freedom and endless possibility, an always expanding frontier in which citizens—as well as the United States itself—could realize their manifest destinies. But that myth is also tragically hollow, just as fully a mirage as a rock candy mountain.[27] (Shortly before his death, Stegner also published an essay collection for which the hobo song provided the title: *Where the Bluebird Sings to the Lemonade Springs: Living and Writing in the West* [1992].)[28]

IV

How and when did Blair/Orwell first hear—or hear about—"The Big Rock Candy Mountains"? We do not know. That question turns on other questions. Was some traditional, oral version of the ballad in circulation in England in the late nineteenth century? How much transatlantic borrowing existed in the Anglophone hobo subcultures?[29] I can find no firm evidence that the song was known or unknown in Britain, either at the time of Jack London's tramping at the turn of the century or later.

I cannot establish when Blair/Orwell might have encountered "The Big Rock Candy Mountains." Most likely it occurred on one of his tramping expeditions. At least one of these down-and-out experiments even predated his underclass submersions during 1928–1930. The first of his letters in the four volumes of his *Collected Essays, Journalism and Letters (CEJL)*, written in the summer of 1920 when he was seventeen and still a student at Eton, begins: "I have a little spare time, & feel I *must* tell you about my first adventure as an amateur tramp. Like most tramps, I was driven to it." He proceeds to recount how, while returning to his family's summer home, he missed a train and had to spend the night in a farmer's field. The letter ends: "I am very proud of this adventure, but I would not repeat it" (*CEJL* 1: 11–12). It is possible that on this sortie, or

239

Big Rock (Sugar)candy Mountain?

Jack London tramped throughout London's impoverished East End almost three decades before Eric Blair did on many of the same streets. Jack London published the story of his experience in *The People of the Abyss* (1903), a book that Blair/Orwell esteemed highly. London was a prominent influence on Orwell in other matters too, particularly in Orwell's evolving attitudes toward totalitarianism.

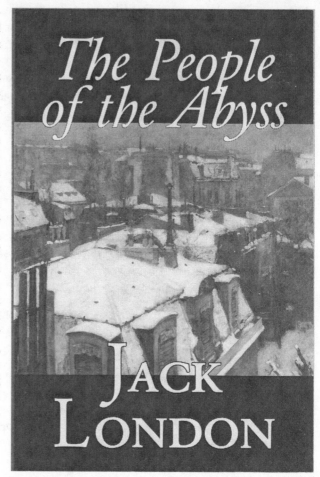

The People of the Abyss

JACK LONDON

in conversation with his friends and classmates who expressed interest in his "adventures," that Eric Blair might have heard about "The Big Rock Candy Mountains" even before Haywire Mac's 1928 recording.[30]

More probable, however, is that Blair became familiar with the hobo song sometime between 1928 and 1932 in the course of his periodic immersions in the tramping underworld.[31] Beginning in October 1928 and continuing intermittently until he finished *Down and Out* in late 1932, he shared the hard existence of the down-and-outers for periods ranging from a single night to a full month.

At first Blair immersed himself in the severe poverty of the East End of London, putting on a tramping outfit as Jack London had done and wandering among the indigent.[32] Blair's conception of being a tramp was essentially a visual one. He had found that clothes do indeed *un-*

make the man, and he had a regular tramp outfit, which was no more than some old rags that he kept at his cousin's apartment:

> He kept a suitcase of ancient clothes at Ruth Pitter's for the purpose—and disappeared into the streets. A day or two later (sometimes longer) with a minimum of explanation as to where he had been and what he had seen and done, he would reappear, bathe, change clothes, become Eric Blair again. As Blair he would spend a bit more time in London, going out to dinner with Miss Pitter, dropping in for a cup of tea over the gas fire at the *Adelphi* office in Bloomsbury Street, staying overnight with the Fierzes, before returning to Southwold and continuing with his book. . . . At a friend's house he prepared his clothes, dirtied them, made them authentic-seeming (it is all a little too artful and self-conscious, and so differs radically from the involuntary first experiences that are thrust upon "I" when he arrives in London in *Down and Out*). Then, in his careful disguise he wandered through the East End, and came at last to a common lodging house in Limehouse. He was afraid to go inside, fearful of the working-class denizens of the place, so brutal and threatening as they must seem in the fantasies of any member of his class: what if they should recognize the Etonian under the rags and do violence to him? The image that occurs to him as he stands outside is of entering "a sewer full of rats." But eventually he screwed up his courage and went through the doorway and down the dark passage to the communal kitchen. There a drunken young stevedore was reeling about. He lurched toward Blair, who stiffened in his rags, readying himself for the violence he expected to come next. But instead, the stevedore offered him a cup of tea—that English communion—and called him "chum." He felt it was a baptism.[33]

Soon Blair began to write up his experiences. D. J. Taylor observes: "It is doubtful that there was a clear literary purpose in his mind during his early trips to the East End. He seems to have had only a vague desire to collect information for a book without really knowing whether he would put it to use in a novel, a book of short stories, a series of essays, or a long autobiographical report."[34] Nonetheless, after moving to Paris in January 1929, Blair published his first articles: "A Day in the Life of a Tramp" and "The Beggars of London" in *Progrès Civic*, a French newspaper.[35] He told his literary agent L. I. Bailey a month later that he had a book on "Tramps and Beggars" in preparation. That December *Adelphi* accepted "The Spike." (The term was tramp slang for cheap lodgings

Big Rock (Sugar)candy Mountain?

for transients.) Throughout this period Blair was still working on a draft of *Down and Out* (under the title "A Scullion's Diary") and tramping occasionally in London and its environs.[36]

Of course, Blair was never really down and out. He could always rely on his parents for help and often returned home to them (or to friends and relatives such as Ruth Pitter) after a night in the abyss. In Paris, his Aunt Nellie was always available in an emergency (though he never seems to have asked for her assistance.) Blair *was* at times penniless, but he was never without a means of extricating himself from poverty, or just getting a hot meal and a warm bath. As Peter Stansky and William Abrahams note in *The Unknown Orwell*, after Blair returned from Paris and resumed his tramping in and around London during autumn 1930, he developed a pattern that alternated tramping excursions with literary activity, all of it designed to support his goal of becoming a writer: "At this point, from the autumn of 1930, an extraordinary, fluctuating pattern of down-and-out writing and living was inaugurated—comfortable Southwold for the manuscript, poverty-stricken London for the experience, the two interacting and alternating until the book had been lived and written."[37] As Stansky and Abrahams explain, Blair had "no schedules, no fixed periods decided upon in advance—so much time allotted for Southwold, so much for London—and he was more often and longer in Queen Street, writing, than he was in London going down and out. But when he wanted to go down and out, he did."[38]

In August 1931, Blair undertook his longest tramping expedition, which included a stint in Trafalgar Square followed by piecework employment in the Kent hop fields for a month. (A few weeks later, he published "Hop Picking" in the *New Statesman and Nation*.) The publication of *Down and Out in Paris and London* in January 1933 represented the fulfillment and endpoint in his samplings of life in the abyss. Eric Blair's self-imposed expeditions among the wretched were over; the author George Orwell had emerged. The search for a literary subject had resulted in the discovery of a literary vocation. Blair the tramp would be fully replaced—and partially effaced—by Orwell the writer.[39]

In *Down and Out*, Orwell is sympathetic yet critical of the tramps whom he meets. Paddy Jacques is a "good fellow," yet "he had the regular character of a tramp—abject, envious, a jackal's character." But Orwell allows that "it was malnutrition and not any native vice that destroyed his manhood." Likewise, beggars are not people who have "sold their honour" but merely lost souls who have "made the mistake of choosing a trade at which it is impossible to grow rich." Bozo the pavement artist is lame, but he is "an exceptional man" who watches for meteors and

The Un(der)examined Orwell

believes that "rich or poor, all was well as long as one could say 'I'm a free man in *here*,'" that is, in the mind.

However deluded or even preposterous, Bozo's sentiment captures well a fundamental conviction in the hobo world[40]—and one that Blair/ Orwell shared during his jauntier moments on the road, such as in "Hop Picking." And Bozo's sense of freedom—the insistence on doing his Orwell-like "as I please" regardless of the physical and emotional hardships that it may entail—is immortalized in the closing lines of "The Big Rock Candy Mountains":

> I'm a-going to stay where you sleep all day
> Where they hung the jerk that invented work
> In the Big Rock Candy Mountains.

Orwell made his living as a political journalist and book reviewer until the popular success of *Animal Farm* in 1945–1946. He developed a limpid, straightforward prose style that has exerted enormous influence on writers and journalists of the last six decades. Although the widely anthologized "Politics and the English Language" is often taught in introductory college composition classes, Orwell originally wrote it as a prose guide for fellow journalists on the staff of the London *Observer*, published by Orwell's friend David Astor.

NATIONAL UNION OF JOURNALISTS

7 John Street, Bedford Row, London, W.C.1

'Phone: HOLborn 2258

Telegrams: Natujay Holb, London

This is to certify that

Mr. GEORGE ORWELL

of The Tribune

is a member of the I. + P. Branch of the National Union of Journalists.

Leslia R. Aldous Branch Sec.

(Address) 66, Priory Gans., N.6.

Member's Sig.

Chapter 13

Literacy and the English Language

Pedagogy is a practical art, and it may be that other teachers have had more success in freshman English composition courses with Orwell's "Politics and the English Language" (1946) than I've had. Yet my reflections here draw not only on my own difficulties with the essay, but also on those of other rhetoric instructors as well as the frustrations of several of my colleagues at the University of Virginia and the University of Texas at Austin.[1] I am convinced that the problem lies not so much with Orwell as with the preparation of our students. But the problem also does, to some extent, lie with Orwell's essay, and even more so with the expectations we teachers have of it and the uses we try to make of it.

Let me address the latter problem first: our varieties of pedagogical experience with the essay. We might profitably assign Orwell's essay for diverse reasons: to promote cultural literacy (it is a justly famous essay),[2] to foster critical thinking, to introduce the plain style, to heighten awareness of euphemism and jargon, to clarify the interconnections between politics and language. Still, none of these uses implies that Orwell's essay is one from which most beginning students are likely to learn how to write better.

And that observation is central to my mixed experience with "Politics and the English Language": I question its suitability as a model for beginning students. We need to distinguish between a fine *essay* and an exemplary student *prose model*. The fact is that the status of "Politics and the English Language" as probably the most widely anthologized essay in beginning composition readers and the most frequently assigned essay in beginning composition classes has much to do with the dynamics of reputation-building and canon formation, which may only bear indirectly on the merits of the essay for any particular task.

I have found that "Politics and the English Language" does not represent an exemplary prose model for beginning and remedial students, though it serves advanced students admirably. Exemplary prose models should be sufficiently accessible to allow readers to imitate the author's writing strategies and to identify with his or her writing situation.

I

The other difficulty with "Politics and the English Language" pertains to the essay itself. I find that it offers advice that may undermine, rather than nurture, beginning students' developing skills.

Take, for instance, Orwell's advice to avoid clichés. "Politics and the English Language" closes with a plea to "send some worn-out and useless phrase—some *jackboot, Achilles heel, hotbed, melting pot, acid test, veritable inferno*, or other lump of verbal refuse—into the dustbin where it belongs." This is invaluable counsel for the more advanced student. But I have found that beginning students don't know that these phrases are worn out—or, sometimes, even what these phrases (or individual words within them) mean.

It is not enough to say, "Well, go ahead and tell them!" Or to say, "Then let them look it up!" No, the problem runs much deeper. In the case of many beginning students who are just entering the academic environment, we are asking too much all at once. Before we burden these students with anxieties about improper usage or the political dangers posed by invoking dying metaphors, we might first encourage these students to play with clichés, to use them (at least in the first month of class) as freely as they wish. Perhaps this experiment would be best handled in nongraded assignments. Thereafter, within limits, we should let them discover how clichés become clichés through overuse. Let them learn for themselves how metaphors tire and die. Let *them* wear them, and let

The Un(der)examined Orwell

them wear them *out*! I have found that, in the course of a semester, beginning students are naturally led to parody the clichés.

II

"Literacy and the English Language" should precede "Politics and the English Language." Not in scale of values, but in point of time. The two are, roughly and in most cases, distinguishable. What Orwell called in "Why I Write" his childlike, irrepressible "joy of mere words" came long before his mature control over the language. Similarly, our students' apprenticeship to literary culture will probably come in stages, as it did for most of us. Orwell assumed in "Politics and the English Language" that his readers knew how to write—if badly. Many of our beginning and remedial students do not know how to write at all. Only after their styles have achieved some level of complexity need we worry overmuch about simplifying them.

For Orwell's "simple" style does not seem simple to them at all. And indeed it is not. As with *Animal Farm*, the plain style of "Politics and the English Language" masks an intricate art of argumentation. Orwell's apparently casual, conversational style projects a plain-man populism that enabled an intellectual to speak as a common man. It is a writing strategy that demands consummate mastery of the language.

Other bits of Orwell's advice in his essay are, I think, also unhelpful for beginning students. Consider, for instance, Orwell's injunction to use short words and to cut unnecessary words. Some of us take such an exhortation as self-evidently, indubitably *right*. But what may aid us in our writing—and perhaps assist our more advanced students—may hamper the progress of beginning and remedial students. Many of them have severely limited lexicons and can't even meet word limits. Rather than issue them too many cautions about verbosity and diffuseness, we might foster in them a linguistic exuberance. Let them first discover and exult in "the joy of mere words"! We could invite those students with small vocabularies, yes, *to be wordy*—and embolden them to go to the dictionary or thesaurus and then experiment with the bounty they discover. (I can verify that this is an excellent way to master a foreign language, and I am sure it also applies to first-language acquisition.) The "joy of mere words" will lead some students, for a time, down the Path of Prolixity. That is fine. As they learn the nuances of their language, they will experience what Orwell calls "aesthetic enthusiasm," the thrills of euphony and exquisiteness. As Orwell knew, the controls of clarity and simplicity can follow.

I realize that these views are a bit quirky. But the student composition is a special academic genre. For the specific task of writing a student essay, it will generally benefit students to have exemplary student prose models rather than to read a classic essay like Orwell's. So my own specific advice amounts to the following.

Do assign "Politics and the English Language" to beginning students if your aim in a particular unit is chiefly social or analytical—that is, to promote cultural literacy or critical thinking, or to present the plain style, or to discuss the niceties of good versus bad usage. But choose another prose model if your aims are, in the narrower sense, mainly rhetorical—that is, to improve the skills of beginning student writers by providing writing models for imitation.

Moreover, be willing to experiment and *see what works*—and what doesn't. For instance, instead of a global, deductive approach to essay writing featuring the presentation of pedagogical guides or literary models such as "Politics and the English Language," with its famous "six rules" for good prose, try a modest, step-by-step, "building blocks" method. Such a "bottom-up," gradualist process is how beginners learn a foreign language—and the skills needed to advance in introductory composition courses (or "remedial" writing classes) may indeed resemble the task of second language acquisition, precisely because they are *writing* courses. The students may be "native *speakers*," but they are not "native *writers*."

So why not first simply teach students what a good sentence looks like? Then proceed to help them write a model paragraph governed by a topic sentence, followed by several pertinent sentences in the body, and a concluding sentence; then assign a short essay made up of such paragraphs, and finally a longer essay. Emphasize the value of patient craftsmanship, of the need to flex and develop the "writing muscle," of literary composition as *process*. Remind them that the prose models that they read in class—and virtually all published work—did not emerge full-blown in the finished form that they are encountering it. Usually it went through a lengthy gestation process. In fact, Orwell himself was known to revise his novels and major essays up to twenty or thirty times before he was satisfied with them. Other leading writers have done the same. It is often intimidating, not just for a beginning writer but even for an established professional, to look at his or her first or second drafts and compare them to a polished classic such as "Politics and the English

The Un(der)examined Orwell

Language." Usually such comparisons serve no good at all: they do a disservice to the reader who feels inferior and gets depressed, and they represent an injustice to the author being read by ignoring or downplaying the arduous labor invested in his or her work.

The kind of experimentation in the introductory composition class that I am suggesting here should be ad hoc and a matter of trial and error. Its virtue as a pedagogy, however, is that it is quite flexible: it is tentative, provisional, and revisable. As a philosophy of composition, even if a very loose one, its maxims consist of practical advice. For instance, stress to the students the importance of formulating what they want to say before rushing to commit their thoughts to paper, but balance that counsel with this reminder: there are very few good writers; there can be good *re*writers galore. Consider showing the students the early drafts of established writers who struggled to find their literary voices and produce finished pieces of work. (Mention that Orwell himself spent more than five years struggling "to be a writer" and during that time destroyed at least two novels and several short stories.) Letting the students inspect writing drafts, rather than read published work exclusively, reduces the likelihood of their discouragement from inadvertent comparisons with professional quality prose. If the teacher later shows the class the published work that emerged from the early drafts, it demonstrates convincingly how a piece of writing can be transformed in the course of the revision process.

So don't recoil from sharing burnished examples of expository prose, whether in the form of journalism or essays. Such models of clear, straightforward argument help student readers recognize what such an argument looks like. Rather, offer such exemplary prose with the caveats already voiced and with gentle reminders about the need to develop the writing muscle and respect the writing process. All this will enable student readers to appreciate better what good prose style and cogent argument require—and thereby assist them in their quest to achieve the same in their own literary endeavors.

III

Some composition instructors also view "Politics and the English Language" as "a key to understanding *Animal Farm*" because "the victim animals allow the pigs to fool them through the misuse of language." Replying to an essay of mine on the use of Orwell's work in English literature and composition courses, a contributor to *College English* writes:

> The other animals should not have been fooled by the pigs' rationalizations but should have insisted upon equality. In other words, they should have been able to analyze the pigs' political language and stopped the corruption of the revolution at its beginning. An even more serious error in judgment is the lack of attention paid to Napoleon's secret training of the puppies, paralleling Lenin's establishment of the secret police. Even the super-intelligent Snowball, caught up in his projects, does not see the threat.

The contributor goes on to elaborate how she teaches the "theme" of Orwell's fable:

> The motto, "The price of liberty is eternal vigilance," is certainly appropriate here, as is Lord Acton's famous dictum "Power tends to corrupt." Why Rodden calls this a "bromide" is a puzzle to me. . . . This theme in *Animal Farm*, far from being a platitude, is a profound truth that ought to be taken seriously. Just ask anybody who has survived totalitarian rule in Europe—or Asia, or South America.

I do agree that Squealer's rhetorical sleights of hand (quite literally with his paintbrush) applied to the Seven Commandments of Animalism—which exemplify the pigs' clever, cynical manipulation of language throughout the fable—facilitate the destruction of the revolution. I also concur that the barnyard animals would have benefited from Orwell's advice in "Politics and the English Language." Yet the application of Lord Acton's dictum to *Animal Farm* is problematic. "Power corrupts" *is* just a "bromide" if it is treated as the "theme" of *Animal Farm*. It is a platitude if that high level of generality is the stopping point for analysis, especially if this pronouncement arrives tacked on to a reading of *Animal Farm*, presenting it as an entertaining story and downplaying the Russian parallels. These parallels are quite specific and unmistakable. *Animal Farm* is a fable *and* an allegory.

Furthermore, dare I ask: Is Lord Acton's apothegm a "profound truth"? Although I have enormous respect for the victims of totalitarian suffering—as reflected in my stories about the Orwellian ordeals of East Germans in Part 2 of this book—I do not think it is persuasive to reply: "Just ask anybody who has survived totalitarian rule in Europe—or Asia, or South America."

The Un(der)examined Orwell

Is "power corrupts" a "profound truth"? Or *was* it? Before, that is, it became something close to one of those worn-out and useless phrases that Orwell rails against in his essay, such as "Achilles heel" or "veritable inferno"? Yes, what would the author of "Politics and the English Language" say about Lord Acton's statement—"if Orwell were alive today?" (to cite yet again a running leitmotif of this study that has itself degenerated into a near-cliché).

I'm not sure. Yet I believe that, as applied to *Animal Farm*, this kind of thinking—treating *Animal Farm* as if it were one of Aesop's fables and affixing a moral (or "profound truth") to it—is worrisome. For it elides the fable's historical correspondences, as if *Animal Farm* were first a general commentary on the corruptions of totalitarian power ("in Europe—or Asia, or South America") rather than, quite specifically, an allegorical fable about postrevolutionary Russian Stalinism.

A historical case in point: At the height of the Cold War, the 1954 film adaptation of *Animal Farm* obscured or deleted many of the historical and biographical correspondences, casting it instead as a general warning on the theme of "power corrupts" and against collectivist experiments, leader worship, and revolutionary dogmatism. This led some film reviewers (who probably hadn't read the book) to interpret it as a direct attack on Nazism or on the British welfare state—precisely what Orwell hoped to avoid by making the allegory so explicit.[3]

Here again, we see the importance of "literacy and the English language," but in a slightly different sense than with Orwell's much celebrated essay. Now we are addressing the issue of *cultural* literacy. Yet the overall point remains the same: "Literacy and the English language" must precede "Politics and the English language"—again not in scale of values, but in point of time. For instance, readers of *Animal Farm* in the 1950s who were not familiar with the major events and personalities of the Russian Revolution and its aftermath could have easily misread *Animal Farm* as a universal critique of power or as a satire of their immediate present in the 1950s. As any teacher today knows very well, the problem has only increased in our own era. I can testify from my own experience in the classroom, both at the secondary school and undergraduate levels, that countless students now read *Animal Farm* as an amusing story and have only the vaguest idea that it is a precisely written, satirical allegory of the rise of Bolshevism. (Sad to say, many secondary school teachers also lack the cultural and historical literacy to place the fable in a rich historical context and explain its detailed correspondences with developments in the early twentieth century.) The challenge is exacerbated

Literacy and the English Language

by the fact that many students will view the 1999 film—or perhaps even the 1954 film—and never bother to read Orwell's book. Of course, this is often the case with contemporary docudramas that bring events of the past to the screen, and it is an ever-increasing, worrisome development when it also occurs with the classics, whether the work be a magnificent tragedy such as *Hamlet* or a little literary gem such as *Animal Farm*.

CHAPTER 14

George Orwell,
Literary Theorist?

Orwell had little patience with literary theory, let alone high-flown philosophical speculation or linguistic analysis. He famously dismissed Jean Paul Sartre as "a bag of wind," and though he admired the novels of Albert Camus, he disparaged existentialism as "a charade." Orwell befriended A. J. ("Freddie") Ayer, yet evidently never discussed any philosophical topic with the founder of logical positivism. Temperamentally empirical-minded and self-admittedly imbued with "a love of concrete things," he showed no interest in academic discussion about Victorian or Russian literature when he corresponded with a Dickens specialist and a professor of Russian, respectively. Doubtless Orwell, if he had lived to hear the term "theory" incessantly blared in literary discussions, would have reached for his revolver.

Orwell was, however, a master rhetorician. He intuitively grasped the art of polemic and the craft of storytelling, and he knew how to combine them: he could make a story tell a powerful argument. *Animal Farm* and *Nineteen Eighty-Four* are two famous "didactic fantasies," in the useful phrase of Alex Zwerdling.[1] Other critics have argued that Orwell contributed significantly to political thought in the 1950s, especially the

Speakwriting at *Minitrue*, or vaporizing the author? Recorded Books has released unabridged editions of *Animal Farm* and *Nineteen Eighty-Four* on eight audiocassettes totaling thirteen hours. Although Recorded Books proclaimed "Orwell's two masterpieces" to be "brilliant satires of totalitarianism . . . as relevant today as when first published," the audio firm ultimately subjected Orwell to what literary theorists term "the death of the author"—or what readers of *Nineteen Eighty-Four* call "down the memory hole." Reflecting the ironic status inversion between print and broadcast media, Recorded Books highlighted not Orwell but the performer reading his work. The recording firm (quoting one reviewer) hailed the narrator of the audiocassettes as "the first true superstar of spoken audio." In a laughable reversal of the relative priority of author versus narrator, Recorded Books quoted a delighted customer: "I owe much to [narrator] Frank Muller and George Orwell for allowing me to feel what the real loss of freedom would feel like."

The Un(der)examined Orwell

"theory" of totalitarianism, with *Nineteen Eighty-Four* amounting to a fictional prototype for nonfiction treatises such as Hannah Arendt's *The Origins of Totalitarianism* (1951) and Carl Friedrich's *Totalitarianism* (1956).

This chapter treats *Nineteen Eighty-Four* as a model of narrative argumentation, an exemplar of how stories can often persuade readers far more effectively than overt, rational arguments. Of course, the historical evidence for such a claim is also copious. Witness the enormous political and social impact of *Nineteen Eighty-Four* in the Cold War era and indeed through to the present day. It is one of those "books that changed the world," in the phrase of the 1935 survey of influential books conducted by Charles Beard and John Dewey.[2]

Our approach to *Nineteen Eighty-Four* as an example of "how stories convince us," and as a literary touchstone for understanding the conceptual dynamics of the rhetoric of narrative, does not of course imply that Orwell consciously designed *Nineteen Eighty-Four* as such—particularly in view of his already-noted disdain for theoretical abstractions. Nor does it suggest that, as an author for whom "political purpose" represented one of the primary motives for writing, Orwell deliberately aimed to create an anti-utopia or novel of ideas that would seamlessly suture concept and craft.[3]

My point is simply this: whatever his conscious aspirations, Orwell succeeded in creating politically aware artworks that illustrate argumentation theory without crudely descending into propaganda. Like Ida Tarbell's Lincoln, one could fairly say that Orwell "got more arguments out of stories"—that is, he attained a greater political purpose—through his "didactic fantasies" than he did in even the greatest of his essays. Or as Tarbell expresses it in her celebrated short story "He Knew Lincoln":

> I tell you he got more arguments out of stories than he did out of law books, and the queer part was you couldn't answer 'em—they just made you see it and you couldn't get around it. I'm a Democrat, but I'll be blamed if I didn't have to vote for Mr. Lincoln as President, couldn't help it, and it was all on account of that snake story of his illuminatin' the taking of slaves into Nebraska and Kansas. Remember it?[4]

I

Let me return to the conceptual question that governs this chapter: How do stories convince? How do stories and "law books" (or essays, cam-

George Orwell, Literary Theorist?

paign speeches, product advertisements, etc.) appeal differently? How do narratives argue?

This chapter addresses these questions. We shall return later to Orwell's work, and in particular to how *Nineteen Eighty-Four* illuminates narrative theory. But let me note here that this triad of questions is important not just for the literary scholar but for everyone. For the "story of our lives" is a central part of our self-talk and of our conversations with others. We live our lives as stories—or as "narratives," as the literary scholars prefer to say. Whatever the term, the fact is that a deeper understanding of the subtle dynamics of storytelling and "narratology" can shed valuable light both on literature and on our lives.

Orwell once observed that Dickens's characters had become part of the "furniture of the Victorian mind." In the latter half of the twentieth century, *Nineteen Eighty-Four* achieved a similar feat that endures today; its language and vision are embedded firmly in our political lexicon and cultural imagination. These developments testify that fictional stories that become woven into our cultural fabric and social mythology both reflect and shape our lives. For the plots and settings of novels, as well as the "storied lives" of fictional characters, influence our lives (and resemble them too). We have much to learn from closer study of literary narratives. Art not only "entertains," as Horace observes in *The Art of Poetry*, it also "edifies." My reflections here aim to illuminate how stories edify us, whereby I also explore the implications of their instruction (or "persuasion").

The three questions in the opening paragraph of this section serve as a broad framework for our inquiry, which I explore from the perspective of rhetorical studies, a field generally devoted to matters of persuasion and argumentation. I advance a conceptual outline for what might be termed "a rhetoric of narrative"; that is, if we consider rhetoric in the classical tradition as "argumentative speech." For these are *rhetorical* questions—not in that they do not solicit answers, but in that they demand rhetorical approaches toward answers.

II

How *do* stories argue? How does the "argumentative process" of storytelling unfold and persuade readers?

A rhetoric of narrative moves by concepts. We may say that a "break" in the rational/emotional chain of propositions, each of which must somehow advance the argument, constitutes "mere narration," or aimless storytelling (as in a tangent or digression). If the break is extreme or continues, we may have a "pure" short story or novel (or rant or free-association dream narrative) rather than a "rational argument." By contrast, a break in the temporal sequence of events, each unit of which furnishes bits of data to the audience, constitutes "argument." The information flow ceases and the narrative content shifts to the stuff of argumentation: advancing claims and contradictions, supplying internal summary and recapitulation, proposing changes in action or attitude.[5]

Of course, these differences will often be more difficult to mark in theory than in practical cases. Rather, the narration/argument distinction is a matter of emphasis, with a Henry James story (or any formalist narrative) closer to the narration pole and an essay/editorial closer to the argument pole. Still, if we were to explore them carefully, we would find that both the Henry James story and the essay contain narrative and argumentative elements. They consist of both patterned events and concepts. Whether operating in the narrative or in the argumentative mode, literature may use description, exposition, ellipsis, pause, summary, and scene-setting either to inform or argue.

In our rhetoric of narrative, meaning is not a coded text but a "hi-fi performance" (e.g., reading a text "aloud"). In the speech act of reading, we develop a speaker-listener relationship. The speaker speaks with an individual, personal voice.

So we are now concerned not just with the *what* of a rhetoric of narrative, but also with the *how*. Our conception of a dynamic speaker-listener relationship, with the speaker helping to shape the communicative act as the speaker adapts to the listener's ongoing reactions, directly raises the question of *how* rhetoric works, *how* it convinces audiences.

How indeed does rhetoric "move" or function? An established definition of rhetoric is that it is "the function of adjusting ideas to people and people to ideas."[6] This process ranges on a continuum between the poles of a complete accommodation of speaker ideas to audience views ("telling people only what they want to hear") at one extreme, to total intransigence at the other ("my facts speak for themselves" or "my viewpoint is the only reasonable/moral/proper one"). The would-be convincing speaker, therefore, must always be adjusting his or her ideas (and self) to the listeners; the listeners are always "measuring the speaker up," bending toward him or resisting him. He projects a certain image to them, and as his discourse proceeds, they reconsider their impressions of him, filling in the missing links of his argument, placing it within the context of their own experience, and relating to it in their own idiosyncratic ways.

George Orwell, Literary Theorist?

III

In *The Rhetoric of Fiction*, Wayne Booth addresses at length our "measuring up" of the speaker/narrator and our forming a certain "image" of him or her. Booth discusses this process as the reader's construction of the author's "second self" and terms this second self "the implied author." The real author "creates not merely an ideal, impersonal 'man in general' but an implied version of himself that is different from the implied authors we meet in other men's works." The implied author is a kind of "official scribe," and "the picture the reader gets of this presence is one of the author's most important effects."[7] However impersonal the author may attempt to be, the reader will construct this picture, says Booth. Seymour Chatman maintains, however, that Booth's implied author has no real voice. "It instructs us silently, through the design of the whole, by all the means it has chosen to let us learn."[8] Technically, Chatman's interpretation of Booth here is not quite accurate, for the implied author establishes norms in the narrative, with his chief method an often subtle use of tone.[9]

It is true that the implied author has no clear voice, however, and this stems from the fact that—despite Booth's avowedly rhetorical orientation—his book conceives narrative as a fictional *world*, not as a communicative act. *The Rhetoric of Fiction* principally discusses the use of fictional *devices*, with rhetoric conceived not primarily as argumentation but as technique or style. This accounts for Booth's repeated preference for the novels of James and Austen over the realist Edwardian master Arnold Bennett.[10]

A more appropriate term for works nearer to my "argument" pole than the "narrative" pole—works which construct not a fictional world that the reader enters but a speaker-listener relationship (as in the essay)—is "the implied orator." At a glance, this may seem a mere substitution of terms. But the "implied orator" actually functions very differently from Booth's implied author, giving a clear impression of a speaking voice.

In many novels, of course, Booth's "implied author" is indeed the proper term, for we have an "author" who does seem to instruct us silently. We may be aware, but only dimly, of a mind arranging the plot and evaluating characters, thereby crafting a fictional world. Yet in more didactic novels, such as Orwell's *Nineteen Eighty-Four*, we are often aware of a presence arranging and evaluating ideas and characters to build a convincing argument. We as readers respond to the arguments that the implied orator advances by proposition and symbol or motif; we care less about the characters' fates or development and more about

The Un(der)examined Orwell

how the characters figure in the narrative's central argument. We care less about Winston Smith and Julia in *Nineteen Eighty-Four* than about where Oceania is headed, whether "The Brotherhood" exists, whether Goldstein and the underground can possibly launch a true revolt, and what *the book* (the bible of the revolutionary Brotherhood) contains.

"Rhetorical" fiction such as *Nineteen Eighty-Four*—political novels, utopias/dystopias, novels of ideas, philosophical novels, satire—seems to most readers to "argue a case," however overtly or covertly. We see and hear an orator painting scenes and presenting examples and propositions, whether or not the narrative is in the first person (as in Fielding's *Tom Jones*) or third person (Orwell's *Nineteen Eighty-Four*) point of view. This narrative priority of the implied orator to shape convincing arguments (rather than richly, seamlessly textured fictional worlds) accounts for what many critics deplore in overtly rhetorical fiction as "unsatisfying" character creation: novels "lacking" dynamic, three-dimensional characters. (As the next chapter will address at length, this is typically regarded as a near-universal deficiency of utopian fiction such as More's *Utopia*, Huxley's *Brave New World*, and *Nineteen Eighty-Four*.)

The implied orator's focus on argument also provokes related objections, including what many critics (such as Booth) unsympathetic to the novel of ideas chide as "the author's intrusive presence." Because the implied orator's argumentative success hinges not only on the quality of his argument, but also on the listeners' belief in his character and good will (the orator's ethos) and on their emotional response to him (pathos), he will necessarily seem (and be) much more immediate and "present."[11] His voice will sound more direct and constant than that of the implied author. But this implied orator is not the author—just as Booth's implied author is not. For we are dealing (in the case of prose fiction) with the act of storytelling—that is, a speaking subject communicating his or her "fictional world of experience" to a listener. "Narrative," or "story," connects speaker and listener through *telling*.

The crucial difference here from Booth's conception is that the implied orator is more (or at least substantially) concerned about the structure of his argument than with the structure of his fictional world (insofar as we can make that distinction here). Of course, we might claim that the most successful arguments are those that are fully integrated within rich fictional worlds, such as in the novels of Fielding, Dostoyevsky, and Tolstoy. But this would not necessarily be true. For the effectiveness of rhetorical fiction depends on the adjusting of ideas to people and people to ideas. It might well be the case that *Nineteen Eighty-Four* would be

George Orwell, Literary Theorist?

a far less effective argument against political tyranny and totalitarianism if Orwell had created a "richer" fictional world with "rounder," more fully realized characters and a less heavily plotted narrative, or a less darkly textured setting. Moreover, it is also the case that the rhetorical effect of *Nineteen Eighty-Four* owes considerably to Orwell's skill in inventing the sooty, grimy setting of Oceania—the bleak apocalypse that Isaac Deutscher referred to as "The Black Millennium"—and communicating his vision so efficaciously to readers. The success of Orwell's argument—the plausibility of his cautionary warning that a totalitarian future such as Oceania was conceivable within thirty-five years—derived from the fact that he composed his novel against the immediate postwar backdrop of a defeated Nazi Germany and a victorious, still expanding Stalinist Russia. In other words, readers in the West knew that a ghastly future such as Oceania could indeed come to pass—"it could happen here," too—because "it" represented merely a transplanted extension of what had existed elsewhere in the 1940s. As Orwell wrote in July 1949 in a vain attempt to rescue *Nineteen Eighty-Four* from co-optation by the far Right and vilification by the far Left: "My recent novel is NOT intended as an attack on socialism. . . . [The] danger lies . . . in the totalitarian outlook of intellectuals of all colours. The moral to be drawn from this dangerous nightmare situation is a simple one: 'Don't let it happen. It depends on you.'"[12]

As we shall see, what Orwell did to vitalize *Nineteen Eighty-Four* and render it so effective and convincing to so many people was to construct an "implied orator"—his trademark, now-famous "plain-man" speaking persona—that his readers could trust. In a world of polemics, propaganda, and deceit—the prevailing ideological climate of the 1930s and '40s—Orwell projected a literary personality much like Cato's *Vir bonus, discendi perditus*, "the good man speaking well."[13] Wrote one reviewer of Orwell's *Collected Essays, Journalism, and Letters* (*CEJL*): "Open [Orwell's books] anywhere and you touch a man very close to your best self, that self that exists for most of us only in wistful imaginings."[14]

Orwell's unique gift for writing with a disarmingly clear and direct literary voice—that is, to transmit a carefully crafted literary personality onto paper—is a singular achievement. It largely accounts for why numerous readers, especially his fellow literary-political intellectuals, have identified so strongly with Orwell, often drawing a portrait of him in their own idealized self-images as a way of addressing their own needs and aspirations. They have thereby sought, however unaware or half-consciously, to bolster and legitimate (if only to themselves) their own

The Un(der)examined Orwell

identities by rewriting Orwell, projecting their own ego ideals onto him and then passionately embracing "my Orwell."[15]

IV

We might also consider these narrative issues from the audience's standpoint. Whereas concepts such as "the implied author" and "the implied orator" proceed from the standpoint of the *storyteller*, concepts such as Wolfgang Iser's "implied reader" conceive narrative issues as proceeding from the receiver. Like Booth, Iser pursues a phenomenological approach that posits a literary "world." Iser's implied reader confronts the literary text as structure and seeks to "bring to light" the work's subject matter in order to "realize" the fictional world (*Konkretisation*). Iser conceives of a story as "something like an arena in which reader and author participate in a game of the imagination."[16]

The scene for the implied orator and the implied auditor is more properly a courtroom. Here they interact as advocate and jury member, respectively. The jury (presumably less so than the judge) will be "convinced" not only by rational argument but also by emotional and ethical appeals. Instead of "realizing a world," the implied auditor weighs appeals and then assents or rejects. Whereas the implied reader's overriding task is to interpret a world and "take an active part in the composition of the novel's meaning," the implied auditor's ambition is to evaluate a case and (re-)actively shape the terms of the argument.[17] According to classical rhetoric, as an auditor listens to the numerous claims made and propositions advanced by the rhetor (or orator), the auditor will determine what Cicero called *statis,* the central or turning point in a case.[18] He or she will decide whether the argument is to turn on a question of fact, definition, value, or quality and then give or withhold his assent accordingly.

Because we as implied auditors (in works closer to my argument pole) are not called upon to "enter a world" so much as to stand apart and evaluate a (rationally based) argument, we may often feel more detached from an overtly argumentative story. We feel distanced, perhaps even alienated. Although the implied orator is "closer" to us than the implied author, we are also fully aware of his presence. We may remain wary and on our guard. In such cases, we do not yield ourselves (except when powerful, effective emotional and ethical appeals are used) quite so readily as we may surrender to a new fictional world. Judging a story from

George Orwell, Literary Theorist?

the conception of "world" rather than "storytelling experience," we thus often conclude that we "couldn't get into the story" because "the author wanted to ram his ideas down [our] throat." Of course, many narratives may fail as rhetoric because they are too shrill and preachy, but viewing prose fiction from a standpoint closer to the argument pole, we evolve a different set of reader expectations. We begin to ask (as we do in lectures or speeches), "What is he driving at? What is the point here?" We begin to wonder about the progress and construction of the argument more than about the strict development of character and plot.

Obviously, we will not be asking these questions about most prose fiction so impatiently or insistently as we do with lectures and essays. But the closer that fiction approaches the "argument" pole (as in satire), the greater our tendency to become "implied auditors" intently listening to our "implied orator." Moreover, powerful nonrational appeals can virtually eliminate orator-auditor distance every bit as much as in fictional worlds entered by implied readers. In these cases, the courtroom does approach the charged atmosphere of the arena—for courtroom drama too can engage a listener body and soul, and in fact courtroom crises are understandably a frequent subject of tragedy and melodrama. The rhetorical situation and the mode of orator appeal will therefore determine the distance of the implied orator and auditor from each other. In general, the greater the distance perceived by the reader, the more the narrative approaches a rationally based argument.

The foregoing discussion of the dialectical exchange between an implied orator and an implied auditor, each one of them framing and responding to argument, serves as an introduction to the *how* of a rhetoric of narrative, as in "How do stories convince *people*?" Or phrased more precisely, "How do implied orators convince listeners through stories?"

We have seen that the answer turns on the extent to which the "story" is rhetorical—on how extensively it "function[s] [by] adjusting ideas to people and people to ideas." In the so-called novel of ideas, the adjustments are quite extensive; in a formalist short story, much less so. Whereas the former more resembles a speaker-listener relationship, the latter constructs a world that the reader enters. As we have discussed, numerous other distinctions enter via these dynamic concepts, all of which advance beyond the *what* of narrative to the *how*. For instance, whereas our *how* of a rhetoric of narrative is exemplified by the formulations of implied orator and implied auditor, our *what* of narrative merely identifies narrative as opposed to non-narrative.

We are now equipped to take another long step toward conceptu-

The Un(der)examined Orwell

alizing our rhetoric of narrative. This step entails taking a sharp turn away from contemporary narrative theory and toward classical rhetoric, whereby we aim to enrich and inform our rhetoric of narrative with relevant insights and distinctions from classical rhetorical theory.

Both our *how* and *what* of a rhetoric of narration can be profitably approached through classical rhetoric's canons. As we shall see, an investigation of the relevance and value of the canons of classical rhetoric to our prolegomena toward a rhetoric of narrative raises numerous complex, protracted issues.

V

My decision to mark narrative as distinct from argument is not arbitrary: classical scholars from Aristotle through Quintilian and beyond considered the *narratio* and *argumentum* to be the two essential parts of *dispositio*, the "disposition" or overall presentation of the case. Classical theorists worked primarily from the model of the forensic (courtroom) speech. Thus *narratio* was the statement of the case; *argumentum* was the "proof" of the case. As Aristotle maintained in *The Rhetoric:* "A speech has two parts. Necessarily, you state your case, and you prove it. Thus we cannot state a case and omit to prove it, or prove a case without first stating it. . . . In Rhetoric we must call these two processes, respectively, Statement and Argument. . . . The indispensable constituents are simply the Statement and the ensuing Argument."[19]

The precise purpose of the *narratio* was to "indicate the nature of the subject on which he [the judge] will have to give judgments."[20] In practice, it was not merely informative but also suasory, "a speech in miniature."[21] Quintilian advised that *narration* functions "not merely to instruct but rather to persuade the judge."[22] Forensic oratory was most appropriate to a statement of the facts since the province of courtroom speech is the past, but deliberative and epideictic (ceremonial) oratory also made use of reciting past events as a basis for recommendations about the future and present—and so *narratio* also came by Quintilian's time to figure prominently in nonforensic discourse.

Although the *narratio* is fundamentally informative, explaining to listeners the circumstances that they need to understand about the subject at hand, the manner of setting forth the facts would predispose the audience toward accepting or rejecting the following argument. Quintilian advised that the *narratio* be brief, plausible, and lucid. Quintilian insisted that "we must aim, perhaps everywhere, but above all in our

George Orwell, Literary Theorist?

statement of facts, at striking the happy mean in our language."[23] Plausibility has much to do with the ethical image and tone of the speaker. Lucidity is gained by what the Greeks called *enargeia*, which refers to the palpability or vividness in the word picture of a scene, and also to the liveliness and emotional impact generated in showing action (rather than merely telling what happened).

Great writers such as Orwell are often rhetorical as well as literary masters who know how to present a compelling *narratio*. In *Nineteen Eighty-Four*, Orwell's descriptive talents support the argumentative ends of his anti-utopian novel. For instance, the following scene depicting Winston's and Julia's first liaison (at the Oceania show trials) is so skillfully rendered that we can imagine the prosecuting attorney for the Thought Police entering it as state's evidence against them:

> They were standing in the shade of hazel bushes. The sunlight, filtering through innumerable leaves, was still hot on their faces. Winston looked out into the field beyond, and underwent a curious, slow shock of recognition. He knew it by sight. An old, close-bitten pasture, with a footpath wandering across it and a molehill here and there. . . .
>
> A thrush had alighted on a bough not five meters away, almost at the level of their faces. . . . It was in the sun, they in the shade. . . . He wondered whether after all there was a microphone hidden somewhere near. He and Julia had only spoken in low whispers, and it would pick up not what they said, but it would pick up the thrush. Perhaps at the other end of the instrument some small, beetle-like man was listening intently. But by degrees the flood of music drove all speculations out of his mind. It was as though it were a kind of liquid stuff that poured all over him and got mixed up with the sunlight that filtered through the leaves. He stopped thinking and merely felt. The girl's waist in the bend of his arm was soft and warm. He pulled her round so that they were breast to breast; her body seemed to melt into his.[24]

This vivid narration is not actually part of a prosecuting attorney's courtroom presentation for the Thought Police in *Nineteen Eighty-Four*. Yet it well could be. There is no disputing the clarity and effectiveness of such a tableau. Its effectiveness is heightened by abrupt contrast; it emerges after more than one hundred pages describing the misery, bleakness, and sterility of Oceania, typified by this passage just two pages earlier:

The Un(der)examined Orwell

A long line of trucks with wooden-faced guards, armed with subma-
chine guns standing upright in each corner, was passing slowly down
the street. In the trucks little yellow men in shabby greenish uniforms
were squatting, jammed close together. Their sad Mongolian faces
gazed out over the sides of the trucks, utterly incurious.... Truckload
after truckload of the sad faces passed. Winston knew they were there,
but he saw them only intermittently. The girl's [Julia's] shoulder ...
was pressed against his.[25]

Placed side by side, these two passages provide us as implied auditors
with a sense of an orator seeking to praise and blame, as in the epideictic speech. The *narratio* as miniature speech, vividly spoken, indicts
not Winston and Julia, but rather the society which makes them seek
love surreptitiously. The first speech also could be entered against the
State; for example, it could properly be given by a prosecutor bringing charges against the government for bugging. Indeed it is the State's
outrageous violation of privacy and decency to which we respond in the
first passage, especially after reading the second. In the second passage,
although the implied orator is initially looking through Winston's eyes,
he then remarks that Winston "saw [the prisoners] only intermittently"
and is preoccupied with Julia. It is the implied orator who has kept his
gaze fixed upon the truckloads of sad faces—and kept our eyes and ears
upon them as well.

As *narratio* functions above, it serves not only to inform but also to
convince. It employs four types of communication that rhetorical hand-
books have traditionally distinguished: description (making verbal pic-
tures), narration (telling stories), exposition (setting forth facts), and argumentation ("applying" the facts). Of course, as we have seen, the types
overlap; still, we may observe that our general category of "narration"
more characteristically uses the first two (as, for example, "narrating the
story of my life"), whereas argumentation is most directly concerned
with the latter pair, what the Romans called *confirmatio* (proof) and
refutatio.

VI

The *argumentum* raises most directly the difficult task
of ordering our points and reflects the contemporary view of *dispositio* as "planned adaptation." The orator is faced with many questions

George Orwell, Literary Theorist?

relating to sequence and significance. Should I refute the other side or present my own arguments first? Should I begin with my weakest arguments and build up to my strongest? The ancients usually advised that refutation precede proof, and that one conclude with the strongest argument. But they stressed that no inflexible rules could be laid down dictating sequence and weight: the best strategy will vary according to the audience and particular situation. Moreover, the ancients presumed that the speaker possessed some relevant knowledge of the audience, based on shared *doxa* (opinion, public consensus) that established varying degrees of communal norms.

It is difficult to illustrate the arrangement and adaptation of arguments in fiction simply by quoting short passages because the ideas proved and refuted are typically embedded in the fiction and developed over several pages or sections. Yet Orwell's *Nineteen Eighty-Four* does contain a few instances of short, enthymematic argument. We have said that the enthymeme as a method of persuasion has the same relationship in rhetoric as does the syllogism as a method of proof in logic. Argument moves also by propositions, with ideas as its defining units. The chief difference between these two forms of reasoning, syllogistic versus enthymematic, is that the former is concerned with deductive truths and the latter with probable knowledge. In both, the ideas are usually presented (at least formally) in three steps: major premise, minor premise, and conclusion. Consider the following instance of syllogistic reasoning.

All men are mortal. (Major premise)
Socrates is a man. (Minor premise)
Socrates is mortal. (Conclusion)

The degree of certainty is much stronger in this syllogism than in the following enthymeme derived from a passage of *Nineteen Eighty-Four*:

Everybody is constantly watched in this society. (Major premise)
I am a member of this society. (Minor premise)
I am constantly watched. (Conclusion)

The preceding enthymeme is extracted from the following passage from *Nineteen Eighty-Four*:

Outside, even through the shut windowpane, the world looked cold. Down in the street little eddies of wind were whirling dust and torn paper into spirals, and though the sun was shining and the sky a harsh

The Un(der)examined Orwell

blue, there seemed to be no color in anything except the posters that were plastered everywhere. The black-mustachioed face gazed down from every commanding corner. There was one on the house front immediately opposite. BIG BROTHER IS WATCHING YOU, the caption said, while the dark eyes looked deep into Winston's own. Down at the street level another poster, torn at one corner, flapped fitfully in the wind, alternately covering and uncovering the single word INGSOC. In the far distance a helicopter skimmed down between the roofs, hovered for an instant like a blue-bottle, and darted away again with a curving flight. It was the Police Patrol, snooping into people's windows. The patrols did not matter, however. Only the Thought Police mattered.

. . . Any sound that Winston made would be picked up by the telescreen; moreover, so long as he remained within the field of vision which the metal plaque commanded, he could be seen as well as heard. There was of course no way of knowing whether you were being watched at any given moment. . . . It was even conceivable that they watched everybody all the time.[26]

Whereas the syllogism leads to a necessary conclusion from universally true premises, the enthymeme leads only to tentative conclusions (though often expressed as certainties) from probable premises. In our example from *Nineteen Eighty-Four*, though the conclusion drawn about life in Oceania is highly probable, the degree of certainty we have about the major premise here is not complete. But if we accept the major premise, doubtless we will also accept the conclusion.

The enthymeme is often discussed as a "truncated syllogism" because one of its premises may be missing yet is invariably supplied by the audience (as with the missing element in an elliptical construction). In other words, one proposition is implied rather than stated, and this proposition is often the enthymeme's vulnerable link.

The following is an enthymeme derived from the above passage with a suppressed premise. "Only the Thought Police matter [are truly terrifying] because they can see beyond physical windows into your mind." Here we have an enthymeme, in the sense of both a truncated syllogism and a deductive argument based on probable premises. The truth of the minor premise here—"The Thought Police can see beyond windows into your mind"—could be confirmed or refuted. The probable premise resides in the unexpressed proposition, "Only seeing into your mind, not privacy invasion, is truly terrifying." We all "know" (or *believe*, according to our culture's shared *doxa*) that the latter proposition is not

George Orwell, Literary Theorist?

universally true. But we also know that "mind control" or invasive psychological methods (what we might term "psycho-invasion") *are* truly terrifying.

It is, in other words, probable by comparison that in a world where eavesdropping and a lack of physical privacy are the norm, state invasion of the mind is the final, terrifying prospect. Indeed, in a ruthlessly totalitarian state, the prospect of maintaining an intact mind (a "house of Being" free from intrusion) is the only form of personal privacy, and therefore the only terrifying invasion, that remains. For all practical purposes, that probability is sufficient to convince us at the novel's end that the Ministry of Love and Room 101 must contain some utterly inconceivable and inhumane means of mental torture and control.[27]

To sum up: we have seen *how* argument "moves": it is advanced by a progression of ideas ordered in an enthymematic chain. This chain may serve either to prove or refute. Thus, the narrative's development is shaped not so much by the necessities of plot and character as it is bound to rational suasion.

VII

Let us reformulate our main question and approach it from a different angle: How do stories *persuade* us? How do they "move"—and move us? The short answer: by analogies.

If argumentative movement in narrative can be characterized primarily as logical, we may characterize persuasive movement as primarily analogical (Gk. "according to" some "ratio" or comparative "relation") and psycho-logical (Gk. a spirit-relation, i.e., a connection perceived by the imagination). As the narrative weaves images and moves from motif to motif, it appeals primarily to the reader's imagination, not to his or her reason. Another way of positing this distinction, as exemplified in Burke's *Philosophy as Literary Form*, is that, whereas classical, rationally based *narratio* in the Aristotelian sense argues, a psychologically based rhetoric fosters author-reader (-auditor) identification through aesthetic form.

Burke addresses the "business of interpretation" in the language of classical rhetoric, calling it "argument [or persuasion, actually] by analogy." We persuade by means of oversimplification and "analogical extension": "We oversimplify a given event when we characterize it from the standpoint of a given interest—and we attempt to invent a similar characterization for other events by analogy."[28] The pattern of extension

The Un(der)examined Orwell

involves adding some device or aspect from an unrelated context to the situation at hand, as when, accustomed to walking on level ground, we "invent" a forward swing of our hands for walking uphill. The veteran sailor, however, having learned to shipwalk by taking the rhythms of the sea into account, may inadvertently "roll" when on firm ground. Our extensions may either enable or handicap us.

As with enthymematic chains, it is difficult to illustrate motif chains in short passages from stories. But most readers find that *Nineteen Eighty-Four* addresses them more in the spirit of persuasion than as an argument, as I have distinguished them here. Orwell makes less use of logos than of ethos and pathos. Charged phrases dominate the novel: "Big Brother," "WAR IS PEACE, FREEDOM IS SLAVERY, IGNORANCE IS STRENGTH," "Thought Police," "Enemy of the People," "The Brotherhood," "The Book," "Room 101," "Miniluv," and so on. These and other words possess a hypnotic power that pervades the narrative. Several notable analogical extensions occur as Winston brings elements from the reader's world into the world of *Nineteen Eighty-Four*, whereby Winston finds in dismay that the extensions do not apply—though indeed the implied orator uses them to good persuasive effect.

For instance, Winston hears the prole woman singing a maudlin jingle about the past and thereupon develops a "mystical reverence" for her. He fantasizes that she is singing especially for him and for Julia, and he sees the singer as the incarnation of a proletarian spirit that "would stay alive against all the odds, like birds, passing on from body to body the vitality that the Party did not share and could not kill." From here, Winston's associations pass on to birds themselves. He imagines that the thrush which he and Julia heard on their first afternoon of lovemaking "sang to us." Julia replies: "He wasn't singing to us. . . . He was singing to please himself. Not even that. He was just singing."[29]

She is right. Yet so accustomed is Winston to the carefully orchestrated "Two-Minute Hate" sessions chanted to Big Brother, and to the vapid State hymns intoned by half-drunk Party members under strict supervision in local bars, that he can only conceive of singing as performed for an audience and with a rational (even propagandistic) purpose. Unmediated desire and raw instinct have been purged from his view of the proles by his social experience, which, analogically "chained out," has become what Veblen calls a "trained incapacity."

This incapacity is rendered even more apparent by the narrative's analogizing between Oceania's clocks and language with our own. The clock in Winston and Julia's hideaway above Mr. Charrington's shop is a pre-Oceania antique whose face is not marked according to mili-

George Orwell, Literary Theorist?

tary time. Whereas all Oceania public events, news bulletins, and official Party activities are announced or scheduled by military time (and indeed the novel opens with the clocks "striking thirteen"), this is not the case in the utopian world of the bedroom above Charrington's shop. In this lovers' hideaway with its antique clock, the time never goes beyond twelve. Winston's habit of marking time by Oceania standards, however, apparently causes him to confuse 9 a.m. with 9 p.m., and he and Julia accidentally sleep through the night and miss work the next morning, a technical slip-up that leads to their capture by the Thought Police. Here again, Winston's trained incapacity—viewing the world of the room in Charrington's shop by the standards of Oceania (he had also been standing in the bedroom looking outside on the prole woman singing) causes him to confuse the two worlds.

The implied orator thus persuades us powerfully of the oppressive nature of a world literally run on military time, where the clocks seem to us readers fixed on thirteen—and where people can be convicted of "Thoughtcrime." Of course, this term itself is part of Oceania Newspeak, which Winston can expertly manipulate (and takes pride in his capacity to do so). Oceania is run on words such as *doublethink, duckspeak, INGSOC, Minitrue, Pornosec,* and *facecrime.* "The Revolution will be complete when the language is perfect," one of Winston's coworkers, Syme, declares to him. Yet Winston, despite his proficiency in Newspeak, is deceived into regarding O'Brien and Charrington as honest men, largely because they know so much about the past, particularly the Oldspeak words of his childhood nursery rhymes. His facility with Newspeak blinds him to the duplicitous characters of these Thought Police agents. Once again, it is a matter of analogy between our world and the world of *Nineteen Eighty-Four,* and we as readers—unlike Winston's colleague Syme—see in Newspeak the impoverishment and manipulation of language, not the beauty of its "rigid definition," pristine economy, and greater "self-discipline," in Orwell's satiric description.

The point here is that we can trace how images and words form patterns that carry some clear theme, idea, or dominant impression threaded through a narrative or a section of it—in this case images and words such as "singing," "clock," and particular language motifs. These images and words may or may not be directly "analogous" to the reader's familiar experience. Nonetheless, the reader will draw some conclusion about the narrative as persuasive act by comparing its world with his own.

This fact broadens our concept of the implied orator and auditor, for it expands the range of appeals that the orator uses—to persuade,

The Un(der)examined Orwell

not necessarily to argue rationally. It also alters the nature of the auditor's response and the paradigmatic "scene" of our communicative act. The scene is no longer the courtroom. Now it somewhat approaches the scene posited in Wolfgang Iser's *The Act of Reading*: the "arena." But we are still far from his poetics of narrative and his literary aesthetics. A story that is a communicative act of persuasion remains chiefly a rhetorical narrative. It bears affinities with Iser's "arena," though it is by no means quite like a "playing field of the imagination." Rather, it seems closer to the hustings (i.e., the campaign trail) where candidates typically emphasize ethical and emotional appeals over rational ones, though they also include the latter.[30]

VIII

Are stories arguments? Are narratives persuasive discourses?

Sometimes. If they progress primarily by conceptual chains or by motifs carrying ideas, we may posit, enthymematically, a tentative "yes." But as with the interrelation of *inventio* and *dispositio*, and with the dynamic, dialectical character of the communicative act, the *what* of narrative is not a separate question from the *how*. We must constantly be attentive as to how narratives move if we are to distinguish the modes within them accurately.

Only then will we become aware of how they are moving us.

The statist designs of dystopia: this image of Big Brother from the film adaptation of *Nineteen Eighty-Four*, directed by Michael Radford, reflects Orwell's intention to combine images of Hitler and Stalin in his representation of Oceania's mythical tyrant.

CHAPTER 15

The Architectonics of Room 101

eorge Orwell was an avid reader of utopian literature
long before it became a topic addressed by scholarly associations and PhD dissertations in literary academe.[1]
The utopian visions of H. G. Wells, such as *Men Like Gods* (1923),
shaped Eric Blair's early views of technology and society. Even after Orwell reacted strongly against the "Wellsian World State" in Part 2 of *The
Road to Wigan Pier* (1937), he remained a keen and admiring student
of literary utopias.[2] And yet, his turn against Wells and the optimistic,
progressive character of the Victorian-Edwardian era and their futuristic
utopias prompted Orwell to study carefully the emerging anti-utopian
tradition. Not only did he devour British anti-utopias, such as Aldous
Huxley's *Brave New World* (1932), but he also searched out little-known
utopias in foreign languages, such as Yevgeny Zamyatin's *We* (1946),
which Orwell reviewed for *Tribune*.[3]

Although Eric Blair had valued the utopian aspirations of artificial
languages such as Esperanto[4] and the fraternal implications of creating a natural "universal language" via Basic English, the mature Orwell
later came to see them as threats: a dictator such as Hitler—or even a
conservative imperialist such as Churchill—could, Orwell thought, ex-

ploit a single world language to impose his political will on the entire globe. Thus, despite having been an enthusiast of utopias and the Wellsian World State in his youth, Orwell became a fierce anti-utopian who feared "the streamlined men" of the bureaucratic collectivist utopia, Hilaire Belloc's "servile state."[5]

No genre of writings has greater designs on the world than the utopia, what I might term its "stately designs." (Or "statist designs," as anti-utopian critics such as Orwell might prefer to say.) The very word *utopia*, translated from the Greek, means "no place." But the coinage was also a pun by Thomas More, with "eu" meaning "good." So the utopia is "the good place that is no place," and the challenge for utopian thinkers is to persuade you that their "no place" is preferable to your "someplace." Similarly, *dys* is a Greek negative; hence a "dystopia" is a negative utopia, a "no place" that we all pray will remain such. Certainly all readers of *Nineteen Eighty-Four* have cherished that hope—which testifies to the fact that Orwell's cautionary warning has proven highly effective. History attests to it too: the fact that "1984" never came to pass—and instead the world witnessed the *annus mirabilis* of 1989–1990, climaxed by the fall of the Berlin Wall—owes in some measure to the impact of *Nineteen Eighty-Four*: it failed as a prophecy because it succeeded as a warning.

Let us step back now from discussion of the place of *Nineteen Eighty-Four* in the tradition from utopia to anti-utopia and widen our perspective. If we examine the larger context of utopia as a genre, we can return to *Nineteen Eighty-Four* better equipped to comprehend why it has been a powerful cautionary reminder for millions of readers—even though the subgenre of utopia has been held in relatively low regard in the literary academy. For the utopia is fundamentally a *political* genre. Despite the ascendancy of academic approaches such as "cultural studies" and the popularity of courses such as "the political novel," the reign of literary formalism—which has endured in diverse forms from the New Criticism of the 1930s through to avant-garde movements such as deconstruction, postmodernism, and poststructuralism in the twenty-first century—accounts for the academic disesteem that the subgenre has suffered.

I shall elaborate on these conceptual issues of aesthetic value, but immediately let me state here my aim in this chapter. It is not to explicate *Nineteen Eighty-Four* as a dystopia, nor to focus narrowly on its relation to utopian genre theory. Rather, I seek to address the *tradition*—from utopia to dystopia—to which *Nineteen Eighty-Four* belongs, broaching large conceptual questions about genre that apply to Orwell's *chef d'oeuvre* as well as to other landmarks in the tradition. My aspiration is, therefore, threefold:

The Un(der)examined Orwell

1. To show how the utopian imagination functions, how it reorders the organization of narrative elements as it projects its "no place."
2. To propose an alternate set of aesthetic criteria which might value the utopia for what it tries to do: the architectonics of the utopian imagination is not a sacred temple, an upper House of Being, but a freewheeling town meeting hall, more like a lower house of representatives.
3. To suggest the implications of this revaluation of aesthetic criteria for the larger issues of reputation-building and the hierarchy or perceived prestige levels of literary genres.

I

What is a utopia? It is an ideal community that is deliberately constructed by its designers. It is not a *Gilligan's Island* or a *Fantasy Island*. It is a *political* community. The utopian genre emerges from and is directed to an immediate historical and political context, and it attempts precisely to redesign the political order: it is written for the age, not for the ages. Of course, the same is true—*mutatis mutandis*—of dystopias such as *Nineteen Eighty-Four*: they are cautionary reminders about the horrific consequences of ideologically driven, abstract reconstructions of society. They are warnings for the age, if not always for the ages.

For example, Bacon's *New Atlantis*, Harrington's *Oceana*, Condorcet's *Esquisse*, Bellamy's *Looking Backward*, and Skinner's *Walden Two*—not to mention anti-utopias such as Orwell's *Nineteen Eighty-Four*—have all had a profound influence on world events. *The New Atlantis* served as the direct inspiration for London's Royal Society, *Oceana* influenced the conception of the U.S. Constitution, the *Esquisse* was printed in several thousand copies by Robespierre in an effort to link Condorcet's vision with that of the Jacobins, *Looking Backward* actually launched a political party (the Nationalists), and *Walden Two* (like earlier utopian communitarian experiments) has been the model for numerous postwar communes. *Nineteen Eighty-Four*, of course, is the best-selling political novel of all time, and its early postwar role in McCarthyism and in shaping the West's view of the Soviet Union was immensely significant. All of these are "books that have changed the world," in the title of a famous 1935 survey of influential books conducted by Charles Beard and John Dewey.

The enormous reception and impact of these works is precisely why we should attend to them. Literary critics have often been unable to appreciate the complexity of the utopian tradition, or to account for its enormous popular success, whereas rhetorical critics have seldom given it systematic attention. Utopias are, however, rhetorical works with "stately designs"—and sometimes "statist" designs—on the world. The failure of literary critics to respect utopian literature stems from enduring modernist assumptions about the nature and function of literature: the high value placed on epistemological complexity, stylistic intricacy, careful plot development, and dynamic and rounded characterization. Utopias, however, make direct appeals to readers' emotions.

In the following pages I examine how those appeals are crafted in the course of exploring the rhetoric and aesthetics of utopian literature. My immediate concern is twofold: first, with the architectonics of utopias— their "stately" (or "Stately") designs (i.e., the structural designs of these linguistic "states of mind"); and second, with how their history of underappreciation bears on the critical problem of distinguishing among interpretation, evaluation, and reputation.

II

Rhetorical critics have had much to say about the reception and impact of books and ideas, though they have not typically been influential in shaping literary or philosophical canons. Indeed the neglect of these works is largely a casualty of critical attitudes that equate aesthetic merit with nonargumentative discourse and "transcendent" subjects. Such values reflect the inability of most literary critics to appreciate the complexity and scope of the utopian tradition, or to account for its enormous popular success. This incapacity stems from modernist and, more recently, poststructuralist and other formalist assumptions about the nature and function of literature. In modernist thinking, literature makes no claims, or has no designs, on the world. It does not attempt to change things politically, but merely to represent them mimetically, and it does so in a specific literary language whose claim to value lies in its uniqueness. The sacralized critical vocabulary of the New Criticism and Heideggerian phenomenological criticism discloses this pure, otherworldly conception of art as a transcendent, sacred creation: in the phrase of W. K. Wimsatt, true artworks are "verbal icons" which avoid the "heresy of paraphrase," or in Heidegger's own metaphor, the artwork is a "temple" in which Being dwells.

Consequently, those "impure," time-bound works whose implied

The Un(der)examined Orwell

purpose is to influence the course of history, and which therefore employ a language that is not only not unique but common and accessible to everyone, do not qualify as works of art. Literary works that make continual and obvious appeals to the reader's emotions, communicate a paraphrasable message, and use technical devices that are distinguished by their utter conventionality (e.g., *Nineteen Eighty-Four*'s rat torture scene in Room 101)[6] epitomize the opposite of what "canonized" literature is supposed to be.

I derive this aspect of my argument about utopias from Jane Tompkins's important study in genre theory, *Sentimental Designs* (1986).[7] Great literature, according to the traditional canons of literary modernism from Arnold through Eliot, Leavis, and the New Critics, has no designs on the world. Tompkins's book is an insightful survey of the "sentimental" novel in which she shows how a nineteenth-century domestic novel such as *Uncle Tom's Cabin*, appealing directly to readers' feelings via melodramatic devices, persuaded readers to change their hearts and minds on the slavery issue. *Uncle Tom's Cabin* certainly did have designs on the world, and the ways in which it helped revolutionize race relations and North-South relations are still being felt today.

As I have noted, the utopia has generally not been considered "good literature" according to modernist criteria. It is rarely taught in courses on prose fiction or the novel. Might we instead approach this traditionally "lowly" genre via an antimodernist, pragmatic set of aesthetic criteria different from traditional modernist criteria? Such new criteria would value the utopia according to what it attempts to do: redesign the world. They would address the socially reconstructive character of the utopian imagination. For my purposes, two key questions immediately emerge:

- What is the special structural design of the "utopitect"—the architect of utopia?
- How does the architectonics of the utopian imagination—that which imagines an ideal way of life—make use of the rhetorical imagination?

Utopians deal with the art, in Reinhold Niebuhr's phrase, of "the impossibly possible." The utopian's passionate goal to change people's attitudes makes him or her willing to exchange artistic precision for rhetorical power. "Architectonics" is concerned with balancing the useful and the beautiful, the Horatian equipoise of utility and pleasure. But the utopian willingly chooses the useful over the beautiful to get his message across.

My approach here pivots on the claim that value and reputation are radically contingent: numerous, indeed virtually countless factors condition aesthetic judgments and literary status. Literature comprises not just *belles lettres* embodying enduring themes in complex forms, but also aesthetic endeavors to redefine the social order. We may read novels and stories not only because they manage to transcend or escape the limitations of their particular time and place, but because they offer powerful examples of the way a culture thinks about itself, articulating and proposing solutions for problems that shape a particular historical moment.[8] Utopias, in particular, are books written not to be enshrined in a literary canon, but to win the minds and influence the behavior of wide audiences. These are works which are suspect from the point of view of the literary formalism of T. S. Eliot and F. R. Leavis, which tends to classify works that address political and social change as merely entertaining or propagandistic.

The fact that an artwork engages such issues—poverty, revolution, fascism, socialism, capitalism, technological change, mass culture—is traditionally taken as a sign of its limitations: the more directly it addresses purely local and temporal concerns, the less artistic it is considered to be—not only because it is captive to the fluctuations of history, but also because in its attempt to mold public opinion, it is closer to propaganda than to art. For example, as I noted in *Scenes from an Afterlife: The Legacy of George Orwell*, Orwell is the best-selling political writer in any language, and his last two books have sold fifty million copies, more than any pair of books by a serious novelist of his generation. Yet not a single course in modern British literature taught at the University of Texas includes his work.

Indeed *Nineteen Eighty-Four* is probably the most influential political novel of the century. Likewise another novel, Edward Bellamy's *Looking Backward*—voted the most significant political work in American literature of the previous half century in Dewey and Beard's 1935 survey—is rarely taught in courses in political theory or American literature.

The examples are less significant in themselves than for what they suggest about the peculiar status of the utopia as a literary genre. Indeed, given its variety of forms—novel, romance, philosophy of history, cultural anthropology, religious tract, manifesto, and so on—critics have often expressed uncertainty as to what precisely a "utopia" is at all.

Political philosophers and scientists regard the utopia as insufficiently rigorous or systematic. Or with Hegel in *The Philosophy of Right*, they dismiss the utopia as a useless abstraction, a dream vision not oriented toward the real world. It is short on critical analysis, philosophically

The Un(der)examined Orwell

flabby, and theoretically weak in its exposition of alternative political futures.

Meanwhile, literary critics judge the literary utopia as a *roman manqué*, a failed novel, according to the aesthetic standards of modernism and formalism: psychological intricacy, organic unity, moral ambiguity, epistemological complexity, stylistic density, formal economy, and subtlety of plot construction. Utopias are "bad novels." They feature stereotyped characters, didactic plots, and inadequate dramatic development.

Thus, for example, Orwell's fiction is "stillborn," because it never drew on "a more elevated form of knowledge than was available through mere ideas," in the judgment of Joseph Epstein, an admirer of Orwell. "Except at odd moments, Orwell never quite progressed beyond ideas: their stranglehold suffocates not only *Nineteen Eighty-Four* and *Animal Farm*, but even his less directly political fiction."[9]

Although he is generally an astute critic, Epstein is beholden to an abstract idea himself: the doctrine of modernism. He cannot appreciate Orwell as a "novelist of ideas," contrasting him unfavorably with Henry James, of whom T. S. Eliot famously commented that "he had a mind so fine no idea could violate it." James was indeed a great writer of modernist fiction; but Orwell was after something different in his "didactic fantasies."[10] As he says in "Why I Write" (1946), "political purpose" ultimately became, however reluctantly, his chief motive for writing in "an age like this." If James managed to imbue his fiction with "a more elevated form of knowledge than was available through mere ideas," Orwell clothed ideas in the form of literary fiction that shaped the course of post–World War II history. If James "had a mind so fine no idea could violate it," Orwell possessed a mind so lucid and honest that no ideology could violate it.

Or take another example: B. F. Skinner's *Walden Two*. Critics have pronounced that it fails both as a realistic novel and a work of political theory: the characters (Frazier, Castle, Burris) are stickmen rather than finely delineated, Skinner's behavioristic theory violates the integrity of the fictional world and polemicizes the work, the story line lacks verisimilitude, and the events are implausible and sensationalized. As a political treatise, Skinner's "science of behavior" is not presented systematically or rigorously by Frazier; the fictional form sugarcoats and adulterates the theory; and, whatever one thinks of behaviorism, Skinner as theoretician is much more effective in *Beyond Freedom and Dignity*.

And so, accustomed to the textual standards of modernism's approach to the novel, students often judge *Walden Two* "boring" and "preachy." Until, that is, my Virginia students found out that a *Walden Two* community, Twin Oaks, existed just twenty miles from the University of Virginia, visited it, and saw that its residents were so deeply influenced by the book that they have been willing to build their forty-year-old community according to many of its principles. Likewise, students analyzing Skinner's theories sometimes judge them solely at the level of argument rather than persuasion. They forget to ask why the original *Walden Two* audience was deeply moved by the book, and they forget that classroom analysis is not the normal or only mode for approaching such a work.

Part of the problem in appreciating the utopia, therefore, rests with what the British philosopher Gilbert Ryle calls a "category mistake."[11] We need to recognize how and why the utopia adopts a diversity of forms, and to see it outside the rigid aesthetic categories of the political treatise and the realistic novel.

III

Utopias are trying to do something different, and it is best to see them in their own terms, with an eye toward their own aspirations and excellences. They do not seek primarily to show the complex interrelationship between the individual and society, as does the realistic or psychological novel; or to exhibit the close or thorough reasoning of a political treatise or philosophical essay.

The utopia is an unusual hybrid category partaking of the political and aesthetic: an attempt, in Orwell's words, to "make political writing into an art." Thus the utopia raises from a new angle the old debate of the relations between rhetoric and poetic. Because of restricted space, let me emphasize what I take to be the most interesting domain of the debate: the aesthetics of the literary or fictional utopia. Here then begins our appreciation of the particular cast of the utopian temper and its reordering of the role and priority of narrative elements.

The utopia focuses not on the traditional controlling narrative elements of the novel—character and plot, or even setting—but rather on *idea*. Instead of seeing the utopia as a failed novel compromised by having its characters serve as mouthpieces for ideas, we should see the utopia as a form in which life is breathed into personified ideas, who then do battle and prove that ideas can and do have consequences.

This, then, is the starting point for an aesthetic revaluation: In utopian literature, idea is the controlling narrative element. The rhetorical strategy of the utopia turns on the attempt to persuade the reader to accept the idea; all else—character, plot, setting—is secondary. This

The Un(der)examined Orwell

"controlling statement" establishes a principle of selection and determines the presentation of other narrative elements. Typically, the reader can formulate a statement of the author's political beliefs (i.e., "socialist," "Fabian," "anarchist," or "feminist") because all narrative elements serve this end. The satiric and programmatic functions of the utopia point it outside the literary world to the real world.

Thus, the traditional privileging of character in contemporary fiction gives way in the utopia to characters as vehicles of ideas. Characters in the utopia become "types." For example, in *Walden Two*, Augustine Castle is the skeptical critic of utopia. He is a philosopher, and he is shown to be a naif, inferior to Frazier, the behavioral psychologist-king who has displaced him. Frazier is the advocate and host, articulate and confident. Burris is the questioning guest, or observer, who becomes gradually committed and with whom most readers normally identify.

Characters in utopias, therefore, are standard types: host and guest, or guide and visitor. The visitor is invariably impressed with the wisdom and benevolence of the host, and with the wonders of the new world he or she is visiting; typically the visitor comes to see the advantages of exchanging his or her old world for the new one. Thus do utopias educate visitors.

Education, in the broadest sense, is the subject of all utopias: both the education of the visitor and us readers.[12] The characteristic response of sympathetic liberal readers to Bellamy's *Looking Backward* and Wells's *Men Like Gods* was like that of Lincoln Steffens, who in his report to Bernard Baruch after his visit to Russia in the 1920s announced: "I have seen the future, and it works."

It is quite true that the characters in utopia are typically static and do not develop. But this is no weakness. In the near-perfect world that the classic utopias project, time has stopped, and history is at an end. The tragedies and uncertainties that make for exciting characters are no more—and this is regarded as a small price to pay. Perhaps conflict is necessary for dynamic, rounded characters. The guest in William Morris's *News From Nowhere* notes that in such a boringly happy world as that of London 2003, human beings seem "paler," lack personality, are less colorful—they no longer are like characters out of an old nineteenth-century novel.

Likewise, the flat characters of anti-utopias reflect no shortcomings in artistic achievement. For in a world so oppressive as *Nineteen Eighty-Four*, it is virtually necessary that Winston Smith not be a full, rich human being. He has been drained of his humanity and reduced to a type by the omnipotent system.

In other words, the novel's traditional portrayal of complex, dynamic characters is, in the utopia, replaced by a single, complex, fascinating hero: the hero of utopia—and the antihero of dystopia—is the system. It is the central character about whom everyone talks, and the fates of individuals are less important to the reader than the fate of the system, the proposed social program. It is analyzed and scrutinized throughout. One falls in love with, or hates, the omnipresent system.

The utopian author thus seeks a balance between reader identification with character, often through romance conventions, and a Brechtian novel of externality, in which the reader stands outside, detached, looking over characters' shoulders and engaging in an analysis of the institutions of the utopia. The goals of psychological realism and careful character development, which empower the psychological or realist novel, would in utopian fiction deflect attention away from a continuous comparison between the system in the reader's society and the utopian society. Our concern with individual characters in the utopia exists only insofar as we identify their fate with or against the system. Our interest in the individual must be kept below our concern for the system; otherwise it might undermine our willingness to acknowledge that, in utopia, the community is more important than the individual.

Plot too changes in utopia. It becomes an engagement of ideas between characters. The dramatic tension of the plot is a discussion of ideas because the characters are mouthpieces for concepts, and all the structural conflicts of these worlds are resolved. And there is no extended conflict precisely because classic utopias mark the end of history. As Morris demonstrates in *News From Nowhere*: "Plot is what happens when history is conflict." In the utopia, however, plot is the intellectual process of discovery by the observer or guest and, therefore, the reader: the plot tracks the course of the argument between Castle and Frazier, and the struggle of Burris to decide whether to stay or leave Walden Two.

Plots in utopia are often episodic, as in *News From Nowhere* or *City of the Sun* and *The New Atlantis*; characters are quickly introduced and disappear; plot and character reveal only what is necessary to the doctrinal statement. Here again, what might seem to be flaws in plot from the standpoint of the realistic or psychological novel become plausible strengths in utopian fiction. Utopian plots are often stock and contain *deus ex machina* devices. But this arises because problems of social reconstruction require plots which are often repetitive and slightly improbable; a socialist or feminist revolution will likely possess discontinuities

The Un(der)examined Orwell

at many levels with the present, and neither one is a probable development. So the norms of probability and formal economy of a Proustian or Faulknerian novel are actually inappropriate; the utopia deliberately violates such norms because a radical solution to political problems will not be possible within those norms. Utopian scenes are openly heuristic and didactic, rather than mimetic; they do not attempt to transcribe in detail an arc of events as they "actually happen" in society. Rather, they provide models for remaking the social and political order in which events take place.

Wilde remarked of Dickens's *Old Curiosity Shop*: "One would have to have a heart of stone not to laugh at the death of Little Nell." Many readers feel the same about the torture of Winston Smith with rats in Room 101 in *Nineteen Eighty-Four*, or the death of John Savage in *Brave New World*. But the scenes are unforgettable; just as the deaths of Little Eva and Uncle Tom in *Uncle Tom's Cabin* made a point about slavery, these scenes make their point about the horrors of the system in these anti-utopian nightmares.

Finally, setting in utopias is not a reflection of characters or plot, as in the traditional realistic novel, but a method of presentation of the new system. Somehow, the visitor must be taken on a "tour" of the new world. The panorama of its excellences must be shown. The journey device is central to utopian settings, for it allows the encyclopedic, anatomical form of presentation needed.

The setting thus allows the skeletal idea of the utopia to be convincingly clothed: the setting reveals a whole—it does not show particulars in formation. All crucial institutions must be sketched—family, sexual relations, form of government, work and leisure, level of technology—if the reader is to choose this "no place" over his or her "someplace." Because the presentation of the setting is so crucial to the utopian author's aspiration to convey an attractive vision of "no place" (or to sound a compelling warning about the perils of this "bad place"), the setting is usually a vibrant, idealized spectacle (or a hellish nightmare in anti-utopias). For instance, in the case of *Nineteen Eighty-Four*, the fact is that the setting, Oceania, is the multifaceted, titanic antihero. Whereas Winston and Julia are essentially one-dimensional, flat characters, Oceania is larger than life, extraordinarily complex, and ingenious in the range and variety of its torture instruments, surveillance devices, and diabolical slogans. Let us not forget that the national anthem of this superstate is "Oceania, 'tis of thee." Orwell omits to mention its lyrics; if the reader will permit me a stint at *Minitrue*, let me suggest *à la* Winston an opening refrain:

The Architectonics of Room 101

> Oceania,
> 'tis of thee
> Wasteland of tyranny
> 'Fore thee I cringe

This dehumanizing wasteland, Oceania the Un-Beautiful, is the cynosure of all eyes, as if the telescreen were always turned toward it, as if "Big Brother Is Watching You" also referred to the collective fixation of us readers on this infernal setting. Indeed, it is as though *our* eyes join Big Brother's in riveted horror on the tyrannical antihero—in a mesmerized or gaping stare at this Medusa-like monster, the perverted Wellsian, a.k.a. Orwellian, World State.

IV

The foregoing sketch toward an architectonics of the utopian imagination—briefly showing how well-conceived utopias carefully reorganize the relationship of narrative elements in fiction in the service of idea—is meant to indicate how fictional utopias construct "states of mind": mental states that might become political states by influencing the emotional and intellectual states of readers. This cartography of the utopian vision demands that readers approach utopias not primarily by way of formal criteria such as complexity, organic unity, character development, and dramatic interest, but rather by a new set of rhetorical criteria. And here the moment is opportune for moving to my second main point: a rationale for an alternative set of aesthetic criteria, rhetorically oriented, for valuing the utopian fiction.[13]

Utopias invite criteria that address what utopias *do* in the world. In that light, the questions asked of a utopia should first attend to personal reader response—that is, to what responses the work evokes in the reader's world—in terms of the reading experience as well as public action.

- Does the utopia alter our vision of how to live the good life?
- Is its "romance of the future" a personally compelling one?
- Is the projected image of social harmony or cultural unity one that will promote better conditions for individuals to pursue happiness, virtue, wealth, and salvation?

Second, we should inquire about the work's larger institutional and social reception history:

- Has the utopia provoked readers to reevaluate their ideas about social arrangements?
- What kind of public impact has the utopia had?
- How has it been received by real readers?
- What has been the "life" of utopia in history?

These questions alert us to the fact that utopias must be approached contextually—not just textually, not just via intrinsic criteria, but via their life in history. Bellamy's *Looking Backward*, Skinner's *Walden Two*, and Orwell's *Nineteen Eighty-Four* were written for the world of action and should be evaluated in relation to it, and all three have exerted an influence utterly disproportionate to their literary merit as judged by formalist criteria of novelistic excellence. We need to examine the connection between utopias and social movements: how and why *Looking Backward* launched the Nationalist Party of the 1890s, how and why *Walden Two* stimulated dozens of experimental utopian communes in the 1950s and '60s, how *Nineteen Eighty-Four* helped change the course of Western debate about socialism and anticommunism in the 1950s.

Appreciation of context allows us to assess how a work succeeds or fails on the basis of its "fit" with the features of its immediate context, how it fulfills the social-psychological needs/desires of a historical moment, how it provokes a change of heart and mind in an audience—not in relation to unchanging formal, psychological, or philosophical standards of complexity and artistic truth. Personal response and historical impact become the new criteria for utopian achievement.

The task of looking to reception history also entails examining the perversions of utopian thought in the very real world of action. For utopias are indeed sometimes not only "stately designs" but "statist designs." Bolshevism and Nazism were utopian visions in the eyes of their leaders and supporters. Given the "fit" or "needs" of a historical moment, the utopia may lend itself to exploitation as a way of bolstering a political program or devising an intellectual pedigree. Works live because of what people do with them—including distorting them.

Creative treason, in the phrase of sociologist Robert Escarpit, happens when an adaptation or translation of a work "betrays" the work, and yet the result is to lend it a new lease on life for a new audience.[14] But what I might call "septic treason" is poisonous betrayal, whereby (for example) some utopias continue to live but in mangled form, ideologically defaced: for example, Thomas More's *Utopia*, claimed by the socialists like Karl Kautsky of the German Social Democratic Party and utilitarians like the followers of Mill; Campanella's *City of the Sun*, exalted by the Mensheviks and Bolsheviks; and Orwell's *Nineteen Eighty-Four*, exploited by the John Birch Society and other rabid anticommunists.

V

The larger issue, on which I will close this chapter, is the implication of this perspective on the utopia for the complex question of generic hierarchy and the politics of reputation.

- Why is utopian fiction noncanonical?
- How do works achieve canonical status?

In *The Politics of Literary Reputation*, I argued that artistic reputation arises not alone from the intrinsic merit of one's work, but rather from a complex of factors that makes works visible initially and then maintains them in their preeminent position. One of my special interests has been how historical contingencies have shaped the value and repute accorded to a single author, George Orwell. Here I am concerned with a related topic: the value and reputation accorded to an entire genre, the utopia. In both instances my argument is this: We should see artistic productions not, in Jane Tompkins's phrase, as "the ineffable product of genius," but as the bearers of a set of national, social, economic, institutional, and professional interests; they are not a matter of indisputable excellence, but the product of innumerable, and only partly recoverable, historical contingencies.[15]

Appreciating the reception history of a work or genre means appreciating how history is not a backdrop against which one admires the artist's skill in transforming the raw materials of reality into art. Instead history becomes the only way of accounting for the enormous impact of works whose force may escape the modern reader. In order to understand that force, it will be important, as densely and richly as possible, to reconstruct imaginatively the context from which a work sprang and the specific problems that it addressed, thus avoiding dehistoricizing the work with a "presentist" bias. Ultimately the critical task within literary academe amounts to engaging in institutional history: a critical institutional history of ourselves as critics who shape values and reputations.

In the case of the utopia, as so often in political discourse, we must learn to value not what separates this work from others as "unique." Rather, the imperative is to prize what it shares in common with other works of its historical moment. For a utopia's impact on the culture at

The Un(der)examined Orwell

large depends not on its escape from the stock and the familiar, but on its tapping into a storehouse of commonly held assumptions. As Tompkins has noted, the works that become "exceptional"—in the sense of reaching an exceptionally large audience and driving exceptionally deep into the political consciousness of a generation—do so not because they depart from the ordinary and conventional, but because they *embrace* what is most widely shared.[16] And what is most widely shared is familiarity with character types, with conventional plots, with the everyday settings and truisms of life. The typicality of these narrative elements in a literary utopia, put in the service of a compelling idea, does not make them bankrupt and stale but produces intense reader response.

Utopias generate passion for an idea. None of the foregoing means that we should uncritically admire that idea: there are dehumanizing aspects of anti-utopias, and even, in many instances, of utopias. I am not endorsing willy-nilly the utopian imagination.

But utopias should be taken seriously; the effect they have on readers, including students in a classroom, is often transfiguring. In a culture that lives more by its shoestrings than by the stars, which tends to undervalue community and prize rugged individualism, utopias point to what might be. And so, when it comes to axiology and art, to literature which is socially conscious and politically committed, let me paraphrase a favorite author of mine: some genres are more equal than others.

Utopias are societal melodramas through which we come to care passionately about both a vision and its hero, the system, which promises a different way of life. Therefore, when one sets aside modernist demands—for psychological complexity, moral ambiguity, epistemological sophistication, stylistic density, formal economy—and attends to how a utopia argues for social change, a different sense of literary excellence emerges and produces a different sense of what constitutes successful characters and plots.

Allergic though he certainly was to literary theory and conceptual wrangling about genre, I believe that Orwell would have been sympathetic to this argument. After all, his oeuvre demonstrates that, in practice, his craft of fiction ran along similar tracks. (As I have proposed elsewhere, this literary lineage might be termed the nonformalist "Other Great Tradition" of the British novel, also thereby a non-Leavisite tradition stretching from realistic novelists such as Defoe and Fielding up through Samuel Butler and the Dickens of *Hard Times* to Wells, Bennett, and Galsworthy.)[17]

Indeed the civil engineering of Oceania—the architectonics of "Room 101"—attests that Orwell crafted the setting of *Nineteen Eighty-Four* with sturdy materials steeled for the world of action and for social change. On this view, critics of the utopia should relinquish the critical perspective that values art according to whether or not it achieves a universal, timeless idea of truth and formal coherence, and should move instead toward a notion of works doing work, artworlds acting in the world. Like good pragmatists, that is, critics of the utopia should ask: "What does the utopia *do*?" rather than "How does this literary work mean?"—and thereupon they should pursue the worldly experiences, aesthetic and otherwise, that emerge from this difference.[18] Utopias—and anti-utopias such as *Nineteen Eighty-Four*—do a particular kind of political work within a particular social and historical context, expressing and shaping that historical context.

The enormous political and cultural impact of *Nineteen Eighty-Four* testifies indisputably to this. So we should value the work it does do, for the contribution it makes to our changing lives. It is a rhetorical work written to and for the age, not the ages, written to and for us, not posterity.

It is an artworld—with state-ly designs on our world.

CHAPTER 16

The Review Orwell
Never Wrote?

One of Orwell's biographers, Gordon Bowker, has speculated about "the biography that Orwell never wrote."[1] A measure of Bowker's stimulating essay is that it provokes numerous conjectures on the part of the reader. As Peter Davison has observed: "What is more important than dreaming up what might have been is whether an essay prompts the reader to think and so leads him or her forward."[2]

In that spirit, on finishing Bowker's essay, I immediately posed the following thought experiment: Let us assume that Orwell never would have written his autobiography. His onetime housekeeper Susan Watson claims that Orwell told her that only he could write his life story accurately—and that he would never do it. If we grant this proposition, then the related question—which places Orwell in his familiar position of book reviewer—might arise: What might Orwell have said about the lives of him written by his biographers?

Drawing on the valuable insights and choice Orwell quotations in Bowker's essay, let me now venture to speculate about "the biographical review Orwell never wrote."

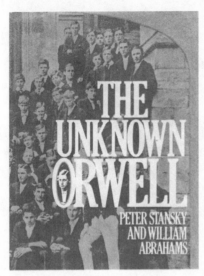

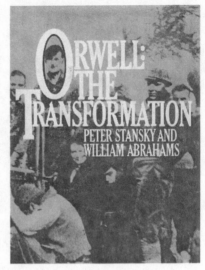

Stansky and Abrahams's two-volume biography of Orwell, published in the 1970s, covered his life until the age of thirty-four. Bernard Crick's *George Orwell: A Life* (1980), the "first complete biography," represented a pioneering attempt to reveal the man beneath the myth and separate Orwell from "Orwell." What might the author of "Confessions of a Book Reviewer" have had to say about these and the subsequent biographies devoted to him?

The Un(der)examined Orwell

I

First it must be acknowledged that Orwell had a low opinion of biography. Bowker believes that Orwell was "certainly not antagonistic to the genre, as some have suggested." Antagonistic? No. But he was quite wary about its potential abuse. That is why he specified in his will that he wanted no biography. As I have noted elsewhere, Richard Rees, who served as Orwell's literary executor along with Sonia Orwell, told biographer Peter Stansky that Orwell's wariness reflected a fear that he might be written up "extravagantly or luridly." In part, Orwell was reacting against the rise of muckraking, tendentious "biograficion." Lytton Strachey's antiheroic *Eminent Victorians* (1918) and the popularity of Freud among intellectuals gave rise in the 1920s and '30s to what Virginia Woolf initially heralded as "The New Biography" and what detractors soon termed "Stracheyism." Less-gifted followers of Strachey soon gave biography a bad name among many serious writers.

Back to my thought experiment. As Bowker points out, Orwell once wrote that "the qualities needed for a biographer are piety and wit." D. J. Taylor's *Orwell: The Life* (2003) is probably the wittiest. It is certainly the quirkiest and most amusing, with most chapters followed by an excursus on idiosyncratic topics ranging from Orwell's distinctive facial and vocal features to his alleged paranoia and obsession with rats. Taylor's biography may be a bit short on piety, but it is so in all the ways that Orwell is likely to have approved. Orwell never advocated "piety" before the biographical subject. Rather, he insisted on respect for the biographer's craft, which demands intellectual integrity when narrating and evaluating a life. These tasks should be guided by the available historical evidence and imbued with a balance of the sympathetic and critical imaginations.

Above all, as Bowker notes, Orwell preferred "the analytical, interpretative method" of biography, which he praised in Lewis Mumford's *Herman Melville* (1929). Orwell also valued what Bowker refers to as the "empirical method" yet did not "believe in all circumstances" that it "alone should be relied upon." Given these commitments, Orwell would have been gratified by the first complete biography of him written by Bernard Crick, *George Orwell: A Life* (1980), which includes a lengthy introduction defending what Crick called his "biography of externality," a quasi-Brechtian approach governed by respect for the factual, the quotidian, the datum.

Yet I suspect that Orwell would have wished that Crick—a political scientist who always sought to integrate social science, political philosophy, and cultural criticism—had written a biography that had risked more of

Dissatisfied with Crick's biography of Orwell, which devoted much attention to Orwell's political and social views, the Orwell Estate commissioned Michael Shelden to write *Orwell: The Authorized Biography* (1991), which stressed his literary sensibility and achievement (*left*). Taking a very different approach to that of the previous biographers, Jeffrey Meyers's *Orwell: Wintry Conscience of His Generation* (2000) probed Orwell's psychology and disclosed the darker side of his genius (*right*).

the "analytical" and "interpretative." As Bowker notes, Orwell remarked about Leon Trotsky's biography of Stalin that some "inherently probable" historical claims (such as Trotsky's view that Stalin ordered the murder of Lenin) were permissible to advance even if near-impossible to prove conclusively. On that view, Orwell might have preferred that Crick had ventured a bit further beyond the available historical evidence and advanced some conclusions, however tentative, about Orwell's own personal history—even if Crick lacked sufficient evidence to prove them definitively (such as the long-standing scholarly ruminations about whether or not Orwell ever shot an elephant, attended a hanging, and so on).

By the same criteria, I believe, Orwell would have admired the work of Michael Shelden's *Orwell: The Authorized Biography* (1991) for its judicious exercise of sympathetic imagination combined with the "analytical, interpretative method." But here, I think, Orwell might have wished for a larger measure of factual detail, precisely the kind of empirical approach that Crick's biography outstandingly represents—and perhaps a bit less speculation without firmer evidence to support it.

The Un(der)examined Orwell

II

What about the other Orwell biographies? Bowker goes on to observe that Orwell's view of biography was "refreshingly free of theoretical dogma," and he notes that it is rather unlikely that Orwell would have had much patience with what might be termed "Marxist biography." Undoubtedly true. So it seems likely that he would have found the Marxist—some invidious critics have called it "neo-Stalinist"—biography of him by Scott Lucas (*Orwell* [2003]), objectionable (even apart from the fact that Lucas displays virtually unremitting hostility, bereft of any human sympathy, for his biographical subject).

Last but not least, Orwell would have probably disapproved of "psychobiography," as Bowker observes, whether approached via Freud, Jung, Adler, or any more contemporary school of psychotherapy. Would he have therefore harbored reservations about the otherwise excellent biography written by Bowker himself, *Inside George Orwell* (2003), which exhibits a sensitive balance between the "empirical method" and the "analytical, interpretative method"? Might he also have voiced similar concerns about Jeffrey Meyers's *Orwell: Wintry Conscience of His Generation* (2003), which relentlessly probes Orwell's psyche, drawing heavily on psychoanalytical concepts that undergird judgments about Orwell's "masochism" and "death wish"?

The centenary year of Orwell's birth, 2003, witnessed the publication of three new and very different biographies of him: Gordon Bowker's pathbreaking, scholarly *Inside George Orwell*; D. J. Taylor's idiosyncratic, perceptive *Orwell: The Life*; and Scott Lucas's combative, avowedly skeptical biographical critique, *Orwell*.

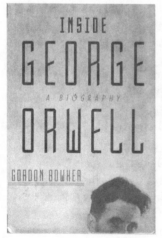

The Review Orwell Never Wrote?

Such assessments—and such language—would have probably elicited a sharp (if defensive) response from Orwell. Or perhaps just his sardonic, deep-throated (tubercular?) laughter. Both responses are conceivable from him.

And yet: One pauses here, because it is also the case that Orwell was always very interested in the psychology of creativity and authorship. Furthermore, his first wife, Eileen Blair, studied Jungian psychology at London University and pursued a master's degree in the field. Bowker and Meyers are not the kind of "biografiends" that Orwell castigated (the coinage owes to James Joyce) who engage in "psycho-autopsies."

So it's also possible that Orwell would have regarded the scholarly snooping into his private life by Bowker and Meyers, if at times excessive or too intrusive, nonetheless justified and illuminating in the main. If that is correct, then he might have wished that the two-volume biography by Peter Stansky and William Abrahams, *The Unknown Orwell* (1972) and *Orwell: The Transformation* (1979), possessed a deeper psychological understanding of the development of Blair into Orwell. Both volumes skillfully integrate the empirical, analytical, and interpretative methods. But they lack much psychological depth. Of course, Stansky and Abrahams labored under two large difficulties. They were the first scholars to attempt a biography of Orwell. Moreover, they were hobbled by the decision of Orwell's widow, Sonia, to refuse all rights to quote from his published or unpublished work. His insistence in his will on no biography notwithstanding, Orwell himself might have granted them such permission. After all, Rees had suggested to young Peter Stansky that the Americans undertake the biography. Stansky and Abrahams had originally planned merely to write about the involvement of Orwell and other British writers in the Spanish Civil War.

III

I have discussed the history of Orwell biography in my first book, *The Politics of Literary Reputation: The Making and Claiming of "St. George" Orwell* (1989), which takes the story of his "afterlife" up until the close of the 1980s—that is, before the appearance of the biographies by Shelden, Meyers, Bowker, D. J. Taylor, and Lucas (and before the second, revised 1992 edition of Bernard Crick's biography). Let me close by alluding to my 1989 study in response to Douglas Kerr's thoughtful reply to Bowker's essay. Kerr writes: "Gordon Bowker's en-

The Un(der)examined Orwell

joyable essay reminds us of Orwell's request that his biography should not be written. Are such requests ever heeded, I wonder?"[3]

In a word: No. My answer today is no different from my conclusion of two decades ago about the lessons of Orwell biography. Fame makes biographical treatment inevitable. The only question is when, not if.

The history of Orwell biography points to important issues beyond Orwell's own case, raising not only legal but also cultural, ethical, and professional questions about the writing of biography in the post-Stracheyan age. Probably the legal right to personal privacy (and personal property) should have prior claim when disputes between author/executor and scholar/biographer arise. . . . The case of Orwell suggests why and how, when a figure achieves a certain stature, the writing of his or her biography can only be delayed by restrictive measures, not prevented. Biographical treatment reflects, not just builds, reputation; a "FAMOUS WRITER" will eventually receive either a good or poor biography, not avoid one.[4]

Jacintha
1948

Jacintha Buddicom in 1948, shortly before she got in touch
with her childhood friend and intimate adolescent companion,
Eric Blair, whose marriage proposal on his return from Burma
she rejected, but who had come to seem to her "less imperfect
than anyone else I ever met." In hindsight, she emphasized her
"memories of the joy and fun Eric and I shared. Knowing each
other's minds so totally insured that I would never marry unless
the 'single oneness' could be found again."

CHAPTER 17

The Life Orwell
Never Lived?

C ould there possibly be anything more of significance
still to be said about George Orwell's life? This book
has largely devoted itself to "the un(der)examined
'Orwell'"—the shadowy or veiled chapters of the legend, not the life.
However, Peter Davison has boldly undertaken the latter task—and, with
the publication of *Orwell: A Life in Letters* (2010), has scored another
literary and editorial triumph.[1] After having compiled and superbly edited the twenty-volume *Complete Works of George Orwell* in the 1980s
and 1990s, he subsequently published three more books that readers
of Orwell value: two edited volumes, *The Lost Orwell* (a supplementary
volume to *The Complete Works*) and *The Diaries of George Orwell*; and
the single best short study of Orwell's literary career, *George Orwell: A
Literary Life*.

Now Davison has collected Orwell's letters, along with a few heretofore unpublished items (by Orwell, or by others about him). Davison
has organized the material chronologically and annotated it carefully,
thereby providing the reader with a judicious overview of Orwell and
his oeuvre. The result is a compelling collection which effectively serves
as the autobiography that Orwell vowed he would never write. Davi-

Orwell's episto-
lary "autobiog-
raphy"? *Orwell:
A Life in Letters*
(2010), edited by
Peter Davison,
appeared on the
sixtieth anniver-
sary of Orwell's
death.

ORWELL

A LIFE IN LETTERS

son's new volume is an important contribution for Orwell biography
and scholarship. *Orwell: A Life in Letters* should take its place beside
the five major biographies by Sir Bernard Crick, Michael Shelden, Jeffrey Meyers, Gordon Bowker, and D. J. Taylor as an indispensable re-
source for understanding George Orwell and his times.

Culled from Davison's twelve previous volumes of Orwell correspondence, *Orwell: A Life in Letters* contains nearly 500 letters and is the
twenty-ninth volume of Orwelliana that Davison has written or edited.
He selected this correspondence from among the 1,700 letters that he
published in volumes 10–20 of *The Complete Works of George Orwell*
(1998) and in *The Lost Orwell* (2006). Among the items from the latter
are Eileen Blair's letters to Norah Myles, her Oxford University class-

The Un(der)examined Orwell

mate and close friend. The new collection also includes significant new material, in particular a letter written by Jacintha Buddicom (1901–1993), a teenage sweetheart of Eric Blair's and a friend of his family, which shows their relationship to have been far more serious than originally supposed.

I

The Jacintha letter is the big news in Davison's collection. In hindsight, it is clear that Jacintha misrepresented her relationship to Eric in her memoir *Eric & Us* (1974).[2] She maintained there that neither of them had any "romantic emotion" for the other, and she took the secret of their shattered love with her to the grave in 1993. One aspect of the secret was an incident that occurred on one of their long

The twenty-six-year-old Jacintha Buddicom (*far right*), after leaving her infant daughter Michal Madaleine, born in 1927, with her solicitor, who was entrusted to give Michal to Jacintha's uncle and aunt, Dr. Noel and Mimi Hawley-Burke. The father escaped abroad as soon as he discovered that Jacintha was pregnant. Michal later emigrated to Canada and had six children, but she was tragically killed in an automobile accident in 1997. The happiness of the new parents and the grief of Jacintha are evident in this picture, taken by a street photographer.

The Life Orwell Never Lived?

walks in Rickmansworth, a Hertfordshire town northwest of London, where both the Blairs and Buddicoms had rented a holiday home in 1921. Jacintha describes it as an assault equivalent to a rape attempt.

This much was already known as a result of the postscript published by Dione Venables, Jacintha's first cousin, in a new edition of *Eric & Us: The Postscript Edition* (2006).[3] The Venables edition established that Jacintha's relationship with Eric was more important than scholars realized. Mrs. Venables also reveals that Eric returned from Burma in 1927 with an engagement ring for Jacintha, but she refused to see him. Predictably (and quite understandably), Blair assumed that she had not forgiven him for his conduct during their walk in 1921, only weeks before he sailed for Burma. Jacintha's reason was not Eric's misconduct, however, but rather a tragic event during his absence: the recent birth of an illegitimate child, whom she had handed over for adoption after the father abandoned her.

Eric and Jacintha never met again, and Blair never knew the real reason why he had been rejected. Their only communication occurred in early 1949, less than a year before Orwell's death, when Jacintha wrote to him after having learned (from her Aunt Lilian) that the author of *Animal Farm* and *Nineteen Eighty-Four* was none other than Eric Blair. After an exchange of letters, Orwell and Jacintha had three telephone conversations in February and March 1949. Dione Venables's postscript addresses all this, and it is invaluable especially because it explains how Jacintha's jumbled feelings prevented her from seeing Eric in 1927.

The other part of the secret is disclosed more fully in a newly published letter in *Orwell: A Life in Letters*. In an exchange with a cousin in May 1972, Jacintha expresses her deep remorse about Eric. Her anguish reveals the poignancy of the sexual mores of post–World War I England, a code that made it difficult for her to cope with her illegitimate pregnancy and Eric's return from Burma. Jacintha confesses that she is writing *Eric & Us* "in the hope of ridding myself of a lifetime of ghosts and regrets at turning away the only man who ever really appealed on all levels."[4] In her letter, which she wrote to comfort a cousin who had conceived a child out of wedlock (and terminated the pregnancy), Jacintha describes her regret about spurning Eric.

> How I wish I had been ready for betrothal when Eric asked me to marry him on his return from Burma. He had ruined what had been such a close and fulfilling relationship since childhood by trying to take us the whole way before I was anywhere near ready for that. It took me literally years to realize that we are all imperfect creatures but

The Un(der)examined Orwell

that Eric was less imperfect than anyone else I ever met. When the time came and I was ready for the next step it was with the wrong man and the result haunts me to this day.[5]

Jacintha also vouchsafes that she was quite unprepared and indeed shocked and angered when she read *Nineteen Eighty-Four* in June 1949. Jacintha became convinced that Julia, Winston Smith's lover, was a portrait of herself. In her letter to her cousin, Jacintha writes: "He [Orwell] describes her with thick dark hair, being very active, hating politics—and their meeting place was a dell full of bluebells." Jacintha was devastated by what she regarded as Orwell's literary act of vengeance. She concludes: "In the end he absolutely destroys me, like a man in hobnail boots stamping on a spider. It hurt my mother so much when she read that book that we always thought it brought on her final heart attack a few days later. Be glad that you have not been torn limb from limb in public."[6]

Was Jacintha in fact the inspiration for "Julia"? Not of course if one considers her renewal of contact with Eric to have been a possible factor; the manuscript of *Nineteen Eighty-Four* was already at the printer in mid-February 1949, so Orwell could not have based Julia on the sudden reentry of Jacintha into his life. She bases much of her argument that she is the model for Julia on the bluebell dell, which was "our special place." But did Orwell share this memory through all the decades? Perhaps bluebells did not exert the same emotional force in his life as in hers, or perhaps the breakup was a permanent source of sadness for her but not for him. Nevertheless, Jacintha avers that she is "certain" that Julia "is clearly Jacintha."[7] Of Winston Smith and Julia, she writes:

> . . . their meeting place was a dell full of bluebells. We always wandered off to our special place when we were at Ticklerton which was full of bluebells. They die so quickly if you pick them so we never did but lay amongst them and adored their heavy pungent scent. That very bluebell dell is described in his book and is part of the central story.[8]

How seriously should we take Orwell's February 15 letter to her? If we read his lines with a sympathetic nod to Jacintha's viewpoint, her suspicions gain a much stronger footing. Orwell says that he "can't stop thinking about the young days with you and [her siblings] Guin and Prosper and things put aside for twenty or thirty years. I am so wanting to see you."[9] Even though Jacintha's sudden reemergence in Orwell's life had

The Life Orwell Never Lived?

nothing to do with the characters in *Nineteen Eighty-Four,* which had already been written, Eric had never forgotten her. She was his dearest childhood friend and his first great passion, and their letters and conversations in 1949 make clear that he cherished their shared past. It seems possible, then, that Orwell based Julia partly on Jacintha's persona because she had endured in his memory so strongly.

II

Although the 1972 Buddicom letter is the major item of interest in the unpublished epistolary material, disclosing that the 1921 parting between Eric and Jacintha haunted her (and perhaps even him) for life—and may have inspired Orwell's most famous female character—*Orwell: Life in Letters* sheds new perspectives not just on Orwell's personal life. It also provides insight into the development of his political outlook. For instance, in a previously unknown letter to the writer-editor Richard Usborne, written in August 1947, Orwell furnishes a thousand-word summary regarding the evolution of his thinking on the warring ideologies of the day. Most important is his remark that "there is not much to choose between Communism and Fascism."[10] Despite Orwell's status as the leading literary Cold Warrior of the West, critics and historians have not claimed that Orwell viewed communism as an evil equivalent to Nazism and fascism—not even his conservative or neoconservative admirers. Thus the statement to Richard Usborne represents an unexpected revelation.

Davison also highlights another "un(der)examined" aspect of Orwell's work: his sense of humor. (Or in Orwell's phrase, quoting Mr. Micawber, "the hollow mask of mirth.") Scattered throughout the letters are examples of Orwell's dry, wry humor. Dismissing the idea of an intelligent left-wing comic book for children because left-wing ideologues are hopelessly solemn or earnest, Orwell notes that "Boys of the OGPU, or The Young Liquidators" would not do. Probably "nobody would read them," he said, adding that "it would be the worse if they did."[11]

A related discovery in Davison's new volume is found in some letters by Orwell's first wife, Eileen, to her friend Norah Myles (1906–1994), several of which display Eileen's own sense of humor. For instance, she writes bemusedly about Orwell and his family, whom she characterizes as "on the shivering verge of gentility."[12] She also wrote before she married him that his family "all adore Eric and consider him quite impossible to live with...."[13] Different as Eileen and George were, however, they got along surprisingly well. Her letters to him in the weeks before she died in March 1945 establish the depth of her affection for him. They should prompt readers who are doubtful about the success of the marriage to reconsider their views. Eileen's letters reveal a side of her (and Orwell) not fully recognized. Thanks to Davison's inclusion of Eileen's letters, she emerges as a real person. Although her correspondence with Norah Myles appeared in *The Lost Orwell*, they fit comfortably within Davison's chronological approach, thus fleshing out the autobiographical aspect of the book. (Moreover, published by Timewell Press, *The Lost Orwell* had a small circulation, and its new material remains unknown to the general public interested in Orwell.)

Orwell's letters also disclose another, very human side of him—his deep love for his adopted son Richard. Although some of their friends were skeptical about whether George and Eileen would be good parents, they proved surprisingly responsible. Orwell's letters to his friends after Eileen's death show how much he enjoyed fatherhood. He wrote constantly about Richard's doings: his weight, what he was eating, his slowness to talk, his talent with things mechanical. Orwell's joy about fatherhood appears in his references not only to his own son but also to his friends' children. His advice possesses Orwell's characteristic quirkiness. When Rayner Heppenstall's child was born, Orwell told him to make sure and give him a good name. "People always grow up like their names. It took me nearly thirty years to work off the effects of being called Eric."[14]

When Julian Symons and his wife had a baby, Orwell writes in a congratulatory note: "They're awfully fun in spite of the nuisance & as they develop one has one's own childhood over again." And then, showing he had thought seriously about child-rearing, Orwell added: "I suppose one thing one has to guard against is imposing one's own childhood on the child."[15]

III

Let me return, in closing, to the Eric-Jacintha relationship and its import for our understanding of Orwell's "life in letters"—that is, to "Eric, Jacintha—& Us." And here let me anticipate the topic of this book's conclusion, which speculates about the course of Orwell's life "if he had lived" beyond January 1950, the month of his premature death at the age of forty-six. Exploring issues associated with Orwell's political legacy rather than his personal life, the conclusion meditates on

Dione Venables, 2008, first cousin of Jacintha Buddicom and publisher of the Blair/Orwell Forum website.

that pensive subjunctive, "If He Had Lived." It conjectures about Orwell's spectral presence in posthumous events as it proposes a counterfactual afterlife. I beg the reader's patience if I conduct a similar thought experiment here with regard to Blair/Orwell and Jacintha.

The Eric-Jacintha relationship raises fascinating questions about the man and writer "If . . ." For the material about Jacintha could drastically alter our conception of Orwell's life. The new disclosures raise intriguing questions: What if Eric Blair had married Jacintha Buddicom? According to Mrs. Venables, Jacintha confided that Eric had asked her to marry him before he went to Burma; he was hoping that she would wait for him as a betrothed girl.[16] Mrs. Venables elaborates:

He had a plan. He saved his salary for those five years. Just look at the letters of those with whom he had served in the Burma Police Force.

The Un(der)examined Orwell

They all make a point of saying that he kept himself to himself, was a bit of a skinflint, and seemed to prefer the company of the "locals." He was saving his salary so that he had a nice nest egg at the end of the five years. He could then afford to have another go at asking Jacintha to marry him. Sadly, it never happened. . . . But he had come back to England, well equipped to make a formal proposal to Jacintha. The fact that those five years, during which he grew into a mature man, had carried the image of Jacintha every time he put money aside, meant that he would never quite exorcise her from his mind.[17]

In light of all this, let us inquire again: How do we interpret Orwell's remark in his February 1949 letter that he could not "stop thinking about the young days with you . . . and things put aside for twenty or thirty years"? Perhaps he too—just like Jacintha—ruminated on those days, fantasized about them, indeed stowed them away for future use, ultimately expressing them via the creation of Julia in *Nineteen Eighty-Four*. If so, then Jacintha truly was the model for Julia—and not Sonia Brownell, Orwell's second wife, whom most scholars have until now regarded as the original for Julia. (My own view now is that Julia is a composite of Jacintha, Sonia, and one or more of Orwell's other lovers.)

The speculations are endless. We could reimagine Orwell's entire life and work on the basis of this new information about Jacintha's cameo appearances in it: her exit from Blair's early life and her brief reappearance at Orwell's end. Her significance thus shifts from the minor status of a forgotten, platonic childhood friend to the role of leading lady—as potential wife and/or unrequited lover and soul mate. On this latter view, her limited presence in Blair/Orwell's life changes radically its arc and shape. We may even wonder whether "Eric Blair" would have become "George Orwell" at all. Jacintha was the oldest nonfamily friend who continued to know Orwell as "Eric." Perhaps he would have retained his birth name as his pen name—influenced by his wife's preference—and what might that have meant for "George Orwell"?

And that latter question concerns not just the narrow topic of a pen name. Both Jacintha's family and Eric's mother were campaigning in 1921 for Eric to sit for the entrance exam to Oxford. Jacintha says that he was becoming receptive to the possibility—and only the Rickmansworth incident, which (temporarily) alienated the families and rained opprobrium on Eric, nixed the plan. That left Burma as his sole option—a form of punishment and exile, as it were, at least from Jacintha's viewpoint.[18]

The Life Orwell Never Lived?

If Eric had attended Oxford, would he have ever gone to Burma? The prospect seems extremely unlikely. Would he have ever seen a hanging or shot an elephant? No—and probably never written about them either. And what else might he have never written? Or written instead of such work?

Human error, tragic misunderstanding, bathos, and revenge: this is indeed the stuff of tragicomedy. It could be part of a melodramatic plot by Thomas Hardy, something akin to the star-crossed fates of Tess and Angel.

Yes, Orwell's afterlife continues to amaze. It represents a literary second act nonpareil.

CHAPTER 18

The Centenarian,
Our Contemporary

The following interview was conducted on May 1, 2003, for "The Connection," a cultural program on National Public Radio, at the downtown office of its Boston affiliate. The occasion, of course, was the approach of the centennial of George Orwell's birth on June 25. I found it interesting to converse about Orwell with the NPR staff and listeners who called "The Connection" to express their views about Orwell. The edited transcript below represents a valuable record of their responses to his work. Indeed their remarks about Orwell's politics and his ongoing topicality shed revealing light on his current standing among present-day readers. One of the notable features of the transcript is that, despite the sea change in world affairs and in Anglo-American culture during the last half century, Orwell's work continues to engage the wider reading public, not just literary academics and politically minded intellectuals. The range of responses also shows that everyone has his or her own Orwell, or "Orwell." The transcript also shows the kinds of attitudes that "ordinary people"—not academics or pundits—have toward Orwell: they are admiring but not uncritical, deeply engaged with the moral questions that preoccupied Orwell.

The text below is edited from the full transcript. A prominent topic was the US-led invasion of Iraq, whose military phase was just concluding. Much of the dialogue concerned the question of Orwell's possible statements and even positions regarding the Iraq war, as well as speculation about his thinking on a host of subjects and events topical on the occasion of his centennial. The questions capture a controversial moment in Orwell's reception history at the dawning of the twenty-first century.

Hosted by Gail Harris, the program opened:

Fact or fiction: "War Is Peace? Freedom Is Slavery? Ignorance Is Strength? There are no American infidels in Baghdad. We have them surrounded in their tanks. Be assured: Baghdad is safe and protected."

Well, if you guessed the first three sentences came from George Orwell's novel Nineteen Eighty-Four *and the second three were delivered weeks ago by the Minister of Information of the Iraqi government, then you're right. And the line between the two is even shorter than . . .*

GH: *I have to ask you first, what would George have made of the statements by the former Iraqi minister?*

JR: Orwell would certainly have classed his remarks as an instance of Newspeak, though he might have also added that there's "Bushspeak" and "Blairspeak" too. There is a great deal of doublethink and doublespeak on both sides of the debate about the Iraqi invasion. And I imagine that Orwell would have targeted both sides for their doublespeaking—though that doesn't mean he'd equate Bush or Blair with Saddam.

GH: *In the larger scheme of things, why do you think Orwell remains—a century after his birth—such an important literary figure?*

JR: There are a number of reasons. One is this: he was virtually alone among his literary generation in his grasp of certain trends of the time and in his genius for encapsulating them in language that became usable for slogans and popular catchwords. "Newspeak," "thoughtcrime," "doublethink," "Big Brother Is Watching You"—all these slogans from *Nineteen Eighty-Four*—as well as those from *Animal Farm*—became screaming anticommunist headlines during the Cold War and are part of the West's political lexicon today. Orwell gave voice to currents that were already under way and managed to do so in arresting, quotable language.

GH: *He was not a pacifist, however? You have to wonder whether he*

The Un(der)examined Orwell

would have supported the war in Iraq because Saddam Hussein exemplified exactly what he seemed to hate most.

JR: He was not a pacifist, though the question of "where Orwell would stand today" on Iraq is a complicated one. After all, he's been dead for fifty-three years! What might he have observed? Probably Orwell would have pointed to the fact that, just as there were in *Nineteen Eighty-Four*, there are shifting alliances in the past two decades involving the U.S. and Iraq—after all, we backed Iraq in the 1980s and even sold weapons to Saddam. In the novel, Oceania, Eurasia, and Eastasia shift from one side to another just as Nazi Germany and Stalinist Russia did in World War II. The 1939 Nazi-Soviet pact established them as allies before June 1941, when Hitler invaded Russia.

GH: *And Orwell was actually against the war, before it began?*

JR: Yes. Orwell was certainly antiwar in 1938. With the war's outbreak in September 1939, however, he became strongly antipacifist—and, in fact, an English patriot. What's important here to emphasize, however, is that Orwell became a patriot during World War II largely because he felt that this could be a revolutionary war—a form of "war socialism" that could usher in socialism in Britain and also lead to the demise of the Empire and British imperialism. In fact, he was quite explicit that English patriotism did not mean British nationalism or imperialism; it was no defense of neocolonialism. He hoped that Britain would suffer a series of defeats sufficiently minor, so that it could remain strong enough to defeat Hitler—and yet sufficiently major to remove Churchill and the Conservatives from power and introduce a Labour Party [i.e., socialist] government. That hope was, in fact, realized in the 1945 British elections.

But his overall attitude toward the war represents a very different conception of patriotism from the nationalism of admirers who promote Orwell as a defender of the status quo. Orwell was careful to distinguish between "patriotism" and "nationalism" in "Notes on Nationalism" (1945). Patriotism was a matter of cultural sentiment and in no way involved imposing one's values on other peoples (which he might have accused [President George W.] Bush and [Defense Secretary Donald] Rumsfeld of doing in Iraq and elsewhere). Nationalism was a rather aggressive politics that included the ultimate imposition of one's values on other people.

GH: *And why do we even care? And why are people even fighting about this all these years later?*

JR: It is because Orwell still seems relevant, despite all the changes in the Zeitgeist that have occurred in the decades since his death. If you Google the following phrase, you'll find that ordinary readers as well as journalists and intellectuals repeatedly pose the question: "If Orwell Were Alive Today?" In fact, I often imagine that there are these placards waving in front of me emblazoned "W.W.G.O.D," not unlike those in some Christian funda-

The Un(der)examined Orwell

mentalist rallies heralding "W.W.J.D." "What Would George Orwell Do?" the airwaves and newspaper headlines wonder. And in some respects that question is voiced even more loudly and insistently than previously. For two reasons: one is that those readers who ask that question today are from a generation so far removed from Orwell's own that the historical context for understanding his situation is lacking. So they feel liberated to invent any kind of "Orwell" to respond. Secondly, no one has replaced him. Of all the potential candidates one can imagine, they seem like small fry compared to "the Big O."[1] In fact, this year has witnessed numerous proposals nominating someone as "Orwell of our time." Yet no fully satisfactory candidate has emerged. And that's because George Orwell has been canonized: he's now "St. George Orwell," the patron saint of postwar England, the patriot and the defender of British values. And he's also "St. George" the pure stylist, the prose guardian and indeed "prose laureate" of the West, the author who wrote in a language that has become a model of clear, simple writing.

GH: *But had that been said to his face, don't you think he would have snorted and stomped out of the room?*

JR: Yes—or laughed sardonically. Orwell was no "saint." He was a human being like all of us, with all of the contradictions of a flawed human being. He was a decent man and reportedly a good, faithful friend. At the same time, he led a somewhat conflicted personal life, as his numerous infidelities during his marriage to Eileen attest.

TOP LEFT: Through the myopic eye of Prophet Orwell: was George wrong about the personal computer?

TOP RIGHT: The revolution *will* be televised (and advertised!). During the countdown to Orwell's title date, the socialist writer was recast as a capitalist moneymaker. Cashing in on the "Profit Orwell," numerous firms and stores spun ambitious advertising campaigns off "1984." One of the most audacious was Einstein Moomjy Carpet Store in New York: "19.84 for a revolutionary new carpet"!

BOTTOM LEFT: W.W.G.O.D.? campaign buttons ("Orwell in '84!!") and other materials were produced by a Pennsylvania public relations firm when it launched the "Orwell for President" campaign in 1983. Nominated that year on April Fool's Day, Orwell was promoted as "the *doubleplusungood* candidate."

BOTTOM RIGHT: "If Orwell Were Alive Today!" The editor of the *Binghamton Sun-Bulletin* (New York), Steve Jones, invented "The 1984 Board Game." According to Jones, "the object of the game is to avoid being killed before 1985." Among the stops on the game board are "Down with the Big Brother," "Doublethink," "Junior Anti-Sex League," "Vaporized," and "Goodthink." The game features seventeen rules. For instance, rule no. 5 specifies: "A player landing on the square Junior Anti-Sex League must proceed immediately to the nearest Thought Police station."

The Centenarian, Our Contemporary

GH: *Let's start with his birth into the English middle class. His name was Eric Blair. He went to Eton and then he spent almost the rest of his life trying to declass himself. He was a man pursuing downward mobility in a time when many people were not interested in going in that direction.*

JR: Yes, he joked about himself as being from the "lower-upper-middle class." He had a sufficiently genteel upbringing to get into Eton—Britain's leading public school—and before that he attended a prep school of some distinction. However, his family had no money. One of the reasons why Orwell entered the Indian Imperial Police after graduating from Eton was that his father had served as a policeman in India in the Empire police. Orwell, of course, served in Burma.

The Burmese experience transformed him into a strong anti-imperialist—and, of course, another question posed today is, "How would Orwell apply his conception of imperialism to our situation?" Would Orwell the anti-colonialist and the anti-imperialist regard the current war in Iraq as an instance of American imperialism? Or would he regard the post-imperialist world, represented by governments such as Robert Mugabe's Zimbabwe, as even more unjust than the British Empire? After all, Orwell died before the African and most Asian colonies were liberated—perhaps he would have distinguished between what some scholars called "progressive" and "regressive" colonialism? Such are the conjectures.

GH: *How did he make that shift from being Eric Blair to George Orwell?*

JR: He actually proposed a number of pseudonyms, apparently in a rather casual fashion to his publisher, one of which was H. Lewis Allways. People have often joked about what his legacy might be if he had adopted that name. Imagine it: "If H. Lewis Allways Were Alive Today." Somehow it rings a bit flat!

Blair apparently preferred "George Orwell" because a small river, the Orwell in Suffolk, flowed near his home and because of St. George's associations with England—St. George the dragon slayer. His publisher accepted his choice. One of the reasons that Orwell decided on a pseudonym was that he was a bit anxious about his forthcoming first book, *Down and Out in Paris and London* [1933]. He had just turned thirty, and his stories about trafficking with tramps and minors would be getting back to his parents and his relatives. He thought it might be easier for him personally to have a pseudonym, so that his family wouldn't be ashamed of him when they heard about the contents of his book.

GH: *And yet his tombstone says "Eric Blair"?*

The Un(der)examined Orwell

JR: "Here Lies Eric Blair" is engraved on his tombstone. He used that name in official circumstances all his life. Ironically, his second wife, Sonia Brownell, whom he had married three months before his death, took the married name "Orwell."

GH: *Isn't it interesting that on that tombstone there isn't anything, not even in parentheses, identifying him as George Orwell?*

JR: Indeed. There is a sense in which Orwell embraced Eric Blair as the identity for his personal life, whereas George Orwell was his literary personality. And that literary identity would live on in his books—in fact, in the leather-bound *Collected Works* that he dreamed would be published— and so it didn't need to be etched in stone.

GH: *Let me ask you: What's your take on Orwell and women?*

JR: I don't believe he was a misogynist. As I have said, he was no saint; he was a man of his time. If one looks to the context of the period in which he was writing—the 1930s and '40s—one sees that he was rather like most of his contemporaries. The Depression, fascism, and the approach of war dominated people's concerns. He was not ahead of his time on feminism and women's rights. Unfortunately, there is an expectation that someone who has been lionized so much and who was ahead of time on other significant issues (such as imperialism, fascism, and Stalinism) should have possessed the same kind of progressive views about women.

I believe he was anti-feminist, but not anti-woman. Orwell was a man of his time on gender issues, not a misogynist.

Let me also add: George Orwell is not the same as the posthumous figure of "Orwell," the mythic "St. George Orwell," the canonized saint whom everyone is invited to admire. People look to others as role models and often want to see them as exemplary models on all kinds of diverse issues. This idea of an intellectual genealogy or "tradition" is a very understandable urge. But we need to practice caution. We must develop an ethics of admiration and detraction—that is, responsible ways of admiring and criticizing.

GUEST CALLER: *I think it doesn't matter today about where he stood on World War II. We should look at his work. At least to those books that are relevant to our situation today: most interesting is the idea in* Nineteen Eighty-Four *of perpetual warfare. I think perpetual warfare will continue so long as it distracts people and prevents them from concentrating on problems that are closer to home. I don't worry about the war with Iraq, but I feel that he would have objected mightily to some of the euphemisms—for example, "collateral damage." So I would like your opinion on that.*

The Centenarian, Our Contemporary

JR: I do agree that it is crucially important to keep the attention on Orwell's literary work and not get caught up with debates centered on his personality, either involving his literary personality or the life of the man. On the other hand, the reality is that George Orwell has been enshrined as a model. So there are issues pertinent to his biography that should not be ignored.

On the issue of *Nineteen Eighty-Four*'s relevance to American culture, we must remember that Orwell titles his dictatorship's national anthem "Oceania, tis of thee"; he also calls its currency "dollars," not rubles or pounds. In a June 1949 letter about his intentions in the novel, he stressed that he was not merely writing about the degenerative tendencies of English socialism, but also what he called "100 percent Americanism." That letter is sometimes taken as Orwell's warning against the rise of what became McCarthyism several months later. *Nineteen Eighty-Four* was primarily targeted against Stalinism, but Orwell was also pointing out that there were totalitarian tendencies on the Right and the Left within the western democracies.

GUEST CALLER: *Going back to* Nineteen Eighty-Four, *the telescreen is in every apartment and house so that Big Brother can watch you. And I think one application to the world today is that within the past year some young lady has set up a website where she can be watched twenty-four hours a day.*

GH: *Assuming anyone cares to—*

GUEST CALLER: *Yes, but it brings up the possibility of governments maintaining that we should have this arrangement to protect us from terrorists. What Orwell foresaw in theory is now reality, given that the technology is available.*

GH: *What about that, John? Are we now living in a world that Orwell really predicted?*

JR: Certainly there are features of *Nineteen Eighty-Four* that seem to be realized today in the democratic West, not just in dictatorial or one-party states. The similarities between what Orwell wrote in *Nineteen Eighty-Four* and current reality are why people often call him a "prophet." On the other hand, many post–World War II events contradict the scenarios of *Nineteen Eighty-Four*. For instance, if anything, we do not—especially not in the West—live in a rundown empire overwhelmingly populated by starving masses. There are indeed shifting alliances and "perpetual warfare," with the United States often fighting proxy wars abroad rather than committing our own troops. Yet the U.S.-led invasions and U.S. occupation forces in Afghanistan and Iraq contradict such easy generalizations.

On the other hand, Orwell thought that capitalism was doomed. At times he feared that a totalitarian state was on the horizon. Today, the world looks nothing like that. Capitalism is not dying: it is flourishing. And there is no longer a Cold War confrontation between two (or three) great superpowers.

GH: *John, let me ask you about Orwell's literary style. It demonstrated a new way of writing about serious subjects. He was very clear, he used short words. I am wondering whether that was the BBC influence at work, or simply a matter of how he always thought and how he wrote.*

JR: Even as a working journalist penning book reviews and writing about intellectual topics, Orwell wrote simple, lucid prose. Until the early twentieth century the predominant literary style tended toward the ornate. For instance, consider the prose style of Samuel Johnson. Orwell helped popularize the journalistic idiom in belles lettres. He wrote about intellectual topics in short, concise, fast-moving sentences, which has also become the basis of today's "business English." At the same time, he constructed a literary persona of a salty, honest, straightforward author.

GH: *—of a working man.*

JR: Yes, Orwell's is a kind of working man's English, and that of course is another reason for his special masculine appeal. Orwell is so significant as a writer's guide or "prose guardian" because he can be consulted in essays such as "Politics and the English Language," in which he criticized language corruption and warned against the propaganda of *Nineteen Eighty-Four*; and at the same time he can be imitated as a prose model (or "prose laureate") who exemplified a refreshingly direct, clear style. And yes, his two-year stint at the BBC helped him hone this clear, clean style.

GH: *I could add that he hated it there! He worked there during the war and apparently couldn't wait to get out. He really did paint a bleak picture of life there in* Nineteen Eighty-Four.

GUEST CALLER: *I have a question about* Animal Farm. *I am currently studying it in my English 12 class. And we all want to know where the Seven Commandments come from. Were they just his idea? Or are they derived from some other writing?*

JR: The seventh commandment, which is "revised" by Squealer, actually derived from a forgotten short story [Philip Guedalla's "A Russian Fairy Tale" (1928)]. Orwell simply adapted the line and integrated it into *Animal Farm*. He sometimes is criticized as a plagiarist for doing that with-

The Centenarian, Our Contemporary

out attribution. The seventh commandment reads: "All animals are equal, but some are more equal than others."

In general, however, the Seven Commandments of "Animalism" are allegorical. "Animalism" can be equated with Stalinism or Marxism-Leninism, the "state religion" of the USSR. Orwell gave "Animalism" seven commandments; of course, in the Old Testament, Moses receives ten. The number wasn't important for Orwell to match. He just wanted to invoke the idea. The first six commandments in *Animal Farm* are not based on anything specific. They are targeting how language is corrupted, manipulated, and turned inside out. They anticipate the three great "commandments" of *Nineteen Eighty-Four*: "War Is Peace, Freedom Is Slavery, Ignorance Is Strength."

GH: *I take it that this course is English 12 that you're probably a senior in high school. How are you enjoying the book?*

GUEST CALLER: *I really enjoyed the book. It's a lot like* Nineteen Eighty-Four. *They both are really great novels that are relevant today.*

GH: *John, would those of us who encountered Orwell in high school or perhaps in college be well served in going back and rereading both* Nineteen Eighty-Four *and* Animal Farm *as grown-ups? I found myself leafing through both of them and really getting more out of them this time.*

JR: Yes. And that is the mark of great literature. One can return to it, reread it, and derive deepened understanding and pleasure. Going back to those two books, we can find how we have changed as readers. We discover new dimensions of the books—and that is the difference between literature and propaganda, or between literature and sub-literature (or "kitsch").

By the way, if Orwell had died *before* the publication of *Animal Farm* (1945) and *Nineteen Eighty-Four* (1949), both of which appeared during the last four years of his life, I doubt we would be having this conversation. He'd be a little-known writer who published some early, arguably rather mediocre, realistic novels during the 1930s. He'd be regarded as a good journalist who wrote a few superb essays. That would be the end of it. The fact is that *Nineteen Eighty-Four* and *Animal Farm* are a crucial part of his reputation today. Orwell's moral and political stature largely rests on the significance of these last two books.

GUEST CALLER: *When I think about Orwell and his legacy, I think of the second half of* The Road to Wigan Pier *and about the coal miners in England. And he is pretty derogatory. He talks in harsh language about other socialists. Do you think Orwell was successful as an empowering writer, as*

The Un(der)examined Orwell

one who increased dialogue within the mainstream? Or just a writer who questioned authority?

JR: *The Road to Wigan Pier* is a very controversial work. Nowadays, he is castigated by many leftists for its criticisms of British socialists as trendy and superficial, what we might today term their "radical chic." Orwell is also derided on the Left for not having exhibited progressive views of women, both in *Wigan Pier* and elsewhere. Obviously he is not regarded today as having empowered all groups—although the controversies about him suggest that he has certainly promoted discussion in the mainstream as well as in alternative media.

All this raises the recurrent question, "If Orwell were alive today, where would he stand?" Take the issue of feminism. The editor of *The Complete Works of George Orwell*, Peter Davison, has done a little study in which he discusses several dozen works contemporaneous with *The Road to Wigan Pier* and examines how much attention they devote to working-class women. And there is almost none. Here again, Orwell was a man of his time. The standard view of coal mining was that it was a masculine profession. He wasn't ahead of his time.

We have this chronic problem when we exalt someone as a secular saint. Orwell was a human being with foibles and flaws. Nowadays, we emphasize the flaws. However, we run the risk of overemphasizing them. Taking Orwell down a few pegs is often a strategy—consciously or unconsciously—for elevating oneself. Let's instead value what he got right, openly debate what is disputable in his work, and fairly criticize what he got wrong, all the while acknowledging that he was no hero or saint but simply a person of his time.

If He Had Lived . . .

"**[I]**f one imagines him as living into our own day," wrote Orwell about Jack London in 1945, "it is very hard to be sure where his political allegiance would have lain. One can imagine him in the Communist Party, one can imagine him falling victim to Nazi racial theory, and one can imagine him the quixotic champion of some Trotskyist or Anarchist sect."[1] Indeed it is interesting to ponder what Orwell's response to world events might have been had he lived another decade—or even several more—and confronted the different political and social issues that emerged after midcentury. "If he had lived," mused Irving Howe in 1968, "he would today be no more than sixty-five years old. How much we have missed in those two decades!" Howe went on to envisage the spectacle of Orwell's pungent invective skewering the politicians of the times: "Imagine Orwell ripping into one of Harold Wilson's mealy speeches, imagine him examining the thought of Spiro Agnew, imagine him dissecting the ideology of Tom Hayden, imagine him casting a frosty eye on the current wave of irrationalism in Western culture! . . . The loss seems enormous."[2]

A few years later, W. H. Auden expressed a similar regret, though he hesitated to prophesy Orwell's posthumous stands. "Today [1971], reading his reactions to events," wrote Auden, once a victim of Orwell's attacks on "the pansy Left," "my first thought is: Oh, how I wish that Orwell were still alive, so that I could read his comments on contemporary events!" Auden, after pronouncing Orwell a "true Christian," ran through his list: drugs, trade unions, birth control, nationalization, and student demonstrations. "What he would have said I have no idea," Auden concluded. "I am only certain he would be worth listening to."[3]

Agreed. Precisely because so many readers[4] have been "certain he would have been worth listening to," this conclusion ventures—at the risk of temerity, hubris, and foolhardiness—to do just what Irving Howe dared and Auden judiciously sidestepped: to forecast Orwell's "comments on contemporary events," that is, "what he would have said."

Today historians are fascinated by the concept of "counterfactuals." The judicious use of counterfactuals in historiography raises the question "what if" yet scrupulously avoids drifting into the realm of fantasy. The "what ifs" posed must possess a plausible logic, whereby they also furnish new insights into historical issues or turning points.[5] As we shall see, applying such a historiographical tool for biographical purposes to a major literary/cultural figure such as George Orwell enables scholars to gain a greater appreciation for his work and what he sought to do.[6]

If George Orwell (1903–1950) had received his biblically allotted three score and ten, he would have died in 1973. If he had lived until the title date of his great anti-utopian novel, *Nineteen Eighty-Four*, he would have been eighty-one. If he had survived to become a venerable centenarian—an admittedly unlikely prospect, given his history of poor health—he would have witnessed the US-led invasion of Iraq in 2003.

By the time of Orwell's death in January 1950 at the age of forty-six, he had already become a highly respected political journalist, an internationally renowned novelist, and a nondoctrinaire socialist with a deep antinomian streak in his temperament. A patriot yet never a nationalist, an adamant political radical though a cultural traditionalist, Orwell's progress from public school boy to Imperial Burmese policeman to impecunious freelance writer had shaped his political and social views by the early 1930s. Given Orwell's preference for plainspeaking and straightforward prose, it is likely that whatever stance he took would be clearly and directly stated. The contrarian element in his makeup was far too strong for him ever to fall in line rigidly with either the Left or Right.

If He Had Lived . . .

II

On some issues the posthumous Orwell's likely response to events is somewhat more easily foreseeable, though the inevitable hazards of historical analogies and the temptations to misread the past warrant emphasis.[7] Consider the postcolonial situation of the 1950s, when a wave of national independence movements first swept through Africa and Asia. Orwell was a firm anti-imperialist, even dating back to his autobiographical essay "A Hanging" (1931), his novel *Burmese Days* (1934), and his classic, oft-reprinted literary memoir, "Shooting an Elephant" (1936). Orwell's service in the Indian Imperial Police in Burma had soured him forever on the idea of Empire. To him it was little more than a pretense for exploiting Asians and Africans in favor of the white race. Throughout his mature years he advocated the withdrawal of the British Raj from India. He would have cheered the hauling down of the Union Jack throughout the rest of the British Empire in the late 1950s and early 1960s.[8]

What position would he have taken on the Cold War? (The Oxford English Dictionary credits Orwell as one of the first to use the term.) Long before Orwell's death, the battle lines had been clearly drawn: by the winter of 1949–1950, the Cold War was fully under way. In fact, because of the sweeping success of *Animal Farm* (1945) and *Nineteen Eighty-Four* (1949)—both of which immediately sold hundreds of thousands of copies, became US Book-of-the-Month Club selections, and were widely translated—Orwell was viewed as a spokesman for the anti-communist cause.

Uncompromising though his hatred of Stalinism and left-wing orthodoxy indeed was, his reputation as a Cold Warrior dismayed Orwell in a certain respect. Outside the London literary scene, where his dissident leftist stance was generally well understood, his criticisms of the Soviet Union and communism were often misinterpreted, deliberately or not. For instance, in the United States and on the Continent, his independent, anti-Stalinist politics was exploited by some conservatives to defend capitalism and repudiate the very idea of socialism. Especially after the publication of *Nineteen Eighty-Four* in June 1949, Orwell strove—with only partial success—to clarify that he supported democratic socialism in general and the British Labour Party in particular.[9]

In June 1950 the Korean War erupted. Its outbreak would have confronted Orwell with a clear choice: support armed defense against communist aggression or remain quiescent. During World War II, Orwell had rejected pacifism as a politically irresponsible position. As he wrote in "Notes on Nationalism" (1945): "Pacifism, as it appears among a section of the intelligentsia, is secretly inspired by an admiration for power and successful cruelty."[10] Orwell would have had no difficulty endorsing the Labour government's decision to take military action against the North Korean communist regime.

As the Korean War dragged on until its negotiated settlement in mid-1953, however, it sharpened a Cold War split on the London Left that had already emerged during Orwell's lifetime between liberal anticommunists (including his friends Arthur Koestler, Stephen Spender, and Richard Crossman) and (mostly Stalinist) radicals who believed in a postwar version of the old 1930s Popular Front position of "No enemies on the Left."

Orwell certainly would have sided with his anticommunist colleagues. As early as 1948, Orwell had derided the Labour MP, Konni Zilliacus, as a Soviet sympathizer on the grounds his views were "barely distinguishable from that of the CP . . . and that when Soviet and British interests appear to clash, [he] will support the Soviet interests."[11] Without doubt Orwell would have remained resolutely anticommunist had he lived, because no significant postwar developments occurred within the communist world that would have shaken his convictions. If anything, Khruschev's denunciation of Stalin in his "Secret Speech" at the USSR's Twentieth Party Congress in February 1956, followed by the Soviet invasion of Hungary that November, would have only reaffirmed Orwell's contempt for communism and its fellow travelers on the Left. (A decade later, Leonid Brezhnev's pronouncement—the so-called Brezhnev Doctrine, whereby no Warsaw Pact "ally" could withdraw from the Soviet system, an edict which the USSR brutally applied in its decision to invade Czechoslovakia in May 1968—would only have reinforced Orwell's anticommunist convictions.)

Although the Korean War split the British Left, anticommunism was never as potent a political force in Britain as it became in the United States during the 1950s.[12] As a vigorous supporter of free speech, even for Stalinists, Orwell would have castigated Senator Joseph McCarthy's anticommunist crusade during 1950–1954. One has only to look at the American intellectuals with whom Orwell agreed, such as the radical critic Dwight Macdonald or the editors of the left-wing *Partisan Review* (known as *PR*, for which Orwell wrote as their London wartime correspondent)—all of whom were sharp critics of McCarthy—to recognize where Orwell would have stood.[13]

If He Had Lived . . .

III

And yet, given that his *PR* colleagues were hopelessly divided about the issue a dozen years later, where would Orwell have stood on the Vietnam War? Given Orwell's bedrock anticolonialism, which predates and always undergirded his antimercantilism, the answer is clear, even though today's neoconservatives (such as Norman Podhoretz) highlight his antipacificism and anticommunism to argue differently: Orwell would have opposed US military involvement as a new form of Western neo-imperialism, or as a mere reversion to some outdated species of colonialism. Whatever America's intentions in Southeast Asia, Orwell would not have repudiated the perspective expressed in "Shooting an Elephant." Imperialism, he insisted, enslaves not only the subalterns but also the masters.

Nonetheless, Orwell would never have veered toward the opposite pole and into pious or naïve rhapsodies in Red. He would have avoided romanticizing Ché Guevara, Mao Zedong, or Ho Chi Minh, a common tendency on the Left—especially within the New Left and the student movement—throughout the West in the late 1960s. Orwell hadn't been taken in by the talk of "Uncle" Joe Stalin in the 1940s. He would have dismissed the café Marxist patter in the 1960s about Ché and Mao and Ho ("the George Washington of Vietnam") as equal nonsense.[14]

If he drew the line on endorsing US conduct in Vietnam, would his Cold Warrior politics nonetheless have led him to participate during the 1950s and '60s in the clandestine activities of the anticommunist Congress for Cultural Freedom (CCF)? This international organization, which was secretly funded by the CIA, included on its British and American steering committee many of Orwell's London friends (e.g., Spender, Malcolm Muggeridge, Fred Warburg) and his *PR* colleagues (e.g., Macdonald, Diana Trilling, Sidney Hook). The CIA connection was exposed in February and March 1967 by the antiwar New Left magazine *Ramparts*, much to the embarrassment of the liberal anticommunist intelligentsia.[15]

Orwell would have backed the activities of the CCF as the rather mild "dirty work" of cultural politics—a necessary, if regrettable counterpropaganda initiative if Western democracies were to battle effectively the unscrupulous, no-holds-barred, totalitarian tactics of USSR tyranny. He would not have associated the CCF with McCarthyism, let alone viewed its funding source as rendering it equivalent to a Soviet propaganda organ. (CCF publications—such as *Encounter* in London and *Der Monat* in Berlin—were recognized for their literary quality and po-

The Unexamined Orwell

litical independence by noncommunist intellectuals across the ideological spectrum.)

On CCF matters, Orwell's commitment to anticommunism would have proven decisive. He would have behaved toward the CCF as he did toward the Labour Party's Information Research Department (IRD), a case in which Orwell's distrust of communism led him—if the step is evaluated with the historical hindsight of decades—into one of the most controversial actions of his career. In May 1949 Orwell responded to a request from an old friend, Celia Kirwan, sister-in-law of Arthur Koestler, by sending her a list of thirty-eight people whose political allegiances he suspected. She was working for the IRD, a new Foreign Office agency that carried out democratic, pro-Western propaganda. (He felt deep affection toward her too; indeed he had proposed marriage to her in 1945.)

For years Orwell had kept a private notebook annotated with the names of more than one hundred probable communists or (in the shorthand expression) "FT," fellow travelers. Orwell's hostility to Stalinism and its British intellectual adherents dated from even before the Spanish Civil War in 1936–1938. He had long argued that destruction of the myth that the Soviet system was a legitimate form of socialism was necessary "if we want to revive the Socialist movement." He also believed (with justification, as British government files later revealed) that English communists and their sympathizers were behind many of his difficulties in finding a publisher for *Animal Farm* in 1944.

When Kirwan requested his short list of political unreliables, Orwell had no qualms giving her a sample of his suspects. Orwell told Kirwan that, in his opinion, the thirty-eight people on his list were all "crypto-communists, fellow-travelers or inclined that way and should not be trusted as propagandists." Among the names on his list were the actor Charlie Chaplin; Kingsley Martin, editor of the *New Statesman* and a long-time bête noire of Orwell's; D. N. Pritt, a Marxist MP who was expelled from the Labour Party because of his pro-Stalinist obeisance; the political economist Harold Laski; and the popular novelist J. B. Priestley.

When this list became public in 2003, many critics of Orwell accused him of betraying socialism. Christopher Hill, the English Marxist historian, declared that the list showed that Orwell was "two-faced." According to the left-wing journalist Paul Foot, the existence of such a list showed that Orwell had taken "a McCarthyite position toward the end of his life." The Labour MP Gerald Kaufman went, if anything, even further, trumpeting: "Orwell was Big Brother too."

If He Had Lived . . .

Was this accurate? Hardly. Orwell's actions bore no resemblance to McCarthy-type slander and blacklisting. First, Orwell was a sincere anti-communist, not someone trying to exploit the issue for his own advancement. Secondly, most of the people on his list were indeed of doubtful loyalty. For instance, Orwell named Peter Smollett, born Peter Smolka of Austria, as a possible Russian agent. Here, as in so many other political judgments, Orwell was prescient. When the KGB archives were opened in the 1990s, they disclosed that Smollett was a Soviet mole who had been recruited by none other than Kim Philby—and who (*mirabilé dictu!*) had mobilized his publishing connections to block acceptance of *Animal Farm* during the war.

Was Orwell nonetheless a hypocritical sell-out of his own side, a traitor to the Left? Not at all. Orwell's list was simply intended to alert Kirwan that these people should not be hired for pro-Western propaganda assignments since their loyalty to England was questionable at best. To tar Orwell with the brush of McCarthyism because he opposed paying anti-Western critics to write prodemocratic polemics is strained beyond reach. Moreover, none of the people on Orwell's list had their careers harmed (Chaplin, for example, wound up living in England and was even knighted; Priestley remained a beloved and best-selling writer for years).[16]

Related to the complex matter of Orwell's Cold War stand is the issue of "where Orwell would have stood" on the Campaign for Nuclear Disarmament (CND) in the late 1950s and 1960s. That question arose chiefly among young British leftists of the generation succeeding Orwell. Here, Orwell's views in essays such as "You and the Atom Bomb" (1945) would have likely prevailed: he would have supported deterrence. Without belligerent rhetoric or cynical *realpolitik*, he would have voiced the need for pragmatism in the face of totalitarian evil—a stance resonant with his likely pro-CCF stand. But he would have tempered his call for nuclear deterrence after Stalin's death in March 1953, and especially by the 1980s. He would have parted company with pro-nuclear hawks and opposed the Reagan administration's acceleration of the arms race, urging instead—however great the risk to his reputation as a tough-minded anticommunist—that both the United States and the USSR hammer out a workable, verifiable treaty. On these thorny questions of disarmament and détente, Orwell's democratic socialist stance would have resembled the politics of his close friend and fellow *Tribune* editor, Labour leader Aneurin Bevan, who sided with Hugh Gaitskell in a controversial 1957 speech and supported, with qualification, the Labour Party's decision to deploy nuclear weapons. Bevan was severely castigated by many leftists for his pragmatic policy stand—even by some former *Tribune* colleagues. Both young and Marxist and noncommunist leftists saw Bevan in 1960 as an accommodator to Gaitskell's "gradualism," which had led the Labour Party into a blind alley.

Here again, it is important to stress that Orwell was a democratic socialist first and an anticommunist Cold Warrior second. He embraced the latter stand in his role as "conscience of the Left," in the phrase of his admiring *Tribune* colleague John Atkins, whereby he sought to defend and protect what he regarded as the basic values of socialism: freedom and justice for all. Orwell's outrage invariably focused on *la trahison des clercs*; his criticism was almost always directed at social*ists*, not social*ism*: he mercilessly attacked their lies and orthodoxies because he wanted socialists to be worthy of socialism. A "conscience" of the Left does criticize from within; and though Orwell may sometimes have been a guilty or excessively scrupulous conscience, he flayed the Left in order to strengthen it, not to weaken or abandon it. The motives for his assaults thus bore no resemblance to those of the anticommunist conservatives who adopted him (such as the John Birch Society, which adopted "1-9-8-4" as the last four digits for the phone number of its national headquarters).

The point is a crucial one: Orwell was never an "anticommunist" or "Cold Warrior" as those terms came to be understood in liberal-Left intellectual circles during the McCarthy era—that is, a knee-jerk dogmatist of the far Right. He was that outstanding, uncommon, historically situated, intellectual phenomenon: the "antitotalitarian." He hated all tyrannies, whether of the totalitarian Right in fascist Spain or Germany, or of the totalitarian Left in Stalinist Russia. His louder, more frequent castigation of the latter owed to his view that Western democracies (especially the Western intelligentsia) were beholden to communist orthodoxy—and in danger of becoming "Ingsoc." This immediate threat oriented his antitotalitarian stance, which he broadly shared with the independent leftists associated with *Partisan Review*. Or, as Julian Symons, his friend and fellow *Tribune* writer, once put it, Orwell stood with that tiny, distinctive cluster of wartime and early postwar intellectuals, the "premature anti-Stalinists."[17]

IV

If we look beyond the era of liberal anticommunism and the Vietnam War, the international scene is more complicated. In

If He Had Lived . . .

the 1970s and 1980s, the thawing of the Cold War first ushered in a period of East-West détente, but then soon gave rise to renewed hostilities as Reaganism, the Soviet invasion of Afghanistan, and the breakdown of disarmament negotiations all mutually reinforced US-Soviet tensions.

Where would Orwell have come down on such issues as the nuclear freeze, NATO missile deployment in Western Europe, and the civil war in Nicaragua? Despite Orwell's opposition to pacifism during World War II, his English patriotism, and his loathing of the Soviet Union, he would probably have taken nuanced positions on all these issues. He would have opposed the nuclear freeze as an unjustified unilateral step by the West, advocating instead that NATO deployment proceed in the absence of suitable Soviet concessions. But he would have opposed US policy in Nicaragua on anti-imperialist grounds similar to his Vietnam War position. Skeptical though he would have remained about fuzzy-minded neutralist thinking, let alone fatuous procommunist (or Euro-communist) rhetoric, he would not have dismissed the peace movement as pacifist/neo-isolationist, nor regarded détente as a simple-minded accommodation to "Soviet imperialism."

And what about the subject of our concluding chapter in Part 3, "The Centenarian, Our Contemporary"? In the unlikely event that Orwell had survived into the twenty-first century, how would he have responded to the events of September 11, 2001, and thereafter? Would he have endorsed the Bush administration's war on terrorism? And the Obama administration's modified reaffirmation of it? Or would he have emphasized the abridgment of Americans' civil liberties, the US government's violation of prisoners' rights in Guantanamo Bay (and elsewhere), and American mishandling of the Iraq War and the subsequent occupation?

Neither a hawk nor a pacifist, Orwell would have taken stands congruent with his positions on deterrence, disarmament, and anti-imperialism. He would have drawn a sharp distinction between the US-led invasions of Afghanistan and of Iraq, pushing for constructive engagement until official provocation from Baghdad occurred. The events of September 11 would not have furnished a sufficiently compelling reason for him to endorse an invasion of Iraq, let alone would the mere suspicion of Saddam Hussein's possession of weapons of mass destruction. Nevertheless, Orwell would have endorsed the West's campaign against Islamic fundamentalism (or "Islamofascism," as Christopher Hitchens terms it) and the fight against al-Qaeda—stopping short, however, of backing policies that violated prisoners' rights or compromised any provisions in the 1945 charter of the UN Declaration of Human Rights. All the while, Orwell would have averred that, in facing the geopolitical clash of civilizations dawning in the twenty-first century, he stood squarely on the side of the Americans and the West—and that he rejected the politics of equivalence. He would have recalled his stance expressed in "Toward European Unity" (1947), when he granted that if a united Europe could not arise betwixt the Cold War superpowers, Russia and the United States, "I would always choose America."[18]

V

What might Orwell have concluded about the course of his afterlife and its complex interconnections with his life? It is impossible to say. Surely he would have remarked on, and possibly disavowed or even derided, the unintended consequences that flowed from his writings; noted the differences between what others have written about him and what he himself wrote; and commented on those camps and/or movements with which he felt most at home among the plethora that have been linked to him.

In expressing his convictions and reservations about the misinterpretations and distortions of his work by subsequent generations, he may also have had much to say about the larger issue of what historians call the "use of the past."

Perhaps Orwell would have also distinguished, as do cultural historians, between "history" and "heritage." Both terms involve the past, but our heritage is that sense of pastness perceived as continuous with our present, a past that feels familiar and even second nature to us because much of it still remains in the present, as well as in ourselves. To "appreciate our heritage" does not typically require significant labor. One does not struggle to discover or ascertain an authentic past. It is also true that the line between heritage and legend (or myth or folklore) is often a very fine one, since heritage is largely based on perceptions, impressions, and feelings about the past.

By contrast, "history" concerns a past that may be quite discontinuous with our present and feel quite inhospitable. Moreover, historians are usually preoccupied with unearthing and certifying "the authentic past," or at least with engaging in a search for the truth about what happened "back then" (or, at a minimum, what likely scenarios might have transpired). For historians, as well as biographers, the psychic hold of a

If He Had Lived . . .

people's heritage often interferes with this historical quest—as historians' caveats and suspicions about the value of historical hindsight (e.g., *post-facto* interviews, oral history evidence) attests.[19]

Indeed, the boundary between Orwell's own posthumous history and heritage is, ironically, also a fuzzy one, a version of what Erik Erikson termed in his distinguished study of Luther's psychosocial development "half-legend, half-history." Nonetheless, what the careful cultural historian of Orwell's politicized reception can pronounce with authority is the following.

The evidence of Orwell's reception history establishes that from the Cold War to the era of détente to the events of September 11, he has proven a writer, as he once remarked of Dickens, "well worth stealing." Indeed, Gracie Fields's vaudeville refrain from the 1930s, "He's dead but he won't lie down"—which Orwell chose as the epigraph for his novel *Coming Up for Air* (1939)—might well serve as his own epitaph. Scarcely a major Anglo-American issue has gone by since 1950 that has not moved someone to muse, "If Orwell Had Lived. . . ." Orwell himself was not above speculating about the posthumous politics of writers ranging from Swift to Dickens to Jack London. (In fact, Orwell's "Interview with Jonathan Swift," which he conducted as a BBC broadcaster in 1942, was his own attempt to give a dead man a contemporary voice. There he gets Swift to comment on the condition of England and world affairs in the 1940s.)

So can one credit (or censure) Orwell himself with furnishing a precedent for the opinionated, quite debatable conjectures here? Perhaps. In any case, if other readers likewise cannot resist the lure, let them now bestow "St. George" with a different counterfactual (after)life.

The Unexamined Orwell

Notes

As indicated in the notes below, selective use has been made of the Michael Josselson Papers and the Nicolas Nabokov Papers, both of which contain unpublished material pertinent to several chapters of this study. These collections are archived at the Harry Ransom Center (HRC) at the University of Texas at Austin, and I have cited them according to box and folder numbers.

Introduction

1. Similarly, his cultural criticism is dismissed as "undertheorized" despite its topical affinities with current academic critical approaches. On this view, he was a pioneering cultural critic—and one of the first literary intellectuals to publish serious studies of popular art. Indeed, he is even regarded as a forerunner of the Birmingham School of British Cultural Studies (and exerted direct influence on members of its first generation, such as E. P. Thompson, Raymond Williams, and Richard Hoggart). But his work bears little relation to the heavily theoretical, Eurocentric cultural studies of the present-day literary academy.

2. Scott Lucas, "Deconstruct This: George Orwell," *Chronicle of Higher Education*, 30 May 2003. The other two interviewees were Scott Lucas, professor of American Studies at Birmingham University, and Daphne Patai, professor of Spanish and Portuguese at the University of Massachusetts at Amherst. Lucas is the author of *George Orwell and the Betrayal of Dissent: Beyond Orwell, Hitchens, and the New American Century* (London: Pluto Press, 2004), and *Orwell* (London: Haus Publishing, 2003), among other books. Patai has published *The Orwell Mystique: A Study in Male Ideology* (Amherst, Mass.: University of Massachusetts Press, 1984).

3. See chapter 12, "W.W.G.O.D.?" in John Rodden, *Scenes from an Afterlife: The Legacy of George Orwell* (Wilmington, DE: ISI Books, 2003).

4. See, for instance, Mike Peters, "A Toxic Mix of Lies and Doublespeak," *Washington Post*, 6 September 2008.

5. And yet even today, Orwell is arguably—at least among deceased authors—the political writer most esteemed by Anglo-American intellectuals. For example, in *Public Intellectuals* (2001), Richard Posner exalts Orwell as the model intellectual of the twentieth century and compares contemporary intellectuals (usually unfavorably) to him. Posner calls Orwell "the exemplary figure" for "much of the best public intellectual work in the past," which "has consisted of seeing through the big new political and economic nostrums." Posner, *Public Intellectuals: A Study of Decline* (Cambridge, MA: Harvard UP, 2001).

Posner also constructs a list of leading public intellectuals based on citation counts from database searches. Ranked number 5 by media mentions, Orwell is the highest-ranking deceased intellectual on Posner's media list of the top 100 public intellectuals, and one of only two dead intellectuals (along with George Bernard Shaw, at number 17) who make the top twenty. Moreover, the first seven so-called intellectuals on Posner's list, which was compiled in the mid-1990s, are really policy wonks or prominent political figures rather than intellectuals, such as Henry Kissinger, Daniel Patrick Moynihan, George Will, Lawrence Summers, William J. Bennett, Robert Reich, and Sidney Blumenthal. The first bona fide intellectuals on the list are Arthur Miller (at number 8) and Salman Rushdie (at number 9). William Safire (at number 10) was, like George Will and Sidney Blumenthal, in the public eye because his syndicated column ran in hundreds of newspapers and offered him access to the powers-that-be in Washington. Like most of the other names at the top of Posner's media list of the 1990s, he is seldom cited today.

It is an interesting reflection of Orwell's lower status in the academy, which prizes cultural (especially avant-garde) theory, that he does not even rank among Posner's top 100 public intellectuals by scholarly citations during 1995–2000, a list that is headed by names such as Michel Foucault, Pierre Bourdieu, Jürgen Habermas, and Jacques Derrida. The first American on this list is Noam Chomsky, with Richard Rorty and Edward Said barely making it into the top twenty-five.

6. Raymond Williams, *Politics and Letters* (London: New Left Books, 1979), 134. The significance of the sudden expansion of Orwell's reputation in the 1950s is crucial to an understanding of these developments. For Orwell exemplified during his life what could be termed "optimal marginality," and he exemplified "optimal centrality" posthumously. That is to say, he began as a marginal figure, a "pre-mature anti-Stalinist," but he died as the leading cold Warrior of his generation, a symbolic cultural battleground at "the bloody crossroads where literature and politics meet," in the phrase of Lionel Trilling. By the 1950s, as Raymond Williams acknowledged, "Down every road that you traveled, Orwell seemed to be waiting."

So "marginality" can be advantageous. Although Orwell did not attend university, let alone Oxford, he had opportunities (Burma, Parisian low life, tramping, dishwashing, Wigan, Catalonia) that he seized and developed into major advantages. It is thus crucial to see the context within which an author writes and lives (the "reception scene" of his work, as I have argued in *The Politics of Literary Reputation*). Some contexts will lurk in the shadowy past—or get lost in the memory holes of history. These contexts may be historical, generational, cultural, class-oriented, gendered, racial, and so on. What rise to a peak visible from a vast distance are distinctive textual rather than contextual features: the prose style, the narrative skill, the plotting, and the power of characterization. Their prominence and availability prove very useful for the literary critic. But they represent a disadvantage for the literary and cultural historian because reputation is a matter very different from interpretation or evaluation. The reputation of a work and author owes much to context, whereas the latter two aspects of criticism are textual matters. The literary historian must look "around" a work, not so much "at" it or "into" it. He or she must reconstruct the reception scene because that scene will usually illuminate seemingly unmotivated, mysterious, purely "individual" achievements.

We are all products of history and community, of opportunity and legacy. The reception scene and cultural community inscribe structures of contingencies that constrain whether and how one can achieve reputation. Viewed in its full context of emergence and development, the formation of reputation is neither exceptional nor enigmatic, nor attributable to a vague posterity or a mystical "test of time"; rather it deals with how reception scenes foster conditions that enable or limit reputation of a certain kind.

7. This plain fact has not, however, stopped critics on the Left, such as Daphne Patai, from insisting that Orwell *should* have foreseen events decades following his death and possessed the clairvoyance to have safeguarded his work from legions of grave-robbers and mantle snatchers. She thus blames Orwell, rather than ideologically motivated right-wing critics, for the polemical, exploitative ends to which they have put his work—and never mentions that left-wing critics have similarly abused Orwell's writings for different ends and in

different ways. As Patai writes: "Nor can one argue that Orwell is 'not responsible' for the conservative political uses of his work."

Such an insistence on Orwell's foreknowledge or prescience is quite unlike Orwell's own generous practice in his literary criticism. For instance, while noting that Charles Dickens had become a writer "well worth stealing," especially by Catholics and conservatives of the 1930s, Orwell derided such critics who would ransack and bowdlerize Dickens's work to promote their political goals. Nonetheless, even with respect to such abuses, he extended a certain magnanimity, granting that such literary theft was near-inevitable when a figure gained the stature and popularity of a Dickens.

Orwell himself occupies a place in the cultural imagination of our time rather like Dickens did in Orwell's day, except that Orwell's reputation is arguably far bigger and more diverse—and certainly more ideologically tainted. But Patai is not alone in her view that writers should be able to anticipate the shape of things to come and booby trap, as it were, their work in such a way as to prevent later generations from burglarizing and looting it. As Louis Althusser notes, in a passage cited by Patai: "A great artist cannot fail to take into account in his work itself, in its disposition and eternal economy, the ideological *effects* necessarily produced by its existence."

Yet Althusser then draws back from his own edict, explicitly admitting that the "failure" is that of the critic, not the artist: "Whether this assumption of responsibility is lucid or not is a *different* question." Unfortunately, it is a question that neither Patai nor Althusser, nor like-minded critics, ever pursue. They do indeed impose an "assumption of responsibility" on the artist and disavow their judicial responsibilities as critics themselves. Their approach does not just fall short of being "completely lucid"; it is polemical, presumptuous, and irresponsible. For they simply make such theoretical pronouncements and do not engage in the laborious, often difficult trench work of the journeyman historian—that is, gathering the necessary empirical evidence that would support or refute their contentions.

See Daphne Patai, *The Orwell Mystique*, 216; and Louis Althusser, "Cremonini, Painter of the Abstract," *Lenin and Philosophy and Other Essays* (New York: Monthly Review Press, 1971), 242.

8. *Collected Essays, Journalism, and Letters of George Orwell*, vol. 1, 413.

9. Scott Lucas, "Deconstruct This: George Orwell," *Chronicle of Higher Education*, 30 May 2003.

10. See especially my three full-length works devoted to the phenomenon of Orwell's fame: *The Politics of Literary Reputation: The Making and Claiming of St. George Orwell* (New York: Oxford UP, 1989), *Scenes from an Afterlife,* and *Every Intellectual's Big Brother* (Austin: University of Texas Press, 2007).

Not only Orwell's reputation but also the subject of reputation generally have received belated, much-needed attention within the literary academy. When I began to study Orwell's reputation in the early 1980s, little had been written about it—and nothing of a systematic, comprehensive kind. Nor, perhaps surprisingly, had the literary academy devoted any interest to the dynamics and formation of reputation. Impressionistic criticism was virtually all that existed, usually single-author studies in which scholars treated "critical reception" (based on a scattered collection of an author's book reviews and scholarly articles).

As I explained in my second edition of *The Politics of Literary Reputation* (New Brunswick, N.J.: Transaction, [1989] 2002), this state of affairs owed to a long-standing matrix of structural and professional forces, all of which acted to "repress" reputation into near-invisibility as a topic worth of inquiry.

In brief: Traditionally, the study of reputation has been widely neglected by literary scholars because they had configured the institution of criticism to exclude the idea that literary reputations exert decisive influence on literary interpretation and value. The norms of literary criticism and theory thus required that literary scholars hallucinate a fixed canon of "star" reputations in the artistic firmament. This consensus—a kind of "Emperor's New Clothes" phenomenon that rendered reputation an invisible issue—derived support from impressionistic, often hollow, pseudo-conceptual claims about the "test of time" and the "verdict of posterity." But the interpretive communities in the literary academy that held to the prevailing consensus have weakened in the last two decades, so that the systematic study of reputation as a social process has attracted considerable attention in recent years. This is welcome news. For, like it or not, reputation *does* exert influence on our values and inter-pretations—not just pertaining to artworks but also to our daily lives—and thereby generates significant consequences that warrant scrutiny. The study of reputation allows us to become more aware of the social processes that govern our affairs, and thus ultimately enables us to make better-informed decisions.

For a fully developed argument of this position, see John Rodden, *The Politics of Liter-ary Reputation* (New York: Oxford UP, 1989), especially chapters 1 and 2.

11. For an excellent critique that addresses both the aspirations and limitations of my work in reputation studies devoted to Orwell, see Anna Vaninskaya, "The Orwell Century and After: Rethinking Reception and Reputation" *Modern Intellectual History* 5, vol. 3 (2008): 597–617.

12. The expression is from one of Orwell's fiercest Marxist critics, Isaac Deutscher, "*1984*—The Mysticism of Cruelty," *Russia and Other Essays* (New York: Grove, 1960), 263. The essay originally appeared as "Orwell" in *The Observer* in December 1954.

13. Especially for polemically minded journalists and casual readers of his work, and even more so for nonreaders whose acquaintance is limited to broadcasts about him, "Orwell" is an intellectual brand name. In this respect, references to "George Orwell" carry a certain ca-chet of authority, or confer a distinct aura of credibility, or burnish one's own reputation with enhanced moral or literary integrity—a form of appropriation conducted at the considerable price of bleaching Orwell and his work of any incompatibilities with the cause or product he is being grave-robbed to sponsor.

14. See Peter Stansky and William Abrahams, *The Unknown Orwell* (London: Consta-ble, 1972).

15. Ben Wattenberg, host of the PBS program "The Orwell Century," March 2002.

16. I discuss the concept of "reception scene" in *The Politics of Literary Reputation*, 75, 87, 91, 93–94, 99, 486.

17. A further word about how my approach to Orwell's afterlife may enrich biography (and historiography) is apposite here. Especially in the case of the chapters in Part 1 ("If the Mantle Fits. . . ."), as well as in the conclusion, the conditions and constraints of Orwell's posthumous fame exert a shaping influence. Let me briefly note the underlying conceptual issues here.

When it comes to discussing an afterlife, and in the case of reputation more generally, the cultural historian must give proper emphasis to the significance of timing. Indeed, as I have argued elsewhere, "being in the right place at the right time" is the single most important factor in the sociodynamics of the reputation process. The terms "volcanic moment" and "*loci* of the momentus," both of which are essential to my rhetoric of reception, conceptual-ize this claim. If an author suffers a "neglected" or "stillborn" reputation, it typically has very little to do with the quality or merit of his work, despite the insistence of numerous impres-sionistic critics and avowedly untheoretical historians who insist on "posterity" or the "test of survival" as near-infallible guides to whether a writer gains a reputation, posthumously or otherwise.

Careful study of reputation-building invariably reveals that such faith is misplaced: the failure to acquire a reputation is not due to an author's literary achievement, but rather largely because the requisite timing (and placement) is off. That is to say, the author and his work have never, as it were, "gotten into proper position" for a "takeoff" or "launch." In such cases, the enabling factors required in society and culture to propel a "literary ascension" (to the level of cultural "star" status) are not yet available. One may say of the author and his work that "their time has not yet come"—and perhaps it never will.

"Getting into position" is chiefly a matter of the necessary enabling factors converging in such a way as to create, so to speak, a "liftoff effect," whereby the author and his work are flung or cast to a level beyond the downward gravitational pull of the everyday tide of onrushing news events, nowadays the infotainment "stream of history." Hurled above this information tsunami into the transcendent, longer-enduring "statusphere," the author or work may thereafter orbit at a supernal cultural altitude almost effortlessly, riding on this higher gravitational momentum, as it were, carried along by journalists' allusions, scholarly exegeses, critical studies, commercial uses and abuses, and the like.

Orwell's posthumous reputation is the quintessential modern example of this phenomenon. First *Animal Farm* benefited from a volcanic moment: what can be called the "little bang" of its Book-of-the-Month Club selection in August 1946, which coincided with the onset of the Cold War; after Orwell's death, his decisive posthumous volcanic moment occurred: the 1953 BBC adaptation of *Nineteen Eighty-Four*, which catapulted its sales volume from 150 copies per week in December 1953 to several million copies per year by the late 1950s. This BBC telecast can be termed the "big bang" in Orwell's reception history. Particularly in this latter case, Orwell's reputation profited from the "law of accelerating returns." This law, whose effect is most pronounced in the upper reaches of the statusphere, governs the dynamics of paradigm shifts in those regions. It posits that paradigm shift rates increase substantially, even geometrically, at these higher reputational altitudes. If the enabling factors that catapulted an author and his work into those spheres maintain themselves, their location in the statusphere will continue and perhaps even become fixed and enduring—or what we now term "canonical." In Orwell's case, albeit with periodic attenuations, the enabling factors have persisted with remarkable steadiness and even received overpowering reinforcement during the 1984 countdown (his second great posthumous volcanic moment, effectively another altitude-sustaining big bang) and, to a much lesser extent, the run-up to the 2003 centennial.

18. Of all post–World War II writers in the West, probably only Albert Camus rivals Orwell in such an intellectual "pentathlon."

19. The title of Part 2 is, of course, a nod to Orwell's famous essay "Politics and the English Language" (1946)—the pedagogical uses of which I take up in Part 3. It is worth noting that Orwell's neologisms and linguistic experiments in *Nineteen Eighty-Four* partly derive from his close observation of Nazi Germany, both as a BBC broadcaster (1941–1943) and an *Observer* war correspondent in newly occupied Germany (March–April 1945). Orwell partly based Newspeak on his experience at the BBC as a broadcaster combating Nazi rhetoric. Of course, to a certain extent Newspeak was first and foremost a satire on Basic English, given its philosophy of simplifying the English language by narrowing it to just a few hundred words. But the propagandistic, deliberately manipulative language of Newspeak is clearly also indebted to the wartime rhetoric of Nazism, to which Orwell was exposed on a daily basis during his stint at the BBC in the early 1940s. That was also the time at which he

conceived his vision of *Nineteen Eighty-Four*, and he was certainly well aware of what was happening in East Germany after the war.

As I discussed in a previous study, the themes of "Politics and the German Language" even include literary watchdog groups dedicated to exposing "Orwellian rhetoric" *auf deutsch*. Since 1977, the highly regarded Society for the German Language (GDS), based in Wiesbaden, has selected a "Word of the Year." Among the winners since then are the following: 1991: *Besserwessi* (know-it-all western German); 1992: *Politikverdrossenheit* (fed up with politics); 1994: *Superwahljahr* (super-election year); 1997: *Reformstau* (reform congestion); 1999: *Millennium* (millennium); 2002: *Teuro* (the costly euro); 2005: *Bundeskanzlerin* (female chancellor); 2009: *Abwrackprämie* (cash for clunkers bonus).

Other German literary organizations have publicized an "Unword of the Year." The GDS has not participated in the Unword contest since 1994. After the jury criticized Chancellor Kohl for his expression *kollektiver Freizeitpark* (collective amusement park), the GDS publicly censured the jury, whereupon the Unword jury accused the GDS of not wanting to offend political conservatives and formed itself as an independent board, formally titled "Linguistic Criticism in Action for the Unword of the Year." (The jury consists of the chairman, Hans Dieter Schlosser, three language scholars, and several journalists.) Now the GDS only participates in the annual selection of the Word of the Year. Charges of the Unword jury's liberal bias has raged for years. The most heated ideological debate involved "culture lite," which received 70 percent of the public votes for Unword of the Year in 2000. Yet the Unword jury selected the right-wing extremist expression *national befreite Zone* (nationally liberated zone).

20. See also John Rodden, *Scenes from an Afterlife: The Legacy of George Orwell*, Part 2.

21. It is worth noting that *Big Brother*, the TV reality show, began on Channel 4 in the UK and became a big hit there before being adapted for American TV. There are also Australian and South African versions. See the website http://directory.google.com/Top/Arts/Television/Programs/Reality-Based/Big_Brother/, or the official website, whose opening graphic ends with the warning "*Big Brother* is always watching": http://www.channel14.com/entertainment/tv/microsites/B/bigbrother/index.html.

Chapter 1

1. The opening paragraphs of this chapter are paraphrased and revised from my book *The Politics of Literary Reputation* (New York: Oxford UP, 1989), 63–64. Reviewers have repeated Trilling's characterizations of Orwell (especially "virtuous man") almost ritually. Some critics have even argued that Trilling's introduction single-handedly established Orwell's reputation in the United States. In *George Orwell: A Critical Heritage*, editor Jeffrey Meyers calls Trilling's introduction to *Homage to Catalonia* "probably the most influential essay on Orwell." See Jeffrey Meyers, *George Orwell: A Critical Heritage* (New York: Routledge, Kegan and Paul, 1975), 34.

2. At the very moment when, in the summer of 1952, Trilling's introduction to *Homage to Catalonia* was eliciting critical raves just as ecstatic as for the book itself, he was also ruminating about the implications and consequences of his own literary fame: "I hear on all sides of the extent of my reputation—which some even call 'fame,'" he wrote in his journal. "It is the thing I have most wanted from childhood—although of course in much greater degree—and now that I seem to have it I have no understanding whatever of its basis—of what it is that makes people respond to what I say, for I think of it as of a simplicity and of a naiveté

almost extreme." Quoted in "From the Notebooks of Lionel Trilling," *Partisan Review* 51 (Fall 1984/Winter 1985). The entry was dated 23 July 1952.

3. As his intellectual and personal life manifested in other, similar ways, Trilling deeply admired the apparent ordinariness of Orwell, his "not being a genius." And yet another side of Trilling associated genius with originality and creative talent, and ultimately Trilling sided with that part and fully committed himself to it. And yet again: Trilling's self-lacerating journal entries show the toll that this commitment exacted. Probably the battle never ceased to rage in him. Just months before he completed his essay on Orwell, he confided in his journal in mid-1950—after delivering his much-discussed lecture "Wordsworth and the Rabbis" at Princeton University:

> Feeling of total alienation from the academic profession and that I must not any more identify myself with it at such occasions. But I must in all things declare myself and go on being "brilliant," and if necessary, wrong, extreme. The sense that I fall between the two categories, of the academic and the man of genius & real originality, but better to make a full attempt toward "genius."—To learn to make no concessions of a personal social kind toward the academic, but also not to signalize in a personal way my separation from it.

Quoted in Louis Menand, "Regrets Only: Lionel Trilling and His Discontents," *New Yorker*, 29 September 2008, 80.

4. What became, one wonders, of the class paper on Orwell that Trilling says his Columbia graduate student, who, as Trilling acknowledged, first had called Orwell "a virtuous man," was also writing at the time? The essay was never published, but the student went on to become an associate editor of *Partisan Review* and professor of English at Columbia University. The nameless student was Steven Marcus (letter to the author, 16 December 1986).

5. Trilling's essay, "A Jew at Columbia," was first published posthumously. It appeared in *PR* in March 1976 and was reprinted in *The Last Decade: Essays and Reviews 1965–75*, ed. Diana Trilling (New York: Harcourt Brace Jovanovich, 1979), 230–231.

6. While a Columbia University professor (1916–1937), American educator John Erskine (1879–1951) helped launch the Great Books movement with works such as *The Moral Obligation To Be Intelligent* (1921).

7. Ironically, the "heroism" and "virtue" attributed to Trilling, which in their lavish expressions were mainly a posthumous phenomenon, represented a reversal of how he was regarded during much of his lifetime, especially later in his career. Younger members of the New York "family" disliked Trilling because of his longtime disdain and denial of a Jewish literary identity and his lack of any critical perspective on America's postwar rise to global dominance. What chiefly mattered to Trilling, they perceived, was that intellectuals (like himself) receive more respect. This accommodationist streak in Trilling is highlighted by Russell Jacoby in *The Last Intellectuals*, which speaks of Trilling's role in "reconciling a depoliticized intelligentsia to itself and the social status quo." In a similar vein, Alfred Kazin speaks disapprovingly of Trilling's "exquisite sense of accommodation." "For Trilling," says Kazin, "I would always be too Jewish, too full of my lower-class experiences." The rhapsodies about Trilling's "heroism" and "virtue" occurred against this background and came mainly from outsiders or non-Jewish members of the *PR* circle (such as John Holloway and William Barrett).

8. As we shall see, the subsequent intellectuals' slugfest over "the James Trilling affair" concerned not just a son's filial impiety, but rather involved large issues about intellectual

celebrity and posthumous reputation directly relevant to the afterlives of both Lionel Trilling and George Orwell.

9. "I have one of the great reputations in the academic world," Trilling wrote in his journal after being promoted to full professor in Columbia's English department in 1948. "This thought makes me retch." Quoted in Menand, "Regrets Only," 80.

How much more unsavory for Trilling today if he knew that his "great reputation" no longer has much to do with any serious attention to his work, but rather merely to the way in which celebrity and a "star system" have come to characterize academic life, just as they now do in every other domain of American culture.

Chapter 2

1. Orville Williams [John Lukacs], "Dwight Macdonald: Another Orwell?" *America*, 17 May 1958: 224–227.

2. Michael Wreszin, *A Rebel in Defense of Tradition: The Life and Politics of Dwight Macdonald* (New York: Basic Books, 1994).

3. Macdonald was the only member of the New York Intellectuals closely acquainted with Orwell. A generous portion of their extensive correspondence during 1942–1949 appears in *The Complete Works of George Orwell*, edited by Peter Davison, vols. 16, 17, 18.

4. *The Collected Essays, Journals, and Letters of George Orwell* (*CEJL*), ed. Sonia Orwell and Ian Angus (New York: Harcourt, 1968), vol. 1, 528.

5. My own efforts to pay a centennial tribute to Macdonald were among the few exceptions. See, for example: "Memorial for a Revolutionist: Dwight Macdonald at 100," *Society* 44 (5) (August 2007): 51–61; "Dwight or Left," *The American Prospect* 17 (3) (March 2006): 45–48; and "Rebel with a Cause: Dwight Macdonald, A Centennial Tribute," *Commonweal* 133 (4) (February 2006): 9–10.

6. See, for instance, Gertrude Himmelfarb, "The Trilling Imagination," *Weekly Standard*, 21 February 2005. An academic conference devoted to Trilling was also hosted by the University of Louisiana at Lafayette in November 2005.

7. Perhaps McCarthy was not, however, so much an outsider as Macdonald. Late in life she revealed in her autobiography that she had a Jewish grandmother. See her *Intellectual Memoirs: New York, 1936–1938* (New York: Harcourt Brace Jovanovich, 1992). Among the other nominees for the role of the representative figure of the group have been Lionel Trilling, Philip Rahv, and Delmore Schwartz. See Barrett, *The Truants*.

8. See Mary McCarthy, "Portrait of the Intellectual as a Yale Man," in *The Company She Keeps* (New York: Harcourt Brace, 1942). For Macdonald's opinion of *The Oasis*, see *A Moral Temper: The Letters of Dwight Macdonald* (New York: Ivan R. Dee, 2001). Macdonald was not the only friend of McCarthy, however, or the only model, upon whom the male protagonist of "Portrait of the Intellectual as a Yale Man" was based. John Chamberlain, another Yale graduate and the book critic for the *Wall Street Journal* and contributor to several Luce publications, was the physical model for Jim Barnett, the naïve, guileless Stalinist intellectual. Other facets of Jim Barnett were based on Robert Cantwell and Malcolm Cowley, who were Yale men too.

Macdonald was also the model for Mike, the bewhiskered intellectual whom children mistake for Uncle Sam in McCarthy's story "The Hounds of Summer," originally published in the *New Yorker* in 1962. See *The Hounds of Summer and Other Stories* (New York: Avon, 1981).

For more on McCarthy's portraits of Macdonald in her fiction, see Carol Brightman, *Writing Dangerously: Mary McCarthy and Her World* (New York: C. Potter, 1992); and Frances Kiernan, *Seeing Mary Plain* (New York: W. W. Norton, 2000).

9. As the Depression deepened its hold in the United States, Macdonald began a rapid intellectual evolution toward the far Left, growing angrier year after year about the failings of American capitalism. And so it was not surprising that in June 1936, after the editors of *Fortune* scrapped one of his articles, a highly critical study of United States Steel Corporation, Macdonald resigned. This was no minor gesture. At the time, Macdonald was making $10,000, an almost princely sum for anyone in the depths of the Depression.

Macdonald's resignation impressed Mary McCarthy, who observed in *The Oasis* about Macdougal Macdermott, the editor of a radical libertarian magazine that resembles Macdonald's *politics*: "[T]en years before, he had made the leap into faith and sacrificed $20,000 a year and a secure career as a paid journalist for the intangible values that eluded his empirical grasp." Mary McCarthy, *The Oasis* (New York: Random House, 1949). See also Carol Gelderman, *Mary McCarthy: A Life* (New York: St. Martin's, 1988).

10. In Trotskyist jargon, a "degenerated" worker's state was a dictatorship of the proletariat that had regressed to a form of collectivism in which bureaucracy and authoritarianism perverted and usurped political power. That devolution was purportedly the fate of the USSR as control of the Soviet Communist Party passed from Lenin's to Stalin's hands.

11. Michael Wreszin, *A Rebel in Defense of Tradition: The Life and Politics of Dwight Macdonald* (New York: Basic Books, 1994), 83.

12. Ibid., 83.

13. But Macdonald was not alone among Trotskyists in his enthusiasm for Joyce or selection of a Party name based on a clever literary allusion. (Another Trotskyist contemporary was known as "Blake Lear.")

14. *Partisan Review* was originally founded in 1934 as a magazine of the John Reed Club, which placed it under the auspices of the American Communist Party. For the early history of *PR*, see Terry Cooney, *The Rise of the New York Intellectuals: "Partisan Review" and Its Circle* (Madison: University of Wisconsin Press, 1986). See also Alexander Bloom, *Prodigal Sons: The New York Intellectuals and Their World* (Oxford: Oxford UP, 1986); Alan Wald, *The New York Intellectuals: The Rise and Decline of the Anti-Stalinist Left from the 1930s to the 1980s* (Ann Arbor: University of Michigan Press, 1987); and Neil Jumonville, *Critical Crossings: The New York Intellectuals in Postwar America* (Berkeley: University of California Press, 1991).

15. The anticommunist "vital center liberalism" of the New Deal, promoted by centrist liberals such as Arthur Schlesinger, Macdonald insisted, was ineffective in confronting the great danger represented by postwar Stalinism. Macdonald's attacks on liberals, labor, and the New Dealers were relentless; he referred to them as the "liblabs," a term of sneering ridicule meant to impugn the wishy-washy complacency of postwar liberal democracy.

During World War II and after, Macdonald maintained a steady barrage of invective against the liblabs for their view that the war and its aftermath would redeem the Wilsonian dream of a rationalized and peaceful world order—indeed, that the war was a democratic crusade that would globalize the New Deal. By contrast, Macdonald saw the war as an old-style power struggle between the Western democracies and the totalitarians.

16. Wreszin, *Rebel*, 193.

17. Macdonald, "Trotsky Is Dead," *Partisan Review* 7 (September–October 1940), quoted in Wreszin, *Rebel*, 206.

18. Macdonald, *Memoirs of a Revolutionist: Essays in Political Criticism* (Cleveland: Farrar, Straus and Cudahy, 1957) and *Against the American Grain* (New York: Random House, 1962).

19. Even after submitting his SWP resignation, Macdonald continued to contribute occasionally to Trotskyist publications, writing a number of articles for the journal *New International*—mostly labored pieces of Marxist exegesis which, in the words of Macdonald biographer Stephen Whitfield, "have sunk of their own weight into oblivion." See Whitfield, *A Critical American: The Politics of Dwight Macdonald* (Hamden, Conn.: Archon Books, 1984).

20. This point warrants elaboration. What was at stake in Macdonald's battle with Phillips and Rahv before the breakup in 1943 was not so much their opposing positions on the war, but the fact that the editors had an agreement that the magazine would have no position on the war, even though editors and contributors would be able to express themselves as individuals. Rahv and Phillips reneged on this agreement, blocking almost any kind of antiwar commentary after Pearl Harbor. The disagreements, which went back to 1937, were largely about risk-taking. Rahv and Phillips were afraid the FBI would shut them down (not an unreasonable assumption). Macdonald wanted to speak out anyway, as he did when he finally launched *politics*.

21. Gregory D. Sumner, *Dwight Macdonald and the Politics Circle: The Challenge of Cosmopolitan Democracy* (Ithaca, N.Y.: Cornell UP, 1996).

22. Macdonald enlisted a distinguished international group of writers on the Left to contribute to his new magazine (including a number of Americans, such as Paul Goodman and C. Wright Mills). Macdonald wanted *politics* to become the vehicle for an intellectual exchange between America and Europe. (Nicola Chiaromonte became Macdonald's close friend and tutor on European political and cultural affairs.) Possessing a clearly defined internationalist as well as radical stance, *politics* would become (in Macdonald's words) a "transplanted spore of European culture" (quoted in Wreszin, *Rebel*) in the American body politic. Macdonald was something of a snob about European intellectuals, believing them more politically and culturally sophisticated than their American counterparts. The role of *politics* was, in effect, to Europeanize provincial American culture.

23. Sumner, *Dwight Macdonald.*

24. "A Note on Wallese," *politics* (March–April 1947). See also Macdonald, *Henry Wallace: The Man and the Myth* (New York: Vanguard, 1948), 24.

25. Macdonald, "Why Politics?" *politics* 1 (February 1944).

26. Ibid.

27. "The Root Is Man," *politics* 3 and 4 (April and July 1946): 194–197. Deepening Macdonald's political disillusionment were personal problems: his marriage was falling apart, and the work of putting out *politics* had lost its appeal. He drifted into a passionate affair with the novelist Joan Colebrook that left him alternately exhilarated and depressed. He eventually divorced Nancy, with whom he had two sons, and married Gloria Lanier, the wife of an old friend, in 1952. This second marriage was a qualified success, though Gloria was never an intellectual comrade-in-arms, as Nancy had been.

28. Wreszin, *Rebel.*

29. See Macdonald, "Comment on Simone Weil, 'Factory Work,'" *politics* 3 (December 1946).

30. Wreszin, *Rebel*, 302.

31. Another personal relationship that influenced Macdonald's turn to anarchism in the mid-1940s was with Paul Goodman, whose sexual libertarianism and anarchic sensibility ultimately contributed to the breakup of Macdonald's marriage to Nancy. Like Goodman,

Macdonald became a vociferous defender of individualism and personal freedom, including sexual. In that connection, a related formative influence on Macdonald's anarchism was Wilhelm Reich. Macdonald gave Reich space in *politics* to explain his controversial Organotherapy, which also fit with Macdonald's anarcho-pacifist, communal interests and his emerging bohemian radicalism. Macdonald accepted Reich's critique of the connection between sexual repression and totalitarianism. See Wreszin, *Rebel*, 286, 351. For Goodman's assessment of Macdonald, see Paul Goodman, "Our Best Journalist," *Dissent* 5 (Winter 1958): 82–86.

32. Wreszin, *Rebel*, 366.

33. Ibid., 88, 452. By 1958, Irving Kristol could write about a brief yet fierce critique of American culture by Macdonald (which appeared that autumn in *Dissent*): "It is even more infantile than Dwight usually is. But I don't think you need have any worries about its causing malicious gossip in New York. . . . I think things have reached the stage where Dwight just isn't taken as seriously as he used to be." Letter from Irving Kristol to Michael Josselson, 7 November 1958. Michael Josselson Papers, HRC, box 22, folder 7. On the circumstances surrounding Macdonald's *Dissent* essay and his relationship with Kristol, see note 35.

34. William Barrett, *The Truants: Adventures among the Intellectuals* (New York: Anchor Press and Doubleday, 1982), 221.

35. Macdonald published his essay in *Twentieth Century* after *Encounter* had withdrawn its acceptance and rejected the piece. Macdonald suspected that *Encounter*, a London-based magazine supported by an American foundation and affiliated with the anti-Soviet Congress for Cultural Freedom (CCF), had reversed its acceptance on political grounds because his piece was sharply critical of Eisenhower-era America. Macdonald voiced his suspicions in a short *Dissent* essay in autumn 1958. The issues were especially complicated because Macdonald had served as an editor of *Encounter* (1956–1957) and because its main editor (who had accepted and then rejected "America! America!") was Irving Kristol, a friendly acquaintance and fellow New York Intellectual. Kristol was indeed under political pressure from the CCF and its administrative secretary, Michael Josselson. On first reading the piece, an enraged Josselson wrote to John Hunt, a CCF staff member who was soon to be promoted to executive secretary of the international office of the CCF in Paris, that Macdonald's essay "America! America!" was "the most anti-American piece I have ever read and belongs in *Literaturnaya Gazeta*." Josselson to Hunt, 27 May 1958. Michael Josselson Papers, HRC, box 22, folder 7.

Five months later, Josselson wrote from the CCF offices in Paris to Kristol about "Dwight's little introduction to his 'America! America!' in *Dissent*." Josselson ridiculed Macdonald's "too exhibitionist articles about his Marxist days" that had appeared in *Encounter* and "his exhibitionist pieces about America that you and Stephen [Spender] were wrong in accepting in the first place. Dwight is mistaken if he thinks we were afraid of losing the support of some of the Foundations if *Encounter* published his silly piece about America. I don't know how he ever got that idea." Josselson to Kristol, 30 October 1958. Michael Josselson Papers, HRC, box 22, folder 7.

But Macdonald was right in his surmise, both about the "foundation" support generally and about the fate of his essay in particular. In 1967, news broke that the CCF (and its magazines, such as *Encounter*) had been funded from the outset by the CIA. Later it became known that Josselson himself was on the CIA payroll. Josselson, who remained on friendly terms with Macdonald throughout all their political disagreements, wrote to him: "In the whole business there's nothing I'm ashamed of—except for that letter I wrote you about your *Encounter* piece on American life. My very next trip to the US showed me how much more you were in touch than I was. I am sorry to say I didn't apologize to you then and there." Josselson to Macdonald, 15 March 1967. Michael Josselson Papers, HRC, box 26, folder 4.

36. Macdonald, *Against the American Grain*, 273.

37. Wreszin, *Rebel*, 310–312. A few other members of the New York Intellectuals—Fred Dupee, Mary McCarthy, and James Burnham among them—were not Jewish. But as in the case of the New York Trotskyists of the 1930s and 1940s, most of the *Partisan Review* circle was overwhelmingly Jewish. They referred to Dwight and the other non-Jews as "our distinguished goyim."

38. Wreszin, *Rebel*, 317.

39. For example, writing for *Esquire* in August 1960, Macdonald unleashed an avalanche of criticism from the Jewish community in response to his negative essay-review of *Ben Hur*, *King of Kings*, and *The Greatest Story Ever Told*. Macdonald wrote that the Jewish community's financing of these movies was aimed at assuring that the Romans would be "the fall goys" for the crucifixion of Jesus, for there were "no ancient Romans around and there are many Jews and fifteen million dollars is fifteen million dollars." Similar to the controversies a generation later about Mel Gibson's movie *The Passion of the Christ*, Macdonald was charged with anti-Semitism for branding the Jews as "Christ-killers"—though his defenders argue that he was just being contrarian, going against the grain as always. On this episode, see Wreszin, *Rebel*, 410.

40. For a glimpse of Macdonald's close personal relationship with Arendt, see their correspondence in *A Moral Temper: The Letters of Dwight Macdonald*, ed. Michael Wreszin (New York: Ivan R. Dee, 2001).

41. McCarthy, *The Oasis*.

42. Hannah Arendt, "He's All Dwight," *New York Review of Books* (1 August 1968).

43. Dwight identified strongly with his college students. He dwelt in a nonhierarchical psychological environment, and the student culture easily enabled him to show his modesty by refusing to be an authority figure for young people—while at the same time resting assured that the students would be flattered by his modest insistence on their treating him as an equal.

He was in fact a true democrat who treated others as equals. But his democratic ethos was often driven by an inveterate tendency to equalize authority and by an unwillingness to accept that any hierarchical structure could have a reasonable purpose. Equalizing authority reflected his desire for unlimited freedom. He didn't want to be the boss, and he didn't want to be under a boss, so he equalized authority to avoid being told or avoid telling others what to do. (He was therefore attracted by the security of belonging to a group of like-minded people, but the only time when he truly experienced this without diverse conflicts was when he gathered them around himself as the hub of *politics*.)

Under such circumstances, *politics* could only be a one-man operation; the Macdonald organization had to be an "ad-hocracy" that functioned on an egalitarian, first-name basis. Individuality, experimentation, and creativity were the order of the day. The editorial, marketing, sales, and finance departments were Dwight and his wife, Nancy, whose inheritance bankrolled the venture.

44. It was in this sense that Macdonald was a Peter Pan figure, an eternal child who never quite landed on the planet because he never fully accepted the value of sticking it out, the necessity of persistent, focused effort to actualize his dreams. Although he would have been grounded by a commitment to a major, long-term project as his ultimate life work, his intellectual promiscuity would not permit that. He needed a tether to complete a project worthy of his talent—that is, a daily routine that would have developed a firm habit of self-discipline.

45. He was both gifted and burdened by a habit of splitting attention among different interests—a great strength for an imaginative editor or a prolific journalist, but a crippling hardship for an author of book-length manuscripts. It was as if his capacity to endure the painstaking writing process exhausted itself at the length of an essay and thus rendered the goal of writing a book unthinkable. He was a marvelous editor and teacher of expository writing; yet like many editors, he seems to have dealt with his frequent writing blocks by channeling his energy into the literary activities of others as a close reader of their work. James Atlas credits Macdonald with having practically coauthored large sections of Atlas's biography of Delmore Schwartz; Irving Howe credits Macdonald with nothing less than having "taught me how to write."

46. In *Public Intellectuals*, Richard Posner raises the question of why intellectuals are so often wrong, especially when they write outside their narrow subfield of academic expertise. He argues that one reason is that they are not "penalized" for being wrong by a loss of any kind. Posner wants such public intellectuals to pay at least a reputational price for being wrong. He believes that more responsible public intellectual discourse will emerge if intellectuals are held accountable for their predictions and claims and not given a "free pass" on sundry topics just because they happen to be expert in an unrelated field; he cites the fact that many people consider the work in linguistics of Noam Chomsky to somehow justify his political arguments about topics ranging from the Vietnam War to politics in the Mideast. Posner argues that, however valid and compelling Chomsky's scholarly work in linguistics, it ultimately bears no relation to his political discourse and should not influence the reader's opinion of it.

Whatever one's view of Posner's argument, it is indisputable that Macdonald paid a steep price for "being wrong": he lost his reputation, even within radical intellectual circles. See Richard Posner, *Public Intellectuals: A Study of Decline* (Cambridge, Mass.: Harvard UP, 2001).

47. One related factor that explains Macdonald's near-invisibility in American intellectual culture is illuminated by a comparison with Irving Howe. Macdonald founded a political journal that lasted just five years—and witnessed regular publication in only the first two. By contrast, Howe edited an intellectual quarterly, *Dissent*, that is nearing its seventh decade of publication and has become a landmark in American politics and letters, especially in the radical tradition. For this reason, it seems far more likely that Howe's legacy will endure, at least until *Dissent* expires, whereas Macdonald has had no direct successors to continue the *politics* heritage or champion him. Although numerous contributors affiliated with *Dissent*, or even those writing against its positions, continue to cite Howe, scholars in cultural studies and media studies rarely cite Macdonald's essays on mass culture or his critiques of "midcult." Unlike the work of Theodor Adorno, Macdonald's work has not entered the academy, where it might acquire canonical endurance. So when the events that occasioned Macdonald's mass culture criticism exited the scene, his work vanished from public discussion along with them.

48. Macdonald, *Discriminations: Essays and Afterthoughts, 1938–1974* (New York: Grossman, 1974), 336.

49. Milosz expressed this observation in his review of the 1953 edition of *The Root Is Man*, which Macdonald had arranged to have printed as a pamphlet. The remark originally appeared in Czeslaw Milosz, *Beginning with My Streets: Essays and Reflections*, quoted in Sumner, *Dwight Macdonald*.

50. For a discussion of the origins and dissemination of this phrase, see *The Politics of Literary Reputation*, Chapter 5, 229–231.

51. Sumner, *Dwight Macdonald*, 5.

52. Quoted in Sumner, *Dwight Macdonald*, xiii.

53. See Christopher Hitchens, *Letters to a Contrarian* (London: Basic Books, 2000), 123.

Chapter 3

1. Richard Rorty, *Achieving Our Country* (Cambridge, Mass.: Harvard UP, 1998).

2. Josephine Woll, "Remembering Irving Howe," *Dissent* (Fall 1993): 541.

3. Hilton Kramer, "Socialism Is the Name of Our Desire," *Twilight of the Intellectuals* (Chicago: Ivan R. Dee, 1997).

4. The phrase—intended facetiously as a counter to all "the quasi-religious eulogies"—is Jeremy Larner's in his memoir of Howe, "Remembering Irving Howe," *Dissent* 40 (4) (Fall 1993): 539–542.

5. Alexander Cockburn, "A Few Tasteless Words about Irving Howe," *Nation*, May 14, 1993, 822.

6. See Howe, "A Moderate Hero," *Partisan Review* (March 1955): 21–30. Here Howe rejected the view of most liberals that Orwell should be seen as a "good" man, a "conscience," or a "saint." Such characterizations, Howe thought, softened or spiritualized Orwell's angry radicalism. His Orwell, Howe insisted, was no "man of truth"—he was a political figure: an honest radical.

7. Howe, "As the Bones Know," in *Decline of the New* (New York: Harcourt, Brace, and World, 1970), 97, 103.

8. See Howe, *A Margin of Hope* (New York: Harcourt, 1982).

9. Ibid., 217–218, 238, 242.

10. Ibid., 232, 321–322.

11. Howe, interview, 9 October 1983.

12. Trilling, introduction to *Homage to Catalonia* (London: Secker and Warburg, 1986), xvi, xviii.

13. See also Howe's attack on Trilling's view of Orwell in "A Moderate Hero." Too "cozy" with the conservative spirit of the mid-'50s, liberal critics such as Lionel Trilling, V. S. Pritchett, and John Atkins were unnerved by the gritty, irascible, even ill-tempered side of Orwell, claimed Howe. Unable to fathom Orwell's "desperation," they sought to remake him into "a moderate hero," "a down-at-the-heels Boy Scout who voted Labour." Likewise, lacking Orwell's own "fiery" imagination, they were incapable of understanding his passion for justice and decency, so they recast it in moral terms as a species of "sainthood."

As we saw in chapter 1, Trilling had memorialized Orwell as a "virtuous man" in his introduction to the first American edition of *Homage to Catalonia* (1952). But such a figure was too soft for Howe, nothing like his image of a combative Orwell, his refreshingly immoderate hero, his "revolutionary personality." See Howe, "A Moderate Hero," 22–24.

14. Podhoretz, "If Orwell Were Alive Today," *Harper's* (January 1983): 32.

15. Campus speeches on Orwell, conference talks and radio interviews about Orwell, a *New Republic* cover story, a new and expanded edition of *Nineteen Eighty-Four: Text, Sources, Criticism*, the edited volume *1984 Revisited: Totalitarianism in Our Century*: in 1983–1984 Howe seemed to be the designated American keeper of the Orwell flame. Howe became increasingly identified with his "intellectual hero" during the last decade of his life, even as he himself gained a reputation beyond intellectual and academic circles as a result of his widely acclaimed bestseller, *World of Our Fathers* (1976).

16. Sanford Pinsker, *Georgia Review* 45 (Winter 1991): 802–803.

17. Lewis Coser, *Dissent* (Fall 1993). Quoted in John Rodden, ed., *The Worlds of Irving Howe* (Boulder: Paradigm, 2004), 331.

18. Nonetheless, the story of Howe and *Dissent*'s hostility toward the New Left—and the mutual acrimony that developed—makes the rehabilitation of Howe's reputation on the progressive left in the 1970s and '80s—the fact that he gained the esteem of such former New Left stalwarts as Todd Gitlin—all the more remarkable.

19. Quoted in Gerald Sorin, *Irving Howe: A Life of Passionate Dissent* (New York: New York UP, 2002), 313n24. Bellow's remark appears in a letter to their mutual friend Al Glotzer, an erstwhile Trotskyist comrade, written at the time of Howe's death in 1993. Bellow, who had veered rightward into neoconservatism since the 1960s, was criticizing Howe and *Dissent*, which Bellow regarded as a backward-looking, stodgy, behind-the-times relic of social- ism. Bellow wrote to Glotzer: "He struck me as rather quaint, like an old-fashioned lady, who still cans her tomatoes in August."

20. Philip Roth, *The Anatomy Lesson* (New York: Farrar, Straus and Giroux, 1983), 474.

21. Several of the leading figures associated with *Partisan Review*, "the house organ of the American intellectual community" in the early post-World War II era—among them Trill- ing, Rahv, Delmore Schwartz, and Mary McCarthy—have also been nominated by various observers as the archetypal "New York Intellectual." See, for instance, William Barrett, *The Truants: Adventures Among the Intellectuals* (New York: Anchor Press/Doubleday, 1982). (The characterization of *Partisan Review* is by Howe's friend, the liberal historian Richard Hofstadter, in his *Anti-Intellectualism in American Life* [New York: Vintage, 1963], 394.)

22. Robert Lowell, *Notebook 1967–68* (New York: Farrar, Straus and Giroux, 1969).

23. Philip Nobile, *Intellectual Skywriting: Literary Politics and the New York Review of Books* (New York: Charterhouse, 1974), 135–136.

24. Nobile, *Intellectual Skywriting*, 13.

25. They take, as it were, two-thirds of Howe's corpus and approve it: "Two cheers for Irving Howe." Or sometimes less: Edward Alexander, in *Irving Howe: Socialist, Critic, Jew,* gives one rousing cheer for Howe's work—or at best one and a half cheers: socialist—no; critic—yes; Jew—yes (*Yiddishkeit*) and no (Israel). Alexander's harshest criticism of Howe's politics is for his support of the Israeli left and the peace process—and his castigation of what he regarded as Israeli militarism in the guise of national defense. For Alexander, Howe was critic first, then socialist and Jew. Alexander sees Howe as a great critic, but a misguided political thinker—who exhibited a misconceived politics that reflected a refusal to grow up— and a false friend to Israel. Alexander, an English professor, especially identifies with Howe the literary critic and strongly endorses his preservative, traditionalist positions on the liter- ary canon and his hostility to postmodernism and deconstructionism. (The Old Left and neoconservatives are closest on positions with regard to culture and literature. They tend to share a respect for the classics and literary canon—and even for conservative modernist writ- ers such as Pound and Eliot.) In addition to his biography of Howe, see Alexander's *Irving Howe and Secular Jewishness: An Elegy* (Cincinnati: University of Cincinnati Judaic Studies Program, 1995).

26. Although Howe was an anti-Zionist before the Arab-Israeli Six-Day War in 1967, he developed strong links and friendships in Israel in the 1970s (and even married an Israeli woman). During his last two decades, Howe was a strong and articulate, if critical, supporter of Israel.

27. See Edward Alexander, *Irving Howe: Socialist, Critic, Jew* (Bloomington: Indiana UP, 1998), chapter 2.

28. Hasia R. Diner, "Embracing *World of Our Fathers*: The Context of Reception," *American Jewish History*, vol. 88, no. 4 (December 2000): 449. The American Jewish community celebrated *World of Our Fathers* as an act of homage to American Jewish history and as a Semitic version of Alex Haley's *Roots*, another bestseller in the bicentennial year. Diner recalls that the Jewish community centers "staged 'Lower East Side' fairs to accompany his presentations, and the strains of Klezmer music wafted from the social halls at the reception afterwards."

Howe's New York Intellectual colleagues also welcomed *World of Our Fathers* enthusiastically, and even most of the neoconservatives in his community lauded it. As Daniel Bell wrote in a letter to Michael Josselson (whose activities with the CIA-sponsored Congress for Cultural Freedom had drawn Howe's fire): "I write because Pearl [Bell's wife] is deeply immersed in Irving Howe's *World of Our Fathers* that she is reviewing for the *New Leader* next week. We take turns reading aloud sections of the book to each other and break down in alternate fits of laughter and tears. It is hard to recapture our parents' lives and to recall our own childhoods." Letter from David Bell to Michael Josselson, 3 February 1976. Michael Josselson Papers, HRC, box 19, folder 6.

29. Quoted in Diner, "Embracing *World of Our Fathers*," 453.

30. Roth, *The Anatomy Lesson*, 482.

31. Mitchell Cohen, *Dissent* (Fall 1993); *New Republic*, 12 May 1993; Robert Kuttner, *Dissent* (Fall 1993); Leon Wieseltier, "Remembering Irving Howe (1920–93)," *New York Times Book Review*, 20 May 1993, 31.

32. Matthew Frye Jacobson, "A Ghetto to Look Back To: *World of Our Fathers*, Ethnic Revival, and the Arc of Multiculturalism," *American Jewish History*, vol. 88, no. 4 (December 2000): 473–474.

33. Joseph Dorman, "World of Our Fathers," *New York Times Book Review*, 2 March 2003, 13.

34. Ronald Radosh, "A Literary Mind, a Political Heart," *Los Angeles Times Book Review*, 6 April 2003, 10.

35. See Alexander, *Irving Howe*, 9.

36. As we have seen, Howe's friends and junior colleagues certainly embrace the analogy. Richard Rorty and Josephine Woll are two very different examples, each of whom is quoted in the opening paragraph of this chapter.

37. See my book *George Orwell: The Politics of Literary Reputation* (New Brunswick: Transaction, [1989] 2002).

38. His biographer, Gerald Sorin, calls Howe "a hero of sorts," applying Howe's remarks about Silone's "heroism of tiredness" to Howe himself (*Irving Howe*, xiv).

39. Howe, *Leon Trotsky* (Penguin: New York, 1979), 161.

40. On Howe's high estimate of Norman Thomas—as a politician and speaker rather than a writer—see *A Margin of Hope*, chapter 5.

41. Howe, *Leon Trotsky*, viii.

42. Ibid., 192–193.

43. Howe wrote in his preface to *Leon Trotsky*: "I have remained a socialist. I have found myself moving farther and farther away from [Trotsky's] ideas and he remains a figure of heroic magnitude" (viii).

44. Ian Williams, "An Ex-Maoist Looks at an Ex-Trotskyist: On Howe's *Leon Trotsky*," in John Rodden's *Irving Howe and the Critics* (Lincoln: University of Nebraska Press, 2005), 37.

45. Howe also used the phrase in the 1980s and '90s to characterize radical professors

who favored multiculturalism and postmodernism over the classical literary canon and the traditional liberal arts curriculum.

46. One measure of the influence of Howe's 1954 essay is that a book by Alan Valentine appeared later that year under the title *The Age of Conformity* (Chicago: Regnery Press, 1954). An essay by John W. Aldridge also appeared in the *American Scholar* in 1956: "American Literature in an Age of Conformity."

47. Quoted in Sorin, *Irving Howe*, 161.

48. I quote from Howe's essay "Silone: A Luminous Example," in *Decline of the New* (New York, 1970), 290. The essay was first published as "Silone and the Radical Conscience," *Dissent* 3 (Winter 1956): 72–75. It was revised and reprinted in *Politics and the Novel* and *Decline of the New*.

49. A further measure of Howe's regard for Silone was that he and Lewis Coser dedicated *The American Communist Party* (1958) to "Ignazio Silone and Milovan Djilas—two men who more than any other stand for the attempt to create a non-Communist radical opinion in Europe."

50. Howe, *Decline of the New*, 290.

51. Ibid., 284.

52. Ibid., 285–287. This tension between the attractions of power and purity was one that Howe also carried throughout his life—as a radical who wrote for Henry Luce and *Time*, as a critic of conformist bourgeois life who became a chaired professor of English, and so on.

Howe obviously found inspiration in Silone's public example of how to creatively maintain and balance these oppositions. What then would he have had to say about the shocking disclosures of the late 1990s about Silone's preference for means to ends, and his choice of expediency over morality, as an Italian socialist? Silone's radical credentials and noble image as a pillar of anti-fascism have been soiled by chilling evidence, discovered not long after Howe's death, in the files of the Italian fascist secret police revealing that he was an informant under the code name "Silvestri" from 1919 to 1930. In fact, the staggering truth is that "Silvestri" was the longest-serving and probably most important fascist agent within the Italian Communist movement.

Other documents establish that Silone was knowledgeable about CIA funding of the Congress for Cultural Freedom and other anti-Soviet cultural activities of the Western intelligence services in the "cultural Cold War"—activities that Howe castigated in "This Age of Conformity" and in *Dissent*'s pages throughout the 1950s and '60s. In light of these findings, Howe's praise of Silone sometimes rings most ironically: "The memory of [Silone's] refusal to accommodate himself to the fascist regime stirred feelings of bad conscience among literary men who had managed to become more flexible. Alas, men of exemplary stature are often hard to accept. They must seem a silent rebuke to those who had been less heroic or more cautious" (*Decline of the New*, 288).

53. The recurrent theme of Howe's essays in Part 4 of *Decline of the New*, which consists of three substantial essays, is heroism. Orwell is his "intellectual hero" (269), Silone his "hero of tiredness," and T. E. Lawrence exemplifies the entire "problem of heroism" (294–325).

54. Howe, *Decline of the New*, 293.

55. Wilson was one of the senior lecturers invited to teach the Christian Gauss seminars in the spring of 1953. Howe was selected as a junior lecturer, and he attended Wilson's sessions. Years later, Howe turned down a submission to *Dissent* from Wilson, who, rather than hold a grudge, "teased him about being turned down by a magazine that didn't even pay." See Sorin, *Irving Howe*, 94, 147.

56. Howe, "A Man of Letters," collected in *Celebrations and Attacks* (New York: 1979), 221.

57. Howe, *A Margin of Hope*, 168.

58. Edmund Wilson, *The Triple Thinkers* (New York: Oxford UP, 1948), 71. See also Janet Groth, *Edmund Wilson: A Critic for Our Time* (Athens: Ohio UP, 1990), passim; David Castronovo, *Edmund Wilson* (New York: F. Unger, 1984), 33–42; and Jeffrey Meyers, *Edmund Wilson* (New York: F. Ungar, 1995).

59. The collection's title derived from Wilson's essay "The Politics of Flaubert," and it was intended to provide Wilson with a unifying theme for his numerous fugitive pieces addressing such disparate figures as Paul Elmer More, A. E. Housman, Christian Gauss, John Jay Chapman, Marx, and Ben Jonson. In addition to the aforementioned quartet of main nineteenth-century figures (Pushkin, James, Shaw, Flaubert), the highlights of *The Triple Thinkers* are the introduction to Pushkin (including Wilson's own prose translation of "The Bronze Horseman"), theoretical studies of "Marxism and Literature" and "The Historical Interpretation of Literature," and Wilson's interpretations of the dramas of "Morose Ben Jonson," in which he subjects the Jacobean dramatist to speculative psychobiography.

60. I am well aware that the unpolitical Flaubert would have been unlikely to characterize Howe, or Wilson himself—at least during his Marxist phase in the 1930s, when the first edition of *The Triple Thinkers* (1938) was published—as a "triple thinker." Flaubert opposed socialism, the goal of social equality, mass education, universal suffrage, and revolutions in general. Wilson quotes Flaubert's 1853 letter to Louise Colet: "The triple thinker . . . should have neither religion nor fatherland, nor even any social conviction" (73–74).

61. Howe's triple thinking flowed, therefore, from his involvement in three different worlds; that is, from the seriousness he brought to politics, literature, and Jewish life. But he was hardly orthodox in any of those worlds. He was political, but his radicalism marginalized him in liberal and conservative America. He loved literature, but his disdain for professionalized "lit crit" made him an outsider in the literary academy. He was Jewish and valued his roots, but he could not accept a rejection of universalism and nationalism at the expense of the Palestinians. His insights and his own outsider status were linked. Howe's boundary crossing helps explain not only his originality and intellectual contributions, but also his many conflicts and enemies.

62. See Howe, "The New York Intellectuals," *Commentary* (March 1968).

63. During the reception after his 1986 lecture at Virginia, Howe chatted with several of us at length about *Politics and the Novel* (1957) and whether it might be time to reissue his landmark study. "There's been nothing like it since then," a few of us agreed. And, in fact, Howe did come to reissue it in 1992—perhaps gently nudged by our enthusiasm for the book.

64. See Howe, "Ballet for the Man Who Enjoys Wallace Stevens," *Harper's* (May 1971): 102–109. See also Sorin, *Irving Howe*, 177–178, 222–223, 270, 286.

65. Daniel Bell, *Dissent* (Fall 1993): 517.

66. Irving Howe, "The Range of the New York Intellectuals," 287, in Bernard Rosenberg, ed., *Creators and Disturbers: Reminiscences by Jewish Intellectuals of New York* (New York: Columbia UP, 1982).

67. But some of Howe's contemporaries among the New York Intellectuals—and even a few *Dissent* colleagues—believe that Howe's pride about dispensing with a doctoral degree betrayed a defensiveness that masked an insecurity. He felt vulnerable, they maintained, because academic scholars had often cited his lack of a PhD in order to demean his literary criticism as amateurish.

68. See Sorin, *Irving Howe*, 146–147.

69. Leon Wieseltier, memorial address on Howe, delivered 24 May 1993.

70. Irving Howe, *Thomas Hardy* (New York: Macmillan, 1967).

71. Howe's supporters on the organized Left in the 1970s could best be described as coming from the Democratic Socialist Organizing Committee (DSOC), a group that merged with a small New Left group called the New American Movement (NAM) in the early 1980s. It is important to acknowledge Howe's political involvement in this strain of American socialism, even though literary criticism and *Dissent* became more central to his life and work than organized socialism after the late 1940s.

72. Howe, *World of Our Fathers*, 645.

73. Just a year before his death, in his preface to the 1992 edition of *Politics and the Novel*, Howe wrote that his 1957 study "was written at a moment when I was drifting away from orthodox Marxism. . . . I still hold firmly to the socialist ethos which partly inspired this book, but the ideology to which these essays occasionally return no longer has for me the power it once had" (7).

74. On the genre of the anecdote, see my book *The Politics of Literary Reputation* (New York: Transaction Publishers, [1989] 2001), 126, 132.

75. Dickstein is quoted in the *New York Times* obituary on Howe, 7 May 1993. See also Howe, introduction to *A Critic's Notebook*, 12.

76. Howe, *A Critic's Notebook*, 316.

77. Ibid., 315–316. Occasionally Howe also lost his precarious balance between the aesthetic and the ethical, with the latter overwhelming the former. And indeed, maintaining his much-prized "moral poise" depended chiefly on keeping his literary poise. Howe was blessed with a power rarely given to a critic, a power difficult to control: he had the literary equivalent of "perfect pitch." His ear for good prose style was nearly faultless. He possessed both an exquisitely fine sense for the rhythm and cadence of sentences and a superb judgment about *le mot juste*. These talents proved ideal equipment for a literary critic.

But Howe's concentrated energy could become a sharp weapon when it contracted and overfocused on the foibles of an adversary or homed in on isolated details of an ideological dispute. He was marvelous when he related an easily overlooked particular to the big picture, but he could be cutting and wounding when he became preoccupied with small concerns. Under such circumstances, he could use morality as a club. Such was arguably the case with Tom Hayden and the young New Leftists, whom he blasted when they visited him and *Dissent* in 1965. On that episode, see Todd Gitlin, *The Sixties: Years of Hope, Days of Rage* (New York: Bantam Books, 1987), 171–176.

78. Howe, "The Fate of Solzhenitsyn," collected in *Selected Writings* (New York: Harcourt Brace Jovanovich, 1990), 459, 463.

79. Introduction to *The Best of Sholem Aleichem*, ed. Irving Howe and Ruth R. Wisse (Washington, DC: New Republic Books, 1979), xvii. Sholem Aleichem was also a "culture hero" of Howe's, but less a personal, intellectual hero (unlike Trotsky, Orwell, Silone, and Wilson) than a nineteenth-century spirit of the age. Howe wrote of Sholem Aleichem: "I think of him as a culture hero in the sense that Dickens and Mark Twain were culture heroes. For he embodies the culture of eastern European Jews at a time of heightened consciousness" (12). See also Howe's essay "Sholem Aleichem: Voice of Our Past," collected in *A World More Attractive* and in *Selected Writings*.

80. Irving Howe and B. J. Widick, *The UAW and Walter Reuther* (New York: Random House, 1949), 199. Howe's portrait of Reuther resembles a description of Howe's own former commissar self who had been in thrall to Trotskyist sectarian politics—a life that Howe, by 1949, had largely ended: "Reuther eats, sleeps, and talks union. He is as close to a political machine as any man alive today. He has forgotten how to relax and how to play. Reuther

is characteristic of a generation of radicals that came to feel leftist politics is a dead end but could not throw off the moral compulsions that had led them to such politics" (201). By all accounts of his acquaintances, this passage could also describe Howe's own struggle at midcentury to work through his Trotskyist past.

81. Fittingly enough, in the last article he published in *Dissent* during his lifetime, Howe proposed "two cheers for utopia"—two, not three—yet genuine, heartfelt cheers nonetheless. Howe, "Two Cheers for Utopia," *Dissent* 40 (Spring 1993): 131–133.

82. Indeed, my own view is that Howe's critical legacy will ultimately have more to do with his revival of *Yiddishkeit*, including the American Yiddish poets, than with the politics of the novel or his valiant attempt to salvage and renew American radicalism. Robert Boyers and others have built on the strand of Howe concerned with the politics of the novel, but there has been no systematic attempt as yet to honor and further develop his contributions to Yiddish literature and culture.

83. The New York "elders" sometimes compared with Howe include Lionel Trilling, Philip Rahv, Sidney Hook, Dwight Macdonald, Harold Rosenberg, and Hannah Arendt. Even after their deaths, Howe was often cast in their shadow via unfavorable comparison. Or he was criticized as "too polemical" or "too prolific." In the 1980s he attained the status of a monument on the liberal-Left, but his reputation went into eclipse even before his death. (It is significant that whereas Trilling's obituary appeared on page 1 of the *New York Times*, Howe's notice was run on page 22 of section D.) The appearance of two excellent biographies in the last few years, Edward Alexander's *Irving Howe: Socialist, Critic, Jew* (1998) and Gerald Sorin's *Irving Howe: A Life of Passionate Dissent* (2002), have brought Howe back into the public eye and more than redressed the previous decade of relative neglect.

The peak of Howe's recognition and broad influence occurred in the late 1970s and early '80s, between *World of Our Fathers* (1976) and *A Margin of Hope* (1982)—just as the height of Trilling's fame in the 1950s also occurred long before his death. In the wake of the success of *World of Our Fathers*, which received the 1976 National Book Award, Howe and Libo edited a popular, illustrated volume of history, *How We Lived: A Documentary History of Immigrant Jews in America, 1880–1930*. Really a coffee-table book, it was selected in 1979 as a main choice of the Book-of-the-Month Club. It was also a selection that year of the History Book Club, the Jewish Book Club, and the Jewish Publication Society. By contrast, *Selected Writings* (1990), a collection of Howe's best essays across more than forty years, received only scattered attention, with no efforts to sum up Howe's career. By the mid-1980s, the vogue for theoretical academic criticism meant that concerns in the literary-academic world had moved beyond Howe's method-less, "amateur" criticism.

84. Howe, "Writing and the Holocaust," *New Republic*, 27 October 1986, 34.

85. Howe, "This Age of Conformity," in *Steady Work*, 319. The essay originally appeared in *Partisan Review* (January–February 1954).

86. Ibid., 323.

Chapter 4

1. Hitchens was the only one in the top five under the age of sixty on the *Prospect* list. (Ahead of him were Noam Chomsky, Umberto Eco, Richard Dawkins, and Vaclav Havel.) Of the top ten nominees, the only other intellectual born after World War II was Hitchens's long-time friend, the novelist Salman Rushdie. More than 20,000 people voted in the poll.

As Hitchens himself would doubtless agree, public opinion polls are not a reliable barometer of intellectual substance—Hitchens is certainly not a popular figure on the Left or even liberal-Left. But such polls may indeed be an accurate index of visibility or notoriety—and no one can dispute that Hitchens scores high on both measures.

2. One index of Hitchens's celebrity was the rumor that he had been the model for Tom Wolfe's hard-drinking British journalist Peter Fallow in *Bonfire of the Vanities* (1987).

3. Of course, another similarity between Orwell and Hitchens—as Alexander Cockburn and other leftists have pointed out ad nauseam—is that Orwell named names to the IRD, and Hitchens signed an affidavit testifying that his friend Sidney Blumenthal committed perjury before Kenneth Starr's committee during the Monica Lewinsky investigation.

4. Despite periodically sharp clashes and bruised relationships with prominent fellow leftists (such as Alexander Cockburn, Edward Said, and Noam Chomsky), a perception of their common right-wing enemies (such as Kissinger, Mother Teresa, and the Ayatollah Khomeini) kept their alliance loosely intact throughout the 1990s. This fact also induced fellow leftists to tolerate Hitchens's apostasies as those of a self-described "unaffiliated radical." The Blumenthal affair was the first major conflict between Hitchens and the Left; 9/11 and its aftermath triggered the break. Nonetheless, the war on terrorism is, for Hitchens, a war against theocracy and religious fundamentalism, which is why he could both support Bush on Iraqi intervention and castigate him as a born-again religious fanatic.

5. On these and other comparisons between Hitchens and Orwell, see John Rodden, "Fellow Contrarians? Christopher Hitchens and George Orwell," *Kenyon Review* (Fall 2006). See also Christopher Hitchens, *Hitch-22: A Memoir* (New York: Twelve, 2010), esp. 72–73, 163, 171–172, 328–329.

6. Hitchens, "Taking Sides," *Washington Post*, 14 October 2002.

7. In *Salon*, the electronic magazine, the editors asked Hitchens: "If one were to look at your writing, say, since Sept. 11, there are threads of Orwell in it, aren't there? Whether or not they're cited." Hitchens answered: "Well if someone wanted to say that, I wouldn't feel I had to repudiate it." Cited in Scott Lucas, *George Orwell and the Betrayal of Dissent* (London: Verso, 2003).

8. As Hitchens mentioned to me in May 2003, both his British and American publishers rejected his own original, preferred title: *George Orwell: A Power of Facing*. That subtitle derives from Orwell's "Why I Write" (1946), and it forms the theme of Hitchens's closing reflections in his book.

9. Andrew Sullivan, *The Times* (London), 30 September 2000. Sullivan is a gay Catholic. Like Hitchens, he tends rightward on numerous geopolitical issues, but he is a radical on most social issues, such as legalizing homosexual marriage.

10. Ron Rosenbaum, "The Man Who Would Be Orwell," *New York Observer*, 23 March 2002.

11. Certainly Hitchens is no antagonist of "the birth controllers" as Orwell was, but his severe criticism of Western sexual mores is most unusual on the Left. How many *Nation* contributors consider the separation of sex and childbearing morally problematic? Consider this passage: "The post-1945 generation has been, at least until recently, free of the fear of untreatable disease and mass unemployment. It more or less grew up knowing that sex and procreation could be easily separated—the first generation in human history for which this was true." Christopher Hitchens, "The Baby-Boomer Wasteland," *Vanity Fair* (January 1996).

Hitchens's mother, Yvonne, reportedly aborted the fetuses that she conceived before and after Christopher; some observers have suggested his moderate pro-life stand has a biographical basis. In any case, Hitchens—again like Orwell—is careful not to equate his criticism of sexual irresponsibility with support for the Church. (In the pages devoted to his mother in his memoir, *Hitch-22*, Hitchens does not address these rumors or his views of abortion and birth control.) See his "Minority Report," *The Nation*, 24 April 1989, 546.

12. In *Letters to a Young Contrarian* (New York: Basic Books, 2001), Hitchens is careful to identify himself as an "antitheist" rather than an agnostic or atheist. He writes: "I not only maintain that all religions are versions of the same untruth, but I hold that the influence of churches, and the effect of religious belief, is positively harmful" (55). Indeed, Hitchens explains about his cordial relationship with his conservative Tory brother Peter (who opposed the 2003 Iraq war strongly): "The real difference between us—and it's an unbridgeable one—is that he's a believing Christian. I have many political disagreements with all kinds of people, but they are irrelevant compared with the ones between me and anyone who is a religious believer." Quoted in Ginny Dougary, "Friendship and Betrayal," *The Times* (London), 17 July 2002. Hitchens was baptized as an Anglican and educated at a Methodist boarding school with compulsory religious instruction, "but I also had a Jewish mother who was once married to a distinguished Rabbi (who I suspected to be a secret Einsteinian agnostic)" (59). On Hitchens's rearing and education, see *Hitch-22*, 47–82.

13. Hitchens has supported the Left's opposition to Zionism. He agreed with Edward Said on the Palestinian question (see their co-edited volume, *Blaming the Victim* [New York: Verso, 1988, reprinted in 2003]). In a posthumous review of Said's *From Oslo to Iraq and the Road Map*, Hitchens wrote: "It may well be . . . that the whole Zionist enterprise was a mistake to begin with and that Palestine should be a political entity that awards citizenship without distinction of ethnicity or religion. (For what it's worth, I think so too.)" "Polymath with a Cause" *Washington Post*, 15 August 2004.

14. See Hitchens's essay on Trotsky, "The Old Man," in *The Atlantic*, where he writes with nostalgia: "Even today a faint, saintly penumbra still emanates from the Old Man."

15. Hitchens has occasionally expressed respect for Lenin, especially during the 1960s. He was certainly no Leninist by the mid-1970s, though he retains a degree of admiration for the socialism of Lenin's rival, Rosa Luxemburg. On Hitchens's youthful regard for Lenin, see his review of Isaac Deutscher's little book on Lenin, "Prophet Silenced," *New Statesman* (July 1970): 811. Hitchens is also a vocal admirer of C. L. R. James, who was both a Trotskyist and a Leninist.

16. As one former comrade from their International Socialist days in the 1960s (who is still a member of the Socialist Workers Party) wrote me: "One thing I have always felt to be absent from his Orwell pose is any genuine sympathy for the underdog, for those at the bottom, the poor, the working class, etc. I don't think Hitchens has ever had a *Down and Out* or *Wigan Pier* in him. Self-indulgence and self-advertisement have always seemed his hallmarks to me even when I have agreed with him."

17. On Blair/Orwell's "antinomianism," see Bernard Crick, *George Orwell: A Life* (Boston: Little, Brown, 1980), 311–315; and Peter Stansky and William Abrahams, *The Unknown Orwell* (London: Constable, 1972), 124–128.

18. Hitchens, *Letters to a Young Contrarian*, 102.

19. In an interview that I conducted with Hitchens in 2003, he demurred when asked if Saddam Hussein's Iraq amounted to a "Big Brother" state. Hitchens told me:

It was a temptation after the great moment of 1989—the implosion and collapse of a one-party state as a theory and practice—to say that the age of totalitarianism was over with the twentieth century.

But probably the most conspicuous feature of contemporary world affairs is the confrontation with aggressive totalitarian leadership. A recent engagement with it—which extended from 1992 to this year—is the case of a twelve-year on-and-off war with Saddam Hussein, a war with global implications. What looks like an inescapable confrontation with Kim Jong II's North Korea—with the additional terrifying prospect of nuclear totalitarianism—is now looming. And we are still digging up the graves from the Milosevic era in the Balkans.

So, though I like to avoid clichés as much as the next writer, I know of no writer of any quality who's been able to visit Baghdad or North Korea and avoid the use of the term *Orwellian*. It's simply inescapable. These are places where the citizen is the property of the state, where terror is the theory and practice, where constant aggression and hatred are inculcated and continuous regimentation is employed. It's quite extraordinary to find how one is reaching for the terms Orwell taught us.

Orwell saw what the smallest details of a dystopian system would be. Not just the hermetic nature of the state, for example, but the rapidly shifting political allegiances that the state demands of people. Yesterday Eurasia was our ally, today we're at war with Eurasia. We never were at war with Eurasia, after all.

Of course, the American public hasn't been drilled to love Saddam Hussein or even until recently to hate him. But the political Establishment has been able to move with suspicious ease from having Saddam as a patron and a client to declaring him Public Enemy No. 1. I don't know if that quite meets the strong test for applying the word "Orwellian"—any more than I'm sure that taking extraordinary measures on the home front for national security quite meets [fair criteria for applying] the "Big Brother" test either.

I think, however, that the word ["Orwellian"] has to be considered, debated, and perhaps discarded. Still, that's an example of its inescapability.

Later, in the same interview, he added:

Those of us who regard ourselves as being in George Orwell's debt are both pleased and displeased when his name comes up. People say that this latest method of surveillance, or this latest campaign against smoking, or anything that requires a government intervention in the life of a citizen, is another step towards the Big Brother State or *Nineteen Eighty-Four*.

Very often at that moment one's compelled to say, "Well, it's good to know that people are aware of the totalitarian temptation and of the tendency of the state, as it were, to take liberties. But it may be ill-advised to [equate that with] the extreme model of *Nineteen Eighty-Four* or Big Brother." Or if someone says, "Much more of this and we'll be living on Animal Farm." There is something absurd about that comparison.

[Such references are] a compliment to Orwell in the sense that he continues to live in people's minds, to inhabit people's memories and emotions. But I think he would be very scornful of the employment to which he is put. Just as he was when *Reader's Digest*—and after his death the CIA—made use of his books, not just for Cold War anticommunism, but sometimes to campaign against democratic socialism or the New Deal.

In other words, it is probably the vice of dystopian writing that its vividness makes it too easy to use for propaganda. In order to defend Orwell, one must be at odds with the people who use the term "Orwellian."

See John Rodden, *Every Intellectual's Big Brother* (Austin: University of Texas Press), 206–207, 224–225.

20. George Monbiot is a British environmental and political activist and a *Guardian* columnist. Probably his best-known book is *Captive State: The Corporate Takeover of Britain* (2000), which argues that corporate participation in British politics seriously threatens democracy.

Chapter 5

1. For Lukacs's views of Macdonald, including his friend's resemblances to Orwell, see "Dwight Macdonald: Another Orwell?" *America* (published under the pseudonym "Orville Williams"), 17 May 1958, 224–227; and Lukacs, "Dwight Macdonald," *Chronicles* (November 1998): 14–16.

2. See Lukacs's comments on Orwell's distinctions, in works ranging from *Historical Consciousness* (1968) to a 1992 *American Scholar* essay ("American History: The Terminological Problem"), both of them excerpted in *Remembered Past: John Lukacs on History, Historians, and Historical Knowledge*, ed. Mark G. Malvasi and Jeffrey O. Nelson (Wilmington, DE: ISI Books, 2005), 44, 107.

3. Lukacs, "The Legacy of Orwell," *Salmagundi* 71 (Fall 1980–Winter 1981): 121.

4. Ibid.

5. See Lukacs, "The Totalitarian Temptation," *Commonweal*, 22 January 1954, 394–399.

6. Lukacs, "The Legacy of Orwell," 122.

7. Ibid.

8. Ibid.

9. In a 1977 essay in *University Bookman* ("What Is Happening to History?"), Lukacs quotes this passage from Orwell's novel: "History was the hardest thing to teach them. . . . A boy of the middle classes, no matter how poorly educated, has at least a mental picture of a Roman senator, of an Elizabethan Englishman, of a French courtier. . . . But for these children these words were incomprehensible, they could not imagine them at all." Lukacs observes tersely: "This condition no longer prevails (perhaps, in part, because of television)." See Malvasi and Nelson, *Remembered Past*, 692.

10. Malvasi and Nelson, *Remembered Past*, 377–378.

11. Ibid., 432.

12. Ibid., 581–582. Elsewhere Lukacs quotes Hitler to underscore his point: "'I was a nationalist,' Hitler wrote in *Mein Kampf* about his youth, 'but I was not a patriot.'" Malvasi and Nelson, *Remembered Past*, 107.

13. Ibid., xx.

14. Lukacs, "The Intellectual in Power," *Salmagundi* 71 (Winter 1981): 264.

15. See Lukacs, "Polish Omens," *New Republic*, 29 November 1980, 14–17; and "Easter in Warsaw," *National Review*, 12 June 1981, 658–665.

16. His parents divorced when Lukacs was eight, and he was raised Catholic by his mother, a recent convert to the faith. Because of his mother's intense admiration for the cultural history and social values of Albion—she sent him to an English boarding school before World War II—the young Lukacs not only acquired the German that educated Hungarians learned but also mastered English, a skill that would prove invaluable in the future.

17. Lukacs, "Lessons of the Hungarian Revolution," *Commentary* (September 1956): 233–250.

18. Lukacs, "The American Conservatives," *Harper's* (January 1984): 44–49.

19. Lukacs's writings on the Cold War first brought him into contact with Kennan, whose fundamental outlook on Cold War diplomatic history Lukacs shared. Their half century of friendship culminated in two serious studies of Kennan's ideas: *George F. Kennan and the Origins of Containment, 1944–46* (1997), which features their lengthy correspondence, and Lukacs's biographical vignette, *George Kennan: A Portrait* (2007).

20. Lukacs, *Churchill's Great Speech* (2009).

21. As Lukacs states in one interview, he believes that teaching undergraduates has made his writing more compelling and more accessible to a wide audience. "It took me a long time to recognize that my undergraduate teaching at Chestnut Hill helped my writing. I had to explain to undergraduates and describe complicated things simply but not superficially. So I think it became a great asset to my writing." John Rodden and John Rossi, "John Lukacs: Visionary, Critic, Historian," *Society* (Fall 2007).

22. On the difficulties and compromises involved in undergraduate teaching, see John Lukacs, "What 'Moonlighting' Reveals: Certain Problems of American College Teachers," *University Bookman* (Summer 1961): 86–90.

23. Malvasi and Nelson, *Remembered Past*, 688–689.

24. Rodden and Rossi, "John Lukacs."

25. Lukacs has also made a noteworthy foray into imaginative literature, *A Thread of Years* (1998), which represents a fresh and distinctive blending of history and literature. Lukacs called this work "his most extraordinary book." He had long wanted to write a work that combined old-fashioned narrative history with narrative fiction.

But in *A Thread of Years*, as always for Lukacs, scholarship and history take priority over literary imagination and fiction. Lukacs doesn't put words in the mouths of famous historical figures, as happens with so many historical novels, but instead creates a succession of what he calls "vignettes." Each of these thumbnail portraits forms a tableau of a particular age at a particular time, with Lukacs the historian-participant intervening to conduct a charged dialogue with the characters whom he has created. Recurring themes featuring both American and European settings—such as the rise of Hitler, the Great Depression, World War II, and the Cold War—emerge as Lukacs gives voice to fictional figures who lived during the years 1901–1969 in America. Still, although *A Thread of Years* was widely praised, Lukacs has no interest in writing a sequel. He says flatly: "I don't think I could do it."

26. "A Conversation with John Lukacs," *Pennsylvania History* (July 1997): 275.

27. Lukacs, "It's Halfway to 1984," *New York Times Magazine*, January 2, 1966; quoted in Malvasi and Nelson, *Remembered Past*, 523.

28. Lukacs, "Intellectuals, Catholics, and the Intellectual Life," *Modern Age* (Winter 1957–1958): 40–53.

29. In 1953 Lukacs published one of the first serious studies of the diplomatic history of Eastern Europe between the two World Wars, *The Great Powers and Eastern Europe*, which showed how the neglect of Central and Eastern Europe by the major powers created a political vacuum into which Nazi Germany and Stalin's Russia moved in the 1930s and '40s. Convinced that Soviet rule in Eastern Europe was culturally untenable, and that the Cold War conflict was being interpreted through a distorted ideological lens, Lukacs elaborated this argument in his landmark study, *A History of the Cold War*, which contends that Russian nationalism and Stalin's determination to regain Czarist Russia's possessions lost after World War I represented the twin keys to understanding the emergence of the USSR's battle with the West. The contributing role of Marxist-Leninist ideology to the origin and development of the Cold War was secondary to that of Russian national interests, Lukacs maintains.

30. For a thought-provoking meditation on the prospect of Hitler's triumph, see Lukacs's essay in counterfactual history, "What If? Had Hitler Won the Second World War," in *The People's Almanac #2*, edited by David Wallechinsky and Irving Wallace (New York: Bantam Books, 1990), 394–397.

31. Lukacs, *The Hitler of History* (New York: Knopf, 1997).

32. On Lukacs's dissent from conventional opinion on these issues, see "The Fifties: Another View: Revising the Eisenhower Era." *Harper's* (January 2002): 64–70.

33. Except for a book review in *National Review* in 1998, however, Lukacs had ceased writing for both it and *American Spectator* by the early 1980s, due apparently both to personal and political differences with their editorial stances. Since then he has further distanced himself from most American conservatives and has sharply criticized their Cold War hero, Ronald Reagan, whom Lukacs has labeled "superficial, lazy, puerile." American conservatives—and most especially the leading neoconservatives at *Commentary*—are not political or social traditionalists, Lukacs argues, but simply frightened liberals.

34. See Lukacs, "Intellectuals, Catholics, and the Intellectual Life," 40–53.

35. Rodden and Rossi, "John Lukacs."

36. Lukacs, "The Legacy of Orwell," 123.

37. See Lukacs, "What Solzhenitsyn Means," *Commonweal*, 1 August 1975, 296–301.

38. Lukacs's pessimism is also traceable to his sense of apocalyptic crisis at the end of a half millennium. "Fear and hatred are prevalent among us, manifest and evident in the increasing savagery . . . in and around our everyday lives," he warns in an admonitory voice in *Outgrowing Democracy*. That tone resounds even more loudly in *Democracy and Populism: Fear and Hatred* (New Haven: Yale UP, 2005). As Lukacs puts it, per the title of one his books, we are "at the end of an age." The magnificent epoch of bourgeois culture that lasted for the better part of five centuries has ended and we face an uncertain future. According to Lukacs, who seconds Tocqueville in *Democracy in America* and Orwell in *Nineteen Eighty-Four*, citizens must maintain a "salutary fear" and "keep watch and ward for freedom" (Malvasi and Nelson, *Remembered Past*, 524).

39. Rodden and Rossi, "John Lukacs."

40. Ibid. Lukacs's *Historical Consciousness*—along with its successors, *The Passing of the Modern Age* (1970) and *At the End of an Age* (2002)—assesses modes of historical writing ranging from nineteenth-century progressivism to contemporary variants of quantitative history, psychohistory, Marxist history, and positivist epistemological history, all of which fail, Lukacs contends, because they ignore the cardinal law governing twentieth-century physics: perfect "objectivity" is impossible because we invariably participate in whatever events we observe.

41. Malvasi and Nelson, *Remembered Past*, 689.

Chapter 6

1. See Peter Schneider, *The German Comedy: Scenes of Life After the Wall* (New York: Farrar, Straus and Giroux, 1991), 12.

2. Most studies are translations of official GDR publications or UNESCO-sponsored colloquia, published variously by the GDR Ministry of Education, by the UNESCO Commission of the GDR, or by Panorama (the GDR public relations agency). For a representative list of these items, see Val Dean Rust, *Education in East and West Germany* (New York: Garland, 1984). For two short works focusing on GDR polytechnic education, see

H. Klein, *Education in a Socialist Country: Report on Educational Policy in the GDR* (East Berlin: Panorama DDR, 1974) and Mina Moore-Rinvolucri, *Education in East Germany* (Devon: Newton Abbot, David and Charles, 1973). For relevant English-language scholarship on GDR education, see works by Sterling Fishman, *Estranged Twins: Education and Society in the Two Germanys* (New York: Praeger, 1987) and by Gregory Wegner, "The Legacy of Nazism and the History Curriculum in the East German Secondary Schools," *The History Teacher* 25 (4) (1992).

3. See Pete Grothe, *To Win the Minds of Men* (Palo Alto, Calif.: Pacific Books, 1958).

4. During the 1970s and '80s, more than a million copies of *Animal Farm* and *Nineteen Eighty-Four* were sold in West Germany. On the German reception of Orwell, see Rodden, *Politics of Literary Reputation* (New York: Oxford UP, 1989), 288–303. See also Klaus Höpcke's article on *Nineteen Eighty-Four* in *Einheit* (January 1984).

5. Helmut Findeisen, editor of *Zeitschrift für Anglistik und Amerikanistik* (Leipzig), personal conversation, 20 October 1991.

6. Heinz Osterle, quoted in Rodden, *Politics of Literary Reputation*, 290.

7. As historian Golo Mann wrote in his review of *Nineteen Eighty-Four* in the *Frankfurter Rundschau*: "Especially for Germans, *1984* is like a fantastic nightmare. . . . [P]erhaps more than any other nation, we can feel the merciless probability of Orwell's utopia" (quoted in Jeffrey Meyers, *George Orwell: The Critical Heritage* [London: Routledge, 1997]).

8. See Rodden, "Varieties of Literary Experience: The Prophetic Visions of *1984*," *Zeitschrift für Anglistik und Amerikanistik* (East Germany) (Spring 1990).

9. Peter Grothe also notes that, throughout the 1950s, East Berlin readers would travel to West Berlin libraries and borrow *Nineteen Eighty-Four*. He claims that the novel was among the books most frequently on loan in West Berlin before the erection of the Berlin Wall (Grothe, *To Win the Minds of Men*, 207).

10. For an insightful analysis into how disillusion with liberal democracy led Weimar intellectuals to embrace a politics of both the radical Left and the radical Right, see Jerry Muller, *The Other God That Failed* (Princeton, N.J.: Princeton UP, 1987). On the consequences of a collapse of faith in a proletariat or nation, see Lutz Niethammer et al., *Die Volkseigene Erfahrung* (Berlin: Rowohlt, 1991).

11. From Louis Fürnberg's "Our Song" (1946).

12. Hans Mieskes, *Die Pädagogik der GDR, Band II* (Oberursel/Taunus: Finken-Verlag, 1971), 308. I was also reminded that Vladimir Ilych Ulyanov and Eric Arthur Blair not only died on the same day (January 21), but that each man also borrowed his *nom de guerre* from local rivers (the Lena is a tributary in west-central Russia; the Orwell flows through Surrey, outside London). The anniversary of Lenin's death was widely commemorated in the GDR. Until the 1970s, annual GDR school memorials honored him in special red "Lenin corners" of classrooms, which were outfitted with communist altars and Bolshevik accessories.

Chapter 7

1. I have told their stories in detail in two recent studies of Germany, *The Walls That Remain: Eastern and Western Germans Since Reunification* (Boulder: Paradigm Publishers, 2008) and *Dialectics, Dogmas and Dissent* (University Park: Pennsylvania State UP, 2010).

2. By contrast, consider the GDR ratio of citizens to *Stasi* (GDR secret police) informers and agents: 6.5 to 1. By the time of the GDR's dissolution in 1990, when its population totaled 16 million, the *Stasi* had 91,000 permanent and 174,000 unofficial employees, of which

109,000 were spies. Richard Price notes that the GDR had "the highest ratio of secret police to population of any state in history. If unpaid informers are taken into account, some estimates put the ratio of the *Stasi* and their informers as high as one to every 6.5 citizens—considerably higher than Stalin's Russia or Hitler's Germany." Historians of Nazi Germany reckon that there was one Gestapo agent per 2000 citizens, and in Stalin's Soviet Union there was one NKVD agent per 5,830 citizens. In its forty-year existence, the GDR generated as many documents and files as the whole of German history since the Middle Ages. See Richard Price, "Caricature of Socialism," *Workers Action*, no. 28 (February 2005).

3. George Orwell, *The Road to Wigan Pier* (London: Gollancz, 1937), 211.

4. I met quite a few eastern Germans who said that their Christian faith and their membership in church groups inspired them to endure the considerable risks and ordeals of political protest. Many of them were willing to give up Party positions or endured vilification by the Party because of their belief in the existence of a genuine, humanistic socialism. (Theirs was what Orwell termed "democratic socialism"—which, on the basis of respect for the dignity of the individual, posits a form of socialism valuing both justice and liberty equally. It thereby places the human being in the center of things, rather than economic collectivism—and thereby avoids state socialism's inveterate emphasis on Party slogans and mass rallies.)

This allegiance to a combination of Christianity and socialism professed by both prominent GDR dissidents and rank-and-file protesters was very typical in the East German middle classes, who inherited this attitude from the upper and middle classes of prewar German society. Especially in the Protestant east of Wilhelmine Germany, Christian and humanistic values were enshrined before World War II.

So the old-fashioned Stalinist socialism of the SED ultimately came under pressure from three directions: the tradition-oriented Christian middle class who valued personal liberties and individual rights; the educated, secular, "modern" classes who prized *Bildung* (education, culture) above all else; and the lower-middle/working classes, who above all wanted a higher standard of living.

5. Social scientists have established that this claim is plausible. As the research of my colleague James Pennebaker at the University of Texas has shown in clinical situations, storytelling can help heal people suffering from various effects of trauma. See Pennebaker, "Telling Stories: The Health Benefits of Narrative," *Literature and Medicine* 19 (2000): 3–18.

6. That has been my experience as I have observed the healing process set in motion by public acts of forgiveness. See, for example, my essays "Forgiveness, Education and Public Policy: The Road Not Yet Taken," *Modern Age* 46.4 (Fall 2004); and "Nuremburg at 60: Steps Toward Reconciliation by the Son of Hitler's Bodyguard and Brother of His Would-Be Assassin," *Journal of Human Rights* 5.2 (July 2006).

7. For reports on the George Orwell Centennial Conference, see Jeanette Tust, "Wofür bekommt man heutzutage 10 Jahre Haft?" *Der Stacheldraht* (July 2003): 7.

8. In her study of trauma and guilt in novels about the wartime bombing of Germany, Susanne Vees-Gulani addresses how trauma, storytelling, and public encounters of narration lead to psychosocial health. See Vees-Gulani, *Trauma and Guilt: Literature of Wartime Bombing in Germany* (Berlin and New York: Walter de Gruyter, 2003).

For a popular book on the GDR that tells several gripping tales and thereby profiles the human costs of the *Stasi* dragnet in ways similar to the present work, see Anna Funder, *Stasiland: True Stories from Behind the Berlin Wall* (London: Granta, 2003). Two other books covering similar ground are Peter Richter's *Blühende Landschaften* (Goldmann: München, 2004) and Allison Lewis's *Die Kunst des Verrats: Der Prenzlauer Berg und die Staatssicherheit* (Würzburg: Verlag Königshausen and Neumann, 2003).

Chapter 8

1. For my reflections on how the excesses of GDR ideological orthodoxies bear comparison with the doctrinal battles over textbook policy in the Texas public schools, see "Illiberal Education," *Texas Observer*, 7 January 2005.

2. *Mathematik 2* (Berlin, 1968), 117.

3. *Mathematik 4* (Berlin, 1968), 109.

4. *Mathematik. Klasse 4. Unterrichtshilfen* (Berlin, 1978), 12.

5. *Mathematik 4*, 65–67.

6. *Mathematik 4*, 109.

7. *Mathematik 5*, (Berlin, 1968), 108.

8. *Mathematik 7*, (Berlin, 1967), 176.

9. *Mathematik 4*, 55.

10. *Mathematik. Klasse 4. Unterrichtshilfen*, 127.

11. Ibid., 146.

12. *Mathematik 9* (Berlin, 1979), 158.

13. Ibid., 126.

14. Ibid., 100.

15. Ibid., 189.

16. Ibid., 128.

Chapter 9

1. Certainly I do not want to imply that GDR textbooks were nothing but agitprop. Yet even a casual glance through them makes clear that a significantly greater part of them than in the case of Western schoolbooks is devoted to ideological claims that were usually advanced in far sharper, blunter terms than in their Western counterparts. These facts need to be acknowledged and evaluated, while avoiding both red-baiting and whitewashing.

Maintaining that critical stance is especially important when one assesses the GDR geography curriculum. The importance that GDR educators accorded geography reflected its significance in molding what I have elsewhere termed "textbook Reds"—particularly through its emphasis on socialist virtue—can hardly be exaggerated. See my "Creating Textbook Reds," *Society* (November/December 2004).

2. Among other researchers, scholars affiliated with the Georg Eckert Institute of Textbook Research in Braunschweig (western Germany) have conducted studies since the 1960s on German textbooks. (See their website at http://www.gei.de/.) For a sample of their scholarly studies that differ from my own, see Georg Stober, ed., *Der Transformationsprozess in Ost-Deutschland und in Polen*, Schriftenreihe des Georg-Eckert-Instituts (Braunschweig: Georg-Eckert-Institut, 2003); and Verena Radkau Garcia and Heike Chr. Matzing, eds., *Zehn Jahre nach der Wiedervereinigung—die DDR im Geschichtsbewußtsein der Deutschen*, vol. 22 (2000). See also "Deutchlandbild und Deutsche Frage" (ed. Wolfgang Jacobmeyer), *Studien zur internationalen Schulbuchforschung*, vol. 43 (1986), which specifically addresses GDR geography textbooks.

For related articles, see also Jürgen Bambach, "The Transformation of East German Education: A Comparison between the Federal States of Berlin and Brandenburg," *European Education* 25 (2) (Summer 1993): 58–65; Jeffry M. Diefendorf, "Teaching History in the Polytechnical Schools of the German Democratic Republic," *History Teacher* 15 (3) (1982):

347–362; and Ilse Spittmann and Gisela Helwig, *DDR Lesebuch: Stalinisierung, 1949–1955* (Köln: Verlag Wissenschaft und Politik Berend v. Nottbeck, 1991).

3. Early editions of the fifth-grade geography text *Lehrbuch der Erdkunde für die 5. Klasse* were subtitled "The German Democratic Republic, Our Socialist Fatherland." Here and elsewhere, M-L educators, following Stalin, conveniently forgot Marx and Engels's ringing words in the *Communist Manifesto* that a communist "has no fatherland."

4. See *Atlas der Erdkunde*. A related "march" is depicted later in the atlas via four historical maps (1914, 1922, 1949, 1961). They highlight "socialist countries" in bright red and "young nations" (newly independent states) in pink. The map is titled "The Collapse of the Imperialist Colonial System in Africa and Asia."

5. *Geographie 5*, 6.

6. *Unterrichtshilfen für den Geographieunterricht in der 5. Klasse*, 10–11.

7. Ibid., 19.

8. *Geographie 5*, 51.

9. *Unterrichtshilfen für den Geographieunterricht in der 5. Klasse*, 161.

10. The SED abolished the old *Land* system of German states and principalities in 1952. It was formally reintroduced to eastern Germany after German reunification in October 1990.

11. In the first edition of 1960, however—before de-Stalinization swept the GDR—the city is still referred to as "Stalinstadt." The strong ideological flavor of the 1960 text reflects the historical crisis of the moment. Whereas the 1980 edition stresses the close working relationship between Eisenhüttenstadt and iron ore locales in the Soviet Union, the 1960 edition treats Stalinstadt as a showcase city of socialism:

A new and beautiful city, Stalinstadt, has been built in the vicinity of the iron ore factory in a former forest area.

In Stalinstadt there are only HO—and consumer stores. They are, like all buildings of the city, socialist property. All skilled workers—tailors, carpenters, painters, etc.—are also members of comrade associations. That is why Stalinstadt is a socialist city, the first of our Republic. It is a model for our socialist cities. (*Lehrbuch der Erdkunde für die 5. Klasse* [1960], 66)

12. *Geographie 5* (1980), 11.

13. Chapters on other cities are similar. For instance, the chapter on Dresden opens: "Dresden was cruelly destroyed on February 13, 1945, by American and English bombers. In a single night, the city was transformed into a river of flames. Tens of thousands of people were killed, irreplaceable cultural objects were destroyed" ([1967], 167). The 1960 edition goes even further in its denunciation of the bombings and concludes by thanking "our Soviet friends" for refurbishing the "art treasures" of the Dresden Art Museum: "Every visitor, when viewing the paintings, should be reminded of the magnanimous deed of our friends, the Soviets" (133). The text makes no mention of how Dresden's art treasures wound up in the USSR in the first place (the Soviet occupation army seized hundreds of paintings), or that the USSR refused to return many paintings and charged the GDR exorbitant prices for those they did return.

14. *Geographie 5*, 52–53. The language was even stronger in the 1960 edition: "Through the fault of the imperialists, Berlin is divided into two parts" (70).

15. *Geographie 5*, 53.

16. Ibid., 52.

17. Ibid., 161.

18. *Geographie 6*, 8.

19. Ibid., 9–10. As elsewhere, the 1960 edition makes a similar point in stronger language via a story of a delegation of GDR coal miners who visit the BRD:

> The people speak German like us at home. Here too there are signs and billboards. But they say: "Drink Coca-Cola! Tank up with Shell!"
> No flags on the houses, no word about peace and reunification. We realize: Yes, we've crossed the border all right! (5)

20. *Geographie 5*, 10. *Arbeitsmaterialen 6*, a seatwork handbook that features questions based on maps, has several exercises of the same sort. This handbook series was in use in all grades of POS geography.

21. Ibid., 55.

22. Ibid., 91–92.

23. Ibid., 98–99.

24. Ibid., 166.

25. *Geographie 7*, 10–11.

26. *Geographie. Klasse 7. Unterrichtshilfen*, 12, 29. Teachers are advised to show a film about the Russian Revolution, *The Russian Miracle*. Here and elsewhere, teachers are told to stress the "legacy" that young socialists have inherited from the revolutionaries of 1917 and "the overwhelming successes in all areas of life" that the USSR has achieved. The teaching guide makes clear that geography teachers belong to the cultural cadre:

> A strong accent on the emotional moment [1917] should flow from the teacher with an exemplary partisan demeanor. The teacher can fulfill the assignment of the syllabus, which should build [these] convictions [in youth]: Strengthen feelings of friendship toward the Soviet Union, heighten pupils' respect for the achievements of the Soviet working people, educate technicians and scientists and produce certainty in them of the firm alliance between our Volk and the peoples of the Soviet Union. (35)

27. *Unterrichtshilfen* (1st edition, 1968), 133.

28. *Geographie 7*, 130.

29. *Geographie 7* (1st edition, 1968), 155.

30. *Geographie. Klasse 7. Unterrichtshilfen* (5th edition, 1978), 13.

31. *Geographie 7* (1st edition, 1968), 155, 159.

32. See also, however, the detailed unit on Cuba, titled "The First Socialist State of the Americas," 166–173. Among the "educational emphases" of the Cuba unit, notes the eighth-grade teaching guide, should be:

> 1. Hatred toward aggressive US imperialism and strengthened conviction of the unstoppable march of socialism.
> 2. Deepening of the perception that oppressed and exploited peoples will win their political and economic independence through the revolutionary transformation of productive relations.
> 3. Strengthening of the recognition that, under socialist relations, the consequences of imperialistic exploitation and oppression can be quickly overcome. (115)

33. *Geographie 8* (1979), 9–10.

34. But this explanation is cited as just a single instance (no. 3) in the chapter's list of the eleven "neocolonial methods of the imperialistic countries." The 1978 teaching guide for *Geographie 8* conveniently summarizes them:

1. Export of capital (foreign or "developmental" aid) with political and economic stipulations.

2. Export of capital or investments of monopolies in order to take control of the economy.

3. Exploitation of dependence on exports and imports for economic and political blackmail.

4. Support of reactionary forces (including the preparation of putsches against progressive governments).

5. Dispatch of advisors and educators to expand political and economic influence.

6. Military aid (arms and advisors) to influence the military apparatus.

7. Ideological poisoning through the distribution of anticommunist and pro-capitalist ideas.

8. Support of right-wing political parties and labor unions as opposing forces to progressive movements.

9. Exploitation of cultural, religious, and economic institutions of the imperialistic states for ideological, political, and economic influence.

10. Joint measures of the imperialistic states through the use of collective institutions (e.g., the World Bank) and alliances (e.g., the Common Market).

11. Classical methods of colonialism also applied (e.g., aggression . . .) (64)

35. *Geographie. Klasse 8 Unterrichtshilfen*, 63.
36. *Geographie 8*, 72–75.
37. Ibid., 75, 78.
38. *Geographie. Klasse 8. Unterrichtshilfen*, 15.
39. *Geographie 8*, 111.
40. *Geographie. Klasse 8. Unterrichtshilfen*, 73, 85.
41. *Geographie 8*, 86–88.
42. Ibid., 109.
43. Ibid., 111.
44. Ibid., 110–111, 126. Exercises in the 1968 edition also alert pupils to "important concepts" such as "conglomerate," "slum quarter," "seasonal worker," "exhaustion of the soil," "soil erosion," "petrochemical," "plantation," "slave system," "racial discrimination," "land reform," "indentured servitude," and "great estates" (105–140).
45. Ibid., 135–136, 145.
46. *Geographie. Klasse 8. Unterrichtshilfen*, 69.
47. Ibid., 73.
48. Letter to the author from Stefan Schwarzkopf, 6 May 2004.
49. *Geographie. Klasse 9. Unterrichtshilfen* (1978), 113. Earlier editions of ninth-grade geography textbooks are more concrete and go further:

The Soviet Union and China show us most clearly how Nature can be changed for the welfare of all people and, through the careful respect for natural laws, the geographical milieu can be constantly improved. In our GDR too, the first socialist state on German soil, we can almost daily gather examples of this. That gives us the certainty that a restructuring of nature, through a thorough knowledge of all her appearances and contexts, is only possible in socialism. (*Lehrbuch der Erdkunde für die 9. Klasse. Grundzüge der allgemeinen physischen Erdkunde* [1961], 132)

50. Quoted in ibid., 6.

51. See *Lehrbuch der Erdkunde für die 9. Klasse. Ökonomische Geographie sozialistischer Länder* (4th ed., 1967).

52. See *Geographie 10. Ökonomische Geographie der sozialistischen Staatsgemeinschaft und der GDR* (2nd edition, 1979) and *Ökonomische Geographie der beiden deutschen Staaten* (6th edition, 1967).

53. *Ökonomische Geographie der beiden deutschen Staaten 6* (1967), 107–117.

54. *Geographie 10*, 5–6.

55. Ibid., 9.

56. *Geographie. Klasse 10. Unterrichtshilfen*, 37, 47, 97.

57. See *Lehrbuch der Ökonomischen Geographie. Klasse 10a, 10c, 11b* (4th ed., 1967).

58. See, e.g., "Cuba's National Democratic Road of Development from a Half-Colony to the Building of Socialism," *Lehrbuch der Ökonomischen Geographie: Teil 2 (Klasse 11a, 11c, 12b)* (5th edition, 1967), 121–132.

59. *Lehrheft der Erdkunde für die 11. Klasse der erweiterten Oberschule, Teil II* (1961), quoted in Peter R. Lucke, *Lehrbuch der Erdkunde in der Sowjetzone* (Bonn/Berlin, 1964), 45.

Chapter 11

1. For example, Cyril Connolly observed in August 1973 in *The Sunday Times* that (unlike himself), both Orwell and Hemingway possessed an ability to "pare words down to the bone." Quoted in Jeremy Lewis, *Cyril Connolly: A Life* (London: Jonathan Cape, 1997), 569.

2. Orwell did not approve of Hemingway, especially in the 1930s, both for literary and political reasons. In a 1935 review, he wrote: "*Criss/Cross* is American and 'tough.' 'The tough' American books would make one exclaim that Hemingway has a lot to answer for, were it not that their very number suggests that Hemingway is merely a symptom and not a cause."
Orwell elaborated a year later:

Fast One is also an American book, but of a somewhat different type. The blurb describes it as a "whirlwind of double-crossing, ambush, and murder." Here is a specimen paragraph: "The little man came into the room quickly and kicked the side of Kells's head very hard. Kells relaxed his grip on Rose and Rose stood up. He brushed himself and went over and kicked Kells' [*sic*] head and face several times. His face was dark and composed and he was breathing hard. He kicked Kells very carefully, drawing his foot back and aiming, and then kicking very accurately and hard." This kind of disgusting rubbish (hailed as genius when it comes in a slightly more refined form from Hemingway) is growing commoner and commoner.

Just before leaving for Spain in December 1936, Orwell also voiced sharp criticism of Hemingway's politics: "Hemingway, on the other hand, is treated rather respectfully (because Hemingway, you see, is rumoured to be toying with Communism)."

3. On the explosion of Orwell's critical and public reputation in the early postwar years, see John Rodden, *The Politics of Literary Reputation: The Making and Claiming of "St. George" Orwell* (New York: Oxford UP, 1989). Also see my *Scenes from an Afterlife: The Legacy of George Orwell* (Wilmington, DE: ISI, 2003).

4. Letter from Ernest Hemingway to Cyril Connolly, 15 March 1948. This letter is in the Connolly Collection at the University of Tulsa, along with telegrams sent in the mid-1940s from Hemingway to Connolly.

5. Hemingway and Connolly first met in Paris in 1929—when Eric Blair was scraping along as a scullion and clochard. (Ironically, Connolly never met Blair in Paris after arriving in 1929, even though they resided only a couple of streets away from each other. They had no contact after Eton until Blair/Orwell got in touch after Connolly had reviewed *Burmese Days* admiringly in the *New Statesman* in July 1935.

When Hemingway arrived in London in May 1944 as a war correspondent, Connolly quickly sought him out and volunteered to introduce him to literary friends at a party in Bedford Square. According to Michael Shelden, they proceeded to "strike up a friendship; they drank together, and talked long into the night." It was during this visit that Connolly invited Hemingway to write a "Cuban Letter" for the regular feature in *Horizon* titled "Where Shall John Go?" (Hemingway agreed to do the piece, but he never came through with it.) Shelden also reports that Connolly took Hemingway to visit Lady Emerald Cunard and that when she inquired about his opinion of Russia, he answered in exasperation: "There is the pro as well as the con about Russia. As with all these fucking countries." Cited in Shelden, *Friends of Promise* (London: Hamish Hamilton, 1989), 120.

Connolly was one of Hemingway's early champions. For instance, reviewing Hemingway's *Men Without Women*, he called Hemingway "easily the ablest of the wild band of Americans in Europe" whose stories combine "ferocious virility" and "strong silent sentimentality." Connolly also lauded Hemingway's *Green Hills of Africa*. Cited in Jeremy Lewis, *Cyril Connolly: A Life*, 180, 443, 455.

Later, however, Connolly voiced stern criticism of Hemingway's fiction. Connolly pronounced *To Have and Have Not* "morally odious" and judged that Hemingway's "writings on big-game hunting, his flashy he-man articles in *Esquire*, and his attitude to criticism have alienated a great many people." Connolly was even harsher in his judgment of *Across the River and Into the Trees*, calling it a "thoroughly bad book." Just four years later, however, Connolly exalted *The Old Man and the Sea* as "the best story Hemingway has ever written" and compared him flatteringly to Flaubert. Quoted in Jeffrey Meyers, *Hemingway: A Biography*, 295, 458. See also Cyril Connolly, *Sunday Times* (London), 3 September 1950.

6. Orwell's view of *The Unquiet Grave* was decidedly less enthusiastic. Orwell called it "a cry of despair from the Rentier who feels that he has no right to exist, but also feels that he is a finer animal than the proletarian." See the London *Observer*, 14 January 1945.

7. *The Unquiet Grave* was published in 1944 in the United Kingdom and in the United States in the spring of 1945. It was reviewed in the *New York Times* by Carlos Baker on 7 October 1945.

8. Hemingway fought in France with the 4th Infantry Division during a few months in mid-1944 as the Allies were sweeping eastward into Germany. He was much admired as a fearless soldier by his military superiors, and he often boasted (he himself is the sole source for this statistic) that he killed 122 "krauts," which he referred to as his "122 sures." Hemingway was actually attached as a correspondent to Colonel "Buck" Lanham's regiment of the 4th Infantry Division, but he was always heavily armed and was often in the thick of battle.

9. Adopting the persona of Palinurus, Aeneas's helmsman on his Italian voyage who fell asleep while steering the ship, Connolly composed a confessional masterpiece, *The Unquiet Grave*.

10. Harvey Breit (1913–1968) was a columnist and assistant editor at the *New York Times Book Review* in the 1940s and '50s, and it was in his official editorial role that he proposed the *Catalonia* review to Hemingway. In 1950 Hemingway developed a friendship with Breit on the basis of their shared enthusiasms for baseball and boxing. By the end of the year, Breit felt close enough to Hemingway to request authorization to write his biography. Hemingway declined because "too many women" were still alive (among them his mother and all his wives) and because he feared that too much thinking about himself would stifle his work. On the friendship with Breit, see Carlos Baker, *Ernest Hemingway: A Life Story* (New York: Scribner, 1969), 485–487.

Breit was also acquainted with several members of the so-called New York Intellectuals as a result of his membership on the advisory board of *Partisan Review* (*PR*), which was known in Europe as *Horizon's* "American cousin" and ran pieces by many of the same contributors. (Orwell, for example, both wrote a regular "London Letter" for *PR* during 1941–1946 and contributed some of his best essays to *Horizon*.) A social democrat, Breit was in broad sympathy with most of the political positions voiced by Orwell, Connolly, and Hemingway during the early postwar period.

Breit was a poet, editor, playwright, literary critic, and reviewer. Probably his best-known work is a drama in three acts, *The Disenchanted* (1959), based on a novel by Budd Schulberg and co-authored with him. Breit also wrote *The Guide*, which was running on Broadway at the time of his death in April 1968. A frequent contributor to the *New York Times Book Review* on contemporary British and American authors, Breit also often did profiles and interviews with well-known authors. These were collected in a book entitled *The Writer Observed* (1956), consisting of sixty portraits and interviews with leading authors (including Hemingway). The collection reflected Breit's association with many prominent literary figures and featured his thoughts on the writing craft and his literary gossip with numerous distinguished American and British writers.

11. Coming from Hemingway, this was high praise indeed. As Meyers observes: "The only contemporary books he disinterestedly praised were [e. e.] cummings's *The Enormous Room* (published by Liveright in 1922), [Isak] Dinesen's *Out of Africa*, and Orwell's *Homage to Catalonia*." See Meyers, *George Orwell: Wintry Conscience of a Generation*, 416. This contention by Meyers is not entirely accurate given that (as we have already seen) Hemingway also voiced high admiration for *The Unquiet Grave* in his 1948 letter to Connolly.

12. Unlike most foreign soldiers and literary men who fought on the Loyalist side in the Spanish Civil War, Orwell did not join the ranks of the well-armed International Brigades, financed by Stalin's USSR. Rather, he fought with the Party of Marxist Unification, known as P.O.U.M., a motley independent Communist militia under the leadership of the French Trotskyist André Nin.

13. Granville Hicks reviewed *Homage to Catalonia* glowingly in the *New York Times* on 18 May 1952.

14. Hemingway to Harvey Breit, 16 April–May 1952. The original of the Breit letter is in the Hemingway Collection of the John F. Kennedy Library at Harvard.

15. As we will later discuss in more detail, sources are in conflict as to which hotel Hemingway stayed at in Paris. Carlos Baker reports that he lodged at the Ritz; Paul Potts and Gordon Bowker merely say that the meeting occurred at the Ritz. But most other Orwell

biographers and scholars claim that meeting occurred at the Hotel Scribe. Since the location of the encounter was apparently Hemingway's hotel room, the differing accounts about where Hemingway was lodging represent a notable discrepancy.

16. Ibid.

17. Ernest Hemingway, *True At First Light: A Fictional Memoir* (New York: Scribner's, 1998), 139–140.

18. Ibid. In *True at First Light*, Hemingway adds: "I wished Orwell were still alive and I told G. C. about the last time I had seen him in Paris in 1945 after the Bulge fight and how he had come in what looked something like civilian clothes to room 117 of the Ritz where there was still a small arsenal to borrow a pistol because 'They' were after him."

Hemingway works in this anecdote about Orwell in conversation with a visitor, G. C., who constantly refers to Hemingway as "General" (139).

19. See Paul Potts, *Dante Called You Beatrice* (London: Eyre and Spottiswoode, 1960).

20. Ibid.

21. On Saunders's treatment of George and Sonia Orwell, see Rodden, *Scenes from an Afterlife*, chapter 2.

22. From D. J. Taylor, *Orwell: The Life* (London: Chatto and Windus, 2003), 344.

23. Shelden is the only biographer to cite the 1948 letter from Hemingway to Connolly. He also refers to Potts's *Dante Called You Beatrice*, but he reports all of this straight, without questioning or qualification.

24. Baker, *Hemingway*, 442. Inaccurately referring to Orwell in March 1945 as "famous," Baker wrote that Hemingway reported, "with what truth it is impossible to say, that one of his visitors was the famous George Orwell, whom he had last seen in Barcelona. Orwell looked nervous and worried. He said that he feared that the Communists were out to kill him and asked Hemingway for the loan of a pistol. Ernest lent him the .32 Colt that Paul Willerts had given him in June. Orwell departed like a pale ghost."

25. Ibid.

26. Townsend Ludington, *John Dos Passos: A Twentieth-Century Odyssey* (New York: Dutton, 1980), 373.

27. In a hard-hitting critique of Baker's work, William Kimbrel refers to "the public persona" that had "attracted Baker" to accept Hemingway's *A Moveable Feast* (1964) as "an authoritative source for information on Hemingway's life in Paris." Kimbrel concludes: "Baker attempts to sustain the illusion of his own neutrality while [also engaged in] continual collusion with his subject to preserve the myth." See William W. Kimbrel, Jr., "Carlos Baker and the 'True Gen,'" and *The Hemingway Review* 16 (1) (Fall 1996): 90. See also "Carlos Baker on Hemingway," in Charles F. Madden, ed., *Talks with Authors* (Carbondale: Southern Illinois UP, 1968), 73–88.

28. Meyers, *George Orwell*, 416.

29. Orwell certainly knew Hemingway's work. As we have seen (note 2, 364), in a September 1935 review in the *New English Weekly*, he expressed a low opinion of some of what he called "the tough American books . . . that Hemingway has a lot to answer for." But Orwell regarded *For Whom the Bell Tolls* highly. He also was angered (though not surprised) when he found out that the communists and their sympathizers in liberated France refused to allow the novel to be republished. Given all this, it is difficult to imagine Orwell omitting mention of any substantial contact with Hemingway. See *The Complete Works of George Orwell*, ed. Peter Davison, vol. 10 (London: Secker and Warburg, 1999), 397.

30. In *Cyril Connolly: A Life*, Jeremy Lewis writes that Hemingway and Connolly met in Paris in 1929 (211).

31. Baker reports that Hemingway had been staying at the Ritz since January 1945, 441–442. As we have already noted, Hemingway's March 1948 letter to Connolly indicates that Hemingway did sometimes stay at the Ritz (e.g., around the time of the Paris liberation).

32. Malcolm Muggeridge, *The Infernal Grove: Chronicles of Wasted Time*, vol. 2 (New York: Morrow, 1974).

33. Philips was a wealthy Australian and the chief financial backer of the independent Left journal *Polemic*—to which Orwell contributed a few of his best short essays. Philips claimed that Orwell feared he could be the target of a communist assassination. Bowker notes: "Orwell's paranoia about communists was not just fear of spies and eavesdroppers, but of assassins too, the sort who had found and murdered others in Paris and even in America" (331). Since the end of the war, and especially since *Animal Farm* had been published, Orwell had felt the need to arm himself.

34. Gordon Bowker to John Rodden, 3 October 2007. In his Orwell biography, Bowker makes much of this and cites Hemingway's report without reservation:

Rather more curious was his encounter with Ernest Hemingway, which revealed a greater anxiety than his health, women, or Wodehouse preying on his mind. According to Hemingway, Orwell came looking for him at his room at the Ritz, and told him that he was afraid he was going to be assassinated by the Communists.... The summary justice handed out by Communists immediately after the liberation must have been on his mind as well as assassinations carried out in Paris by Comintern agents during the Spanish Civil War. His paranoia would only intensify after the publication of *Animal Farm*, the more so because Hemingway had asked him to return the pistol to its original owner when he left France. (370–371)

35. Quoted in Jeffrey Meyers, *Hemingway: A Biography* (New York, 1985), 413. Meyers adds:

During his lifetime, the Hemingway legend took hold and replaced reality. Matthew Bruccoli has noted "how difficult it is to establish the truth about virtually everything involving Hemingway, how difficult to differentiate the public Papa from the private writer." Everyone believed that Hemingway had Indian blood, was kept out of school for a year to play the cello, ran away from home, injured his eye while boxing, associated with gangsters, had affairs with the actress Mae Marsh and the spy Mata Hari, fought with the Italian *Arditi*, was fitted with an aluminum kneecap, kept a mistress in Sicily, reported the battles of the Greco-Turkish War in the wilds of Anatolia. Yet virtually all the drinking, boxing, hunting, fishing and fornicating stories are exaggerations or fantasies. He began to brag more as writing became increasingly difficult; changed from listing the numbers of fish caught and game shot to the number of Krauts killed; said his current command consisted of maid, butler, houseboys, and gardeners. His letters to [Colonel "Buck"] Lanham revealed the worst side of his postwar character: the crude language, the obsessive replay of military adventures, the compensatory bragging. (416–417)

36. Hemingway, quoted in Frank Scafella, ed., *Hemingway: Essays of Reassessment* (New York: Oxford UP, 1991), 4–5.

37. Mark Schechner, "Papa," *Partisan Review* 49 (2) (1982): 213–223. See also Townsend Ludington, "Papa Agonistes," *New Republic*, 2 May 1981, 35.

38. Carlos Baker phrases it more diplomatically in the 1972 edition of his *Hemingway:*

The Writer as Artist (originally published in 1952): "In providing an account of Hemingway's career for the period 1951–1961, the emphasis must fall far more upon what he did than upon what he wrote" (328). The critical consensus about the displacement of Hemingway's energies from the literary to the social—and the fact that this shift became virtually his sole claim during the period to public attention—has only solidified since the 1970s. See Carlos Baker, *The Writer as Artist* (Princeton, N.J.: Princeton UP, [1952] 1972).

Meyers adds in *Hemingway: A Biography* (1985): "As Hemingway began to experience and suffer the betrayal of publicity, he realized that success could be as humiliating as failure, and was well aware of the dangers of corruption, but could not always avoid them. The transformation from private to public man, spurred by wealth and fame, began to take place in the early 1930s. It helped to explain the gradual decline of his writing after *A Farewell to Arms* and the sharp descent after *For Whom the Bell Tolls*" (240). See also Carlos Baker, ed., *Hemingway and His Critics: An International Anthology* (New York: Hill and Wang, 1961).

39. See Earl Rovit, "On Psychic Retrenchment in Hemingway." In Frank Scafella, ed., *Hemingway: Essays of Reassessment* (New York: Oxford UP, 1991), 181–188.

40. On Hemingway's reputation during these years, see Jeffrey Meyers, ed., *Hemingway: The Critical Heritage* (London: Routledge and Kegan Paul, 1982); and Robert O. Stephens, *Ernest Hemingway: The Critical Reception* (New York: Ben Franklin, 1977). Delbert E. Wylder also writes: "After World War II, Hemingway became increasingly hostile to a number of critics. Yet, doctoral dissertations had to be written and critical works published, and the pressures on Hemingway became greater and greater. The *Letters* make clear that he not only refused to cooperate with those critics who insisted on doing biographical studies (especially if the studies were psychologically oriented), but actively tried to interfere with their publication." See Delbert E. Wylder, "The Critical Reception of Ernest Hemingway's *Selected Letters, 1917–1961*," *Hemingway Review* 3 (1) (Fall 1983): 58.

41. Jeffrey Meyers, "Review," *Virginia Quarterly Review* 60 (1984): 591. Also in Meyers, *Hemingway: A Biography*, 240.

42. *The Old Man and the Sea* was published entirely in the 1 September 1952 issue of *Life*. More than five million copies of the magazine sold on newsstands in two days. It was also a Book-of-the-Month Club selection. In March 1954 Hemingway accepted an award from the American Academy of Arts and Letters, and in May *The Old Man and the Sea* won the Pulitzer Prize for Fiction. In July Cuba awarded him its highest order, the Order of Carlos Manuel de Cespedes. In October he received word that he had won the Nobel Prize in Literature. But the prizes of 1954 were largely overshadowed for Hemingway by two tragic, near-fatal plane crashes during his African safari trip to Kenya that January.

43. This interview is collected in Lillian Ross, *Portrait of Hemingway* (New York: Simon and Schuster, 1961).

44. See, for instance, both Dwight Macdonald's savage caricature of Hemingway's style, "Ernest Hemingway," collected in *Against the American Grain* (New York: Random House, 1962); and E. B. White's parody of *Across the River and Into the Trees*, published as "Across the Street and Onto the Grill," *The Second Tree from the Corner* (New York: Harper and Row, 1954).

45. The following passage from the posthumously published, never-completed novel *The Garden of Eden* (1986) ostensibly chronicles the writing difficulties of a young author, David Bourne. But they actually describe Hemingway's own writing block during his last decade, one that increased considerably after the plane crashes in 1954:

> He had started a sentence as soon as he had gone into his working room and had completed it but he could write nothing after it. He crossed it out and started an-

other sentence and again came to the complete blankness. He was unable to write the sentence that should follow although he knew it. He wrote a first simple declarative sentence again and it was impossible for him to put down the next sentence on paper. At the end of two hours it was the same.

46. Quoted in Jeffrey Meyers, *Hemingway: A Life Into Art* (New York: Rowman and Littlefield, 2000), 136.

47. Meyers draws attention to Hemingway's boasting and to the costs of "the Hemingway legend. It was sometimes difficult for him to be a writer, lover, sportsman and warrior, to fulfill everyone's high expectations, to be Ernest Hemingway everyday. He may have created the Papa persona because he felt more comfortable in a role than as himself. The name Papa kept people at a distance and was used by courtiers. During his lifetime, the Hemingway legend took hold and replaced reality." Meyers, *Hemingway: A Biography*, 240–241.

48. Macdonald's essay was originally published in *Encounter* (January 1962). It was reprinted under the title "Ernest Hemingway" in Macdonald, *Against the American Grain*, 167–184.

49. For example, not until *For Whom the Bell Tolls*, published in October 1940, did Hemingway publicly express hostility toward Stalinists such as the Comintern functionary André Marty and communist icon Dolores Ibarrori (the Madrid radio broadcaster known as "La Pasionaria"). Moreover, when the USSR joined the Western Allies in World War II after the Nazi invasion in June 1941, Hemingway once again pulled his punches against "Uncle Joe" Stalin and the Soviets.

50. Meyers elaborates his Hemingway/Orwell comparisons in *Hemingway: A Biography*:

> Hemingway's portrayal of the French political commissar, Andre Marty, in *For Whom the Bell Tolls* shows that he was well aware of the Communist horrors in Spain. He and Orwell were among the very few writers who were honest enough to criticize the Communists from the Left point of view (though Hemingway did not criticize them until after the war) and both writers were reviled by the Communist press. Hemingway condemned Max Eastman, James Farrell and Edmund Wilson for remaining in New York and attacking everyone who went to Spain as a tool of Stalin. . . . Yet some of Hemingway's emotional and political limitations become apparent when he is compared to Orwell, who thought telling the truth was more important than winning the war. (324–325)

Hemingway was not capable of Orwell's political insight and largely abandoned interest in politics after his side lost the war in Spain.

51. See also, for instance, his other two collections of verse from the 1940s: *A Poet's Testament* (London: Whitman Press, 1940) and *A Ballad for Britain on May Day* (London: Modern Literature, 1945). Whatever else be the case, it cannot be said that Potts was a braggart. In the 1978 preface to the second edition of *Instead of a Sonnet*, he opens by saying: "These few poems, if indeed they are poems at all, are not terribly good. The poetry of the English language would be no poorer without them and it is unfortunately no richer because of them." Potts's first selection, "Edited from Gettysburg," continues in this vein: "To read my verse is to share my failure; it is but the weakling harvest of an exciting spring" (4). Potts dedicated the second edition to two Irish women friends and "to the memory of George Orwell." See Paul Potts, *Instead of a Sonnet* (London: Tuba Press, 1978).

52. Derek Stanford, "The Flag of Failure," *Time and Tide*, 4 June 1960, 646. See also Stephen Spender, "The Problem of Sincerity," *Listener*, 26 May 1960; and Hugh G. Portis, "My Loneliness," *Spectator*, 20 May 1960.

53. See Paul Potts, "Don Quixote on a Bicycle: In Memoriam, George Orwell, 1903–1950," *London Magazine* 4 (3) (1957): 39–47.

54. Potts and Connolly were acquainted through correspondence. See, for instance, the admiring letters from Potts to Connolly during the mid-1950s, which are held in the Connolly Collection at the University of Tulsa.

In one letter written from Hampstead, Potts solicits Connolly's help in finding a publisher for *Dante Called You Beatrice*. Potts asks Connolly to read the full manuscript. It is therefore quite possible that Connolly read "Don Quixote on a Bicycle" even before its publication in 1960. Potts writes:

Dear Cyril Connolly,
I have a manuscript of 75,000 words. I have written it and rewritten it and then written it again.

Will you read it? There is absolutely no question that it is good enough not to be a joke to ask you. Now get this straight—

There are some lovely things in it about you. They were not put there for you to read in a manuscript, but as you know, life makes us ask favors. I can't yet get a publisher.

That letter (ca. 1958–1959) follows, ironically, a flattering letter of 6 March 1956 in which Potts asserts that he has always strenuously avoided asking Connolly for any favors.

Dear Cyril Connolly,
I've often wanted to write you the following note, but during the years you've either been editing or reviewing and might have looked as if I wanted a favor.

I can't tell you how much your work has meant to me. You've got the finest mind in English literature today. On reading your Victor Hugo made me [sic] rush into this note, but I mean it, I have said it, a bit better and at great length, in the book which I am just finishing and which is coming out at last. I put no address and so you won't have to answer!

55. See, for instance, the letter from Breit to Connolly ca. 1959, when Breit was staying at the Connaught Hotel as his new play, *The Disenchanted*, was about to be staged in London. The letter is located in the Connolly Collection at the University of Tulsa.

56. Sir Bernard Crick to John Rodden, 21 February 2007.

57. Doubtless Hemingway was unaware when he was recasting his tale of meeting Orwell for the memoir that would eventually be posthumously published as *True at First Light* that he and Blair/Orwell had lived just a few streets apart for several weeks in 1928. Quite possibly, they really did meet back then! One can even imagine Hemingway, possibly feted at a literary luncheon to celebrate the success of *The Sun Also Rises*, being served by Orwell the busboy. The prospect is a delicious one. What new storylines for his "fictional memoir" might Hemingway have imagined—and for that matter, Paul Potts too—if he had known in the 1950s that he and Orwell had resided in Paris just minutes away from each other? Both Hemingway and Potts could have been even freer in their fantasies!

Chapter 12

1. For information about Harry "Haywire Mac" McClintock, see Hal Rammel, *Nowhere in America: The Big Rock Candy Mountain and Other Comical Utopias* (Chicago: University of Illinois Press, 1990). McClintock always contended that he first wrote the song in 1895 after hearing stories about hobo adventures during his early tramping days throughout the American South in the early 1890s. McClintock lost a lawsuit over the issue of copyright and never received any direct royalties from his original recording, because it was ruled that the lyrics were in the public domain.

McClintock's travels took him around the world, and eventually, in 1925, he began a weekly radio show through which he later popularized his recording of "The Big Rock Candy Mountains."

2. On these recruitment efforts, see George Milburn, *The Hobo's Hornbook* (New York: Ives Washburn, 1930), 62–63. "Ghost Tales" were stories that a hobo would invent in order to entice a boy to join him on the road and do much of the hobo's begging for him.

3. In the 1950s, McClintock referred to his 1928 recording as "the cleaned-up version." See Rammel, *Nowhere in America,* 27.

4. In hobo slang, a "punk" was a boy apprenticed to an elder tramp, who was also known as a "jocker." A "tree" was a code word for a boy or male youth. A "homeguard" was simply someone with a fixed abode and some form of employment—that is, a person with a settled life. In many bawdy versions of the ballad, the penultimate line reads: "To be buggered sore like a hobo's whore."

5. The recorded version was published as early as 1930 in Milburn, *The Hobo's Hornbook,* though it had already appeared several times in sheet music form.

6. Orwell, "Songs We Used to Sing," *Daily Mail* (January 1946). See also *The Complete Works of George Orwell,* ed. Peter Davison, vol. 18 (London: Secker and Warburg, 1999), 50–51.

7. Davison, *The Complete Works,* vol. 19, 502–503.

8. Personal communication, 3 November 2008.

9. Orwell, *Animal Farm* (New York: Harcourt, Brace and Company, 1946), 12–13. All further references are to this edition.

10. *Ibid.,* 128–129.

11. In his 1946 essay on James Burnham, Orwell wrote: "History consists of a series of swindles, in which the masses are first lured into revolt by the promise of Utopia, and then, when they have done their job, enslaved over again by new masters." Orwell, *The Collected Essays, Journalism, and Letters* (New York: Harcourt, 1968), vol. 4, 177.

12. See *Animal Farm,* 17, 27.

13. Orwell also attacks the hypocrisy and cynicism of the Church in his depiction of Moses the raven. Moses is first the pet of Farmer Jones and then Napoleon; as Richard Smyer notes, he is the only "in-house animal" on Manor Farm. Moses is thus the only animal to "take up his vices and modes of living" (in Old Major's admonitory phrase) under both Jones and Napoleon—indeed the only creature to break one of the "Seven Commandments of Animalism" even before they are formulated. Orwell's depiction of Moses suggests how the priestly caste, which is vouchsafed the power to mediate and interpret divine law, violates it for its own vested interests. See Richard Smyer, *Animal Farm: Pastoralism and Politics* (Boston: Twayne Publishers, 1988).

14. On several occasions during the 1930s, Stalin tried and failed to reach some accommodation with the Catholic Church, much as Hitler did so successfully in his 1934 concor-

dat with the Vatican. By the war years, however, Stalin had largely succeeded through a mix of sticks and carrots in his efforts to co-opt the Church. After Hitler's invasion of the USSR in June 1941, the antireligious arm of the Komsomol, the Union of the Militant Godless, was disbanded. The *Godless* and the *Antireligionist* ceased publication soon thereafter. In return, leading Russian Orthodox clergy voiced strong support for the war effort, hailed Stalin as "the divinely appointed leader of our armed forces," and helped mobilize the peasants to fight for "Mother Russia." On these points, see Bernard Grofman, "Pig and Proletariat: *Animal Farm* as History," *San Jose Studies* 16, no. 2 (Spring 1990): 5–39.

15. Grofman, "Pig and Proletariat."

16. *Animal Farm*, 128–129.

17. "L'Internationale" was the workers' hymn associated with the First International, the revolutionary workers' organization founded by Marx and Engels in 1863. In *A Reader's Guide to George Orwell* (London: Littlefield, Adams, and Co., 1975), Jeffrey Meyers notes the broad parallels between "Beasts of England" and several passages of "L'Internationale" (1871). Meyers observes:

C'est l'éruption de la fin
Soon or late the day is coming

Paix entre nous, guerre aux tyrans!
Tyrant Man shall be o'erthrown

La terre n'appartient qu'aux hommes
And the fruitful fields of England
Shall be trod by beasts alone.

Foule esclave, debout! Debout!
Rings shall vanish from our noses

Le soleil brillera toujours!
Bright will shine the fields of England. (134)

18. The dream of Cockaigne is the stuff of myth, legend, and folk tale. It is known by many other terms: *Schlaraffenland*, *Pfannkuchenberg* (Pancake Land), *Bauernhimmel* (Peasants' Heaven), *Luilekkerland* (Land of Loafers), Mag-mell (Plain of Pleasure), El Dorado, Bensalem, Lubberland, and numerous others. The Cockaigne motif is extremely widespread, even represented by the gingerbread house in the Grimms' "Hansel and Gretel" fairy tale. Perhaps the most famous variations on Cockaigne are the Golden Age or Elysium, a terrestrial paradise first described in detail in Hesiod's *Works and Days*. Another *locus classicus* is Lucian's *True History*, a fanciful account that includes a utopia of escape known as the Islands of the Blest.

In medieval folk myths about the Land of Cockaigne, the houses are constructed with roofs of sausages, beams of sturgeon, and walls of bacon. Rivers of gravy flow through the town, and roasted geese waddle on the roads, inviting passersby to dine on them. It rains waffles every other day. Brooks and streams run with red and white wines, and gold and silver goblets are strewn plentifully about for any resident's enjoyment. The holidays in Cockaigne include four Christmases, four Easters, four Midsummer Nights, with the Lenten season occurring but once every twenty years. And to ensure that no one harbors any guilt feelings or anxiety about gastronomic excess, the Land of Cockaigne also features a fountain of youth so that nobody ages beyond thirty years old.

On these and other details of the medieval legends associated with Cockaigne, see Gorman Beauchamp, "The Dream of Cockaigne: Some Motives for the Utopias of Escape," *Centennial Review* 25 (Fall 1981): 345–362.

19. On the other hand, "candy" is not necessarily an Americanism: for instance, Graham Greene's novel *Brighton Rock* (1948), which Orwell reviewed, includes a postscript about Brighton rock candy. This reminds us that Sugarcandy Mountain may be informed by all sorts of associations, biographical as well as literary and historical.

20. See Philip Guedalla, "A Russian Fairy Tale" in *The Missing Muse* (New Yorker: Harper and Brothers, 1930), 206.

21. In *The Orwell Mystique*, Daphne Patai contends that Orwell's borrowing of Guedalla's line for *Animal Farm* amounts to "plagiarism." Whether Orwell's sentence is a conscious (or unconscious) borrowing or just a coincidental repetition is uncertain. Quite apparent are their differing functions in the two narratives. Whereas Guedalla's sentence is a forgotten line in the flow of his satire, Orwell's formulation is brilliantly positioned in *Animal Farm* to crystallize and encapsulate the entire sequence of the pigs' "rectifications" in an indelibly memorable sentence. Orwell draws on the full potential of the line to convey dramatic irony to maximum effect, so that it serves as the crescendo of *Animal Farm* and becomes an incessantly quoted touchstone—and even one that itself is endlessly revised and applied to new contexts outside the scope of the fable's events. On the plagiarism charge, see Daphne Patai, *The Orwell Mystique: A Study in Male Ideology* (Amherst: University of Massachusetts Press, 1984), 309.

22. In fact, Eric Blair might well have even heard that, shortly after the release of "The Big Rock Candy Mountains" by Haywire Mac in 1928, several Utah residents, as a joke, erected a large billboard at the foot of the colorful hills near Fishlake National Forest naming them "The Big Rock Candy Mountains." (They also placed a sign next to a nearby spring, dubbing it "Lemonade Springs." The Big Rock Candy Mountain Resort at the base of the hills is a popular tourist spot today.)

Other locales in North America have also adopted the title of the hobo hymn for their own purposes. For instance, one of the peaks in the Capitol State Forest in Washington State was subsequently named "Big Rock Candy Mountain." In addition, a Canadian mine forty miles north of Grand Forks, British Columbia, is known as the "Rockcandy Mine." A large boulder in the South Platte rock climbing area of Colorado is also known as "Big Rock Candy Mountain" because its colored stripes resemble a candy cane. The original and best-known site bearing the name "Big Rock Candy Mountain" does, however, remain the site in Paiute County in west-central Utah, which consists of formerly volcanic rock in various hues of orange, yellow, white, and red.

23. Surely Orwell was familiar with the work of A. L. Lloyd (1908–1982) by reputation, if not personally. Lloyd was in many ways a British counterpart to America's Pete Seeger, and he had already become the most important twentieth-century figure in English folk music by the late 1940s. He was not only a singer, a collector of folk songs, and an arranger and compiler of folk music, but also a working-class, self-educated intellectual and a translator of distinction. Lloyd was especially interested in industrial music and ethnomusicology, including cross-cultural musical transferences. A well-known member of the British Communist Party in the 1930s and '40s, Lloyd too, like Orwell, was much interested in the condition of British coal miners. (He edited two collections of folk songs by and about the coal miners, both of which appeared shortly after Orwell's death.)

Possibly Orwell had some personal contact with Lloyd at the BBC. Lloyd was a scriptwriter and a BBC reporter in the late 1930s and early 1940s who edited and narrated BBC programs devoted to topics ranging from mass unemployment to popular music. (His radio series, "Ballads and Blues," featured performances by a variety of recording artists, especially prominent British folk singers.) Lloyd also worked intermittently for the BBC in the late 1940s, victimized by a political blacklist that was only suspended when special permission to employ him was granted.

Lloyd has been dubbed "the first professional folklorist in Britain." His specialty was, of course, the folk song. Yet he was not only a pioneer who preserved and recorded folk songs in the English language (including songs from the United States and Australia), but also a cultural mediator who introduced singers from Romania, Bulgaria, and Albania to the English-speaking world, many of whom were released on the record label that he co-founded, Topic Records. Possibly Orwell was acquainted with *The Singing Englishman: An Introduction to Folksong* (1944), the first work devoted to folk songs in Britain for more than four decades.

Lloyd may have also come to Orwell's attention when he won the national folk singing contest in 1947, a success that launched an international career that later came to include much-loved albums such as *Come All Ye Coal Miners*. Lloyd began collecting coal-mining songs from the north of England in 1949–1950, the results of which strengthened his conviction that England's folk music tradition was alive and well in some areas and might be revived on a national basis. (Lloyd was also acquainted with two good friends of Orwell, George Woodcock and Reg Groves, both of whom contributed chapters to *Folk: Review of a People's Music*, a collection edited by Max Jones and published in 1945.)

However much Orwell may have respected Lloyd as an autodidact and self-made man, he certainly disagreed with him politically—and Lloyd would doubtless have castigated the first part of *The Road to Wigan Pier* as an antisocialist rant. Lloyd was a follower of the Marxist historian A. L. Morton, a vociferous critic of Orwell. Lloyd's entire approach to the folk song was based on Morton's book, *A People's History of England* (1938), along with subsequent related work in social history by E. P. Thompson.

Lloyd also contributed to both *The Daily Worker* and *Modern Quarterly* and was a staunch anti-fascist. In the 1950s, he became a staffer at *Picture Post*, which was edited by one of Orwell's greatest admirers, Tom Hopkinson, who authored the first full-length study of Orwell's work in 1953. (Hopkinson resisted Cold War pressures in the late 1940s to terminate Lloyd as a staff member because of his Stalinist allegiances.) Much of Lloyd's work appeared under the auspices of the official Communist Party publisher, Lawrence and Wishart. Ultimately Lloyd was an unreconstructed Old Stalinist, and he remained loyal and committed to the ideals of the Party all his life, especially in his analysis of the relation between the British folk music tradition and historical materialism.

For an assessment of Lloyd's career and legacy during the early post–World War II era, see David Gregory, "Starting Over: A. L. Lloyd and the Search for a New Folk Music," *Canadian Journal for Traditional Music* (1999/2000).

24. Orwell continues in a vein that suggests he is fully aware that multiple versions of "The Big Rock Candy Mountains" are in circulation. Orwell writes:

> Songs of this kind have no author and travel from generation to generation, no two versions ever being quite the same. Some of them are extremely ancient in origin; but it is interesting to see that they are still being made up, several in this collection dealing with Hitler and Roosevelt.

Orwell's notice of Lloyd's sixty-page book appeared as part of an omnibus review in *Manchester Evening News,* 22 November 1945. The review is collected in Peter Davison's *Complete Works of George Orwell,* Volume 17, 392–393. The song is not cited anywhere in the index of *The Complete Works.*

Corn on the Cob contained the lyrics of forty-three American folk songs, which were divided into seven separate sections, one of which featured hobo songs. The booklet represented a useful guide and social history of the American folk song. Published by a left-wing press, the booklet celebrated proletarian art, specifically the music of manual workers. One could argue, however, that songs such "The Big Rock Candy Mountains" fit uneasily into Lloyd's ideological thesis. For instance, Lloyd contended: "It is the preponderance of work songs, of songs sung at work or about work, which gives the American folk tradition its special character and makes it different from the tradition of most other countries."

Obviously, "The Big Rock Candy Mountains," which expresses the yearning for a utopia without work, indeed a Cockaigne of bounty and luxury and even profligacy, runs directly counter to the Stakhanovite work ethic of Stalinism that Lloyd defends in *Corn on the Cob.* Nonetheless, Lloyd was an ardent fan of hobo songs, and he justifiably noted that many of the innovators in the hobo folk song tradition were connected with the famed American labor union, the Industrial Workers of the World (IWW), such as Joe Hill, who voiced the hobos' deep grudge "against society and [their] strong desire to get the upper hand and overthrow the wealthy." Lloyd argued that the hobo song belonged to an American folk idiom that spoke to the masses of working-class people and inspired them in their class struggle to subvert capitalism.

25. This impression is underscored by a close reading of Old Major's speech to the barnyard animals before he sings "Beasts of England." His "dream of last night," he says, "reminded me of something I had long forgotten." Years ago, when he was a little piglet, his mother and the other sows intoned "an old song." But they "knew only the tune and the first three words." As Richard Smyer notes, Old Major's claim that he is "certain" of the verses and their hallowed tradition is suspect. Instead, rather like Karl Marx and Vladimir Lenin whom he represents, Old Major may be manipulating truth to instill a revolutionary consciousness in the animals and convert them into political activists. Smyer observes:

> Old Major no sooner mentions the dream than he waves it aside to make way for a political speech delivered to condition his audience to act. And when Old Major finally gets around to the dream, those aspects that might authenticate its primitiveness—the sows' crooning of a merely fragmentary utterance ("they knew only the tune and the first three words") and the ancestral memory of a zoological period before the appearance of *homo sapiens*—become the components of an activist, future-oriented program. The earth devoid of human beings is a condition that "will" be actualized, presumably after humanity has been exterminated; Old Major is dogmatically 'certain' that he knows the whole song of which he heard only three words in his infancy; and in inducing the animals to memorize and sing the lyrics of 'Beasts of England' he is in effect conditioning them to accept the authoritarian dictates of his porcine successors. We may be justified in suspecting that Old Major's secret intention of using his dream to indoctrinate the other animals for the future has led him to falsify the fragmentary nature of the original dream by imposing on it a form of certitude designed to reinforce the ideological content of his speech.

See Smyer, *Animal Farm: Pastoralism and Politics,* 38–39.

26. In addition to the popular rendition by Burl Ives, Tex Ritter also released a version for children in 1948. Later, Pete Seeger made a recording much loved by the folk music community. Numerous recordings of different versions of the song have followed in the last half-century, and as Orwell notes (see note 24), "[I]t is interesting to see that they are still being made up."

27. Wallace Stegner (1909–1993) spent his young adulthood in Utah and always claimed Salt Lake City as his home. He attended the University of Utah as an undergraduate and later returned there to teach. He became one of the most eloquent and honored spokesmen for the American West, and in his semiautobiographical novel *The Big Rock Candy Mountain*, he poetically describes the promise and lure of the American dream of the West. As Forrest and Margaret Robinson have written (*Wallace Stegner* [Boston: Twayne Publishers, 1977]), Stegner's novel is an

> almost epic commentary on the great American dream, one first fully articulated by Thomas Jefferson, of a massive national migration to the wild, fertile, nearly endless territory of the West. For more than a century that dream was a constant of the American consciousness. Born out of pride, acquisitiveness, a sense of national purpose and destiny, an agrarian ideal, a love of wide spaces, open and free, and a longing for purification and redemption, the dream lured millions like Bo and Elsa across the continent. Even for Americans like Herman Melville, who resisted the pull, the frontier was the symbolic stage where a hopeful, exhilarating, definitive national drama would unfold itself. Though Stegner's chapter in the frontier story is a rather late one, it combines the energy, high aspiration, violence, frustration, failure, and renewed though qualified hopefulness that were characteristic almost from the beginning. (118)

In an interview, Stegner himself made explicit the connection between the popular understanding of the "dream of the Big Rock Candy Mountain" and the dream of paradise. Here he specifically discusses how the Mormons of Utah conceive their heaven in terms that resemble Stegner's conception of Big Rock Candy Mountain:

> I don't think there's much difference between a dream of the Big Rock Candy Mountain and the dream of New Jerusalem. One of them is a purely material dream, but you can't say that the Mormon dream of New Jerusalem was entirely unmaterial. They inherit heaven in the flesh, you know, and with all their wives about them, and all their children and descendants and ancestors. It's a very material religion.
>
> The dream of coming west toward New Jerusalem is of course a religious dream. That's Europe's oldest dream, but it's likewise a material dream, and the Mormon Church profited for years and years because it had an almost irresistible double combination to offer the [immigrant] poor of Europe—the black counties of England, the farm communities in Scandinavia, and so on. It offered them for one thing the hope of heaven, and for another free land, as well as the community of support which a lot of them took advantage of and needed. All that potential converts found hard to resist. Bo Mason is never satisfied with anything quite as pedestrian as the dream Mormons would settle for, but he's certainly motivated to keep on toward some ultimate Big Rock Candy Mountain which isn't very different from the streets of jasper and pearl of the New Jerusalem.

See Wallace Stegner and Richard W. Etulain, *Stegner: Conversations with Wallace Stegner on Western History and Literature* (Salt Lake City: University of Utah Press, 1983), 163.

28. In his introduction to *Where the Bluebird Sings to the Lemonade Springs: Living and Writing in the West* (New York: Random House, 1992), Stegner explains for the first time the personal significance of the hobo song and how he came to draw on it for the titles and themes of two of his books:

> I made a novel, *The Big Rock Candy Mountain*, my first and most heartfelt commentary on western optimism and enterprise and the common man's dream of something for nothing. I took the title from the hobo ballad that Harry McClintock, "Haywire Mac," is supposed to have written in 1928, but that I heard my father sing long before that. That vagrant's vision of beatitude—of a place where the bulldogs have rubber teeth and the cinder dicks are blind and policemen have to tip their hats, where there's a lake of stew and of whiskey too, where the handouts grow on bushes and the hens lay soft-boiled eggs—summarized his unquenchable hope as it summarizes the indigenous optimism of the West. I suppose it is proof of the incorrigibility of that spirit that when I began to look for a title for this book of essays about the West, I was drawn back to that same hobo ballad. (xxi)

29. Although such questions are seldom posed by literary scholars, they are critically important to oral historians and sociologists of culture. As we have seen, we cannot be certain as to how wide the diffusion of the ballad was—that is, whether Orwell first encountered it orally, or in print, or in a later commercial recording. The versions of the song available in print and commercial recordings were bowdlerized in relation to the oral versions. "Beasts of England" seems clearly indebted to the ballad, but it is really impossible to know to which version it is indebted. We cannot establish conclusively whether Orwell initially heard the ballad sung live in the street or whether he heard it on a phonograph or the radio—or perhaps encountered it merely via his reading.

The standard reference work for oral historians of Anglo-American folklore—the Roud Folksong Index (which can be accessed via the Vaughan Williams Memorial Library website)—provides no information on whether the song was known in Great Britain before World War II. Nor does scholarship in popular culture studies explore whether the ballad was known in Great Britain or Europe by the time Orwell was tramping in London. All we can say with some assurance is that the relationship between "The Big Rock Candy Mountains" and *Animal Farm* represents an outstanding, heretofore unacknowledged instance in which American folklore in the oral tradition has directly influenced a canonical work of modern British literature.

On these issues, see Richard Phelps's "Songs of the American Hobo," *Journal of Popular Culture* (Fall 1983): 1–21. This is a well-informed article on the subject of hobo songs and American folk music.

30. As Peter Davison has noted, when Eric Blair's boyhood poem on Lord Kitchener was published in 1914, at the age of eleven, in the *Henley and South Oxfordshire Standard*, it "was published a column or two away from a report on the problems posed by tramps." Davison suggests: "This might be a significant juxtaposition that takes tramping and Blair back to St. Cyprian's." Personal communication, 12 December 2008.

31. It is also possible, however, that Orwell encountered "The Big Rock Candy Mountains" at the summer school of the Independent Labor Party (ILP), which he attended at Letchworth in June 1936, shortly after marrying Eileen O'Shaughnessy earlier that month.

Music played a big role in ILP culture, especially at its summer school meetings, and many of its socialist songs expressed sentiments resonant with those of the hobo ballad. For instance, the first stanza of Edward Carpenter's "England, Arise!" begins:

England, Arise!
The long night is over,
Faint in the east
Behold the dawn appear;
Out of your evil dream
Of toil and sorrow—
Arise, O' England
For the day is here.

Such lines as "Out of your evil dream of toil and sorrow" directly echo the sentiments of "The Big Rock Candy Mountains."

Within the context of ILP music culture, we can say that the hobo ballad bears strong affinities with the English tradition of romantic socialist hymns, beginning with Shelley and William Morris (who wrote "The Day Is Coming"), both of whose work was always included in socialist songbooks. In addition to the obvious source for "Beasts of England" in the lyrics of "L'Internationale," it is quite plausible that this socialist tradition of romantic songs also informed the lyrics and sensibility of Old Major's hymn.

32. Eric Blair was a fan of Jack London. It is well known that *The Iron Heel* was a direct source for *Nineteen Eighty-Four*; less widely recognized is that London's *The People of the Abyss* (1903) exerted a strong influence on *Down and Out*. Whereas London limited himself to a single summer in 1902 in the slums of the East End, however, Orwell tramped over a period of almost five years throughout London and in the neighboring counties. It is worth noting, however, that years before publishing *People of the Abyss*, London in his teens was actually a hobo. Starting out from Oakland with Coxey's Bonus Army for its march on Washington, he split off to ride the rails as a hobo, was arrested for vagrancy in Niagara Falls, and spent thirty days in the Erie County penitentiary, where, he claimed, he made his decision to become a writer. All this is recounted in *The Road* (1907).

Blair was also familiar with the work of W. H. Davies, author of *The Autobiography of a Super-Tramp* (1908). Davies reviewed *Down and Out* in the *New Statesman and Nation* in March 1933, praising it as follows: "It is all true to life, from beginning to end." Quoted in *George Orwell: The Critical Heritage*, ed. Jeffrey Meyers (London: Routledge and Kegan Paul, 1975), 44.

On the tradition of middle- and upper-class writers "descending" to explore the underworld of the poor and destitute, see *Into Unknown England, 1866–1913: Selections from the Social Explorers*, ed. Peter Keating (Manchester: Manchester UP, 1976).

33. Peter Stansky and William Abrahams, *The Unknown Orwell* (New York: Alfred A. Knopf, 1972), 273–275.

34. D. J. Taylor, *Orwell* (London: Chatto and Windus, 2003), 146.

35. Blair moved to Paris both to live cheaply while dedicating himself to his writing and to improve his French. He spent eighteen months in Paris, wrote two novels and several short stories (which he later destroyed), and freelanced a few short articles in the Parisian and London press. Early in the winter of 1930 he returned to his parents' home in Southwold and began to write about his down-and-out experiences in London and Paris, some of which would see print and also get reworked into the final version of *Down and Out*.

36. As his book changed and expanded, its title also went through several versions. Originally Orwell called it "Days in London and Paris." In July 1932 he reported that he had proposed such titles to Gollancz as "The Lady Poverty" or "Lady Poverty." Gollancz countered with "The Confessions of a Down and Out." Orwell asked if "The Confessions of a Dishwasher" might be acceptable since he "would rather answer to a 'dishwasher' than 'down and out.'" Shortly before the publication date of January 1933 Gollancz altered his own preferred title to *Down and Out in Paris and London*.

37. Stansky and Abrahams, *The Unknown Orwell*, 273.

38. Ibid.

39. Blair seems to have sought a pseudonym as a cover behind which he could hide from public view, especially from his family, and thereby veil his identity. But his ultimate choice of "George Orwell" as his pen name suggests that he also intuited its potential to provide him with the impetus and psychic space to develop a greater literary self—in fact to grow into an entirely new literary identity far removed from the "failure" and "dandy" of his school years. For Orwell's famous confession that he felt nothing but "failure" throughout his school years, see his essay "Such, Such Were the Joys." On Blair's "dandyism" in his teens and twenties, see Stansky and Abrahams, *The Unknown Orwell*, 100–116.

But "George Orwell" as a pseudonym also turned out to be a bold, if perhaps unanticipated, means of exposure in *Down and Out in Paris and London*. It became the mask of a mask that permitted Blair/Orwell to express far more of himself in the book than he probably would have done so under the name of Eric Blair, even if his concerns about his family's potential embarrassment had played no role. After its publication, the pen name operated not just as a means of self-disclosure, but also as an instrument for self-realization and even self-promotion, whereby it appears finally to have permitted Orwell in his mature work to have nurtured and realized an astonishingly rich, challenging literary personality—in fact to have conveyed, in the estimate of some of his friends, something very close to "the man himself" as they knew him. As George Woodcock expressed it: "I cannot help but feeling from what I remember of Orwell and his conversation [that] he felt that though Blair would die, Orwell might not. The private man would be no more; the literary personality could carry on, sustained on the wings of his own creation." See Woodcock, "Orwell, Blair, and the Critics," *Sewanee Review* 83 (1975): 529.

40. Or as the American hobo "King" Dan O'Brien described his fellow hobos, those "reckless, perambulating soldiers of fortune":

> He is an avowed optimist, laughs a great deal at the gyrations of men, looks upon politicians as tyrants, the clergy as supreme dodgers of things religious, hopes the human race, like whisky, will improve with age....
>
> He swears that when work becomes an art and a joy, he will take off his coat and go to work. (Quoted in "Hobo Hegemony," *Literary Digest* CXXIII (10) (April 1937).

Chapter 13

1. See, for example, Mina Shaughnessy, *Errors and Expectations* (New York: Oxford University Press, 1979); and Cleo McNelly, "On Not Teaching Orwell," *College English* (February 1977). Shaughnessy also cites numerous reservations from six colleagues about using the essay as a teaching tool.

2. Indeed the fame of "Politics and the English Language" has only grown with the passing of decades, attesting that not just *Animal Farm* and *Nineteen Eighty-Four* but also some of Orwell's essays have become measures of English language literacy. The stunning outcome in the case of "Politics and the English Language" is that this essay now performs a unique dual role as both a mini-Baedeker for prose style and a barometer of cultural literacy.

As an example of its latter service, consider the following exchange in "The Ethicist," the in-house column of the *New York Times Magazine*. A reader asked:

> My husband teaches at a private high school, where several students under the influence of marijuana came to an event and consequently were required to miss a day of class. The school called this a "restriction," not a "suspension," so as not to have to report it on college applications. The students were separated from the community for a day without damaging their chances of admission. Was this use of language ethical?

The advice columnist replied:

> Interesting approach. And if students go on a cross-country shootin' spree and are sent to prison, you can call their "separation from the community" "happy fun time." Another way to phrase your question: is it acceptable to use deliberately deceptive language to a college admissions office? I'm going to go with—oh, you know. I'm going to go with George Orwell's "Politics and the English Language." School officials should be required to read it when they're "at the beach."

Randy Cohen, "Truth in Suspension," *New York Times Magazine*, 25 January 2009.

3. On the interpretive confusions and political reception of the 1954 film adaptation of *Animal Farm*, see the chapter "Orwell or the Telescreen" in my book *George Orwell: The Politics of Literary Reputation*, 211–222.

Chapter 14

1. See Alex Zwerdling, *Orwell and the Left* (New Haven: Yale UP, 1974).

2. On the list of influential books compiled by Charles Beard and John Dewey in a 1935 *Publishers Weekly* issue, see Robert B. Downs, *Books that Changed the World* (New York: Signet Classics, 2004), 26–27.

3. If anything, *Animal Farm* reflected such an aspiration, at least in the sense that, as Orwell famously expressed it in "Why I Write," he sought to "make political writing into an art." See "Why I Write," *CEJL* IV: 48.

4. See Ida Tarbell, "He Knew Lincoln," in *The Stories of Ida Tarbell* (New York: McClure, Phillips and Co., 1907), 9.

5. Walter Fisher's theory of "narrative paradigm" advances a different perspective on these issues, especially via his concepts of narrative probability and narrative fidelity. See, for example, Fisher, *Human Communication as Narration: Toward a Philosophy of Reason, Value, and Action* (Columbia: University of South Carolina Press, 1989), chapters 1–3.

6. Donald Bryant, "Rhetoric: Its Functions and Its Scope" in *The Quarterly Journal of Speech* 39: 123–140. See also Wayne Booth, *The Company We Keep: An Ethics of Fiction* (Berkeley: University of California Press, 1988).

7. Wayne Booth, *The Rhetoric of Fiction* (Chicago: University of Chicago Press, 1961), 71.

8. Seymour Chatman, *Story and Discourse* (Ithaca: Cornell UP, 1980), 180.

9. For another, more recent revisionist engagement with Booth's concepts, see Morton Levitt, *The Rhetoric of Modernist Fiction: From a New Point of View* (especially the chapter titled "The Fallacy of the Implied Author") (Lebanon, NH: University Press of New England, 2005). See also the critique by H. L. Hix, *Morte d'Author: An Autopsy* (Philadelphia: Temple UP, 1990).

10. Booth, *The Rhetoric of Fiction*, 147. In his *Rhetoric of Modernist Fiction*, Levitt concentrates his critique of Booth on this limitation in *The Rhetoric of Fiction*. According to Levitt, the strength of Booth's classic study lies in his revealing readings of traditional novels, but his work (despite subsequent revisions) seems outdated to many readers, given that he does not seriously grapple with modernist and postmodernist fiction. Levitt discusses how fictions (and metafictions) reject narrative omniscience, objectivity, and even authorial presence as he analyzes authors and works ranging from Joyce, Mann, and Woolf to Don DeLillo, John Barth, Carlos Fuentes, detective novels, and comic strips.

11. Chaim Perelman, *The New Rhetoric* (Notre Dame: University of Notre Dame Press, 1971). See Perelman's informed discussion of the ethics of rhetoric throughout the opening chapter.

12. Peter Davison, *Orwell and Politics* (London: Penguin Classics, 2001), 499–501.

13. On the narrative tactics used by authors to invent literary personae that invite readers to assume certain roles, see Walter J. Ong, "The Writer's Audience Is Always a Fiction," *PMLA* (January 1975): 9–21.

14. Richard Schickel, "Orwell Emerges Stronger and More Interesting Than Ever," *Chicago Sun-Times*, 20 October 1968.

15. See especially my discussions in Part 1 of several leading American intellectuals' responses to Orwell.

16. Wolfgang Iser, *The Implied Reader* (Baltimore: Johns Hopkins UP, 1978), xi, xiii.

17. Ibid., xiii.

18. Cicero, *Cicero on Orators and Oratory*, trans. J. S. Watson, (New York: Harper and Brothers, 1860), 119.

19. Aristotle, *The Rhetoric*, trans. Lane Cooper (New York: Meredith, 1932), 220.

20. Quintilian, *Institutes of Oratory*, trans. W. Guthrie, (London: Dewick and Clarke, 1805), IV, 2.1.

21. J. Donald Ragsdale, "Brevity in Classical Rhetoric" *Southern Speech Journal* 31 (1966): 21–28.

22. See Quintilian, IV, 2.21.

23. Ibid., 2.45.

24. George Orwell, *1984* (New York: Signet, 1961), 102–103. (In an ironic instance of Newspeak, the American editions of Orwell's novel encapsulated its title in streamlined numerals, "1984.")

25. Ibid., 96.

26. Ibid., 6.

27. For an excellent analysis of Winston Smith as a "political rhetor," see Lloyd Bitzer's "George Orwell's Rejection of Tyrannical Rhetoric" in *Oldspeak/Newspeak: Rhetorical Transformations*, ed. Charles W. Kneupper (Arlington, Tex.: Rhetoric Society of America, 1985). Bitzer's conclusion to his essay confirms the appropriateness of treating Orwell's *Nineteen Eighty-Four* as a touchstone for our investigation into the relation between rhetoric and narrative: "Orwell joins rhetorical theorists, from Plato and Aristotle to Perelman and Burke, who took pains to conceive a rhetoric suited to tendencies toward tyranny."

Edwin Black has also briefly addressed the concept of an implied auditor via his coinage, "the second persona," which treats the relationship between a discourse and the audience that responds to it. Black notes that it "does not focus on a relationship between a discourse and an actual auditor. It focuses instead on the discourse alone, and extracts from it the audience it implies." All rhetorical discourses imply an auditor, and "in most cases the implication will be sufficiently suggestive as to enable the critic to link this implied auditor to an ideology." See Edwin Black, "The Second Persona," *Quarterly Journal of Speech* (56): 109–119.

28. Kenneth Burke, *Permanence and Change* (Indianapolis: Bobbs-Merrill, 1970), 105–107. More recent scholars have developed related concepts that bear on our application of Burkean "analogical extension." For ways in which narrative has been used as a "rhetoric of possibility," in the phrase of some rhetorical scholars, see three essays by John Poulakos, "From the Depths of Rhetoric: The Emergence of Aesthetics as a Discipline," *Philosophy and Rhetoric* 40 (4) (2007): 335–352; "Rhetoric, the Sophists, and the Possible," *Communication Monographs* 51 (1984): 215–226; and "Toward a Sophistic Definition of Rhetoric," *Philosophy and Rhetoric* 16 (1983): 35–48; William Kirkwood, "Narrative and the Rhetoric of Possibility," *Communication Monographs* 59 (1992): 30–47; Maurice Charland, "Constitutive Rhetoric: The Case of the *Peuple Québécois*," *Quarterly Journal of Speech* 73 (1987): 133–150. Also relevant to our discussion is how narratives get rhetorically "reconstructed"; see, for example, Maurice Charland.

29. See *1984*, 182.

30. The term *hustings* (from the Middle English, "court of common pleas") refers traditionally to the public platform on which candidates for the British parliament formerly stood to address the electors.

To substitute a classical concept for the hustings or modern campaign trail, we might also allude here to the Greek *agora* (marketplace) or, more broadly, to the *polis* (political community), where of course orators also made liberal use of emotional and ethical appeals to their audiences.

Chapter 15

1. For instance, despite the relatively low reputation of the utopia within elite circles in literary academe, the Society for Utopian Studies boasts several hundred members and sponsors an international biennial conference attended by dozens of scholars and intellectuals.

2. See Orwell, *The Road to Wigan Pier*. See also Orwell's "Hitler, Wells, and the World State," *CEJL*, vol. 2: 310–315.

3. Marxist critics later accused Orwell of having plagiarized the plot and general idea of *We* and used them in *Nineteen Eighty-Four*, an accusation that proves groundless when one compares the two novels closely.

4. Blair/Orwell's Parisian aunt and her husband were well-known Esperantists. Blair visited them in Paris in 1928. On his view of them, see Crick, *George Orwell: A Life*, 158–159.

5. See Hilaire Belloc, *The Servile State* (London: Liberty Fund Inc., 1912).

6. Other examples of technical devices that are castigated by most critics as "stock contrivances" of literary dystopias include *Looking Backward*'s dream device and *Walden Two*'s journey metaphor.

7. Jane Tompkins, *Sentimental Designs: The Cultural Work of American Fiction, 1790–1860* (New York: Oxford University Press, 1986).

8. My revaluation of criteria appropriate to the utopia is derived from recent work in canon formation, cultural materialism, reputation-building, and the reconceptualization of value by Jane Tompkins, Barbara Herrnstein Smith, Raymond Williams, Terry Eagleton, Howard Becker, Hans Robert Jauss, Stanley Fish, Michael McGee, and other literary and rhetorical theorists and sociologists of art.

9. See Joseph Epstein, "Intellectuals—Public and Otherwise," *Commentary* 109 (5) (May 2000): 46.

10. See Alex Zwerdling, *Orwell and the Left* (Berkeley: University of California Press, 1974).

11. See Gilbert Ryle, *The Concept of Mind* (Chicago: University of Chicago Press, 1949).

12. But the host's pedagogy must be delicately handled if the visitors—and readers—are to be truly edified. If the instruction is too heavy-handed or condescending, they (and we) will simply be put off and conclude that "no place" ought to remain just that. How does the host proceed? More importantly, how does the returning visitor make what is envisioned *there* understood to the natives *here*? The latter is the great dilemma for the utopian time traveler, the guest who ventures into another world, returns to his or her own, and must explain to the natives what he has seen. A literary architect of utopia who wants to have his returning time traveler successfully persuade the "cave dwellers" to sally forth would do well to honor two concepts. Each of them necessitates a heightened sensitivity to rhetoric, to the communicative relationship between the voyager and the homebodies:

    1. Don't startle your listeners with any jarring challenges or shocking revelations about "the world out there."

    2. Build a solid bridge between that "no place" and this "some place," between "out there" and "right here."

13. Here I am most indebted to the work in *Rezeptionsgeschichte* and *Wirkungstheorie* by Hans Robert Jauss and others at the University of Konstanz in West Germany. See, for example, an application of *Rezeptionsgeschichte* in "The Poetic Text Within the Change of Horizons of Reading: The Example of Baudelaire's 'Spleen II'," in *Toward an Aesthetics of Reception* (Minneapolis: University of Minnesota Press, 1982), 139–185. Jauss never explains in this essay how his chosen historical readers (Gautier, Paul Bourget, Huysmans, Sebastian Neumeister) possess authority as influential readers or as "reader-norms," or indeed how their responses constitute anything except their own idiosyncratic experiences.

14. Robert Escarpit, "'Creative Treason' as a Key to Literature," in *Sociology of Literature and Drama*, ed. Elizabeth and Tom Burns (Harmondsworth: Penguin, 1973), 361. Originally printed in *Yearbook of Comparative Literature* 10 (1961): 16–21.

15. Tompkins, *Sentimental Designs*.

16. Ibid.

17. See my chapter "Canonization and the Curriculum," *The Politics of Literary Reputation*, 382–398.

18. For as John Dewey expressed it in *Art as Experience* (1934), the pragmatist asks what experiences the artwork makes available; that is, "what the product does with and in experience." Dewey thereby dissolves the bogus distinction between artworks and daily life. Adapting a famous line from Thoreau's *Walden*, Dewey writes: "Mountain peaks do not float unsupported. They do not even just rest upon the earth. They *are* the earth in one of its manifest operations." This image of the mountaintop expresses the basic theme of *Art as Experience*. According to Dewey, aesthetic experiences do not reside in some Elysium above and beyond our daily experience; rather, they *are* experience in one of its modes or expres-

sions, typically a "heightened" or "elevated" form of experience. (Here Dewey is anticipating the humanistic psychologist Abraham Maslow's famous conception of "peak" experiences.) For Dewey, the category of the aesthetic represents "the clarified and intensified development of traits that belong to every normally complete experience," even though the latter may sometimes exhibit these traits in less vivid or less crystalline fashion. Ultimately, such artworks constitute new configurations of experience—new artworlds—that reconstruct our public as well as private lives as they transform relationships and social practice. As such, a pragmatist aesthetics puts artworks to work in the world—and appraises what I might call the "GNP" (gross noetic products), aesthetic and otherwise, which result.

On Deweyan pragmatism, see *Art as Experience* (1934), collected in *John Dewey: The Later Works, 1925–1953*, ed. Jo Ann Boydston (Carbondale: Southern Illinois UP, 1981), 3, 9, 53. Also relevant is Dewey's *Reconstruction in Philosophy* (1920), in *John Dewey: The Middle Works, 1899–1924*, ed. Jo Ann Boydston (Carbondale: Southern Illinois UP, 1976). For consideration of the relation between pragmatism and utopianism, see Hans Ulrich Gumbrecht's "Aesthetic Experience in Everyday Worlds: Reclaiming an Unredeemed Utopian Motif," *New Literary History* 32, no. 2 (2006): 299–318. Pragmatists have also engaged in innovative readings of Kenneth Burke and have "reconstructed" him as an American pragmatist. See, for example, John McGowan's "Literature as Equipment for Living: A Pragmatist Project," *Soundings: An Interdisciplinary Journal* 86, nos. 1–2 (2003): 119–148.

Chapter 16

1. See the Blair/Orwell Forum website, "Bowker: The Biography That Orwell Never Wrote" (March 2008).
2. Peter Davison, "Reply to Bowker," Blair/Orwell Forum website (July 2008).
3. Douglas Kerr, "Reply to Bowker," Blair/Orwell Forum website (August 2008).
4. Rodden, *The Politics of Literary Reputation*, 152.

Chapter 17

1. Peter Davison (ed.), *Orwell: A Life in Letters* (London: Harvill Secker, 2010).
2. Jacintha Buddicom, *Eric & Us* (London, 1974).
3. Jacintha Buddicom, *Eric & Us: The Postscript Edition* (London: Finlay, 2006), 183–186.
4. *Orwell: A Life in Letters*, 9.
5. Ibid.
6. Ibid.
7. Ibid.
8. Ibid.
9. *Orwell: A Life in Letters*, 445.
10. Ibid., xii.
11. Ibid., 178. "OGPU" was the acronym for the USSR secret police from 1922 until 1934. Formed from the Cheka, the Soviet state security organization, it was initially known as the GPU.
12. Ibid., 67.
13. Ibid., 67.

14. Ibid., 177.

15. Ibid., 399.

16. Mrs. Venables explains:

> Because of various conversations with both Buddicom sisters, I can vouch for the fact that she meant he had made this proposal the last time they spoke before he went to Burma. . . . He spoke to Jacintha on the telephone from Ticklerton when he returned after five years and had rushed over to Shropshire in the hope of seeing her. As she was not there, he managed to persuade [her brother] Prosper to give him her phone number and they spoke then. He mentioned that he had brought her a gift, but she was completely obsessed with her new baby who would all too soon be taken from her. Passionately bonded with her precious Michal, she had no space for anything or anyone else and must have put this over rather more firmly than intended because, apparently, Eric put the phone down with a grim face and left Ticklerton immediately without making his excuses to his hosts.
>
> How sad indeed that over the years she realised her error, and that no one else ever came up to Eric's standard. They had, however, left indelible imprints in each other's minds.
>
> For me, it is one of the saddest true love stories I have ever come across.

Dione Venables to John Rodden, 25 August 2010. But Mrs. Venables does not need to "vouch" for her cousin Jacintha, who is on record as having stated that Blair proposed marriage to her before his Burma departure: ". . . I think he certainly had romantic ideas about me and that he wanted me to be engaged to him before he went to Burma. But I had no romantic ideas about him . . ."

Jacintha's remarks appear in a tape-recorded interview conducted in 1983 for the BBC-TV *Arena* documentary *George Orwell*, produced by Nigel Williams and broadcast in January 1984.

17. Dione Venables to John Rodden, 25 July 2010.

18. Dione Venables, *Eric & Us: The Postscript Edition*, 185. And perhaps from Blair/Orwell's viewpoint, too. The possibility that Orwell might have been interested in applying to Oxford, along with these other circumstances related to Jacintha, adds new dimensions to Orwell's well-known closing to his apparently casual, needling joke in his last letter (15 February 1949) to Jacintha: "Are you fond of children? I think you must be. You were such a tender-hearted girl, always full of pity for the creatures we others shot and killed. But you were not so tender-hearted to me when you abandoned me to Burma with all hope denied" (*Orwell: A Life in Letters*, 445).

Chapter 18

1. On this point, see chapter 6, "Iraq, the Internet, and the 'Big O' in 2003," in Rodden, *Every Intellectual's Big Brother* (Austin: University of Texas Press, 2007).

Conclusion

1. See *The Collected Essays, Journalism and Letters of George Orwell*, ed. Sonia Orwell

and Ian Angus, 4 vols. (New York, 1968), vol. 4, 29. All further references are to *CEJL* in the Harcourt edition, which I have used here (rather than *The Complete Works of George Orwell*, edited by Peter Davison) because it is widely available in an inexpensive paperback edition.

2. Irving Howe, "As The Bones Know," *Harper's* (April 1968): 103.

3. W. H. Auden, "George Orwell," *Spectator*, 16 January 1971, 86. Auden has not been alone in voicing these sentiments about Orwell. Indeed, a historiography of post-World War II events can be constructed via the lens of readers who have prophesied about the posthumous Orwell's likely opinions on contemporary affairs. On the prevalence of such conjectures about Orwell, see, for instance, Rodden, "My Orwell, Right or Left," *Canadian Journal of History*, 24 (April 1989): 1–15; and "WWGOD?" [What Would George Orwell Do?], in *Scenes from An Afterlife* (Wilmington, Del.: ISI Books, 2003), 227–250.

4. Even Orwell scholars have been induced to speculate about the Orwell who might have been. As Gillian Fenwick, Orwell's most recent bibliographer, wrote:

> If George Orwell had been born half a century earlier than 1903 he would have been labeled a man of letters. He would have written for the *Saturday Review*, the *Cornhill Magazine*, the *Encyclopedia Britannica*. He might have edited a monthly magazine, given public lectures on literary or political topics, had a long association with a publishing house. Perhaps he would have stood for Parliament, still keeping his hand in with his writing. His novels, one every three or four years, would have been serialized in popular magazines, his essays collected into volumes every decade or so.
>
> Had George Orwell been born half a century later than 1903, it would have been more difficult to find a single label for him. He might well have been a bright young thing at Wadham College, Oxford, writing poetry in avant garde magazines, speaking at the Union, active in student politics, his first novel published when he was 23 or 24. He might have chosen a career in broadcasting, working on documentaries, producing arts programmes for television, appearing on a late-night discussion show, eventually hosting his own: a popular media figure. He might write screenplays for movies, a regular column in a left-wing magazine, an occasional long article in *The Atlantic*, publish books on travel, local history, a novel every two years, more or less good but guaranteed to sell for his name alone.

See Fenwick, *George Orwell: A Bibliography* (Winchester, UK: St. Paul's Bibliographies, 1998), vii–viii.

5. The use of what Niall Ferguson terms "virtual history," whereby historians imagine alternative outcomes to key events, has been especially popular since the 1970s in historiographical work on modern European history. For several interesting case studies in which historical counterfactuals are applied, see Dmitry Oleinikov and Sergei Kudriashov, "What If Hitler Had Defeated Russia?" *History Today* 45 (5) 1995: 67–70; Bevin Alexander, *How Hitler Could Have Won World War II: The Ten Fatal Errors That Led to Nazi Defeat* (New York: Crown, 2000); Christiano Ristuccia, "The 1935 Sanctions Against Italy: Would Coal and Oil Have Made a Difference?" *European Review of Economic History* 4 (1) 2000: 85–110; Christian Stögbauer and John Komlos, "Averting the Nazi Seizure of Power: A Counterfactual Thought Experiment," *European Review of Economic History* 8 (2) 2004: 173–199; and Ronald Granieri, "Telling It Like It Isn't? Alternative History and International History," *International History Review* 29 (2) 2007: 228–248. See also Gavriel Rosenfeld's *The World Hitler Never Made: Alternate History and the Memory of Nazism*, (Cambridge: Cambridge University Press, 2005).

6. On the use of counterfactual propositions in biographical writing, see Patrick O'Brien, "Political Biography: A Polemical Review of the Genre," *Biography: An Interdisciplinary Quarterly* 21 (1) 1998: 50–57; and Richard Ned Lebow, "Counterfactual Thought Experiments: A Necessary Teaching Tool," *History Teacher* 40 (2) 2007: 153–176. For an overview of the methodological issues generally, see Niall Ferguson, ed., *Virtual History: Alternatives and Counterfactuals* (New York: Picador, 1997).

The use of counterfactuals has been much debated by contemporary historians since the late 1960s. For a spirited defense of their value, see George Murphy, "On Counterfactual Propositions," *History and Theory* (1969): 14–38. For a more skeptical assessment of their place in historiographical writing, see Richard Lebow, "What's So Different About a Counterfactual?" *World Politics* 52 (4) (2000): 550–585. See also Tim DeMey and Erik Weber, "Explanation and Thought Experiments in History," *History and Theory* 42 (1) (2003): 28–38.

7. See, for instance, Alejandro Portes, "Hazards of Historical Analogy," *Social Problems* 28 (5) (1981): 517–519. Historical analogies prove especially alluring for policymakers in the formulation, conduct, and presentation of foreign affairs. See, for instance, Peter J. Beck, "The Lessons of Abadan and the Suez for British Foreign Policymakers in the 1960s," *Historical Journal* 49 (2) (2006): 525–547. Contemporary policymakers have found it nearly irresistible to draw analogies between the origins and development of Nazi Germany and subsequent international crises and issues. See, for example, Arno Mayer, "Uses and Abuses of Historical Analogies: Not Munich But Greece," *Annals of International Studies* 1 (1970): 224–232; Scot Macdonald, "Hitler's Shadow: Historical Analogies and the Iraqi Invasion of Kuwait," *Diplomacy and Statecraft* 13 (4) (2002): 29–59.

History never furnishes precise analogies between the present and the past. Moreover, because a presentist bias is inevitable and the likelihood of fragile or selective memory overwhelming, historical analogies can induce misleading comparisons and become a lazy thinker's substitute for careful political analysis. On these and other dangers in historiography, see Hans Morgenthau, "Remarks on the Validity of Historical Analogies," *Social Research* 39 (2) (1972): 360–364.

On the conceptual issues involved in analogical thinking, see Yaacov Vertzberger, "Foreign Policy Decisionmakers as Practical-Intuitive Historians: Applied History and Its Shortcomings," *International Studies Quarterly* 30 (2) (1986): 223–247; and Luciano Canfora, "Analogie et Histoire," *History and Theory* 22 (1) (1983): 22–42.

8. For an interesting analysis of Orwell's view of Empire, see Emma Larkin, *Finding George Orwell in Burma* (London: Penguin Press, 2005).

9. See Orwell, Letter to Francis Henson, *CEJL*, vol. 4, 16 June 1949, 502.

10. See Orwell, "Notes on Nationalism," *CEJL*, vol. 3, 261–280.

11. *CEJL*, "Two Letters to the Editor of *Tribune*," vol. 4, 193.

12. For an overview of communism in Great Britain before midcentury, see Noreen Branson, *History of the Communist Party in Britain, 1941–1951* (London: Lawrence and Wishart, 1997).

13. Macdonald's estimate of Orwell can be found in "Trotsky, Orwell, and Socialism," *Discriminations: Essays and Afterthoughts, 1938–1974* (New York: Grossman Publishers, 1974).

14. Ian Angus, co-editor of *CEJL* (with Sonia Orwell), speculates similarly that Orwell would have likely condemned both houses—the American architects of Vietnam War policy and the New Left champions of Hanoi. Angus was asked in the late 1960s by the vicar of Christ Church in Albany Street, the prelate who conducted Orwell's funeral service, to ad-

dress his congregation on the topic "What would Orwell have thought about the contemporary world?" Angus declined, he said, because he is "not a public speaker and also because the topic was too daunting." He also writes:

> Re: Vietnam. At the time I considered the Americans should get out of Vietnam, if for no other reason than it seemed clear they had embarked on a war they couldn't possibly win, but I felt very uneasy about the regime that would take over the whole country. Some people I knew over here were enthusiastic supporters of *Ramparts* [the American pro–New Left magazine] and they were fervent in their condemnation of American policy and seemed greatly to admire North Vietnam. I imagined that Orwell would have been totally against what America was doing, but he would have been critical of Ho Chi Minh's ruthless communist government.

Angus concludes that he did not think Orwell would have "taken a romantic view" of Ho Chi Minh. Personal communication, 18 September 2009.

15. On the controversy that raged in the late 1960s about CIA funding of CCF, see Peter Coleman, *The Liberal Conspiracy: The Congress for Cultural Freedom and the Struggle for the Mind of Post-war Europe* (New York: Free Press, 1989).

The close personal connections between CCF officials (such as Michael Josselson, Nicolas Nabokov, and John C. Hunt) and Orwell's friends and intellectual colleagues are noteworthy. For instance, the CCF subsidy to *Encounter* was administered by the British Committee of the CCF headed by Malcolm Muggeridge and Fred Warburg. T. R. Fyvel, Orwell's old friend, was acquainted with Josselson too and had a temporary connection with the British Committee of the CCF. Arthur Koestler, another close Orwell friend, also established a friendship with Josselson based on affection and mutual respect that endured long after Koestler retired from politics and Josselson retired from the CCF.

Given these friendships that Orwell maintained, and especially the important roles in the CCF's British Committee played by Muggeridge (who with Anthony Powell organized Orwell's memorial service in January 1950) and by Warburg, Orwell's publisher, the CCF connection with Orwell might well have been very strong. Both Muggeridge and Warburg were on very friendly terms with Josselson in particular and conducted an extensive correspondence with him. In 1962, Muggeridge wrote to Josselson to ask his help in securing a position in Paris for—of all people—Sonia Orwell. Muggeridge suggested that she would be an ideal editorial assistant on the CCF's French magazine, *Preuves*, noting that she had been "the mainstay" at *Horizon*. Letter from Malcolm Muggeridge to Michael Josselson, 29 December 1962. Michael Josselson Papers, HRC, box 29, folder 5. See also their correspondence about *Encounter* in 1962. Michael Josselson Papers, box 22, folder 7.

And yet, ironically, not only did Orwell's second wife, Sonia, have a near connection with Josselson and the Congress for Cultural Freedom, but Josselson himself engaged Mark Hamilton, the literary agent for the Orwell Estate, as his own book agent. After retiring from the CCF, Josselson undertook to write the biography of Barclay de Tolly, the eighteenth-century Russian imperial general who participated in the Napoleonic wars. For the relationship between Josselson and A. M. Heath and Co. literary agency (Hamilton was director of the firm), see Michael Josselson Papers, HRC, box 29, folder 3.

Warburg, as publisher of Secker and Warburg, undertook a variety of profit-making tasks for the CCF. For instance, his firm bound copies of books for the CCF to distribute, published books serialized in CCF publications, and obtained CCF subsidies for books compatible with the CCF's politics and cultural outlook. Warburg also corresponded with Nicolas

Nabokov, secretary general of the CCF, because he had contracted with him for Nabokov's autobiography, which was to be titled *The Golden Egg*. Warburg referred to it kiddingly as "Holy Nabokov on Holy Russia." Warburg grew frustrated with Nabokov because his globe-trotting and wide-ranging activities as an impresario left him no time or energy to work on his memoirs. Nabokov eventually delivered the manuscript, a dozen years late in 1975, under the title *Bagázh: Memoirs of a Russian Cosmopolitan*. Nicolas Nabokov to Fred Warburg, 12 December 1964. Nicolas Nabokov Papers, HRC, box 12, folder 40. The entire correspondence between the two men about the book is in this folder, ranging from 1962 to 1965.

16. On Orwell's list, see Christopher Hitchens, *Why Orwell Matters* (New York: Basic Books, 2002), 155–170.

17. Interview with Julian Symons, 13 March 1985. See also *The Politics of Literary Reputation*, 310–311.

18. Quoted in Orwell's letter to Victor Gollancz (25 March 1947), in which he writes that in a military showdown between the United States and the Soviet Union, "I would always choose America" (*CEJL*, vol. 4, 309).

19. Numerous and quite different conjectures could easily be advanced about the posthumous Orwell's likely thinking on recent developments. Consider just two movements that arose in the last quarter of the twentieth century: feminism and environmentalism.

On the first issue, Orwell's portrayal of women in his fiction has been sharply criticized by some feminists, as have his personal relationships with some women of his generation. Might he have changed his mind and viewed the women's movement of the 1960s sympathetically? Might he have supported the campaign of feminist liberals such as Betty Friedan and Gloria Steinem, perhaps concluding that (moderate) feminism is a form of humanism? Or would he have sided with conservatives such as Phyllis Schafly and her STOP ERA campaign?

With regard to the environmental movement, one recalls that Orwell was an impassioned lover of nature. Might he have been one of the founders of Greenpeace or an inaugural sponsor of Earth Day?

I leave further speculation on such matters of counterfactual biography to other readers of George Orwell.

The Unexamined Orwell

303–305, 383nn16,18; letter of, to a friend, 299–301

Burma and Burmese, 296, 300, 304, 305–306, 312, 319, 320

Burmese Days (Orwell), 198, 320

Burnham, James, 340n37, 369n11

Bush, George H. W., 83, 94

Bush, George W., 78, 81–82, 83–84, 87, 88, 89, 92, 95, 96, 308, 309, 326; Hitchens's qualified support for, 78, 83, 349n4; and war on terrorism, 81–83, 326, 349n4

Butler, Samuel, 287

Butterfield, Herbert, 107

Cain, William, ix

Campaign for Nuclear Disarmament (CND), 324

Campbell, Roy, 221

Camus, Albert, 19, 36, 207, 253, 333n18

capitalism: and commercializing of "Orwell," 220–221, 310–311, 332–333n17; Orwell's work used as propaganda for, 351n19

Carpenter, Edward, 375n31

Carter, Jimmy, 94, 112

celebrity culture, 26, 181, 336n9; and Hemingway, 218–219; and Hitchens, 348n1, 349n2; and Orwell, 26, 220–221, 335n8; and Trilling, 26, 335n8, 336n9

Central Intelligence Agency (CIA), 82, 94, 351n19; funding of Congress for Cultural Freedom, 322, 339n35, 345n52, 386n15

Chalabi, Ahmad, 81, 89

Chaplin, Charlie, 323, 324

Chatman, Seymour, 258

Chekhov, Anton, 72

Chiaromante, Nicola, 36, 338n22

Chirac, Jacques, 88

Chomsky, Noam, 62, 330n5, 341n46, 348n1, 349n4

Christianity, 356n4

Chronicle of Higher Education, 1, 25

Churchill, Winston: Lukacs on, 98, 106–107, 108, 110, 114, 273, 309; statesmanship of, 103, 107–108

City University of New York, 69; Hunter College, 61

civil rights movement, 37, 171

Cleaver, Eldridge, 49

A Clergyman's Daughter (Orwell), 99

Clinton, Bill, 77, 81, 82, 96

Cockaigne, land of, 228, 231, 232, 233, 234, 239, 370n18, 372n24

Cockburn, Alexander, 56, 59, 78, 81

Cohen, Elliot, 15

Cohen, Mitchell, 61

Cold War, 3, 4, 19, 36, 40, 60, 94, 103, 106, 108, 124, 126, 136, 140, 144, 157, 179, 251, 256, 308, 315, 320, 321, 324, 326, 327, 353n19; "cultural," 209, 322–324, 345n52; influence of, on Orwell's reputation, 320, 330n6, 333n17; origins of, 103, 353n29; Soviet Union and, 106, 124, 324, 353n29; U.S. and, 108, 324

Cold Warrior, 4, 40, 140, 302, 320, 322, 325, 330n6

Collected Essays, Journalism and Letters of George Orwell (*CEJL*; ed. S. Orwell and Angus), x, 239–240, 260

Columbia University, 14, 16, 22, 45, 103, 335n4

Coming Up for Air (Orwell), 328

Commentary, 15, 20, 23, 24, 75

Commonweal, 219

The Communist Manifesto (Marx and Engels), 130

Communists and Communism, 8, 86, 101, 106, 113, 362n2; and GDR leadership (Ulbricht, SED), 120, 127–131, 153, 162, 177, 358n10; and Macdonald, 31–37; and Marxism-Leninism, 128, 143–145, 152–154, 174; and Spain, 197–198, 367nn49,50, 363n12; and USSR, 102, 129, 321

Communist Party of Great Britain (CPGB). *See* British Communist Party

Communist political parties. *See* British Communist Party; DKP; SED

Complete Works of George Orwell (ed. Davison), ix, 199, 212, 297, 298, 317

concentration camps, 180

Congress for Cultural Freedom (CCF), 322–323, 324, 339n35, 386n15

Connolly, Cyril, 200–203, 209, 210, 213, 214, 216, 222–223; relationship of, to Orwell,

The Unexamined Orwell

Harrington, Michael, 43
Harris, Gail, 308
Havel, Vacláv, 348n1
Hayden, Tom, 57, 318
Hegel, G. W. F., 278
Hemingway, Ernest, x, 8, 42, 196, 197–220, 222–224; and attacks on, 216–217; and boastfulness of, 204, 209, 214–215, 367n47; as compared to Orwell in Spain, 217, 219, 367n50; desire of, for recognition, 202, 215–216; and effects of fame on, 215–217; insecurity of, 216–217; and lies and tall stories, 199–200, 204–207, 213–216; literary decline of, 215–217; literary style of, 198, 217; masculinity of, 217; meeting of, with Orwell in Paris, 198–224; myths about, 211–212, 216–217; Orwell on, 198; and plane accident's public image, 205, 215, 219, 366n42; and Spanish Civil War, 197; and unreliable memoirs, 205–207; war and, 201–202; and World War II, 199, 214, 362n8, 367n49; writing block of, 366n45
—Works of: *Across the River and Into the Trees*, 216–217, 219, 262n5; *For Whom the Bell Tolls*, 197–198, 216–217, 364n29, 367n49; *The Old Man and the Sea*, 215–216, 366n42; *The Sun Also Rises*, 224; *True at First Light*, 205, 212, 215, 222, 364n18, 368n57
Heppenstall, Rayner, 303
heroes and heroism, 19, 25, 61–62, 82, 125, 133, 141, 177, 187, 189, 192, 217, 345n53, 354n33; Howe on Orwell, 56–58, 63, 64, 342nn6,13,15, 345n53; Howe on Sholem Aleichem, 73, 347n79; Howe on Silone, 63, 64–66, 344n38, 345n52; Howe on Trotsky, 63–64, 344n43; Howe on Wilson, 63, 66; Lukacs on, 97–100, 107–108, 113; Potts on Orwell, 208–209, 213–214, 222–224; and Trilling as hero, 18, 23, 26, 335n7; Trilling on Orwell, 15, 342n13
Herzen, Alexander, 50
Hill, Christopher, 323
Hill, Joe, 372n24
Himmelfarb, Gertrude, 23–25, 27, 336n6
Hiss, Alger, 106
history: Lukacs on, 103–105, 106–108, 109–

110, 112, 114, 116; and "historianship," 104; as literature, 103–104, 110; physics and, 101, 114, 354n40; professionalization of, 104, 110, 117
Hitchens, Christopher, ix, 7, 54, 76, 77–82, 115, 326, 329, 348n1, 349nn7,8,11, 350nn12, 13, 15; as "contrarian," 80, 82, 115; and International Socialists (IS), 350n16; Orwell as hero of, 79, 351n19; and Taliban, 95; and Trotsky, 80
—Works: *Hitch-22*, 81, 350nn11,12; *Letters to a Young Contrarian*, 80, 81, 350n12; *Orwell's Victory/Why Orwell Matters*, 78; "So Long, Fellow Travelers," 78
Hitchens, Peter, 350n12
Hitler, Adolf, 34–35, 98, 99, 106–107, 110, 114, 115, 272, 273, 309
Ho Chi Minh, 322
Hoffman, Abbie, 49
Holloway, John, 18
Holocaust, 43–45
Homage to Catalonia, 50, 100, 197–198, 203, 214, 217, 363n11; compared to *For Whom the Bell Tolls*, 197–198, 367n50; sales of, 197; Trilling's introduction to, 15–16, 17, 334n1
Homer, 38
Hook, Sidney, 40, 59, 322
Höpcke, Klaus, 125, 355n4
Hopkinson, Tom, 371n23
"Hop Picking" (Orwell essay), 230, 243
Horizon, 109, 201, 203, 386n15
Howe, Irving, 7, 40, 46, 50, 55–75, 212, 318–319, 341n47, 342nn13,15, 343nn18,25,26, 344nn38, 45, 345n46–53, 346nn61,67, 347n77, 348n83; as the "American Orwell," 55–56, 58, 62; character of, 68–71; at City College of New York (CCNY), 69; and Democratic Socialist Organizing Committee (DSOC), 347n71; and *Dissent*, 65, 68, 71, 74–75, 341n47, 343n19, 347n71; and Israeli Labor Party, 60; legacy of, 74–75, 348n82; and literary models, 59, 63–68, 73; and *menschlichkeit*, 71; and neoconservatism, 55–56, 60–62, 70, 343nn19,25, 344n28; and New American Movement (NAM), 347n71; and *Partisan Review*, 57, 64, 66,

Macdonald, Dwight, x, 7, 28, 29–54, 97, 114, 116, 217, 321, 322; anti-Semitic background of, 43; attitudes of, toward Jews, 43–45, 340n39; changes in political beliefs of, 33, 37–40; erratic and unpredictable behavior of, 47–49; on Harrington's *The Other America*, 43; and Howe, 40, 46; and "liblabs," 337n15; as "Macdougal Macdermott," 31, 47, 337n9; and *New International* (Trotskyist journal), 338n19; as "Orlando Higgins," 31; and *Partisan Review*, 32–35; compared to Peter Pan, 41, 52, 340n44; and Phillips Exeter Academy, 43; and *politics*, 29, 36–40; on Revised Standard Version of the Bible, 42; and self-doubt, 46–47, 50; and student movement in 1960s, 48; and Students for a Democratic Society (SDS), 39; and treatment of young people, 340n43; writer's block of, 46–47, 48–50; and Yale University, 43 —Works: *Against the American Grain*, 30, 35, 336n44; "America! America!," 42; "I Choose the West," 40; "Masscult and Midcult," 41–42, 51; *Memoirs of a Revolutionist*, 35, 39, 40; "A Note on Wallese," 36–37; "The Root Is Man," 38, 341n49; "Ten Propositions on the War," 35; "Trotsky Is Dead," 34–35

Macdonald, Nancy, 31, 34, 38, 40

Mailer, Norman, 19, 40

Malenkov, Giorgi, 108

Malraux, André, 207

Mann, Golo, 355n7

Mao Zedong, 322

Marcus, Steven, 17, 335n4

marginalization, 40, 330n6, 346n61

Martin, Kingsley, 78, 323

Marty, Andre, 367nn49–50

Marx, Karl, 34, 39, 99, 124, 130, 143, 232, 346n59, 358n3, 370n17, 373n25

Marxists and Marxism, 1, 50, 97–99, 103, 128, 141, 143, 150, 157, 160, 174–176, 182, 188, 323, 325, 346nn59–60; and Howe, 64–65, 67, 347n73; and Lucas, 2, 4, 293; and Macdonald, 31, 36–40, 53, 338n19, 339n35; and the *Partisan Review*, 34–35

McCarthy, Eugene, 33, 60

McCarthy, Joseph, 106, 110, 321, 324, 325

McCarthy, Mary, 30–31, 44, 47, 50, 336nn7–8, 337n9, 340n37, 343n21

McCarthyism, 6, 19, 32, 110, 275, 314, 322, 323–324, 325

McClintock, Harry ("Haywire Mac"), 225, 226, 228, 234, 369nn1,3, 375n28; and "The Big Rock Candy Mountains," 369n1, 371n22

McHugh, Paul R., 21–22

Melville, Herman, 53, 374n27

Meyers, Jeffrey, ix, 212, 216, 220, 292, 293–294, 298, 334n1, 363n11, 365n35, 365n38, 367nn47,50, 370n17

Micah, Book of, 23, 27

Milburn, George, 369nn2,5

Mills, C. Wright, 338n22

Milosevic, Slobodan, 351n19

Milosz, Czeslaw, 52, 53, 341n49

Modern Age, 353n28, 356n6

Monbiot, George, 84, 353n20

Moore, Michael, 84, 95, 96

More, Thomas, 259, 274, 285

Morris, William, 281, 282, 375n31

Mother Teresa, 81, 349n4

Mugabe, Robert, 312

Muggeridge, Malcolm, 212, 213, 222, 223, 322, 365n32, 386n15

Muller, Heiner, 192

Mumford, Lewis, 34, 291

Mussolini, Benito, 34, 97–98

Myles, Norah, 298, 302–303

Nabokov, Nicolas, 386n15; and *Bagázh*, 387n15

The Nation, 36, 56, 78, 342n5, 349n11; attacks on Hitchens in, 78, 349n3; Hitchens's break with, 78

National Review, 101, 110, 112, 113, 115, 352n15, 354n33

Nazi Germany, 35, 86, 102, 107–108, 127, 131, 182, 192, 260, 309, 333n19, 353n29, 355n2, 367n49, 384n5, 385n7

Nazism, 35, 86, 98, 100, 102, 107, 108, 121, 123, 124, 127, 128, 130, 131, 143, 180, 182, 187, 251, 285, 302, 318, 333n19, 355n2, 367n49, 384n5; and Orwell's postwar German reception, 126, 142, 333n19

Nazi-Soviet pact (Hitler-Stalin pact), 31, 309

neoconservatives and neoconservatism, 36, 58, 70, 75, 82, 95, 96, 302, 322, 343n25, 344n28; and Howe, 55, 59–62, 343n19; and Lukacs, 99, 112, 354n33; and Trilling, 18–19, 24

New Critics, 274, 277

New Deal, 337n15, 351n19

New English Weekly, 364n29

Newfield, Jack, 59

New Left, 18, 32, 36, 46, 48, 59–60, 62, 64, 79, 322, 343n18, 347nn71, 77, 386n14

The New Republic, 22, 36, 61, 78, 101, 342n15

New Statesman and Nation, 78, 242, 376n32

New Yorker, 29, 33, 38, 41, 43, 45, 51

New York Intellectuals, 7, 15, 26, 30, 34, 39, 44, 50, 60, 64, 67, 69, 74, 336n3, 337n14, 339n35, 340n37, 343n21, 344n28, 346nn62,66,67, 348n83, 363n10; and Howe, 59–60, 64, 67, 69, 74; and Macdonald, 30, 34, 39–40, 44, 50; and rift among wartime *PR* editors, 35–36; and Trilling, 15, 26

New York Times, 21–22, 30, 61, 105, 109, 198, 204, 348n83, 363n10, 378n2

Nineteen Eighty-Four, 3, 6, 8, 9, 50, 51, 104, 105, 121, 124–127, 128, 130–131, 136–138, 139–140, 144, 177, 180, 203, 215, 220, 253–255, 256, 258–260, 264, 266–267, 269, 270, 272, 274, 275, 277, 278, 279, 281, 283, 285, 286, 287–288, 300, 301–302, 305, 308–309, 311, 313–314, 315–316, 319, 320, 332n12, 333nn17,19, 342n15, 351n19, 354n38, 355nn4,7,9, 376n32, 378n2, 379n24, 379n27, 380n3; and anti-Stalinism, 126, 260, 314; banned or censored in GDR, 125–126; and genre of utopia, 285; sales of, 278; and social relevance today, 125; and Winston Smith, 125, 138, 224, 259, 281, 283, 301, 379n27

Nobile, Philip, 60

North Korea, 167, 321, 351n19

Nusseibeh, Sari, 91

O'Brien, Conor Cruise, 80

Observer, 203, 213, 244, 333n19

Oglesby, Carl, 59

O'Hara, Dan, 18

Old Left, 59–60, 74–75, 343n25

Orwell, George: and the BBC, 204, 315, 328, 333, 371n23; biographies of, 4–6, 8, 9–10, 199–200, 209–210, 212, 214, 224, 242, 289–295, 365n34; biography, attitude toward, 9–10, 289–295; as book reviewer, 9–10, 234–235, 244, 273, 289–290, 297–298, 315, 361n2, 364n29, 371n19, 372n24; in Burma, 296, 300, 304, 305–306, 312, 319–320, 330n6, 383nn16,18, 385n8; childhood of, 296, 300, 302, 303, 305, 319, 375n30; and Communism, 19, 51, 78, 80, 126, 198, 302, 320, 321–325, 367n50; Communist attacks on, 323, 365n34, 367n50; and conservatism, 80, 97, 302, 319; at Eton, 29, 213, 241, 312, 362n5; and feminism, 1, 313, 317, 387n19; and friendship with Astor, 244; and friendship with Connolly, 203, 213, 222, 223, 362n5; and friendship with Fyvel, 222, 386n15; and friendship with Heppenstall, 303; and friendship with Koestler, 321, 386n15; and friendship with Muggeridge, 212, 222, 223, 322, 386n15; and friendship with Powell, 212, 222, 386n15; and friendship with Rees, 222, 291; and friendship with Spender, 222, 321, 322; and friendship with Woodcock, 221, 222, 371n23; GDR and, 8, 125–127, 131, 135–142, 355nn4,7; and Hemingway, comparisons to, x, 8, 196–200, 203, 206–207, 209–213, 215–219, 224; and imperialism, 1, 80, 309, 312, 313, 322; and integrity, 15–16, 291, 332n13; Left and, 53, 58, 78, 80, 317, 319, 321, 323–325; and list of political unreliables, 323–324; marriage of, to Eileen Blair (née O'Shaughnessy), 203, 213, 294, 298, 302–303, 311, 375n31; marriage of, to Sonia Blair (née Brownell), x, 29, 203, 209, 291, 294, 305, 313; and Marxism, 1, 232, 293, 316, 322; as model stylist, 9, 125,

The Unexamined Orwell

The Unexamined Orwell

CPSIA information can be obtained at www.ICGtesting.com
Printed in the USA
LVOW040723220512

282758LV00001B/1/P